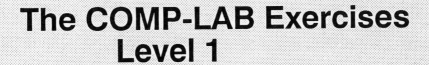

The COMP-LAB Exercises
Level 1

Fourth Edition

Mastering Written English

Mary Epes
Carolyn Kirkpatrick
Michael G. Southwell
York College/CUNY

PRENTICE HALL, Englewood Cliffs, New Jersey 07632

Library of Congress Cataloging-in-Publication Data

Epes, Mary.
    Mastering written English: the COMP-LAB exercises level 1/Mary
Epes, Carolyn Kirkpatrick, Michael G. Southwell. — 4th ed.
      p.   cm.
    Includes index.
    ISBN 0-13-565797-0
    1. English language — Self-instruction. 2. English language —
Textbooks for foreign speakers. 3. English language —
Grammar — 1950- I. Kirkpatrick, Carolyn. II. Southwell, Michael
G. III. Title
PE1112.3.E64 1993
428.2 — dc20
                                                92-32685
                                                  CIP

Acquisitions editor: Carol Wada
Editorial/production supervision: Jenny Moss
Cover design: Maureen Eide
Manufacturing buyer: Bob Anderson
Editorial assistant: Joan Polk
Interior design: Michael G. Southwell, Mary Epes, and Carolyn Kirkpatrick

Previous editions published under the title
The COMP- LAB Exercises: Self-Teaching Exercises for Basic Writing

Printed in the United States of America

10 9 8 7 6 5 4 3 2 1

ISBN 0-13-565797-0

Prentice-Hall International (UK) Limited, *London*
Prentice-Hall of Australia Pty. Limited, *Sydney*
Prentice-Hall Canada Inc., *Toronto*
Prentice-Hall Hispanoamericana, S.A., *Mexico*
Prentice-Hall of India Private Limited, *New Delhi*
Prentice-Hall of Japan, Inc., *Tokyo*
Simon & Schuster Asia Pte. Ltd., *Singapore*
Editora Prentice-Hall do Brasil, Ltda., *Rio de Janeiro*

Contents

To The Teacher

Mastering Written English is a self-teaching text designed to acquaint students with the forms and conventions of written English in a way that is consistent with current thinking about writing pedagogy. It provides 12 modules of exercises that students can complete on their own, outside of class, allowing them and their teachers to spend their limited class time on other writing activities. The modules are truly self-instructional; invariant answers to every exercise are provided in the back of the book. This approach grew out of our work with error-prone basic writers at CUNY; the exercises have been evolving for more than 16 years in response to our students' experience and comments, and to the comments of other teachers who have used the first three editions with their students. They reflect, as well, our own developing understanding of students' needs in the dimension of written language acquisition. In this fourth edition, we have revised the sentence structure sequence (Modules 6, 10, and 12) to add work on sentence formation and punctuation; we have made changes throughout to increase our emphasis on practice with forms in sentence and paragraph contexts; and we have added new appendixes on spelling and possessive forms.

As the subtitle suggests, *Mastering Written English: The COMP-LAB Exercises Level 1* has a companion text for more advanced students, *Writing & Editing: The COMP-LAB Exercises Level 2*. The books are designed for the two levels of college developmental writing that many colleges, like our own, offer. For these schools, the two texts provide a natural sequence, in which learning from Level 1 is reinforced and extended at Level 2. In other settings, teachers should choose one book or the other according to their students' preparation and reading level. *Mastering Written English* has been written for students at the first developmental level, those who enter college with little prior writing experience and whose language background is likely to be either nonstandard English or ESL (often a nonstandard variant of that other language).

We believe that instruction in written English is important, even essential, at the basic writing level. Yet students' needs in the dimension of composing are equally pressing, and we agree with theorists who emphasize that a writing course must be based on **writing**. Our answer to these conflicting demands on instructional time and attention has been to design this self-instructional program as a **complement** to classroom work on the writing process. The subtitle *The COMP-LAB Exercises* reflects our view of the modules as a laboratory component for a developmental writing course, whether students complete the exercises as homework or in a writing lab (as they do at York College).

Self-Instruction and Perceptual Skills

The self-teaching approach has many virtues, the most obvious of which are practical. As noted above, class time that might otherwise be given over to instruction in basic rules and conventions is freed for activities that truly demand a teacher's guidance: work on the rhetorical aspects of writing and on the more complicated principles of syntax. Then, too, the self-instructional approach teaches a great deal (both explicitly and implicitly) about learning how to learn. Students move at their own pace, developing habits of monitoring their own progress and level of understanding.

Most important of all, however, is a dimension which we ourselves have increasingly come to appreciate: Self-instruction offers perceptual practice that cannot be provided in any other practical way. Checking sentences in their own handwriting against the printed Answers in the back of the book forces students to shift awareness from meaning to form. In so doing, they develop and exercise perceptual skills that are crucial for successful editing of their own writing.

The Writing Process

We want to underscore our commitment to a process-oriented and communicative view of writing. The literature of our profession is rich with suggestions for treating basic writing in an intellectually stimulating way, using workshop approaches, word processing, theme-based reading/writing assignments, and collaborative learning activities of many kinds. Students who use this book should be doing a great deal of writing besides the exercises included here; the Instructor's Manual contains our suggestions for coordinating classroom-based writing activities with what students are learning in the modules. And to reinforce this classroom learning, the Writing Tests at the end of each module have been redesigned in this new edition to lead students more explicitly through steps in the writing process.

Some Practical Suggestions

Assigning the Modules. For most basic writing classes, we recommend assigning all twelve modules in the order they appear in the book. The modules start with visual conventions, features that are easy for students to "see," and move step by step into areas of increasing difficulty. The modules are cumulative; for example, once syntax is introduced, considerable attention to syntax is integrated into the word-form modules that follow. Thus all of the modules are likely to be valuable even for students who don't seem to need exercise on a particular feature. The Instructor's Manual contains suggestions for classroom activities to anticipate and reinforce what students are learning in the modules. However, for a heterogeneous class in which students have a wide range of needs, each module is sufficiently self-contained that modules can be assigned selectively.

Managing the Self-Teaching Approach. While it's true that the self-teaching approach can free instructional time for writing activities, it will serve you best if you take time to help students learn to use it. The introductory section How to Use This Book is an important orientation; we urge you not to skip it as self-evident. Remember that most basic writing students aren't practiced at learning from the printed page and that the autotutorial approach will be unfamiliar to most. The Writing Test for the How to Use This Book section is a letter to the instructor; this will suggest right away what guidance individual students may need. Then, as students work through the modules, you or a tutor should regularly spot-check their performance on one or two of the more difficult exercises; the module cover page provides for feedback on this checking. Monitoring students' self-corrections alerts you to students' difficulties, and your attention underscores for students the importance of attending to details on the page.

Instructor's Manual

The *Instructor's Manual* discusses briefly the philosophy of this self-instructional approach. It offers more detailed advice about managing self-instruction in classroom-based teaching or in a writing lab, as well as module-by-module comments and suggestions for related classroom activities. As noted above, the *Instructor's Manual* also contains suggestions for writing assignments and for responding to students' papers in a way that reinforces and builds on the learning of the modules. It includes for each module an Alternate Writing Test and a Review Exercise (a feature-focused proofreading exercise). The *Manual* is available on request from your Prentice Hall representative, or write to: Developmental English Editor; College Division, Prentice Hall; 113 Sylvan Avenue, Route 9W; Englewood Cliffs, NJ 07632.

Acknowledgments

As we've prepared this new edition of *Mastering Written English*, we've been preparing also a second edition of *Writing & Editing*, the Level 2 text. For both, we owe thanks to the teacher-reviewers who commented on our work at various stages: Charles Boyd, Genesee Community College; Donna Cheney, Weber State University; Gary N. Christensen, Macomb Community College; Ellen Dugan-Barrette, Brescia College; Donna Grout, Lincoln University; Susan Lagunoff, St. Louis Community College-Florissant Valley; Emily Lamb, West Virginia University-Parkersburg; Karen McClaskey, New Community College of Baltimore; and Len Roberts, Northampton Community College. We want them to know that we found their comments helpful and took their suggestions seriously even where we decided on other solutions. Thanks also to those who responded to a query about their use of the COMP-LAB texts: Wendell Affsprung, New Mexico Military Institute; Jan Gerzema, Indiana University Northwest; Rhonda Gilliam, Bellevue Community College; Anne Ogle, North Greenville College; and our York College colleagues Elaine Baruch, Rachel Donner, Samuel Hux, Dorothy Parker, and Mildred Ware.

We'd like to acknowledge once more our special debt to long-time reviewers and critics Stan Frick, Beverly Lowry, and Dorothy Smith, of Midlands Technical College in South Carolina; and Lee Churchill, of Indiana Vocational Technical College. Their intimate understanding of how students learn is matched only by their ability to zero in on our own lapses of attention.

In Carol Wada, Prentice Hall and we have acquired a new developmental English editor who is a pleasure to work with, putting us in touch with users' needs and responding sensitively to our questions and problems. We are grateful as well to Phil Miller, who has seen us through five revisions of our two texts and guided us to many sensible decisions, sometimes against our will.

Finally, we thank the family members and friends who have sustained us through the travails of this revision.

MTE, CGK, MGS

To the Student

As you start using this book, we want to encourage you to make your own writing growth a personal priority in the coming term or semester. It's obvious that practicing writing in a writing class, with your teacher's help and guidance, will help develop your skill as a writer. In the act of setting down your ideas on the page, you will learn (both consciously and unconsciously) strategies for expressing yourself in a way that's increasingly clear and effective.

This book is aimed at another dimension of writing effectively—control over the written language. Many student writers worry about making mistakes. They know there are lots of rules about written English, but they're not completely sure when the rules apply and when they don't. Here, too, we want to stress the value of practice. Many textbooks suggest that learning to write correctly is only a matter of learning the rules. Of course learning the rules is important, but it's essential to learn them in a way that carries over to your own writing.

This self-teaching book grew directly out of the experience of student writers in our classes over the years, what they understood about the written language and what they didn't. The book concentrates on the features that have caused them the most difficulty; it explains the rules, and then it goes on to many exercises in applying the rules. Again and again, you will be asked to rewrite sentences and even paragraphs. As you do this, the forms of written English will become familiar, and your eye will grow accustomed to noticing details on the page. Mastering written English, like learning to play the guitar or to play tennis, is very much a matter of internalizing what you're learning, making it completely your own. You try, and probably make mistakes, and try again, and yet again, until doing it right becomes easier. Eventually, doing it right even becomes automatic.

As you work your way through these exercises, we hope you'll find (like many students who have used the exercises over the years) that you're beginning to enjoy writing more. A tennis player who has control of his or her strokes can begin to think about how to win the game. A guitar player who knows the chords can begin to develop an individual style. In the same way, when you don't have to worry about making mistakes in your writing, or about knowing how to correct them when you check over your work, you'll find it easier to focus on your ideas and communicate them more effectively.

MTE, CGK, MGS

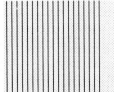

How to Use This Book

NAME _____

As you complete each exercise, record your number of mistakes below.

0.1 ____

0.2 ____

0.3 ____

How to Use This Book

Before You Begin

This is a self-teaching book. It is designed so that you work through it at your own speed, checking your own work against the Answers at the back of the book.

Here is what you need to have before you begin:

1. Two different colored pens (we suggest a black one to work with, and a green one to check your answers with);
2. A three-ring notebook; and
3. A good dictionary.

Whenever you use this book, keep these materials handy.

The Parts of a Module

First you need to understand how this book works. Look at the Contents on p. iii at the beginning of the book. Notice that the chapters are called Modules, and that most of them have several parts. Notice also that Answers to all of the exercises are given at the very end of the book. And notice that each page in the book is perforated, so that you can tear it out easily.

Exercise 0.1 Turn to page 205, the first page of Module 9, for a close look at how every module (except Module 1) is put together. Use your black pen to fill in the answers to these questions. (Even when you're absolutely sure of an answer, writing it down helps you remember it.)

1. Each module is about one point of grammar or area of attention for correcting your writing. Module 9 is

   about _____ _____ .

2. The first page of Module 9 (like the first page of every module) is a cover page with spaces where you and

   your _____ keep notes on the module.

3. Next, starting on page 206, there is a section called _____ . This contains

   explanations, examples, and short exercises.

4. In the Rules section, it's easy to pick out the key ideas because each one is printed in a shaded box. Each

   rule has a number (corresponding to the module number) and a _____ to

   make it easy to refer back to that rule later.

5. Look at the end of Exercise 9.1 on page 207. Here you're told to _____

   your work as you go along.

6. To check your work, you'll compare what you've written for each exercise to what is printed in the

   Answers in the back of the book. Turn to page 385 and look over the Answers for Module 9. Write

   here the answer that is underlined for the 3rd question in Exercise 9.4:

   _____ .

7. Turn now to the end of the Rules section of Module 9. On page 215 is a

   _____ _____ to help you to remember the

   ideas included in this module.

8. Look at Exercise 9.12 on page 216, the first of a series of longer one-page exercises in the Practice

   section. At the top of every one-page exercise is a space for your number of

   _____ . This will help you to keep track of how you're doing on the

   exercises. You'll also record this information on the cover page of the module.

9. Exercise 9.21 on page 225 is _____ _____

   _____ . This asks you to apply what you've learned in several modules.

10. On page 226 is a _____ _____ . This asks you

    to write a paper to show that you can apply what you've learned in this module to your own writing.

11. On page 226 (and elsewhere in this book) there are square _____ at the left

    margin. This box means that you must STOP and do something (for example, fill in a blank, underline

    some words, or write some sentences). Then put an ✗ in the box to show that you have completed this

    step. This work is just as important as completing the numbered exercises.

Checking Your Work

These exercises are not tests, but opportunities for learning. Each exercise teaches something you need to know in order to do the next exercise. So **immediately**, as soon as you finish an exercise, check your work on it before you go on. And to get the most out of these exercises, you need to check your work **accurately**, so that you can learn from your mistakes.

Here is the best way to check your work. As you follow these steps to check Exercise 0.1, put an ✗ in each box.

❑ Make sure that your name is on the cover page to this section (page 1). Get your green pen.

❑ Fold the pages containing Exercise 0.1 along the perforations, and tear them out carefully.

❑ Find the answers for Exercise 0.1 on page 339. Compare what you wrote to what is printed in the Answers. Be sure to check **every detail**, including spelling and word endings.

❑ If you made a mistake, don't just mark it wrong or add a letter. Use your green pen to **write in the entire correct answer** above the mistake. Cross out in green any answer that is incorrect.

❑ Count your number of green corrections. This is the number of mistakes you made in doing Exercise 0.1. On the cover page, write in this number. If you didn't make any mistakes, write in the number 0.

❑ After you've checked your work, stop to think about **why** you made a particular mistake. Were you in a rush to finish? Or did you misunderstand a rule, or forget it?

Checking your work thoughtfully will let you know whether you need to slow down or perhaps to study the rules more closely (with special attention to the examples) before you go on.

❑ As soon as you've finished all the work on any page, put it in your three-ring notebook or folder. But don't put it in until you've completed all the work on both sides of the page.

Important: Follow the same steps to check every exercise except the Writing Test at the end of each module. The Writing Test is the only exercise that you cannot check by yourself. Your instructor will mark it for you.

Following Instructions

To get the most out of working on your own, you need to develop the habit of paying close attention to instructions.

Exercise 0.2 Turn to page 67, the Writing Test at the end of Module 3. **Do not do this Writing Test.** Just read the instructions carefully. Then answer these questions.

1. The Writing Test gives you a chance to show that you can apply what you have learned in the module to your own writing. For this test you need to show that you can avoid _____

   _____ .

2. For this Writing Test, you'll write a _____ to a family member or friend, using words from a list.

3. There are _____ words in the list, and you must use every word at least

   _____ .

4. After you use each word, you should _____ it in the note you're writing.

5. After you have finished revising your ideas, you are asked to _____ the words from the list that you used in the note, and write in the number.

6. In this, as in all Writing Tests, it's important to follow the _____ exactly, step by step. Otherwise, you may not really test yourself on applying the rules of that particular module.

Now check your work on Exercise 0.2:

❑   Turn to the Answers in the back of the book.

❑   Correct any mistakes in Exercise 0.2 with your green pen.

❑   Write in your number of mistakes on the cover page of this section. If you made no mistakes, write in the number 0.

Caution: How much you learn from this book depends very much on how carefully you follow the instructions as you work through the exercises. However, sometimes instructions may seem more complicated than they really are. Be sure to follow them step by step, **in order.**

Exercise 0.3 This exercise will help you see how good you are at step-by-step procedures. For the sentence below, do the following: (1) The word at the beginning of the sentence is not capitalized. Underline it. (2) One word has been omitted. Put a caret (∧) where this word belongs. (3) Two words don't make sense. Underline those two words. (4) The period at the end of the sentence is missing. Put it in. (5) In the space above the line, write correctly the words that you underlined, and insert the omitted word. (6) Circle every correction you made.

often a writing mistake is just slip of the pin, but it my badly confuse a reader

Before you look at the Answers for Exercise 0.3, reread the instructions. Consider these questions:

❑   Did you follow each of the six steps in the instructions?

❑   Did you actually write out the words *Often, pen,* and *may* instead of just adding or changing letters?

❑   Did you capitalize *Often*?

❑   Did you write in the word *a*?

❑   Did you draw five circles?

Now get your green pen and turn to the Answers for Exercise 0.3 to check your work. Write in your number of mistakes on the cover page. If you made no mistakes, write in the number 0.

Teaching Yourself

This self-teaching approach places the responsibility for learning on you. Whenever you make mistakes in doing any of the exercises, try to understand **why** your answers were wrong. Did you read the instructions too quickly or too carelessly? Do you need to read instructions more than once to understand them? Did you stop to think about the point of each exercise before you started to work on it?

Whenever you aren't sure why an answer was wrong, **get help**. Ask your instructor, or your tutor, or another student. You won't learn much if you do the exercises carelessly. But if you do the work thoughtfully, you'll soon find yourself gaining more control over your writing.

Good luck with your work in *Mastering Written English*! We hope that you, like the many other students who have used these exercises, will find this self-teaching method both challenging and helpful.

WRITING TEST

NAME _____

PURPOSE	To show that you understand the self-teaching method, and to give you a chance to ask any questions you may have about using this book.

ASSIGNMENT	Write a letter to your instructor explaining how you will work on the exercises in this book. Use this format:

> [DATE]
>
> Dear Professor [NAME],
>
> [YOUR ANSWERS TO THE QUESTIONS BELOW]
>
> Yours truly,
> [YOUR SIGNATURE]
> [YOUR PRINTED NAME]

Check off each step in the writing process as you complete it.

DRAFT	❏	Look back over this module, and re-read *Teaching Yourself* on page 6. On scratch paper, write a rough draft of your letter. Write a couple of complete sentences about each of the following:

- ■ Have you used self-teaching exercises like these before?

- ■ What is your role in this kind of learning?

- ■ What is your instructor's role?

- ■ Where, when, and for how long will you work on your assignment each week?

- ■ What do you hope to get out of this course?

- ■ What other comments or questions do you have?

REVISE	❏	Read over the draft of your letter to make sure that you have written something about each of the questions above. Try to anticipate what your instructor will want to know as you add, take out, or change ideas, words, or sentences. Remember, it's good for a draft to become messy.
EDIT	❏	Read over the draft of your letter again. Correct any mistakes you find.

    ❏   Make sure that your letter is in correct letter format, including use of commas in the opening and closing.

    ❏   Make sure that **every word** is spelled correctly, including your instructor's name and the words *Yours truly*.

FINAL COPY   ❏   Write the final copy of your letter carefully, using blue or black ink and standard-sized (8½ by 11 inch) paper. Better yet, type or use a word processor. Remember that you are now preparing your writing for a reader.

PROOFREAD   ❏   Read your final copy **out loud**. If you find any mistakes, it's OK to correct them neatly by hand. Or if you have used a word processor, go back and correct your mistakes, and then print out a clean final copy.

Attach your final copy to these instructions, and hand them both in.

Three Essential Skills

NAME _____

As you complete each exercise, record your number of mistakes below.

1.1 _____   1.4 _____   1.7 _____

1.2 _____   1.5 _____

1.3 _____   1.6 _____

Module 1: *Three Essential Skills*

This module will focus on three skills that are basic to all clear, correct writing: the skills of **copying accurately**, **proofreading carefully**, and **using the dictionary**.

According to some experts, more than half of students' errors in writing are caused by weakness in these skills. As you learn to copy your notes and drafts accurately, to proofread your drafts carefully, and to use your dictionary thoughtfully and often, you'll find that many of your mistakes will simply vanish from your papers.

This module can only begin to strengthen these three essential skills. But if you work carefully, this whole book will help you to find and correct errors in your own writing, because the self-teaching approach trains your eye to notice details on the page.

1A.   Copy accurately.

A writer's ability to copy accurately is a big plus. On the job (as computer operators know well), errors in copying names, symbols, and even punctuation marks cost time and money. In college courses, you'll often have to copy unfamiliar words, difficult names, complicated formulas, and lists of numbers. The last step in writing a paper is making a perfect copy of your final revision. The following exercise will test your copying skills.

Exercise 1.1 Copy the following names and formulas by writing one letter, digit, or symbol on each blank line. Leave no lines blank except where there are blanks between the words to be copied.

1. Ngapo Khyen *(a Tibetan name)*

    — — — — — — — — — — —

2. Jonkheer Bastinaansz *(a Dutch name)*

    — — — — — — — — — — — — — — — — — —

3. Katsutoshi Harabayashi *(a Japanese name)*

    —

4. antidisestablishmentarianism *(a word meaning "opposition to withdrawal of state support from a church")*

    —

5. floccipaucinihilipipification *(a word meaning "estimating something as worthless")*

    —

6. Shurnarkabtishashutu *(the name of a star, Arabic for "under the southern horn of the bull")*

    —

7. $Ca_2(Mg,Fe)_5(OH)_2(Si_4O_{11})_2$ *(the chemical formula for nephrite, a kind of jade)*

    —

8. T157962789704530739 *(a driver's license number)*

    —

Remember:

❏ Read and follow instructions step by step.

❏ Proofread your work on each exercise carefully.

❏ Tear out the exercise page along the perforations.

❏ Turn to the Answers and correct your mistakes, using a green pen to write in the **entire correct form**. (Don't just change or add a letter.)

❏ Record your number of mistakes on the module cover page. If none, write 0.

❏ Save your exercises in your three-ring notebook or folder.

‖‖‖ 1B.   Proofread carefully.

Proofreading seems as if it should be easy. When you're reading someone else's writing, errors jump right out at you. Unfortunately, that doesn't happen when the writing is your own. Since you already **know** what you mean by what you've written, your eye just glides right past omitted or incorrect letters, words, and punctuation marks. The exercises that follow will help you see how strong your proofreading skills are.

Important: One of the most effective ways to proofread is to read out loud. Train your eye and ear to work together. Listen to the sound of your voice as you look closely at the words. Are the words on the page the correct words? Have any words been left out? Have any **parts** of words been left out?

Exercise 1.2 (1) Read each sentence out loud. (2) Underline any words that are incorrect. (3) Write the entire correct word in the space above the line. Follow this model:

God

The motto of the Treasury Department is "In <u>Gold</u> We Trust."

1. A girl with three younger bothers often has a difficult childhood.

2. In the early evening, the fireworks factory was rocked by a powderful explosion.

3. When his mother walked in with a tiny bundle in her arms, Gerald rushed up to get a good look at his

    new baby sitter.

4. The beat way to prepare this sauce is to beat it vigorously for three minutes.

5. Victor, an experienced electricity from Czechoslovakia, wants to join the local electricians' onion.

Before you look at the Answers for Exercise 1.2, reread the instructions. Consider these questions:

❑ Did you read each sentence out loud?

❑ How many corrections did you make? _____ You should have made six.

Now turn to the Answers to check your work.

You probably did pretty well in finding the mistakes in Exercise 1.2, because mistakes are easy to see in isolated sentences. However, the proofreading exercise that follows may be more difficult. The kinds of mistakes in it confuse readers much more than the obvious ones you just saw. At the same time, they're the kinds that writers have the hardest time seeing when they proofread their own work.

Exercise 1.3 The following paragraph contains no errors. Read it carefully before you try to correct the version that follows.

> Buying property is even riskier than buying used cars. For example, a store by the library in my neighborhood is going to be put up for sale soon. The owner, Hank Dawson, may try to get $90,000 for it, but the value of the property is actually much less than that. A building inspector was in the basement recently and saw termites. He checked the beams and found they were completely rotten and ready to collapse. Buyers, beware! Dawson is a born liar. Whatever claims he makes about that building, you can bet your bottom dollar they're not true.

Here is the same paragraph, but full of mistakes, as a careless student might have copied it. **Without looking back at the original paragraph,** proofread this version carefully. Mark mistakes like this: (1) Cross out any word that has been repeated. (2) Put a caret (∧) if a word has been omitted, and write the missing word in the space above the line. (3) Underline each incorrect word, and correct it in the space above the line. The first three mistakes have been corrected for you.

Buying property is ~~X~~ riskier than buying used <u>car</u>. *(even)* *(cars)* For example, a store be the library in my

my neighborhood is going to by put up for sail soon. The owner, Hank Dawson, my try to get

$60,000 for, but the value of the the Property is actually much less than that. A building

inspector saw in the basement recently and saw termites. He checked the beams and found the

were completely rotten and ready to collapse. Buyers, beware! Dawson is a born liar. whatever

claims he makes about that building, you can bet you bottom dollar they're true.

Before turning to the Answers at the back of the book, answer these questions:

☐ How many corrections did you make in Exercise 1.3? Count them and write the number here: _____

☐ The paragraph in Exercise 1.3 contained 14 mistakes, not counting the three that were corrected for you. If you didn't find all 14, proofread the paragraph again, reading it **out loud**, word by word. **Listen** for mistakes as you read it. Now how many did you find? _____

☐ If you still didn't find all 14, proofread the paragraph once again, this time comparing it to the original. **Look** for mistakes as you compare it. (There are three mistakes that you must actually **see**.) Now how many did you find? _____

Now turn to the Answers to check your work. Remember to use your green pen to correct your mistakes by **writing in the entire correct word.**

Be sure that you:

■ corrected everything that was wrong;

■ corrected it in the right way; and

■ didn't change anything that was already right.

If you over-corrected, use your green pen to **cross out** the change that you should not have made.

Now count your total number of green corrections. This is the number of mistakes you made in doing the exercise. Write this number on the cover page for this module, where you keep track of your work.

Caution: Learning from your mistakes is an important part of this self-teaching method. If you don't use a different-colored pen when you correct your work, it will be hard for you to locate your mistakes. It will also be hard for you to review.

Exercise 1.4 The following paragraph contains no errors. Read it carefully before you go on.

> Today most people know that smoking is a health hazard. But in the motion pictures of the 1920s and 1930s, cigarette smoking appeared to be harmless and even glamorous. Film stars wearing tuxedos and evening gowns lighted each other's cigarettes in night club scenes. Screen detectives chain-smoked as they solved their cases. The children in "Our Gang" pictures sneaked their first puffs behind the barn. To modern audiences watching old movies, the constant presence of this dangerous habit is somewhat disturbing.

Here is the same paragraph, but full of mistakes, as a careless student might have copied it. **Without looking back at the original paragraph**, proofread this version carefully. Mark mistakes like this: (1) Put a caret (∧) if a word has been omitted, and write the missing word in the space above the line. (2) Underline each incorrect word, and correct it in the space above the line.

Today most people know that smoking is health hazard. But the motion pictures of the

1920s and 1930s, cigarette smoking appeared be harmless and even glamorous. Film stars wearing tuxedos and evening gowns lighted other's cigarettes in night club scenes. Screen

detectives chain-smoked as solved their cases. The children in "Our Gang" pictures sneaked

their first puffs behind barn. To modern audiences watching movies, the constant presence of

this dangerous habit somewhat disturbing.

Before turning to the Answers at the back of the book, answer these questions:

❑ How many corrections did you make in Exercise 1.4? Count them and write the number here: _____

❑ The paragraph in Exercise 1.4 contained eight mistakes. If you didn't find all eight, proofread the paragraph again, reading it **out loud**, word by word. **Listen** for mistakes as you read it. Now how many did you find? _____

❑ If you still didn't find all eight, proofread the paragraph once again, this time comparing it to the original. **Look** for mistakes as you compare it. Now how many did you find? _____

❑ What one kind of error is repeated over and over by the writer of the paragraph in Exercise 1.4?

_____

Now turn to the Answers to check your work.

Exercise 1.5 Here is the same paragraph, as it might have been copied by another careless student. **Without looking back at the original paragraph,** proofread this second version carefully. Mark mistakes like this:
(1) Put a caret (⌃) if a word has been omitted, and write the missing word in the space above the line.
(2) Underline each incorrect word, and correct it in the space above the line.

Today most people know that smoking is a health hazard. But in the motion picture of the

1920s and 1930s, cigarette smoking appear to be harmless and even glamorous. Film stars wear

tuxedos and evening gown lighted each other's cigarettes in night club scene. Screen detectives

chain-smoked as they solve their cases. The children in "Our Gang" pictures sneaked their first

puffs behind the barn. To modern audiences watch old movies, the constant presence of this

danger habit is somewhat disturbing.

Before turning to the Answers at the back of the book, answer these questions:

❑ How many corrections did you make in Exercise 1.5? Count them and write the number here: _____

❑ The paragraph in Exercise 1.5 contained eight mistakes. If you didn't find all eight, proofread the paragraph again, reading it **out loud**, word by word. **Listen** for mistakes as you read it. Now how many did you find? _____

14

❑   If you still didn't find all eight, proofread the paragraph once again, this time comparing it to the original. **Look** for mistakes as you compare it. Now how many did you find? _____

❑   What one kind of error is repeated over and over by the writer of the paragraph in Exercise 1.5?

_____

Now turn to the Answers to check your work.

Exercise 1.6 Here is the same paragraph, as it might have been copied by yet another careless student. **Without looking back at the original paragraph**, proofread this version carefully: (1) Put a caret (⌃) if a word has been omitted, and write the missing word in the space above the line. (2) Underline each incorrect word, and correct it in the space above the line.

> Today most poeple know that smoking is a health hazard. But in the motion pictures of the
>
> 1920s and 1930s, cigarette smoking appeared to be harmless and even glamorous. Flim stars
>
> wearing tuxedos and evening gowns lihgted each other's cigarettes in night club scenes. Screen
>
> detectives chain-smoked as they solved their cases. The childern in "Our Gang" pictures
>
> sneaked their frist puffs behind the barn. To modren audeinces watching old movies, the
>
> constant presence of this dangerous habit is somewhat distrubing.

Before turning to the Answers at the back of the book, answer these questions:

❑   How many corrections did you make in Exercise 1.6? Count them and write the number here: _____

❑   The paragraph in Exercise 1.6 contained eight mistakes. If you didn't find all eight, proofread the paragraph again, comparing it to the original. **Look** for mistakes as you compare it. Now how many did you find? _____

❑   What one kind of error is repeated over and over by the writer of the paragraph in Exercise 1.6? (Yes, it's a spelling mistake, but **what kind** of spelling mistake?)

_____

Now turn to the Answers to check your work.

Put an ✗ in the box next to the exercise (or exercises) which you found most difficult:

❑   1.4   (missing words)
❑   1.5   (missing endings)
❑   1.6   (reversed letters)

Important: Your answer to this question suggests the kinds of mistakes you tend to miss in your own writing. Proofread for these kinds of mistakes with special care.

||||| 1C.   Make good use of your dictionary.

The most important single tool for making your writing clear and correct is a good dictionary. In doing these exercises, you'll need to refer to your dictionary frequently, and as a college student, you should carry it with you all the time.

Your instructor may have a preference for a particular dictionary; if not, he or she can recommend a good one. Paperback dictionaries are convenient, but if you use one, be sure that it is complete and comprehensive. Many suitable dictionaries have the word *College* in their titles.

The most important use of a dictionary is to check the **spelling** of words. But there are many other things that you can learn from using your dictionary.

Exercise 1.7 Look up the word *calorie* in your dictionary, and fill in the blanks below. (If you can't fill in all the blanks, you'll probably need a bigger dictionary for your work on the exercises in this book.)

1.   The word *calorie* has _____ letters and is spelled _ _ _ _ _ _ _ .

2.   Each part of a word that is pronounced separately is called a **syllable**. For example, the word *syl-la-ble*

   has three syllables. The dictionary shows that the word *calorie* has _____

   syllables.

3.   The dictionary shows that when you pronounce this word, the _____

   syllable is stressed.

4.   The dictionary gives the abbreviation _____ to show that the word *calorie* is used as a noun.

5.   The first meaning given for the word *calorie* is:

   _____

   _____

6.   To summarize, the five basic pieces of information which the dictionary gives about every word are:

   a.   its S _ _ _ _ _ _ G;

   b.   how many S _ _ _ _ _ _ _ S it has;

   c.   its P _ _ _ _ _ _ _ _ _ _ _ N;

   d.   whether it is used as a verb, an adjective, a N _ _ N, or in some other way; and

   e.   what it M _ _ _ S.

Now turn to the Answers to check your work.

Caution: The rest of this book will help you review the most important rules of written English. But rules are useless unless you can apply them in your own writing. The self-teaching method of these exercises helps bridge this gap between learning the rules and applying them. One of the ways it does this is by developing the skills that you worked on in this module:

1. **Copying:** In many exercises, you must pay close attention to details as you make small but important changes while copying sentences and paragraphs. This kind of practice helps you to be more accurate in all of your own writing.

2. **Proofreading:** In checking your own work, you must compare your handwritten answers to the printed answers. This trains your eye to find mistakes in your own writing.

3. **Using the Dictionary:** In many exercises throughout this book, you must use your dictionary. This teaches you how to check your spelling, how to make sure that the forms of various words are correct, and how to make sure that you are using the correct word, the word that means exactly what you are trying to say.

To use this self-teaching method successfully, you must follow instructions thoughtfully and carefully. There's a good reason for every step in these exercises. If you use shortcuts (like copying from the Answers), you'll just be wasting time. The point isn't to **do** the exercises; it's to **use** them to improve your own writing.

Module 1: *Three Essential Skills*

WRITING TEST

NAME _____

PURPOSE   To show that you can copy accurately and proofread carefully.

ASSIGNMENT   Copy the following paragraph exactly, word for word.

> We often remember, or think we remember, being told not to use the word "I" in our writing. I think this advice is foolish. Sure, I can avoid the word "I," by avoiding writing about my concerns. But why would I ever want to do this? I can't write successfully about something that is of no concern to me; no one can. If I write about something that matters to me, I know I'll have plenty to say, while the ideas will come very hard if I don't care about the subject. And if I care about what I write, I don't make a lot of foolish mistakes that reveal my lack of attention and make me look silly. Further, when what I write means something to me, it can mean something to others as well; they care (or don't care) along with me. So why avoid the word "I"? The advantages of using it are too many.

Check off each step as you complete it.

READ   ❏   The paragraph above contains no errors. Read it, making sure that you understand it completely.

COPY   ❏   Copy the paragraph carefully, without making any changes. For this assignment, do not use a typewriter or word processor. Use blue or black ink and standard-sized (8½ by 11 inch) paper. Write your name in the upper right-hand corner or use whatever heading your instructor requires.

PROOFREAD ❏   Read your copy **out loud**, comparing it to the paragraph above. Be sure that you haven't left out any words or punctuation marks. If you find any mistakes, it's OK to correct them neatly.

Attach your copy to these instructions, and hand them both in.

2 Writing Conventions

NAME _____

As you complete each exercise, record your number of mistakes below.

2.1 ____	2.9 ____	2.17 ____
2.2 ____	2.10 ____	2.18 ____
2.3 ____	2.11 ____	Summary ____
2.4 ____	2.12 ____	2.19 ____
2.5 ____	2.13 ____	2.20 ____
2.6 ____	2.14 ____	2.21 ____
2.7 ____	2.15 ____	
2.8 ____	2.16 ____	

INSTRUCTOR'S COMMENTS

Instructions:

❏ Followed carefully
❏ Not followed carefully enough

Checking:

❏ Careful
❏ Not careful enough to catch all your mistakes
❏ Green pen not used for checking
❏ Entire correct answer not always written in

Writing Test:

❏ Excellent
❏ Good
❏ Acceptable
❏ Not yet satisfactory

Other:

Module 2: *Writing Conventions*

RULES

Writing conventions are a few commonsense rules about how to put words on paper. These conventions are a relatively recent invention.

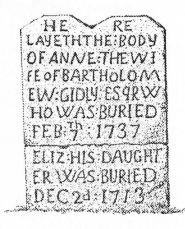

Here is an inscription carved about three hundred years ago on a tombstone at Gidleigh in Devon, England. Most people have trouble reading this epitaph because a few basic writing conventions weren't followed consistently. Some of these conventions are: (1) leaving space between words, but not in the middle of a word, (2) using capital (large) and lower-case (small) letters appropriately, (3) avoiding abbreviations, (4) using standard spelling, and (5) putting a period at the end of a sentence. We take these conventions for granted until we see a piece of writing, like this inscription, where they aren't observed.

Exercise 2.1 Rewrite the inscription, using space between words, capital and lower-case letters, no abbreviations (except for *7th* and *2d*), and a period at the end of each sentence. (Hint: *Esqr* is an abbreviation for the word *Esquire*, a title indicating an English country gentleman, and *Eliz* is an abbreviation for *Elizabeth*.)

_____

_____

_____

_____

Remember: Check your work as you go along, using the Answers in the back of the book. Write in your number of mistakes on the cover page of this module.

Exercise 2.2 Here is a sentence with correct spelling, but without a capital letter at the beginning, space between words, or a period at the end. Rewrite it correctly.

computerswillprobablychangeouroldwritingconventionsandmayhavealreadyintroducedafewnewones

_____

_____

_____

Important: Even if you're sure that you've done an exercise correctly, turn to the Answers and check your work. Comparing what you've written to the printed words in the Answers will help train your eye to notice details on the page.

2A.   Indent the first line of each paragraph distinctly.

1.   To indicate a paragraph, indent about half an inch, or the width of your thumb. Indent five spaces on a word processor or typewriter.

A new paragraph shows that the writer wants to focus attention on something new.

Exercise 2.3 Read the following passage carefully, and then answer the questions.

> The blind and deaf child, Helen Keller, stood by the pump. Water rushed from the spout. As she put one hand under the cold stream, her teacher, Annie Sullivan, spelled the word *water* into the other hand. Using a special code, Annie tapped out each letter of that word, just as she had done so many times before. But to Helen this was just a game. She didn't know that these taps meant words. She did not know what words were. She only knew about things—hot and cold, wet and dry, soft and hard **things**. Suddenly the little girl became very still, with her whole attention concentrated on the sensation of those spelling fingers. At that moment the mystery of language was revealed to her. She understood that those taps meant the wonderful cool thing that was running over her hand. She understood that each thing had a name. Each thing in the world had its own special name—water, trees, flowers, her doll. She took her hand out of the water and tapped its name into the warm hand of her friend. She was almost seven years old and she had just "spoken" her first word.

1. In the first part of this passage, the writer is focusing attention on the fact that the child Helen Keller

    _____ _____ _____ what words were.

2. In the second part of the passage, the writer is focusing attention on the moment when Helen first

    _____ that each thing had a name.

3. This passage would be clearer if it were written as two paragraphs. Insert a paragraph mark (¶) at the

    place in the passage where the writer first focuses the reader's attention on the second idea.

Important: Before you go on, check the Answers to Exercise 2.3.

2. When a sentence ends in the middle of a line, begin the next sentence on the same line.

> The blind and deaf child, Helen Keller, stood by the pump. Water
> rushed from the spout.   **✗**
> As she put one hand under the cold stream, her teacher, Annie Sullivan,
> spelled the word *water* into the other hand. . . .

Never leave space at the end of a line unless it's the last line in the paragraph.

Writing should flow on from one page to the next just as if it were written on a continuous roll of paper. Sentences often begin on the last line of one page and continue on the first line of the next. **Never** leave a space after the last sentence on a page, unless it's the last sentence in a paragraph.

Incorrect:

~~~~ ~~~~ ~~~~~
~~~~.

W~~~ ~~~ ~~~~~~
~~~~ ~~~~ ~~~~

The space after the last sentence on the page is incorrect, because the next sentence doesn't begin a new paragraph.

Correct:

~~~~ ~~~~ ~~~~~
~~~~. W~~~ ~~~

~~~~ ~~~ ~~~~~~
~~~~ ~~~~ ~~~~

This is correct. There is no space after the last sentence on the page.

Important: Don't indent at the top of a page unless a new paragraph begins there.

Exercise 2.4 Rewrite the following passage as two paragraphs, indenting each paragraph distinctly. Start the second paragraph where a new idea begins.

> Anglo-Saxon, an old Germanic language, ranks first among many languages that contributed to our modern English vocabulary. This language, spoken by early inhabitants of England, gave us words like <u>cow</u>, <u>pig</u>, <u>plow</u>, <u>walk</u> – common words associated with outdoor life and the activities of farmers and workers. The second most important source of modern English words is Norman French. This language, brought to England by a conquering army, gave us words like <u>beef</u>, <u>pork</u>, <u>study</u>, <u>dance</u> – more refined words associated with life indoors and the pastimes of a ruling class.

_____

_____

_____

_____

_____

_____

_____

_____

_____

_____

_____

Remember: Before you turn to the Answers to check your work, proofread for spelling, punctuation, underlining, and paragraph indentation.

2B. **Use capital letters for the following:**
   1. The first letter of a sentence;
   2. The word *I*;
   3. The first letter of a name (and a title used with a name); and
   4. The first letter of a word made from a name.

Did I get the right answer?

> *D* is a capital letter because it's the first letter of a sentence.
> *I* is a capital letter because the word *I* is always capitalized.

The retired general teaches at a local college.

> The words *general* and *college* aren't capitalized because they aren't parts of specific names.

Does General Gibson teach at Pomona College?

> The word *General* is capitalized because it's a title used with a name.
> The words *Gibson*, *Pomona*, and *College* are capitalized because they're specific names or parts of specific names.

My brother is studying sociology and English at a Nigerian university.

> The word *sociology* isn't capitalized because it isn't part of a specific course name.
> The words *English* and *Nigerian* are capitalized because they're made from the names *England* and *Nigeria*.
> The word *university* isn't capitalized because it isn't part of the name of a specific university.

Exercise 2.5 Underline each word that should begin with a capital letter, and write the entire correct word in the space above the line. Follow this model:

My   Boston College

my mother works at boston college.

1. when roberto goes to college, he will study psychology and spanish.

2. has your mother made an appointment with the doctor?

3. today i went to see dr. alston.

4. my youngest uncle is an engineer for the sperry corporation.

5. the house where aunt sally was born is on narcissus street.

Exercise 2.6 Underline each word that should not begin with a capital letter, and write the entire correct word in the space above the line. Follow this model:

brother   *power company*
My Brother applied for a job with a Power Company in Santa Fe.

1. St. Mary's is the only Church in the Neighborhood that has a Raffle every Friday night.

2. Our accounting Professor owns stock in the Railroad which was taken over by the Metropolitan Transit

    Authority.

3. The local High School improved its Curriculum by offering new courses in Geography and requiring four

    years of Spanish or another Foreign Language.

2C.   Be sure that your sentences are punctuated correctly and distinctly.

1.   Use a clear capital letter at the beginning of each sentence, and be sure that end punctuation is clear.

College costs are rising, this means many students can't attend full-time.

Because the letter *T* in *This* isn't clearly capitalized, and because the punctuation mark in the middle isn't clearly either a comma or a period, it isn't clear whether this is two correct sentences or a run-on (which is an error).

2.   Use a period at the end of a statement. Use a question mark at the end of a question.

Is the game over **?**

A question mark is used because this sentence asks a question.

I asked whether the game was over **.**

> A period is used because this sentence makes a statement. It tells what I asked.

Don't forget the period or question mark at the end of the last sentence in a paragraph.

Exercise 2.7 (1) Underline each word that should begin with a capital letter, and rewrite it correctly in the space above the line. (2) Write in the correct punctuation mark clearly at the end of each sentence. Follow this model:

Will
<u>will</u> they come tomorrow **?**

1. is it time to go

2. did he ask if it was time to go

3. he asked if it was time to go

4. they couldn't decide whether or not to write the letter

5. did loretta write the letter

3. **<u>Never</u> put a space <u>before</u> punctuation.**
   <u>Always</u> put a space <u>after</u> punctuation.

Put two spaces at the ends of sentences and after colons. Put one space after other punctuation marks.

When I looked at her, ☐ she turned away from me. ☐☐ Then she started to run.
> The ☐ marks where there are spaces.

Important: Parentheses ( ) and quotation marks " " are exceptions to the rule about spacing. Never put spaces after the first parenthesis or quotation mark.

My brother ☐ (the one with the beard) ☐ asked, ☐ "Where are you going?"
> The ☐ marks where there are spaces.

Be especially careful about spacing when you're writing with a typewriter or word processor.

2D. **Avoid most abbreviations.**

    ✗   ✗   ✗   ✗ ✗   ✗
While visiting the <u>U.S.</u> last <u>Oct.</u>, the <u>Fr.</u> architect toured <u>N.Y.C.</u> <u>&</u> photographed many <u>bldgs.</u>
> Avoid abbreviations like these.
> Never use the ampersand sign *&* instead of the word *and*.

While visiting the <u>United States</u> last <u>October</u>, the <u>French</u> architect toured <u>New York City</u> and photographed many <u>buildings</u>.

Spelled out words are easier to read.

Of course, some abbreviations are appropriate in writing. In writing the time of day, use the abbreviations *AM* and *PM* (or *a.m.* and *p.m.*).

Abbreviations of titles like *Sgt.* and *Prof.* are appropriate when used with specific names. The titles *Mr.*, *Mrs.*, and *Dr.* are **always** abbreviated when they're used with a name.

The abbreviation *etc.* is usually acceptable.

Abbreviations like *St.*, *Ave.*, and *Blvd.* and abbreviations of state names are acceptable in specific addresses.

Use a period after most abbreviations except the capital letters used for a state name. If an abbreviation is the last word in a sentence, don't use two periods.

<u>Dr.</u> Mulero has mail delivered to his new address: 725 Tulip <u>St.</u>, Floral City, <u>FL</u> 33417.

Dr. is abbreviated because it's used with a specific name.
St. and *FL* are acceptable abbreviations because they're parts of a specific address.

Many <u>doctors</u> have offices in expensive locations like Boston's Beacon Hill, New York's Park <u>Avenue</u>, <u>etc.</u>

The word *doctors* isn't abbreviated because it isn't a title used with a name.
The word *Avenue* isn't abbreviated because it isn't part of a specific address.
When the abbreviation *etc.* comes at the end of a sentence, only one period follows it.

Exercise 2.8 Rewrite each sentence, changing abbreviations to their written-out forms. But don't change the acceptable abbreviations.

1. L.A. has the worst pollution problem in Cal., and perhaps the worst in the U.S.

   _____

   _____

2. Between Battery Pk. & Greenwich Village, most of the sts. in N.Y.C. have names instead of numbers.

   _____

   _____

3. Dr. Farley's new address is:
        15722 Princess St.
        River Falls, MN 55203

_____

_____

_____

‖‖‖ 2E.   Spell out the numbers *one* through *ten*.

There were <u>26</u> actors on stage and <u>six</u> people in the audience when the performance began.

> The number *26* isn't spelled out because it's more than *ten*.
> The number *six* is spelled out because it's less than *ten*.

For most college and business writing, it's also acceptable to spell out other numbers that can be written as one word, especially round numbers: *twelve, thirty, a hundred, a thousand*.

Numbers in lists and in scientific and technical writing are usually not spelled out.

Numbers are acceptable in words like *11th*, *22nd*, and *33rd* when the numbers are more than ten.

Do not spell out numbers in addresses or dates. But always spell out numbers at the beginning of a sentence.

<u>Nineteen</u> people gathered at <u>6</u> Main Street on July <u>4, 1989</u>.

> *Nineteen* is spelled out because it's at the beginning of a sentence.
> But *6* is not spelled out because it's part of an address, and *4* and *1989* are not spelled out because they're part of a date.

Exercise 2.9 Underline each error in abbreviations and numbers, and write the correct word, number, or punctuation mark in the space above the line. Follow this model:

>   *one*   *England*
> Frances has <u>1</u> brother who lives in <u>Eng.</u>

1. I read only 3 chapters of the book Mrs. Duff lent me, & then I lost it.

2. The prof. in my govt. class assigned one hundred and thirty-three pp. of homework for Tues.

3. When I was 6 yrs. old, we moved to a quiet st. in Phila.

4. 90 people began to picket in front of 10 Downing St., London, on March 9, 1968.

5. She told me to take 1 teaspoonful of cough medicine every four hrs for the next 48 hours.

2F.   In contractions, use an apostrophe to show where letters have been omitted.

it is	→	it☐s	→	it's
are not	→	aren☐t	→	aren't
do not	→	don☐t	→	don't

Apostrophes show where the letters *I* and *O* have been omitted.

will not	→	w☐n☐t	→	won't

The contraction *won't* is irregular.

Contracted forms are more informal than uncontracted forms, but they're usually acceptable in college and business writing.

Exercise 2.10 Write these two-word forms as contractions.

1. it is   _____

2. does not   _____

3. is not   _____

4. I am   _____

5. do not   _____

6. will not   _____

Exercise 2.11 Rewrite each underlined pair of words as a contraction in the space above the line. The first contraction has been written for you.

It's

It is amazing how much we are able to learn about the good old days from old mail order

catalogues. Here is a sampling of their ads between 1912 and 1932:

Model H Motor Car, $348: "We will refund every penny if it will not go fifteen miles an hour."

Baby Grand Piano, $118: "She is a beauty. Delivery? It is free!"

Two-piece Bathing Suits, $1.63: "They are the latest—backless and skirtless." And a model

says, "Where is your courage? I am wearing one. It is the cat's pajamas."

28

Bargains? <u>You are</u> wrong. A person <u>who is</u> making five dollars an hour today <u>would not</u>

have made five dollars a day when these ads were printed.

Exercise 2.12 This paragraph contains contractions that are incorrect because they are missing apostrophes. Underline each incorrect contraction, and correct it in the space above the line. The first error has been corrected for you.

you're
If <u>youre</u> on a diet, its likely that youre counting calories. However, nutritionists are now

saying that calories arent necessarily bad for a person whos trying to lose weight. Theyve

discovered that carbohydrates like potatoes, bread, and cereals have lots of calories, but theyre

full of nutrition, so they dont add pounds quickly. On the other hand, fats like butter arent

nutritious at all, so its easy to gain weight by eating them. Even worse, most people dont realize

how much fat theyre getting in cheese, meat, and ready-made foods. So if youre dieting, youd do

well to remember this: Fats what makes you fat.

2G.   Don't write one word as two words, or two words as one.

1.   Some words are always written in either a two-word form or a one-word form.

These should always be written as two words:

    a lot   all right   even though   in fact   no one

Write these words here, to help you remember them:

_____   _____   _____

_____   _____

These should always be written as one word:

furthermore   however   myself   nevertheless   throughout

Write these words here, to help you remember them:

_____   _____   _____

_____   _____

2. **Other words are sometimes written as one word and sometimes written as two words, depending on what they mean.**

Bill wrote to his mother <u>every day</u>.

> In this sentence, *every* and *day* are two words. They mean "on every single day."

Ginny wore her <u>everyday</u> clothes.

> In this sentence, *everyday* is one word. It means "ordinary" or "commonplace."

Important: If you're not sure whether a word should be written as one word or as two, use your dictionary to look up the one-word form. If the one-word form doesn't have the meaning you want, then you should write the two-word form.

❑   Look up the word *maybe* (the one-word form) in your dictionary. Write the definition here:

_____

❑   Now you know that the word *maybe* (the one-word form) means something like "perhaps" or "possibly."

Put an **✗** in front of the sentence where *possibly* is **not** used correctly:

<u>Possibly</u> Karen is in the library.
You <u>possibly</u> excused.

❑   Now put an **✗** in front of the sentence where *maybe* is **not** used correctly:

<u>Maybe</u> Karen is in the library.
You <u>maybe</u> excused.

> *Maybe* can be written as one word in the first sentence because it means "possibly." *Maybe* cannot be written as one word in the second sentence because it does not mean "possibly."

You <u>may be</u> excused.

> *May be* must be written as two words in this sentence because it does not mean "possibly."

Exercise 2.13 (1) Look up the given one-word form in your dictionary, and write in its definition. (2) Then fill in the one-word and two-word forms.

1. **everyday / every day**

   Everyday means _____ .

   a. _____ most people do their jobs and care for their families.

   b. These _____ activities require commitment, even dedication.

2. **nobody / no body**

   Nobody means _____ .

   a. The court declared Judge Crater dead even though _____ was ever

      found.

   b. Jane had nothing and _____ to call her own.

3. **sometimes / some times**

   Sometimes means _____ .

   a. For criticizing your parents, _____ are better than others.

   b. You are _____ exasperating.

Exercise 2.14 Underline each word that should be two words, or two words that should be one word, and write the entire correct word or words in the space above the line. For help, use your dictionary.

Health care costs so much nowadays that people worry alot about taking care of

them selves. Infact, everyday expenses are so heavy now that almost no body (my self included)

has any money put a side for health emergencies. How ever, I had a high fever to day and

decided that maybe I should see my doctor, who gave me an anti biotic. She said I maybe allright

by to morrow. I certainly hope so, for I donot want to miss an other day at work.

2H.   If you divide a long word at the end of a line, use a <u>hyphen</u> to divide it, between syllables.

In olden times, men commonly kissed or hugged. But modern men show friendship with a <u>hand-</u>
<u>shake</u>.

> The word *handshake* has two syllables, *hand* and *shake*. It can be divided with a hyphen if it occurs at the end of a line.

You cannot divide a word that is pronounced in one syllable, such as *kissed* or *hugged*.

✗

Modern men show friendship with a handshake. But in olden times, men commonly <u>kiss-</u>
<u>ed</u> or hugged.

> Because the word *kissed* has only one sound, it has only one syllable. It cannot be divided. This hyphen is incorrect.

Exercise 2.15 Use your dictionary to rewrite each word with hyphens at the place(s) where it can be divided, and write in the number of syllables in the word. Follow this model:

released   <u>re - leased</u>   <u>2</u> syllables

1. carelessness   _____   _____ syllables

2. revolution   _____   _____ syllables

3. walked   _____   _____ syllables

4. vehicle   _____   _____ syllables

5. athlete   _____   _____ syllables

6. underlined   _____   _____ syllables

2I.   When proofreading your writing, check carefully for omitted words and for words repeated unnecessarily.

Exercise 2.16 (1) Cross out any word which is carelessly repeated. (2) Put a caret (︿) where any necessary word has been omitted, and write it in the space above the line. The first two errors have been corrected for you.

When the ~~the~~ French sculptor Bartholdi offered ^to^ build monumental statue in

in New York Harbor to commemorate the first century American independence,

France promised to pay for constructing the statue, and America agreed to to finance the pedestal. Money poured in from thousands French citizens. In

contrast, Americans were particularly enthusiastic about the project, and

and journalists had to shame New York City millionaires into contributing even a

few dollars from their fortunes. Recently, when Lady Liberty was about to

celebrate her 100th birthday, Americans were much more much generous in

contributing to the monument's restoration.

❑   How many corrections did you make in Exercise 2.16? _____

❑   The paragraph in Exercise 2.16 contained eight errors, not counting the two that were corrected for you.
    If you didn't find all eight, proofread the paragraph again, reading it **out loud**, word by word. **Listen** for
    mistakes as you read it. Now how many did you find? _____

Now turn to the Answers to check your work.

Exercise 2.17 This paragraph contains incorrect words, numbers, abbreviations, and punctuation marks.
Underline each error, and correct it in the space above the line.

today i went to see dr. alston. She told me to take 1 teaspoonful of cough

medicine every four hrs for the next 48 hours. She said I maybe allright by to

morrow.

Now turn to the Answers to check your work.

The sentences in Exercise 2.17 should seem familiar, because you worked with all of them earlier in this
section. If you were unsure about anything in this exercise, that is a sign that you're not doing and checking
your work carefully enough. If you find and correct all your mistakes as you go along, and go back over the
rules to be sure that you **understand** and **remember** them, then you can avoid making the same mistakes again
and again.

2J.   When proofreading your writing, use your dictionary to check <u>spelling</u>.

Spelling is also an important writing convention. Usually there is just one way to spell a word, and you will
find that spelling in the dictionary.

Exercise 2.18 This paragraph contains commonly misspelled words, but no other errors. Underline each misspelled word, and correct it in the space above the line. For help, use your dictionary. The first error has been corrected for you.

automobile

The <u>automobil</u> has changed the landscape and the way we live dramaticly in less than a

hundred years. Citys once were built on rivers, with stores clustered on Main Street. Now

suburban shoping malls and parking lots sprawl for miles along the highways, and it's not unusal

for families to own two or even three cars. Scientists who are studing the enviroment know that

car exaust fumes are a major cause of smog and acid rain. They even beleive that our reliance on

the internal combusiton engine may be contributting to global warming. Yet many Americans

still take thier right to drive for granted, and the avrage person thinks commuting to work by car

is far better than ridding on the mass transit system.

Important: If you made more than one mistake in Exercise 2.18, it would be a good idea to work on Appendix A, which reviews some important spelling rules.

RULES SUMMARY

In the longer one-page exercises that follow, you'll practice applying all the rules which you've learned or reviewed in this module. Before you go on to the longer exercises, check your understanding by filling in the blanks in the Rules Summary below. Fill in the blanks from memory, thinking carefully about what each rule means. If you need help, look back again at the Rules.

A.   Indent the first line of each _____ .

B.   Use capital letters for the first letter of each _____ ; for the word

_____ ; for the first letter of a _____ or a word made from a

_____ .

C.   End every sentence with either a _____ or a question mark.

D.   Avoid most _____ . Instead of *&* write _____ . Use

abbreviations of titles like *Dr.* and *Mr.* with specific _____ .

E.   Spell out the numbers _____ through _____ . Don't spell out numbers in

addresses, dates, or in most _____ or technical writing.

F.   In contractions, use an _____ to show where letters have been omitted.

G.   Don't write _____ word as two words, or _____ words as one. Use your

dictionary to find the meaning of the _____−word form.

H.   If you divide a word at the end of a line, use a _____ to divide it, between

_____ .

I.   When proofreading, check carefully for _____ words and

_____ words.

J.   When proofreading, use your _____ to check spelling.

Now turn to the Answers to check your work. Use these Rules and your dictionary as you go on to do the longer exercises that follow.

Module 2: *Writing Conventions*

PRACTICE

Underline each error in writing conventions, and write the entire correct word, number, or punctuation mark in the space above the line. Follow this model:

> She's
> Shes late again •

1. Among many famous people who never graduated from High School are Alfred E. Smith, the politician,

    & Thomas Edison, the inventor.

2. Why isnt queen Elizabeth coming to Toronto in Aug.

3. Every body in the congregation loves the Preacher at Trinity church.

4. Muhammad Ali earned $ six million five hundred thousand for 1 bout.

5. didnt you lend that library bk. to uncle Philip?

6. As i crossed the ave., some one shouted my name.

7. In 3 min., Megans going to be here.

8. George Patton, an american gen. in world war II, believed he had fought in 6 wars in previous

    incarnations.

9. This Summer I'am planning to enroll in Computer Science 101 in the College near my home.

10. The cassowary & the emu are 2 large australian birds which cant fly.

Exercise 2.20   **Number of Mistakes** _____

Rewrite this passage **as one paragraph,** correcting errors in the writing conventions that were taught in this module. The spelling, grammar, and sentence structure are correct, so **make no other changes.** Hint: the phrase *wonders of the world* should not be capitalized. In your rewritten paragraph, underline every change.

In our History class last week, I gave a report on the Golden Gate bridge in California. I'd heard alot about this bridge, but I wasnt really sure of all my facts. when I said the Bridge was one of the 7 wonders of the world, our Professor asked me what the other wonders were.
Infact, i didn't know, but I guessed the Rocky Mts. No one else in the class even tried to guess. Our teacher laughed & said he'd give us a hint. every single one of the seven wonders, he said, was built by man, and each was built at least 2,100 yrs. ago. After a while, some one guessed 1 right answer, those huge stone pyramids in egypt. But no body could name even one of the other six wonders. Can you.

_____

_____

_____

_____

_____

_____

_____

_____

_____

_____

_____

_____

_____

_____

Important: This passage needed 21 changes or corrections. How many did you find? _____ If you didn't find all 21, try again before you check your work.

Exercise 2.21

Number of Mistakes _____

This paragraph contains commonly misspelled words, but no other errors. Underline each misspelled word, and correct it in the space above the line. For help, use your dictionary. The first error has been corrected for you.

public

      The pulbic arguement between the big lighting companys and groups concerned about the

enviorment has become quite confussing to a lot of people. The power companies claim that

thier experts are studing the situtation. They say that by the year 2000 there will probaly not be

enought power if they can't build any more nuculear plants, and that continueing to use fossil

feuls also adds to enviromental problems. Big bussiness is generaly predjudiced in favor of the

power companies. But many who are intrested in the furture of the planet oppose their plans

because they perdict that overreliance on nucular powers will definately lead to more tradgedies

like the one at Chernobyl in the Soviet Union in 1986. The ordinary citizen dosen't know what

to beleive. Although blackouts and brownouts are ocuring regulerly, hardly any people are

writting to their representatives in Congress about an energy policy, not becuase they're

indiffrent, but because they just don't know what all the seperate issues are, let alone the

answers.

Important: This paragraph contained 30 errors, not counting the one that was corrected for you. How many did you find? _____ If you did not find all 30, try again before you check your work.

Exercise 2.22

1. Look back at Exercise 2.21. What was your total number of mistakes (the words that you marked in green, either misspelled words that you did not find, or words that you corrected wrongly)? Write that number here: _____.

2. If you made no mistakes in Exercise 2.21, skip the rest of this exercise. But if you did make even one mistake, go on to the next step.

3. In the first column below, copy each one of your mistakes. Write it just the way you misspelled it (or left it misspelled). For example, if you made five mistakes in Exercise 2.21, write in five words.

4. In the second column, **use your dictionary** to spell each word correctly.

5. In the third column, **use your dictionary** to rewrite each correctly spelled word with a hyphen between syllables. Follow this model:

INCORRECT SPELLING	CORRECT SPELLING	SYLLABLES
pulbic	*public*	*pub - lic*

INCORRECT SPELLING	CORRECT SPELLING	SYLLABLES
_____	_____	_____
_____	_____	_____
_____	_____	_____
_____	_____	_____
_____	_____	_____
_____	_____	_____
_____	_____	_____
_____	_____	_____
_____	_____	_____
_____	_____	_____

Important: If you tend to make more than one or two spelling mistakes on your papers, it would be a good idea to keep a chart like this one in your notebook, as a personal list of words to study and review.

Module 2: *Writing Conventions*

WRITING TEST

NAME _____

PURPOSE   To show that you can follow basic writing conventions, and proofread for spelling.

ASSIGNMENT   Rewrite the passage below as **three paragraphs**, correcting errors in writing conventions and spelling.

About Writing Conventions

The first and most basic writing convention is the direction of words on the pg. If you dont read any thing but English or some other european language, it probably hasn't occurred to you that words maybe arranged in more than 1 way. But at the dawn of History, writing from rt. to left apparently seemed natural for most people. Infact hebrew still runs from right to left, & Japanese runs from bottom to top. The second basic writing convention, standard spelling, followed the invention of the Printing Press in the 15th cent. Handwritten books were scarce and didnt circulate very far. when local writers spelled words the way they pronounced them, their local readers had no problem. But printed books traveled to distant neighborhoods, so a standard spelling was gradually developed. By 1775, when Dr. Samuel johnson published the first dictionary in english, there was usually just one accepted way to spell a word, even though readers might pronounce it in 2 or 3 different ways. The third basic writing convention, the use of Punctuation marks, wasnt followed consistantly until about two hundred and fifty yrs. ago. For centuries dots were used in random ways, and commas werent used atall. Scribes gradually started to use dots as periods or full stops, showing readers where to pause. However, only in modern times were Commas introduced, to indicate the difference between brief pauses and longer ones.

Check off each step as you complete it.

READ   ☐   Read the passage above carefully. Notice where each new idea is introduced. There are three ideas in all.

EDIT   ☐   Insert a paragraph mark (¶) into the passage above at the place where each new idea begins. There should be three paragraphs.

❑   Review the Rules for this module. In the passage above, underline each mistake in writing conventions, and correct it in the space above the line.

❑   Use your dictionary to find and correct any mistakes in spelling.

COPY   ❑   Copy the corrected passage carefully, using blue or black ink and standard-sized (8½ by 11 inch) paper. Better yet, type or use a word processor. Write your name in the upper right-hand corner, or use whatever heading your instructor requires. Remember that you are now preparing your writing for a reader.

❑   Underline every correction that you made.

❑   Count the corrections that you made, and write the number here: _____ .

PROOFREAD   ❑   Read your final copy **out loud**, comparing it to the corrected passage above. If you find any mistakes, it's OK to correct them neatly by hand. Or if you have used a word processor, go back and correct your mistakes, and then print out a clean final copy.

Attach your final copy to these instructions, and hand them both in.

3 Wrong Words

NAME _____

As you complete each exercise, record your number of mistakes below.

3.1 ____	3.10 ____	3.19 ____
3.2 ____	3.11 ____	Summary ____
3.3 ____	3.12 ____	3.20 ____
3.4 ____	3.13 ____	3.21 ____
3.5 ____	3.14 ____	3.22 ____
3.6 ____	3.15 ____	3.23 ____
3.7 ____	3.16 ____	3.24 ____
3.8 ____	3.17 ____	3.25 ____
3.9 ____	3.18 ____	

Review Exercise A ____

INSTRUCTOR'S COMMENTS

Instructions:

❑ Followed carefully
❑ Not followed carefully enough

Checking:

❑ Careful
❑ Not careful enough to catch all your mistakes
❑ Green pen not used for checking
❑ Entire correct answer not always written in

Writing Test:

❑ Excellent
❑ Good
❑ Acceptable
❑ Not yet satisfactory

Other:

Module 3: *Wrong Words*

RULES

Important: **Wrong words** are not spelling mistakes.

When you make a **spelling mistake,** you've written a word that doesn't exist. You've used the wrong letters, or you've written the right letters in the wrong order. If you try to look up your spelling in a dictionary, you won't find it.

When you write a **wrong word,** the word is correctly spelled, but it's not the correct word for what you mean in that sentence.

✗   ✗
The <u>theif</u> ran over <u>their</u>.

> *Theif* is a spelling mistake for *thief*. You won't find this spelling in the dictionary.
> *Their* is a wrong word. You'll find this word in the dictionary, but *there* is the word
> that would be correct in this sentence.

Exercise 3.1 (1) Use your dictionary to write in the meanings. (2) Then use your dictionary again to fill in the blanks.

1.   In English class, I'm writing a <u>compassion</u> about my first day on the job.

   Compassion means _____ .

   The word that is needed in this sentence is _____ , which means

   _____ .

2.   The <u>hole</u> question is extremely complicated.

   Hole means _____ .

   The word that is needed in this sentence is _____ , which means

   _____ .

3.   Everyone came to the play <u>accept</u> Marvin.

   Accept means _____ .

   The word that is needed in this sentence is _____ , which means

   _____ .

Remember: Check your work as you go along, using the Answers in the back of the book.

Exercise 3.2 Wrong words and spelling mistakes are underlined in these sentences. Above each incorrect word, write SP for a spelling mistake or WW for a wrong word. **Do not guess.** For help, use your dictionary. Follow this model:

WW   SP
I gave the book <u>two</u> my <u>frend</u>.

1. That is <u>know</u> big <u>promblem</u>.

2. She <u>brought</u> a ham <u>sanwitch</u> at the corner delicatessen.

3. <u>Thier</u> class was <u>to</u> large for the room.

4. <u>Their</u> is an important <u>diffrence</u> between spelling mistakes and wrong words.

5. His <u>mine</u> just wasn't focused on what he was <u>writting</u>.

‖‖ 3A.   Do not confuse *and*, *a*, and *an*.

   ‖ **1.**   *And* **joins two words or phrases, and means** *in addition to.*

I ate ham <u>and</u> eggs.
> This sentence means that I ate ham in addition to eggs.

   ‖ **2.**   *A* **and** *an* **both mean** *one.* **They are two different forms of the same word.**

We borrowed <u>a</u> sweater and <u>an</u> overcoat.
> This sentence means that we borrowed one sweater and one overcoat.

Exercise 3.3 Circle the joining word *and* wherever it appears, and underline the two ideas that are being joined. Follow this model:

We saw <u>a zebra</u> (and) <u>an antelope</u> at the zoo.

1. Lex bought a computer and a printer.

2. Then he studied and practiced with his word processing program.

3. After that, he wrote and printed a dozen letters in an hour and a half.

3.   Choose *a* or *an* according to the <u>sound</u> of the word that follows it.

Use *an* before words that start with **vowel sounds** (the sounds of the letters *A, E, I, O,* and *U*).

> Rhoda had <u>an</u> interview that lasted for <u>an</u> hour.
>> *An* is used before *interview*, which starts with the vowel *I*.
>> *An* is also used before *hour*, which starts with a vowel sound, even though it's spelled with the consonant *H*. It's pronounced as if it began with a vowel, like "our."

Use *a* before words that start with **consonant sounds** (that is, any sound except a vowel sound).

> <u>A</u> woman began the struggle for <u>a</u> union.
>> *A* is used before *woman*, which starts with a consonant sound.
>> *A* is also used before *union*, which starts with a consonant sound, even though it's spelled with the vowel *U*. It's pronounced as if it began with a consonant, like "you."

The word *an* can be confusing, because you may hear people say something like "a interview" or "a hour." For each blank below, *an* is correct. Fill in each blank and say the whole phrase out loud, making sure to pronounce the *N* in *an* before the vowel sound.

_____ apple	_____ ugly monster
_____ egg	_____ honor
_____ ice storm	_____ L-shaped room
_____ open door	_____ M for Madison High

The choice of *a* or *an* before letters (as well as before words) also depends on the **sound** of what follows. In the last two examples above, the letters *L* and *M* are consonants, but we pronounce them as if they started with vowels (they sound like "el" and "em").

Exercise 3.4 Fill in *a* or *an*. Say each phrase out loud as you write it, and notice the beginning sound of the next word.

1.	_____ horse		4.	_____ once-in-a-lifetime-chance
	_____ hourglass			_____ ordinary example
2.	_____ service station		5.	_____ X-ray machine
	_____ S-curve			_____ xylophone
3.	_____ umbrella		6.	_____ C on the test
	_____ university education			_____ A on the test

Exercise 3.5 Fill in *a*, *an*, or *and*. Say each answer out loud as you write it.

There is _____ American political party whose symbol is _____

donkey, _____ there is another whose symbol is _____ elephant.

3B.   Do not confuse words that <u>sound</u> alike.

1.   THEN   Use *then* to mean *at that time* or *next*, often as the first word in a sentence.

She shook the present. <u>Then</u> she opened it.
> This sentence means that she opened the present right after she shook it.

THAN   Use *than* to compare two ideas or things.

Beverly has more money <u>than</u> I do.
> This sentence compares the amount of money that she has to the amount that I have.

Than is always used with another word showing comparison, like *more*, *better*, *rather*, and *sooner*.

Exercise 3.6 Fill in *then* or *than*.

1. Sharon liked studying current events better _____ history.

2. _____ she signed up for an archeology course.

3. Her class took a field trip to the Indian pueblos at Santa Clara and Taos in New Mexico;

_____ they visited Mesa Verde National Monument.

4. They examined more _____ a dozen cliff dwellings of the ancient Anasazi

culture which were abandoned mysteriously more _____ 600 years ago.

5. Now Sharon is thinking of majoring in Native American history rather

_____ continuing her studies in journalism.

Exercise 3.7 Fill in *then* or *than*.

When you spend more _____ you earn,

_____ it's time to take out a loan.

2.   TO   Use *to* to mean something like *in the direction of*.

Sheila went <u>to</u> the bank.
> This sentence means that Sheila went toward the bank.

And use *to* with a verb form. This is called an <u>infinitive</u>.

Sheila went <u>to</u> borrow some money.
> This sentence means that Sheila went for the purpose of borrowing some money. *To borrow* is an infinitive.

TOO   Use *too* to mean *also*, usually after a comma.

My brother wanted some cake, <u>too</u>.
> This sentence can mean that my brother wanted cake, and someone else also wanted it. Or it can mean that he wanted cake and also something else to eat or drink.

And use *too* to mean *excessively* or *more than enough*.

It's <u>too</u> windy today for a boat ride.
> This sentence means that it's more windy today than it ought to be for a boat ride.

Notice that *too* has **more than** one *O* and means **more than** enough.

TWO   Use *two* for the number that comes after *one*.

We ordered <u>two</u> books.
> *Two* tells how many books.

Exercise 3.8 Fill in *to, too*, or *two*.

1.   The celebrated orator Edward Everett spoke _____ the crowd at Gettysburg.

2.   He spoke for _____ hours.

48

3.   Abraham Lincoln spoke, _____ .

4.   A photographer stood up _____ take Lincoln's picture.

5.   By the time he had focused his camera, he was already _____ late.

6.   After less than _____ minutes, Lincoln sat down.

7.   It was _____ late _____ capture a great moment of history, the Gettysburg

Address.

Exercise 3.9 Fill in *to*, *too*, or *two*.

Ramon goes _____ the school gym _____ swim because the health

club is _____ expensive. _____ of his friends go there, _____ .

| | | **3.   ITS   Use *its* to mean *belonging to it*.**

Natalie bought a new rake, and then broke <u>its</u> handle.
>   The handle belongs to the rake.

Words that mean "belonging to" are **possessive** forms. The possessive pronoun *its* **never** has an apostrophe.

| | | **IT'S   Use *it's* as a contraction of *it is* (or *it has*, in verb phrases like *it has been*).**

<u>It's</u> a shame he couldn't come.
>   *It's* is the contracted form of *it is*. The apostrophe shows where the letter *I* has been omitted.

The contraction *it's* **always** has an apostrophe.

<u>It's</u> been a long time since I was here last.
>   *It's* is the contracted form of *it has*. The apostrophe shows where the letters *H* and *A* have been omitted.

Exercise 3.10 Fill in *its* or *it's*.

1.   _____ important to check the air pressure in your car's tires every week.

2.   And _____ a good idea to have your car serviced every 5,000 miles.

3.   The garage crew should change _____ oil and oil filter.

4. Every 10,000 miles, your car should have _____ tires rotated.

5. Your car will last longer if _____ not neglected.

Exercise 3.11 Fill in *its* or *it's*.

_____ strange but true that an insect will often eat

_____ mate, or even _____ offspring.

‖‖‖ **4. YOUR**   Use *your* to mean *belonging to you.*

    It's <u>your</u> turn now.
            The turn belongs to you.

The possessive pronoun *your* **never** has an apostrophe.

‖‖‖ **YOU'RE**   Use *you're* as a contraction of *you are.*

    <u>You're</u> always in my way.
            You're is the contracted form of *you are.* The apostrophe shows where the letter *A* has been omitted.

The contraction *you're* **always** has an apostrophe.

Exercise 3.12 Fill in *your* or *you're*.

1. Even if you don't believe in astrology, _____ unusual if you don't know

    what sign of the Zodiac you were born under.

2. Astrologers say that _____ sign in the stars influences

    _____ character and attitudes.

3. For example, if _____ a Leo, _____

    temperament is domineering, like a lion's.

4. And if _____ a Gemini (born under the sign of the twins),

    _____ friends will notice that you have contradictory traits.

5. To tell the truth, doesn't _____ sign of the Zodiac fit you?

Exercise 3.13 Fill in *your* or *you're*.

When _____ anxious, _____

blood pressure sometimes rises.

||| **5.   THEIR**   Use *their* to mean *belonging to them*.

They waxed <u>their</u> car.
> The car belongs to them.

The possessive pronoun *their* **never** has an apostrophe.

||| **THEY'RE**   Use *they're* as a contraction of *they are*.

<u>They're</u> my neighbors.
> *They're* is the contracted form of *they are*. The apostrophe shows where the letter *A* has been omitted.

The contraction *they're* **always** has an apostrophe.

Remember: *They're* means *they are*. So **never** write *they're are*, which would mean *they are are*.

||| **THERE**   Use *there* to mean *at that place*.

Moe left his bike over <u>there</u>.
> *There* tells where he left his bike.

||| Use *there* to begin a sentence, followed by verbs like *is, are, was*, and *were*.

<u>There</u> are two major world powers.
> *There* begins the sentence. It is followed by the verb *are*.

Important: In sentences like these, *there* doesn't mean a particular place. It simply starts the sentence.

Exercise 3.14 Fill in *their*, *they're*, or *there*.

1. Throughout the United States _____ are many young people who dream of

   a future in professional sports.

2. _____ interested in athletics, not _____

   studies.

3. _____ minds are on news stories about huge salaries made by professional

   athletes.

4. So every day _____ out practicing instead of studying in the library.

5. But _____ are few stories about college players who don't make the pros, or

   about high-paid athletes who lose all _____ money to bad investments.

6. Students should be aware that _____ are few things more important than

   _____ college degrees.

Exercise 3.15 Fill in *their*, *they're*, or *there*.

_____ are millions of men who support equal rights for

women, and when the Equal Rights Amendment comes up for a vote again,

_____ going to be _____ at the polls

to cast _____ votes for it.

Exercise 3.16 To review the Rules so far, fill in the appropriate word.

1. its / it's   _____ the last decade of the 20th century.

2. their / there / they're   If these politicians are honest, _____ unusual.

3. your / you're   It saves time if you admit it when _____ wrong.

4. then / than   The door slammed, and _____ he finally understood.

5. to / too / two   The Belmont Sisters will appear on this program, _____ .

6. its / it's   The city is going to amend _____ charter.

7. then / than   Communism collapsed in Russia sooner _____ anyone expected.

8. their / there / they're   _____ are three vacation days this month.

9. your / you're   _____ reading level is a major ingredient of _____

   success at most jobs.

10.   to / too / two   Shakespeare's most famous words are probably, " _____ be or

   not _____ be."

||| **6.   Watch out for other groups of words that sound alike and can cause
        wrong word mistakes.**

✗

Smoking isn't <u>aloud</u> in most classrooms.

Aloud is a mistake for *allowed*. These two words sound alike, but they have very different meanings.

Exercise 3.17 (1) Use your dictionary to write in the meanings. (2) Then fill in the appropriate words.

1.   **passed / past**

   Passed is the past-tense form of the verb _____ .

   Past means _____ .

   Just _____ Rosie's bar, we _____ a big accident.

2.   **know / no**

   Know means _____ .

   No means _____ .

   We _____ that you have _____ time to see us.

3.   **here / hear**

   Here means _____ .

   Hear means _____ .

   _____ comes Joseph to _____ the latest gossip.

4.   **whose / who's**

   Whose is a possessive form meaning "belonging to _____ ."

   Who's is a contraction for _____ .

   _____ the student _____ papers are on the table?

5.   **find / fine**

   Find means _____ .

Fine means _____ .

Harris felt _____ after he was able to _____ the money.

6. **went / when**

Went is the past-tense form of the verb _____ .

When means _____ .

We were relieved _____ Aunt Julia finally _____ home.

| 3C. | Do not confuse words that <u>look</u> alike. |

Some wrong word mistakes are caused by writing a word that has many of the same letters as another, even though it doesn't sound like it.

✗

No one <u>though</u> that we could do it.

Though is a mistake for *thought*. These words don't sound alike, but most of the letters are the same.

Exercise 3.18 (1) Use your dictionary to write in the meanings. (2) Then fill in the appropriate words.

1. **know / now / no**

Know means _____ .

Now means _____ .

No means _____ .

_____ , after years of research, doctors _____

how to prevent polio, but there is still _____ vaccine for the common cold.

2. **bought / brought**

Bought is the past-tense form of the verb _____ .

Brought is the past-tense form of the verb _____ .

My cousin _____ a keg of beer and _____ it to

the party.

3. **quit / quite / quiet**

Quit means _____ .

Quite means _____ .

Quiet means _____ .

Millie is usually a _____ person, but she has

_____ a temper, and once she gets started arguing, it's hard for her to

_____ .

4. **who / how**

Who is a pronoun referring to _____ .

How means _____ .

Anyone _____ goes canoeing should know

_____ to swim.

5. **chance / change**

Chance means _____ .

Change means _____ .

Here's a _____ to _____ your life: Take up

hot air ballooning.

6. **where / were**

Where means _____ .

Were is a past-tense form of the verb _____ .

For a thousand miles, there _____ no mountains

_____ it was possible to ski.

‖‖‖ 3D.   Do not confuse words that are <u>related</u> to each other.

Many mistakes are caused by confusing words that end in *ENT* and *ENCE* (or *ANT* and *ANCE*).

✗

Children see too much <u>violents</u> on television.

> *Violents* is a mistake for *violence*.

The form of a word that ends in *ENT* (or *ANT*) usually names or describes a specific person or thing.

Roy is not a <u>violent</u> person.
Jamillah is the manager's <u>assistant</u>.

> Not *violent* describes Roy.
> *Assistant* names Jamillah's position.

A word that ends in *ENCE* (or *ANCE*) usually names an abstract or general idea.

Roy hates <u>violence</u> in any form.
The motorists needed immediate <u>assistance</u>.

> *Violence* and *assistance* name abstract ideas.

Exercise 3.19 Fill in the appropriate word. For help, use your dictionary.

1. **confident / confidence**

    I have complete _____ in you. I'm _____ that

    you'll succeed.

2. **independent / independence**

    Everyone values an _____ person. However, sometimes it's hard to tell

    _____ from stubbornness.

3. **obedient / obedience**

    My father expects his children to be _____ . However, most parents today

    do not expect total _____ , although they do demand respect.

4. **different / difference**

    What's the _____ between a calculator and a computer? A calculator is

    _____ from a computer mainly because it's used for only one purpose.

5.   **important / importance**

When choosing a career, you must consider what things are most _____ to

you. Do not underestimate the _____ of enjoying what you do.

RULES SUMMARY

In the longer one-page exercises that follow, you'll practice applying all the rules which you've learned or reviewed in this module. Before you go on to the longer exercises, check your understanding by filling in the blanks in the Rules Summary below. Fill in the blanks from memory, thinking carefully about what each rule means. If you need help, look back again at the Rules.

1.   *A* and *an* both mean _____ . Use _____ before words that start with a vowel

sound, and use *a* before words that start with a _____ sound.

2.   Do not confuse words that sound alike.

a.   Use *then* to mean _____ or _____ . Use

than to _____ two things or ideas.

b.   Use *to* to mean something like _____ , and use *to* in an

_____ . Use *too* to mean _____ , or to

mean _____ or *more than enough*. Use *two* to mean the

_____ that comes after one.

c.   Use *its* to mean _____ . Use *it's* as a contraction of

_____ or _____ .

d.   Use *your* to mean _____ . Use *you're* as a contraction of

_____ .

e.   Use *their* to mean _____ . Use *they're* as a contraction of

_____ . Use *there* to mean _____

or to start a _____ .

3.   Do not confuse words that _____ alike or contain many of the same letters.

4.   Do not confuse words that are _____ to each other.

Now turn to the **Answers** to check your work. Use these Rules and your dictionary as you go on to do the longer exercises that follow.

Module 3: *Wrong Words*

PRACTICE

Exercise 3.20   **Number of Mistakes** _____

Fill in *a*, *an*, or *and*. Say each answer out loud as you write it.

According to _____ old story, _____ astronomer claimed that he had

_____ unique power. Whenever he gave _____ order, the sun, moon,

_____ stars always obeyed. But he did not want to use his power in _____

irresponsible way, so he was careful to give commands only at _____ appropriate time.

He explained that if he ordered the sun to rise _____ hour too soon, the crops would

burn up, _____, of course, _____ early moon would confuse the tides. But

on _____ certain evening, to celebrate _____ anniversary, the astronomer

ate _____ enormous meal, drank _____ entire bottle of wine,

_____ didn't wake up until noon the next day. He was amazed to see the disobedient

sun already shining in _____ cloudless sky. Broken-hearted, he retired to his cave

_____ never spoke to _____ heavenly body again.

Exercise 3.21   **Number of Mistakes** _____

Rewrite each sentence, using the appropriate words and underlining them. Follow this model:

> **their / there / they're**   The workers mislaid <u>the</u> tools <u>belonging to them</u>.
>
> <u>The workers mislaid *their* tools.</u>

1. **your / you're**   Where is <u>the</u> dictionary <u>that belongs to you</u>? <u>You are</u> sure to need it today.

   _____

   _____

2. **its / it's**   This show has lost <u>the</u> popularity <u>belonging to it</u>, and so <u>it is</u> time to take it
   off the air.

   _____

   _____

3. **to / too / two**   Diane struggled <u>in the direction of</u> the bus stop. She was carrying <u>fewer
   than three</u> big boxes, and had a full shopping bag, <u>also</u>. This luggage was
   almost <u>excessively</u> heavy for her to handle.

   _____

   _____

   _____

4. **their / there / they're**   The passengers are picking up <u>the</u> luggage <u>belonging to them</u> in the airport.
   Two friends are meeting them <u>at that place</u> to drive them home. <u>They are</u>
   all eager to get going.

   _____

   _____

   _____

   _____

Exercise 3.22   **Number of Mistakes** _____

POSSESSIVE PRONOUNS	CONTRACTIONS	TELLS WHERE OR STARTS A SENTENCE
its, your, their	**it's, you're, they're**	there
The doll lost *its* head. (The head belonged to the doll.)	*It's* lost. (It is lost.)	
Your house is nice. (The house belongs to you.)	*You're* nice. (You are nice.)	
Their house is old. (The house belongs to them.)	*They're* old. (They are old.)	The house is *there* on the corner. (The house is at that place.)
		There is a house for sale.

This paragraph contains errors in *its* and *it's*, *your* and *you're*, and *their*, *they're*, and *there*. Underline each error, and correct it in the space above the line. The first error has been corrected for you.

you're

If your not in the habit of writing down you're ideas and then proofreading what is written

there on the page, its hard for you to see that, although some contractions and possessive

pronouns sound exactly alike, there very different. People who don't write much may not use

apostrophes at all, because they don't realize their importance. Their simply not aware that

every contraction must have its apostrophe to be correct. On the other hand, they're are writers

who treat apostrophes like confetti. They scatter them around in they're writing like

decorations. But there guilty of confusing there readers even more than the writers who leave

apostrophes out entirely. If your ambitious to become a clear and correct writer, it's important

for you to learn the following apostrophe rule and it's application: "Their is a group of words

called possessive pronouns, which mean *belonging to*. These words are never written with

apostrophes. When you use an apostrophe with a pronoun, its always a contraction.

Contractions can also be written as two words."

Important: This paragraph contained 12 errors, not counting the one that was corrected for you. How many did you find? _____ If you did not find all 12, try again before you check your work.

Exercise 3.23

This paragraph contains many wrong words. Underline each error, and correct it in the space above the line. The first error has been corrected for you.

     It's

    <u>Its</u> a interesting fact that many people are much better at speaking then at writing. Their

are some people who can start a riot just by jumping up on a old crate and talking to a angry

crowd. But to few of these born orators are able to write a too-line letter to the newspaper

which it's editor wouldn't find to awkward and ungrammatical to publish. Then there are those

who would rather spend two hundred dollars on telephone calls then two dollars on stamps.

When they pick up a telephone, there chattering away in an instant. An yet when they pick up a

pencil, its likely that they'll chew it for twenty minutes before their able to write a single word.

You may be an excellent speaker, but unless you're able to write your ideas correctly and clearly,

your going to have problems.

Important: This paragraph contained 15 errors, not counting the one that was corrected for you. How many did you find? _____ If you did not find all 15, try again before you check your work.

Exercise 3.24   **Number of Mistakes** _____

Fill in the appropriate word. For help, use your dictionary.

1. **different / difference**   Even when two bottles of wine are made from grapes from the same vines,

there is often a big _____ between them if

they're made in _____ years.

2. **violent / violence**   When teenagers see a lot of sex and _____

on TV and in the movies, their behavior may become more

_____ .

3. **independent / independence**   _____ has its price; to become

_____ , you must learn to live alone.

4. **patient / patients / patience**   I know that _____ is a virtue, but I'm not

very _____ with a doctor who makes

appointments with three _____ in the same

hour.

5. **important / importance**   Is money _____ ? Here's a clue: Only rich

people say that money has no _____ .

6. **confident / confidence**   If you don't lose your _____ , you'll be OK.

Act _____ , and you'll get the job.

7. **obedient / obedience**   Not long ago, _____ was expected of every

wife, but now few brides are willing to make a vow to be

_____ .

8. **silent / silence**   The _____ in the playroom is disturbing.

Those children are never _____ unless

they're into mischief.

Exercise 3.25   **Number of Mistakes** _____

This paragraph contains many wrong words. Underline each error, and correct it in the space above the line. For help, use your dictionary. The first error has been corrected for you.

                       of

An amazing number <u>off</u> people suffer from phobias, or strange fears. After a comet past

over Arizona, a woman how lived thousands of miles away in Maine refused to go out off her

house for five years. She taught a falling stare might land on her. A man in Detroit was terrified

of elevators. He had to fine a new doctor when his old one moved to an office on the 26th floor.

A woman with a violence fear of lightning always hid under the bed during thunderstorms. That

was the only place were she felt safe. A man became terrified of germs, so he when to a store and

brought a surgical mask. He wore it night and day, weather at home or at work. Even thought

people with these phobias are often quit intelligent, they can't except the evidence of facts about

their fears. It's know use telling them how few people are killed by falling stars or elevators or

lightning, or that you're not safe from germs even though you breath though a mask. Their

mines are full of irrational fears; they just can't here you.

Important: This paragraph contained 19 errors, not counting the one that was corrected for you. How many did you find? ____ If you did not find all 19, try again before you check your work.

Exercise 3.26

Now look over all your work on Module 3, especially the corrections you made with your green pen.

❑ Fill in your number of mistakes in using *a*, *an*, and *and* in Exercises 3.3 to 3.5 and 3.20 to 3.25:

	# OF MISTAKES	DEFINITION
a	_____	_____
an	_____	_____
and	_____	_____

❑ Fill in your number of mistakes in using words that **sound alike** in Exercises 3.6 to 3.17 and 3.20 to 3.25:

	# OF MISTAKES	DEFINITION
then	_____	_____
than	_____	_____
to	_____	_____
too	_____	_____
two	_____	_____
its	_____	_____
it's	_____	_____
your	_____	_____
you're	_____	_____
their	_____	_____
they're	_____	_____
there	_____	_____

❑ Fill in the words on which you made mistakes in using words that **look alike** in Exercises 3.18 and 3.20 to 3.25:

WORD	DEFINITION
_____	_____
_____	_____
_____	_____
_____	_____
_____	_____

❑ Fill in the words on which you made mistakes in using **related words** in Exercises 3.19 to 3.25:

WORD	DEFINITION
_____	_____
_____	_____
_____	_____
_____	_____
_____	_____

Important: If you tend to make more than one or two wrong word mistakes on your papers, it would be a good idea to keep a chart like this one in your notebook, as a personal list of words to study and review.

Exercise 3.27   Number of Mistakes _____

Review Exercise A: Spelling, Writing Conventions, Wrong Words

---

This passage contains errors in spelling, writing conventions, and wrong words. Underline each error, and correct it in the space above the line. For help, use your Rules and your dictionary. The first error has been corrected for you.

            a lot
      You hear <u>alot</u> about "the wonders of the world," but only a few people know that this

phrase originally refered to seven wonders in the ancient world. Hardly anybody nowadays can

name these monuments of early civilization. Their is a good reason for this. Just one of these

wonders is still standing, the huge stone pyramids in Egypt. A few people also no about the

second wonder, the magnificent terraced gardens which a king of babylon built to please his wife.

The thrid wonder, a seated statue of Zeus in a temple at Olympia in greece, was made of ivory &

gold, with precious jewels in it's eyes. (If this huge statue could have stood up, it would have hit

it's head on the cieling.) Some fragments of the forth wonder, a Temple dedicated to the

goddess Diana, were found in turkey about a hundred yrs. ago. Earthquakes destroyed all 3 of

the other wonders: a beautiful tomb built for King Mausolus in Turkey, a enormous lighthouse

near the coast of Egypt, and a giant statue of Apollo at Rhodes in Greece. The colossal statue at

Rhodes must have been more spectacular then the Statue of Liberty. According to an old

legend, it stood in the middle of an harbor with its legs spread a part, while ships past between

them.

Important: This paragraph contained 20 errors, not counting the one that was corrected for you. How many did you find? _____ If you did not find all 20, try again before you check your work.

Module 3: *Wrong Words*

WRITING TEST

NAME _____

PURPOSE	To show that you can avoid wrong words, and that you can continue to apply what you have learned in previous modules.

ASSIGNMENT	Imagine that you come home (or arrive at a friend's house) at 10 AM. No one is there. Write a note to a member of your family or to your friend beginning with one of these sentences:

    ❑   I want to use the car tonight.
    ❑   Let's go out to dinner tonight.

In every sentence of your note, use at least one of the following words.

❑	*a*	❑	*its*	❑	*though*
❑	*an*	❑	*it's*	❑	*thought*
❑	*and*	❑	*your*	❑	*were*
❑	*then*	❑	*you're*	❑	*where*
❑	*than*	❑	*their*		
❑	*to*	❑	*they're*		
❑	*too*	❑	*there*		
❑	*two*				

Check off each step in the writing process as you complete it.

DRAFT	❑	Put an ✗ in the box next to the sentence you began with.
	❑	On scratch paper, write a rough draft of your note. **Keep writing until you've used all the words on the list at least once.**
	❑	As you use each word, put an ✗ in the box next to it, and underline it in your note.
REVISE	❑	Read over the draft of your note to make sure that your ideas are clear and sound true to life. Try to anticipate what a reader will need to know in order to understand and believe what you have written. Add, take out, or change ideas, words, and sentences as necessary. Remember, it's good for a draft to become messy.
	❑	After you have finished revising your ideas, count the words from the list that you used and underlined, and write the number here: _____ . You should have used all 19 words at least once. If you did not use all 19 words, write more.
EDIT	❑	Review the Rules for this module. Find and correct any mistakes in the underlined words.

Use your dictionary and the Rules for previous modules to find and correct any mistakes in:

❑   Spelling
❑   Writing Conventions

FINAL COPY   ❑   Write the final copy of your note carefully, using blue or black ink and standard-sized (8½ by 11 inch) paper. Better yet, type or use a word processor. Write your name in the upper right-hand corner, or use whatever heading your instructor requires. Remember that you are now preparing your writing for a reader.

❑   Underline every word from the list in your final copy just as you did in your draft.

PROOFREAD   ❑   Read your final copy **out loud**. If you find any mistakes, it's OK to correct them neatly by hand. Or if you have used a word processor, go back and correct your mistakes, and then print out a clean final copy.

Attach your final copy to these instructions, and hand them both in.

4 Nouns

As you complete each exercise, record your number of mistakes below.

PART 1

4.1 ____	4.7 ____	4.13 ____
4.2 ____	4.8 ____	Summary ____
4.3 ____	4.9 ____	4.14 ____
4.4 ____	4.10 ____	4.15 ____
4.5 ____	4.11 ____	4.16 ____
4.6 ____	4.12 ____	

PART 2

4.17 ____	Summary ____	4.22 ____
4.18 ____	4.20 ____	4.23 ____
4.19 ____	4.21 ____	

Review Exercise B ____

INSTRUCTOR'S COMMENTS

Instructions:

❏ Followed carefully
❏ Not followed carefully enough

Checking:

❏ Careful
❏ Not careful enough to catch all your mistakes
❏ Green pen not used for checking
❏ Entire correct answer not always written in

Writing Test:

❏ Excellent
❏ Good
❏ Acceptable
❏ Not yet satisfactory

Other:

Module 4: *Nouns*

RULES, Part 1: Singular and Plural Forms

4A.   Nouns are words that name things.

The <u>student</u> took a <u>book</u> from the <u>shelf</u>.

> *Student* is a noun because it names who took the book.
> *Book* is a noun because it names what the student took.
> *Shelf* is a noun because it names from what the student took the book.

Nouns often follow words like *the* or *a*.

<u>The student</u> took <u>a book</u> from <u>the shelf</u>.

> The nouns *student* and *shelf* follow *the*.
> The noun *book* follows *a*.

Sometimes there may be descriptive words between *the* or *a* and the noun. These descriptive words tell more about the noun.

<u>The tall student</u> took <u>a history book</u> from <u>the top shelf</u>.

> *Tall*, *history*, and *top* are descriptive words between *the* and *a* and the nouns.

Exercise 4.1 Circle each noun.

1.   A bus finally arrived.

2.   An empty bus finally arrived.

3.   A completely empty bus finally arrived.

4.   The computer has a printer.

5.   The new computer has a broken printer.

Remember: Check your work as you go along, using the Answers in the back of the book.

4B.   A noun which names one thing is <u>singular</u>.
A noun which names more than one thing is <u>plural</u>.

In fifteen <u>minutes</u> , a <u>truck</u> will deliver ten <u>pizzas</u>.

> *Truck* is a singular noun because it names one thing.
> *Minutes* and *pizzas* are plural nouns because they name more than one thing.

Exercise 4.2 (1) Circle each noun. (2) Write S over every singular noun and P over every plural noun.

1. One oak tree may have 17,000 separate leaves.

2. Sixty-three young children crowded into one noisy room.

3. One important idea was discussed for seven long hours.

The **base form** of a word is the form found in the dictionary, without any changes. In this book, base forms are written in CAPITAL LETTERS.

CAR   a <u>car</u>   many <u>cars</u>

> *CAR* is the base form of this noun.
> *Car* is the singular form of *CAR*; *cars* is the plural form.

4C.   Check your writing carefully for the *S* or *ES* ending needed on most plural nouns.

1.   An *S* ending often adds an extra syllable to a noun ending in *E*.

PAGE   one page   several <u>pages</u>

> *PAGE* ends in *E*; the plural *S* ending adds an extra syllable to *pages*.

2.   When the plural form of a noun that does not end in *E* is pronounced with an extra syllable, add *ES*.

WISH   a wish   three <u>wishes</u>

> *WISH* doesn't end in *E*, and the plural form is pronounced with an extra syllable, so add *ES*.

Exercise 4.3 Fill in the plural form of the given noun. Say each answer out loud, as you decide whether to add *S* or *ES* .

1. TRUCK   two _____

2. KISS   a few _____

3. DISH   several dirty _____

4. SHIRT   four new _____

5. BEACH   two sandy _____

3. Add *S*, not *ES*, to make nouns ending in *SK* or *SP* or *ST* plural.

Plural forms with *SK* or *SP* or *ST* may be hard to pronounce, but they don't have an extra syllable. **Never** add *ES* to words ending in *SK* or *SP* or *ST*.

MASK	a mask	several <u>masks</u>
GHOST	one ghost	many <u>ghosts</u>

Masks and *ghosts* have *S* endings and no extra syllables.

		✗
WASP	one wasp	many <u>waspes</u>
		many <u>wasps</u>

Adding *ES* to make *WASP* plural is incorrect.
Wasps is the correct plural form of *WASP*.

Exercise 4.4 Fill in the plural form of the given noun. Say each answer out loud as you write it.

1. GASP   many loud _____

2. RISK   two bad _____

3. TOAST   three _____ to the bride

Exercise 4.5 To review the rules about adding *S* or *ES*, fill in the plural form of the given noun. Say each answer out loud as you write it.

1. DISK   four computer _____

2. EDGE   some sharp _____

3. BUZZ   three _____ on the doorbell

4. WRIST   both broken _____

5. BOX   some big _____

6. TEST   three hard _____

7. STICK   a few broken _____

8. LOSS   several huge _____

Exercise 4.6 This passage contains errors in noun forms. Underline each error and correct it in the space above the line. The first error has been corrected for you.

Austrians
<u>Austrian</u> are fascinated by timepieces. In Vienna, many street have two or three shops that

sell fancy watch of all shapes and sizes, plus clocks made of gold, silver, porcelain, and many

other precious material. In Vienna's Clock Museum are two astronomical clock, each as big as a

room, and several timepiece so tiny that you can't read the number on their faces without a

magnifying glass. The most famous Viennese timepiece is the Anker Clock. Three floor above

the street, twelve life-sized statue of Austrian national heroes march out, and one by one, for

sixty minute, each moves across the clock's enormous face. When the clock strikes the hour,

melody by Vienna's many musical geniuses salute each of these historical figure.

||||| 4D.   Some nouns need spelling changes with a plural ending.

|||| **1.**   **To make the plural form of nouns ending in a <u>consonant</u> + *Y*,
change the *Y* to *I* and add *ES*.**

This is Spelling Rule A2 in Appendix A.

COPY	a clear copy	ten clear <u>copies</u>

Copies is spelled with an *I*, not a *Y*.

|||| **2.**   **To make the plural form of most nouns ending in *IFE* or *F*,
change the *F* to *V* and add *S* or *ES*.**

WIFE	his wife	his two <u>wives</u>
THIEF	one thief	many <u>thieves</u>

Wives and *thieves* are spelled with a *V*, not an *F*.

Some common words ending in *F* don't change the *F* to *V* when you make them plural. When in doubt, look up the plural form in your dictionary. If no special plural form is listed, make the plural in the usual way: Just add *S* without changing *F* to *V*.

| BELIEF | one belief | two <u>beliefs</u> |
| CHIEF | an Indian chief | some Indian <u>chiefs</u> |

Neither *beliefs* nor *chiefs* changes *F* to *V* in the plural.

Exercise 4.7 Fill in the plural form of the given noun. For help, use your dictionary.

1. BABY   some crying _____

2. KNIFE   six sharp _____

3. LEAF   many green _____

4. MEMORY   those fond _____

5. BELIEF   their religious _____

6. WIFE   my cousins' _____

4E.   To make the plural form of most <u>irregular</u> nouns, change the whole word.

| MOUSE | one blind mouse | three blind <u>mice</u> |

Mice is the plural form of the irregular noun *MOUSE*.

Most of the mistakes students make with irregular nouns are caused by just three words. If you check these words carefully when you proofread your writing, you should be able to avoid many mistakes.

MAN	one man	some <u>men</u>
WOMAN	a woman	many <u>women</u>
CHILD	this child	these <u>children</u>

Write the singular and plural forms of these three irregular nouns here:

CHILD   a _____   several _____

WOMAN   one _____   some _____

MAN   that _____   those _____

Important: Never add the regular *S* or *ES* plural ending to an irregular noun.

✗

CHILD   the child   the <u>childrens</u>
                                          the <u>children</u>

Because *CHILD* is an irregular noun, *children* doesn't have a plural *S* ending.

Exercise 4.8 Fill in the plural form of the given irregular noun. For help, use your dictionary.

1. FOOT   four _____

2. MAN   several _____

3. CHILD   three crying _____

4. TOOTH   two loose _____

5. WOMAN   both young _____

6. MEDIUM   all the news _____

4F.   Nouns are usually used with <u>determiners</u>.

1.   Determiners are words like *the* or *a*, that come before nouns,
        and tell <u>which</u> or <u>how many</u>.

<u>A fireman</u> rescued <u>three children</u> from <u>the rooftop</u>.

The nouns *fireman*, *children*, and *rooftop* follow the determiners *a*, *three*, and *the*.

Exercise 4.9 (1) Circle each noun. (2) Draw an arrow from the determiner to the noun. Follow this model:

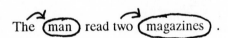

The (man) read two (magazines) .

1.   The boat sank quickly.

2.   One woman donated a cake.

3.   That messenger picked up this package from the store.

||| **2.** A <u>noun phrase</u> is a group of words that includes a noun, its determiner, and often descriptive words telling more about the noun.

<u>A courageous fireman</u> rescued <u>three frightened children</u> from <u>the blazing rooftop</u>.

A courageous fireman, *three frightened children*, and *the blazing rooftop* are noun phrases. Each noun phrase has a determiner, a descriptive word, and a noun.

Exercise 4.10 (1) Circle each noun. (2) Draw an arrow from the determiner to the noun.

1.   These fresh peaches taste good.

2.   I gave her twelve yellow roses.

3.   Some busy women have two different jobs.

4.   A talented teenager made this prizewinning quilt.

||| **3.** In a noun phrase, both the determiner and the noun must be either <u>singular</u> or <u>plural</u>.

Exercise 4.11 (1) Circle each noun. (2) Draw an arrow from the determiner to the noun. (3) Write S over each singular noun and P over each plural noun. Follow this model:

1.   one picture frame   many picture frames

2.   a political speech   some political speeches

3.   that simple task   those simple tasks

4.   this local library   these local libraries

5.   an unusual child   several unusual children

Remember: Determiners tell **which** or **how many**.

Here are some determiners that tell **which**:

BOOK	this book	these books
	that book	those books
	the book	the books

Determiners telling **which** have special singular and plural forms. *These* is the plural form of *this*, and *those* is the plural form of *that*. *The* is used with both singular and plural nouns. Write the appropriate forms of these determiners here, to help you remember them:

THIS   _____ desk   _____ desks

THAT   _____ desk   _____ desks

THE   _____ desk   _____ desks

Here are some determiners that tell **how many**:

BOOK   a book   books
                                some books
                                several books
                                many books

            one book   two books
                                ten books

            each book   all books
            every book

Notice that there are just a few **singular** determiners telling **how many**, but there are many different **plural** ones. Sometimes a plural noun can even be used with no determiner.

He likes to read <u>books</u>.

> *Books* without a determiner means something like "some books."

Exercise 4.12 Fill in the plural form of each noun phrase. Follow this model:

PET   one pet   <u>some</u>   <u>pets</u>

1. RACE   this race   _____   _____

2. LIST   the list   _____   _____

3. MAN   one man   _____   _____

4. TEST   that test   _____   _____

5. STITCH   one stitch   _____   _____

6. WOMAN   a woman   _____   _____

Exercise 4.13 Fill in the singular form of each noun phrase. Follow this model:

PET   some pets   _____a_____   _____pet_____

1. PATCH   those patches   _____   _____

2. PONY   two ponies   _____   _____

3. KNIFE   these knives   _____   _____

4. BOOK   the books   _____   _____

5. RISK   many risks   _____   _____

6. PUSH   pushes   _____   _____

RULES SUMMARY, Part 1

In the longer one-page exercises that follow, you'll practice applying all the rules which you've learned or reviewed in this module. Before you go on to the longer exercises, check your understanding by filling in the blanks in the Rules Summary below. Fill in the blanks from memory, thinking carefully about what each rule means. If you need help, look back again at the Rules.

1. Nouns are words that _____ things.

2. A noun that names one thing is _____ . A noun that names more than one

    thing is _____ .

3. To make most nouns plural, add _____ or _____ to the base form. A plural noun

    with an *ES* ending always has an _____ syllable. **Never** add *ES* to a noun

    ending in *SK* or _____ or _____ .

4. To make the plural form of a noun ending in a consonant + *Y*, change the *Y* to _____ and add

    ES. Some nouns ending in *IFE* or *F* change the *F* to _____ before adding *ES*.

5. To make most irregular nouns plural, change the _____

    _____ .

6. Nouns are usually used with _____ like *a* and *some*, that tell **which** or **how**

    many.

7.   In a noun phrase, both the determiner and the noun must be either _____

or _____ .

Now turn to the Answers to check your work. Use these Rules and your dictionary as you go on to do the longer exercises that follow.

Module 4: *Nouns*

PRACTICE, Part 1

Exercise 4.14   **Number of Mistakes** _____

(1) Circle each noun. (2) Rewrite each sentence, making the nouns plural, and making whatever other changes are necessary. (3) In your rewritten sentence, underline each change. Follow this model:

That (man) sold a (guitar) .

Those men sold ten guitars.

Remember: There are many different plural determiners. Answers like *many guitars*, *some guitars*, or *several guitars* would also be correct.

1.   The woman wrote a mystery story.

_____

2.   That man liked this scarf.

_____

3.   A girl fixed this broken shelf.

_____

4.   This child broke that dish.

_____

5.   A neighbor planted a hickory tree.

_____

6.   The boy cut up one large pumpkin for a pie.

_____

Exercise 4.15

Number of Mistakes _____

Words like *he*, *she*, and *they* are **pronouns**. Pronouns are used to **refer to nouns**.

John sold his car, and then he bought a truck.

> *His* and *he* refer to the noun *John*.

Like nouns, pronouns have singular and plural forms.

The man lost his wallet.

The men lost their wallets.

> *Man* and *his* are singular. *Men* and *their* are plural.

(1) Circle each noun. (2) Rewrite each sentence, making the nouns and pronouns plural, and making whatever other changes are necessary. (3) In your rewritten sentence, underline each change. Follow this model:

The (man) sold his (guitar).

The men sold their guitars.

1. The lawyer won her case.

   _____

2. One neighbor never mowed his lawn.

   _____

3. That child caught a butterfly with his net.

   _____

4. The man made a phone call, and then he left.

   _____

5. This woman earned her master's degree.

   _____

6. Because his wife had gone camping, that man ate out a lot.

   _____

Exercise 4.16 **Number of Mistakes** _____

Remember: Determiners are words like *the* or *a*, that come before nouns, and tell *how many* and *which*.

This paragraph contains errors in noun forms. Underline each error and correct it in the space above the line. The first error has been corrected for you.

parents

Both parent of the newborn quadruplets were returning home from the hospital. For the first 24 hour, two of their four tiny baby had struggled for their lifes. Although still in incubators, now they all seemed to be doing well. So at this moment the parents were worrying more about the many huge bill that were piling up. The mother was asking herself why she had taken those fertility pill. And where, they both wondered, would they get the cash for all the thing on their shopping list—diapers, blanket, shirt, pins, bottle, and countless other basic item? Approaching the front door, the couple saw that all the light were shining in the three rooms of their small house. At first, they were afraid that burglars had been there, but as they looked around inside, their eye widened with surprise. In the living room were four box, each filled with baby clothes, toy, and medical supply. Among other thing were four pairs of bootys, matching sweaters and caps in four different color, and even four little hairbrush. When they picked up a big brown envelope, their neighbor, hiding in the backyard, all shouted at once through the kitchen window, "Open it!" More than fifty check fell out on the table. For a few months, anyway, their worrys about money were over.

Important: This paragraph contained 22 errors, not counting the one that was corrected for you. How many did you find? ____ If you didn't find all 22 errors, try again before you check your work.

Module 4: *Nouns*

RULES, Part 2: Special Problems

4G. Nouns after *of* and *of the* are often plural.

BICYCLE   one of the <u>bicycles</u>
               the seat of the <u>bicycle</u>

   One of the means that there is a group of bicycles, so *bicycles* is plural.
   The seat of the doesn't mean that there are several bicycles, so *bicycle* is singular.

Exercise 4.17 Fill in the appropriate form of the given noun.

1. DISH   Leora broke one of her mother's favorite _____ .

                The handle of the _____ broke off.

2. TEST   Another of those awful _____ was given yesterday.

                Part of that _____ gave me a lot of trouble.

3. QUESTION   One of the _____ was especially tricky.

                The first word of the _____ puzzled me.

4. KNIFE   Every one of those _____ needs sharpening.

                The blade of the _____ rusted in the rain.

Remember: Check your work as you go along, using the Answers in the back of the book.

4H. Some nouns name things that cannot be counted. We call these <u>noncount</u> nouns. They do not have plural forms.

HAPPINESS   Money can't buy <u>happiness</u>.

   Happiness is a noun, because it names something. The abstract quality that it names is
   neither singular nor plural, so *happiness* is a noncount noun.

Nouns naming things that can be counted have both singular and plural forms. Nouns naming things that can't be counted have just one form.

| TABLE | This <u>table</u> is an antique. |
| | These <u>tables</u> are antiques. |

> Tables are pieces of furniture which can be counted, so *TABLE* has both a singular and a plural form.

| FURNITURE | This <u>furniture</u> is ugly. |

> Furniture in general can't be counted, so *FURNITURE* doesn't have a plural form.

Noncount nouns are different from singular nouns. They can be used with no determiner.

| TABLE | We bought a <u>table</u>. |
| FURNITURE | We bought <u>furniture</u>. |

> Because *table* is singular, it must be used with a determiner.
> Because *furniture* is a noncount noun, it can be used with no determiner.

Noncount nouns used after *of* or *of the* can't be plural.

| WATER | They drank a lot of <u>water</u>. |

> *WATER* is a noncount noun; it doesn't have a plural form.

Exercise 4.18 Write in a lot of plus the appropriate noun form. Follow this model:

| BOOK | *a lot of books* |
| KNOWLEDGE | *a lot of knowledge* |

1. IDEA   _____

   INFORMATION   _____

2. EQUIPMENT   _____

   TYPEWRITER   _____

3. SLICE   _____

   BREAD   _____

4. ACCIDENT   _____

   LUCK   _____

5. LEISURE   _____

   HOBBY   _____

6. ASSIGNMENT   _____

    HOMEWORK   _____

Some words may be either count nouns or noncount nouns, depending on their meaning.

EXPERIENCE   Janet has lots of <u>experience</u> with bookkeeping.
              Janet had lots of interesting <u>experiences</u> on her trip across the country.

> *Experience* is a general idea, so it can't be counted.
> *Experiences* are specific events, so they can be counted.

Exercise 4.19 Fill in the appropriate form of the given noun.

1. INTEREST   Sophie has no _____ in spelunking.

    Sophie has so many other _____ that she hardly has

    time to sleep.

2. TIME   Most of the _____ it's better to keep your temper.

    How many _____ must I tell you?

3. EXPERIENCE   _____ may be the best teacher.

    We usually can learn the most from our bad _____ .

RULES SUMMARY, Part 2

In the longer one-page exercises that follow, you'll practice applying all the rules which you've learned or reviewed in this module. Before you go on to the longer exercises, check your understanding by filling in the blanks in the Rules Summary below. Fill in the blanks from memory, thinking carefully about what each rule means. If you need help, look back again at the Rules.

1. Nouns after *of* or *of the* are often _____ .

2. Nouns naming things that can be _____ have singular and plural forms.

3. Nouns naming things that can't be _____ have only one form.

Now turn to the Answers to check your work. Use these Rules and your dictionary as you go on to do the longer exercises that follow.

Module 4: *Nouns*

PRACTICE, Part 2

Exercise 4.20   **Number of Mistakes** _____

Fill in the appropriate form of the given noun.

1. APARTMENT   Neither of the _____ was big enough for a family of

    four.

2. STEEL   A lot of the _____ for the building had rusted.

3. WOMAN   Each of the _____ thought that her child was the most

    intelligent in the class.

4. INFORMATION   How much of the _____ was useful for your paper?

5. COMEDY   That is one of the best _____ the drama club has ever

    staged.

6. MILK   Two quarts of whole _____ daily is no longer

    recommended, even for adolescents.

7. BALLOON   We bought a big bunch of _____ .

8. FURNITURE   There was a pile of broken _____ in the corner of the

    basement.

9. HOMEWORK   Our teacher gave at least two assignments of _____

    every week.

10. BARN   The roof of the _____ was blown off in the storm.

11. LUCK   Happy coincidences are examples of good _____ .

12. VITAMIN   Fresh vegetables are an excellent source of _____ .

Exercise 4.21   **Number of Mistakes** _____

Remember: Like nouns, pronouns have singular and plural forms.

(1) Circle each noun. (2) Rewrite each sentence, making the nouns plural (unless they're noncount nouns), and making whatever other changes are necessary. (3) In your rewritten sentence, underline each change. Follow this model:

The (farmer) needed (advice) about his (problem) .

The farmers needed advice about their problems.

1. This book contained that information.

   _____

2. The boy asked for hockey equipment for his birthday.

   _____

3. One piece of music will not be enough for that ceremony.

   _____

4. The new tenant built some furniture for her apartment.

   _____

5. This car stalled in traffic; its driver couldn't start it.

   _____

6. That woman had much experience with carpentry.

   _____

Exercise 4.22   **Number of Mistakes** _____

This paragraph contains errors in noun forms. Underline each error, and correct it in the space above the line. The first error has been corrected for you.

work-roles

Joe and Gloria often switched <u>work-role</u> before they had their first two childrens. About

three time a month, Gloria used to bring home several of her friend from work, and Joe would

prepare fancy meal for them. He specialized in dish they could get their teeths into. One night

he served thick French onion soup to his two guest. As he mixed their drink, he gave them some

advices about cooking: "When I sliced these onion, I used the sharpest of all my knife. Always

cut the cheese into small pieces. Three dash of salts should be enough for a quart of soup. Keep

many different spice on your shelfs." The women said that his soup was one of the best feast

they had ever eaten. Gloria gave her husband two big kiss as a reward, and after dinner she

helped him clean up the mess. The other two woman went home and told their mens to make

onion soup for them. The next night stomping feets, several loud crash, and excited cry were

heard in the kitchens of these lady. Later they told Gloria that onion soup had turned their

happy marriages into complete wreck.

Important: This paragraph contained 24 errors, not counting the one that was corrected for you. How many did you find? _____ If you didn't find all 24, try again before you check your work.

Exercise 4.23

Number of Mistakes _____

(1) Circle each noun.

A rich local citizen recently bought a beautiful old house, fixed it up, and opened it to the public. A teacher took her seventh-grade class to visit this mansion. One student asked the guide to give her some information about the family who once lived there. The guide told her all about the man and the woman who had built this house long ago. Another child wanted to know more about the furniture, such as the tiny ornate desk, the huge bed, the cradle made of jet black wood, and the six-foot clock which still kept perfect time. Later on, in his English class, a student made up a spooky story about the ghost who still sat at that fancy desk, and rocked that black cradle, and slept in that big bed.

(2) Rewrite the paragraph, making the nouns plural (unless they're noncount nouns), and making whatever other changes are necessary. Remember that a variety of plural determiners is possible to tell **how many**.
(3) In your rewritten paragraph, underline each change. Your first sentence will begin like this: *Some rich local citizens recently bought two beautiful . . .*

_____

_____

_____

_____

_____

_____

_____

_____

_____

_____

_____

_____

_____

_____

Exercise 4.24   **Number of Mistakes** _____

Review Exercise B: Spelling, Writing Conventions, Wrong Words, Nouns

---

This passage contains errors in spelling, writing conventions, wrong words, and nouns. Underline each error, and correct it in the space above the line. For help, use your Rules and your dictionary. The first error has been corrected for you.

bears
Three brown <u>bear</u> had frightened a troop of young scout camping in the forest. When two

rangers arrived to get some informations from the scout leaders about what had happened, some

of the little camper were still as pale as ghost, and others were too scarred to speak. The

childrens said that 3 huge bears had knocked over several table, had torn one of their tent, and

then had run off into a clump of trees. the rangers knew that a adult female bear and it's two

cubs were in the nieghborhood, and they explained that female bears are even more ferocious

than males when there protecting there cubs. One of the leaders admited that the children had

left alot of food out on thier picnic tables, including an apple pie, several loaf of bread, and some

honey. "It's lucky you're not all dead," 1 ranger told all the campers angrily. "Theres nothing

more dangerous then leaving food out when bears are a round. You and your leaders can't be to

careful on these camping trip." The mens left, shaking their heads. They were glad they didnt

have to kill a bear just because some of the camper had acted foolishly.

Important: This paragraph contained 28 errors, not counting the one that was corrected for you. How many did you find? _____ If you didn't find all 28, try again before you check your work.

Module 4: *Nouns*

WRITING TEST

NAME _____

PURPOSE	To show that you can use a variety of noun plural forms correctly, and that you can continue to apply what you have learned in previous modules.

ASSIGNMENT   Imagine that a relative of yours recently won a million dollars in a state lottery and then went shopping to buy presents for five members of the family. Your relative was feeling generous and **always bought at least two of everything;** he or she never bought any single items, but bought everything in sets or pairs or large quantities.

Write a report for your local television station describing what your relative bought.

Check off each step in the writing process as you complete it.

DRAFT   ❏   On scratch paper, write a rough draft of your report. Try to write sentences that sound natural but aren't too complicated. Don't just list what your relative bought; **write at least two sentences about each gift.** Use and underline noun plural forms as you describe each gift.

REVISE   ❏   Read over the draft of your report to make sure that your ideas are clear. Try to anticipate what a reader will need to know in order to understand and believe what you have written. Add, take out, or change ideas, words, and sentences as necessary. Remember, it's good for a draft to become messy.

Make sure that you have used a variety of noun plural forms, not just forms ending in *S*.

❏   After you have finished revising your ideas, count the noun plural forms that you used and underlined, and write the number here: _____ .

EDIT   ❏   Review the Rules for this module. Find and correct any mistakes in noun plural forms.

Use your dictionary and the Rules for previous modules to find and correct any mistakes in:

❏   Spelling
❏   Writing Conventions
❏   Wrong Words

FINAL COPY   ❏   Write the final copy of your report carefully, using blue or black ink and standard-sized (8½ by 11 inch) paper. Better yet, type or use a word processor. Write your name in the upper right-hand corner, or use whatever heading your instructor requires. Remember that you are now preparing your writing for a reader.

❏   Underline every noun plural form in your final copy just as you did in your draft.

PROOFREAD   ❏   Read your final copy **out loud**. If you find any mistakes, it's OK to correct them neatly by hand. Or if you have used a word processor, go back and correct your mistakes, and then print out a clean final copy.

Attach your final copy to these instructions, and hand them both in.

5 Verbs and Verb Phrases

NAME _____

As you complete each exercise, record your number of mistakes below.

PART 1

5.1 ____	5.7 ____	Summary ____
5.2 ____	5.8 ____	5.13 ____
5.3 ____	5.9 ____	5.14 ____
5.4 ____	5.10 ____	5.15 ____
5.5 ____	5.11 ____	
5.6 ____	5.12 ____	

PART 2

5.16 ____	5.20 ____	5.24 ____
5.17 ____	5.21 ____	5.25 ____
5.18 ____	5.22 ____	Summary ____
5.19 ____	5.23 ____	5.26 ____
		5.27 ____

INSTRUCTOR'S COMMENTS

Instructions:

❑ Followed carefully
❑ Not followed carefully enough

Checking:

❑ Careful
❑ Not careful enough to catch all your mistakes
❑ Green pen not used for checking
❑ Entire correct answer not always written in

Writing Test:

❑ Excellent
❑ Good
❑ Acceptable
❑ Not yet satisfactory

Other:

Module 5: *Verbs and Verb Phrases*

RULES, Part 1: Recognizing Verbs

Important: In English grammar, **tense** means **time**.

Dan <u>walks</u> home.
> This sentence is written in **present tense** or present time; it tells what Dan usually does.

Dan <u>walked</u> home.
> This sentence is written in **past tense** or past time; it tells what Dan did in the past.

Dan <u>will walk</u> home.
> This sentence is written in **future tense** or future time; it tells what Dan is going to do in the future.

Exercise 5.1 Write in PRESENT, PAST, or FUTURE to tell the tense of each sentence.

1. The train <u>arrives</u> on time.

   The train <u>arrived</u> on time.

   The train <u>will arrive</u> on time.

2. The train <u>will be</u> early.

   The train <u>was</u> early.

   The train <u>is</u> early.

Remember: Check your work as you go along, using the Answers in the back of the book.

5A. **To find the verb in a sentence, find the word that can change form to show different tenses.**

CALL   Every night my sister <u>calls</u>.
        Last night my sister <u>called</u>.
        Tomorrow night my sister <u>will call</u>.
        > *CALL* can change form to show three different tenses: present, past, and future.

Remember: The **base form** of a word is the form found in the dictionary. In this book, base forms are written in capital letters.

94

Exercise 5.2 (1) Write in PRESENT, PAST, or FUTURE to tell the tense of each sentence. (2) Underline each verb. (3) Then write in the base form of the verb. Follow this model:

She <u>sees</u> the mountains.   <u>PRESENT</u>

She <u>saw</u> the mountains.   <u>PAST</u>

The **base form of the verb** is _____SEE_____.

1.   The flowers bloomed.   _____

     The flowers will bloom.   _____

     The **base form of the verb** is _____ .

2.   Acid rain will destroy living things.   _____

     Acid rain destroys living things.   _____

     The **base form of the verb** is _____ .

3.   These days many adults attend college.   _____

     In the past few adults attended college.   _____

     The **base form of the verb** is _____ .

Exercise 5.3 (1) Rewrite each sentence in the given tenses. (Use a one-word verb for the present tense. Use a one-word verb with an *ED* ending for the past tense. Use a two-word verb with *will* for the future tense.) (2) In the given sentence and in your rewritten sentences, underline each verb.

1.   PRESENT   Mr. Rafael walks fast.

     PAST   _____

     FUTURE   _____

2.   PAST   The skies cleared gradually.

     PRESENT   _____

     FUTURE   _____

3.   FUTURE   The bank tellers will check the total.

     PRESENT   _____

     PAST   _____

||||| 5B.   Every sentence must have a verb.

A group of words that does not have a verb is not a complete sentence.

> ✗ Many foreign students in the United States.
>> This group of words doesn't contain a verb, so it isn't a sentence.

> COME   Every year, many foreign students <u>come</u> to the United States.
>   Last year, many foreign students <u>came</u> to the United States.
>   Next year, many foreign students <u>will come</u> to the United States.
>> Each of these sentences contains a verb.

Exercise 5.4 One word group of each pair is a sentence, and the other is not. Look for a verb in each word group by trying to change its tense. If there is a verb, underline it, and write in SENT for sentence. If there is no verb, write in X.

1.   The grass in the back yard three feet high.   _____

     The grass in the back yard grew three feet high.   _____

2.   Business English is a popular course.   _____

     A popular course, Business English.   _____

3.   The children in the playground.   _____

     The children are in the playground.   _____

Exercise 5.5 Look for a verb in each word group by trying to change its tense. If there is a verb, underline it, and write in SENT for sentence. If there is no verb, write in X.

1.   Happy children.   _____

2.   Children play games.   _____

3.   Nobody called.   _____

4.   It is late.   _____

5.   Good evening.   _____

||| **1.   A sentence can have more than one verb.**

As soon as they <u>finish</u> dinner, they <u>wash</u> the dishes.
This sentence has two verbs, *finish* and *wash*.

Exercise 5.6 (1) Rewrite each sentence in the past tense, using one-word verbs with a *D* or *ED* ending. (2) In the given sentence and in your rewritten sentence, underline each verb.

1.   Many students work slowly but eventually succeed.

_____

2.   When the twins arrive home late, their parents complain.

_____

3.   Every Monday the managers discuss their plans and decide on a course of action for the week.

_____

_____

||| **2.   A contraction always contains a verb.**

<u>They're</u> in the hall.   They <u>are</u> in the hall.
They <u>aren't</u> ready yet.   They <u>are</u> not ready yet.
The contractions *they're* and *aren't* contain the verb *are*.

Exercise 5.7 (1) Circle each contraction. (2) Rewrite each sentence, changing the contraction into two words. In your rewritten sentences, underline each verb. Follow this model:

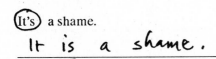

(It's) a shame.
It <u>is</u> a shame.

1.   Where's Inez?

_____

2.   She wasn't at work today and isn't at home now.

_____

3.   There's a memo that I'm eager to get from her.

_____

||||| **5C.   Don't confuse verbs with other words that may seem to be verbs.**

||| **1.   *To* + the base form of a verb is an <u>infinitive</u>. An infinitive is not a verb.
     It never changes form.**

    LIKE   I <u>like</u> to skate.
                      I <u>liked</u> to skate.
                           LIKE changes form to show different tenses, so it's a verb.
                           To skate doesn't change form, so it isn't a verb.

Exercise 5.8 (1) Rewrite each sentence in the past tense, using a one-word verb with a *D* or *ED* ending. (2) In the given sentence and in your rewritten sentence, underline each verb and circle the infinitive. Follow this model:

My dog <u>loves</u> (to swim) .

1.   Sandra plans to type her paper.

_____

2.   Alan wants to climb Mt. Hood.

_____

3.   Trump hopes to build the tallest skyscraper in the world.

_____

||| **2. An *ING* word by itself is not a verb.**

    PRACTICE   Jenny <u>practices</u> diving.
                          Jenny <u>practiced</u> diving.
                             PRACTICE changes form to show different tenses, so it's a verb.
                             Diving doesn't change form, so it isn't a verb.

Exercise 5.9 (1) Rewrite each sentence in the past tense, using a one-word verb with a *D* or *ED* ending. (2) In the given sentence and in your rewritten sentence, underline each verb and circle the *ING* word. Follow this model:

Katie <u>hates</u> (driving) .

Katie <u>hated</u> (driving) .

1. My boss starts working before breakfast.

    _____

2. Bicycling requires stamina.

    _____

3. The scouts like going on camping trips.

    _____

3. Words that show action are not always verbs.

ENJOY   I <u>enjoy</u> skating.
            I <u>enjoyed</u> skating.
                ENJOY changes form to show different tenses, so it's a verb.
                Skating shows action but doesn't change form, so it isn't a verb.

Exercise 5.10 (1) Rewrite each sentence in the past tense, using a one-word verb with a *D* or *ED* ending. (2) In the given sentence and in your rewritten sentence, underline each verb.

1. The jockeys prefer to ride at Hialeah Park.

    _____

2. Walking briskly burns calories.

    _____

3. Cooking and gardening help Yves to relax.

    _____

99

4. Words that are <u>not</u> verbs often look exactly like words that <u>are</u> verbs.

DRINK   They always <u>drink</u> iced tea.
BE   Iced tea <u>is</u> a very refreshing drink.

> In the first sentence, the verb is *drink*.
> In the second sentence, *drink* isn't the verb. The verb is *is*.

Exercise 5.11 (1) Find the verb in each sentence by trying to change the tense of the sentence. Then underline each verb. (2) Write in A or B for the sentence containing the given verb.

1. A. These tiny insects fly ten miles a day.

    B. This tiny fly travels great distances.

    Fly is the verb in sentence _____ .

2. A. My aunt cooks gourmet dinners.

    B. The best cooks prepare simple meals.

    Cooks is the verb in sentence _____ .

3. A. Many dances demand endurance.

    B. Mary dances for the American Ballet Company.

    Dances is the verb in sentence _____ .

4. A. The priest married the couple.

    B. The newly married couple exchanged rings.

    Married is the verb in sentence _____

5. A. Bike races are a new and popular sport in America.

    B. The Portland bike team races every Tuesday evening.

    Races is the verb in sentence _____

Remember: Infinitives are not verbs.
            ING words by themselves are not verbs.
            Some words that show action are not verbs.
            But words that change form to show different tenses **are** verbs.

Exercise 5.12 Find the verbs in each sentence by trying to change the tense of the sentence. Then underline each verb. Be careful not to underline any word that is **not** a verb.

1.   The Lundbergs need to paint their house again.

2.   Skydiving is exciting to watch.

3.   Shouting and screaming, the children rushed into the playground.

4.   Because Miriam hates to hurt anyone's feelings, she ends up telling lies.

5.   Most guests will enjoy eating outdoors.

6.   There's no place like home.

Important: If you missed any verbs in Exercise 5.12, or if you underlined any words that were not verbs, get help right now, before going on to the rest of this module.

RULES SUMMARY, Part 1

In the longer one-page exercises that follow, you'll practice applying all the rules which you've learned or reviewed in this module. Before you go on to the longer exercises, check your understanding by filling in the blanks in the Rules Summary below. Fill in the blanks from memory, thinking carefully about what each rule means. If you need help, look back again at the Rules.

1.   To find the verb in a sentence, find the word that can change form to show different

      _____ .

2.   Every sentence must have at least one _____ .

3.   *To* + the base form of a verb is an _____ , which is never a verb.

4.   An _____ word by itself is never a verb.

5.   Words that show _____ are not always verbs.

Now turn to the Answers to check your work. Use these Rules and your dictionary as you go on to do the longer exercises that follow.

Module 5: *Verbs and Verb Phrases*

PRACTICE, Part 1

Exercise 5.13   **Number of Mistakes** _____

Remember: (1) A sentence can have more than one verb. (2) An infinitive is not a verb. (3) An *ING* word by itself is not a verb.

Find the verbs in each sentence by trying to change the tense of the sentence. Then underline each verb. Be careful not to underline any word that is **not** a verb.

Near the Italian town of Maranello, a blood-red car rockets around a twisting track. The speedometer leaps to 120 miles per hour. The driver pumps the brakes and careens into a hairpin turn. Skidding briefly, he turns the steering wheel sharply to regain his hold on the road. He roars around the track a few more times, and the car screeches to a stop. The driver steps out grinning. This Ferrari passes.

Enzo Ferrari began producing his racing cars in 1929. His trademark was a prancing black horse, the insignia of the Italian flying ace, Francesco Baracca. Ferrari cars started to win racing championships during the next decade. In 1945, Ferrari designed his first 12-cylinder model for everyday use. He developed a system of checks and controls to make certain that every part was perfect, and hired daring designers to create shovel-nosed hoods and swooping fenders. The result was a powerful and almost indestructible machine, so beautiful that thousands of car buffs rushed to buy it, even at extravagant prices.

The next Ferrari which will come out of Maranello will cost nearly $200,000, and it's likely to have a top speed of around 200 miles per hour. The Ferrari factory will produce no more than a few thousand of these cars, and they're sure to disappear from the dealers' shops on the same day they arrive. Then most of them will spend their lives cruising over roads where the speed limit is 55 miles an hour—about one-fourth their capacity. Still, their proud drivers will continue to smile, and to smile again, as heads turn and eyes stare at these aristocrats of the road.

Exercise 5.14

This paragraph is in the past tense. (1) Find the verbs in each sentence by trying to change the tense of the sentence, and then underline them.

In 1992 Jan and Walter were intern doctors at Central Hospital. Medical facts filled their brains, but they had little experience in caring for critically ill people. They worked 36-hour shifts. Just as they tumbled into bed, too weary to shower, their beepers sounded again. Their patients needed transfusions. They had raging fevers. Jan and Walter staggered back to the intensive care unit. Their eyes blurred as they tried to read their patients' charts. They worried about making fatal errors. The resident doctors checked Jan's prescriptions carefully, and the nurses watched closely as Walter's fingers fumbled with the intravenous tubes. The patients just prayed hard that no mistakes slipped by.

(2) Rewrite the paragraph, changing *In 1992* to *This year*, and changing the past-tense verbs to present-tense verbs. (3) In your rewritten paragraph, underline each verb. Your first sentence will begin like this: *This year Jan and Walter are intern doctors . . .*

_____

_____

_____

_____

_____

_____

_____

_____

_____

_____

_____

_____

_____

_____

Exercise 5.15

This paragraph is in the present tense. (1) Find the verbs in each sentence by trying to change the tense of the sentence, and then underline them.

Every two years my friend Madeline receives a summons to serve as a juror in civil court. Madeline loves to read about dramatic trials, but jury duty in civil court is quite a disappointment. Every day for two weeks, Madeline listens to lawyers as they explain their not very exciting cases. In one case, a man collides with a glass door. In another, a woman slips on a rug. These people want compensation for minor bruises and nervous strain. The lawyers ask Madeline what she does for a living, what church she attends, what newspapers she enjoys reading, etc. But they never pick her to be on a jury. They seem to prefer people who smile a lot when they talk and who look at comic books while they wait. Madeline almost dies of frustration and hopes to be called for jury duty in criminal court next time.

(2) Rewrite the paragraph, changing *Every two years* to *Last fall*, and changing the present-tense verbs to past-tense verbs. (3) In your rewritten paragraph, underline each verb. Your first sentence will begin like this: *Last fall my friend Madeline received a summons* . . .

_____

_____

_____

_____

_____

_____

_____

_____

_____

_____

_____

_____

Module 5: *Verbs and Verb Phrases*

RULES, Part 2: Recognizing Verb Phrases

5D. A verb can be one word, or more than one word. A verb that is more than one word is called a <u>verb phrase</u>.

All verbs have both **one-word** forms and **verb-phrase** forms. Verb phrases are used naturally in both speaking and writing to express various time relationships or meanings of a verb.

1. A verb in the <u>future</u> tense is always a verb phrase with *will*.

COOK   Leonard <u>will cook</u> dinner tomorrow.
> *Will cook* is a future-tense verb.

2. A verb in the <u>present</u> tense can be either a one-word verb or a verb phrase.

COOK   Leonard usually <u>cooks</u> dinner.
Leonard <u>is cooking</u> dinner right now.
> *Cooks* and *is cooking* are both present-tense verbs.

3. A verb in the <u>past</u> tense can be either a one-word verb or a verb phrase.

COOK   Leonard <u>cooked</u> dinner last night.
Leonard <u>was cooking</u> dinner for hours.
> *Cooked* and *was cooking* are both past-tense verbs.

Exercise 5.16 (1) Write in PRESENT, PAST, or FUTURE to tell the tense of each sentence. (2) Underline each one-word verb and verb phrase.

1. Sasha exercises every night.   _____

   Sasha is exercising right now.   _____

   Sasha will exercise tomorrow.   _____

2. William was working last night.   _____

   William is working today.   _____

   William works hard.   _____

William will work for me next week.   _____

William worked for me last week.   _____

Remember: Check your work as you go along, using the Answers in the back of the book.

5E.   Every verb phrase has two parts: at least one <u>helping verb</u> and a <u>main verb</u>.

1.   The <u>main verb</u> is the last word in a verb phrase. It tells what a verb phrase is about.

PREPARE   Paula <u>had prepared</u> dessert already.
                 Paula usually <u>does</u> not <u>prepare</u> dinner until at least 7 PM.
                 Paula <u>is preparing</u> dinner now.
                 Each sentence tells about preparing food. *Prepared*, *prepare*, and *preparing* are main verbs.
                 The base form of the main verb in each sentence is *PREPARE*.

2.   <u>Helping verbs</u> are the words in a verb phrase that come before the main verb. They express various time relationships.

PREPARE   Paula <u>had prepared</u> dessert already.
                 Paula usually <u>does</u> not <u>prepare</u> dinner until at least 7 PM.
                 Paula <u>is preparing</u> dinner now.
                 Had, *does*, and *is* are helping verbs.

Exercise 5.17 Study the verb phrases in these sentences. Then fill in the blanks.

1.   I <u>am planning</u> a trip to Canada.

   a.   The **helping verb** in this sentence is _____ .

   b.   The **main verb** in this sentence is _____ .

   c.   The **base form** of the main verb is _____ .

2.   The Economics Department <u>had planned</u> to install a new computer.

   a.   The **helping verb** in this sentence is _____ .

   b.   The **main verb** in this sentence is _____ .

   c.   The **base form** of the main verb is _____ .

3.   <u>Does</u> anybody ever <u>plan</u> to have an accident?

   a.   The **helping verb** in this sentence is _____ .

   b.   The **main verb** in this sentence is _____ .

   c.   The **base form of the main verb** is _____ .

||| **3.   In verb phrases, the helping verb, not the main verb, shows the <u>tense</u>.**

   USE   Someone <u>is using</u> the meeting room now.
                    Someone <u>was using</u> the meeting room yesterday.

                    The helping verb *is* shows that the first sentence is in the present tense.
                    The helping verb *was* shows that the second sentence is in the past tense.

Exercise 5.18 These sentences contain verb phrases in the present tense. (1) Rewrite each sentence in the past tense, changing *is* to *was*, and *are* to *were*. (2) In the given sentence and in your rewritten sentence, underline each verb phrase, and double underline the main verb. Follow this model:

   The roof <u>is leaking</u>.

   <u>The roof was leaking.</u>

1.   Carl is doing research on the last primary election.

   _____

2.   Fewer Americans are registering to vote.

   _____

3.   The candidates are worrying about budget deficits while they are promising not to raise taxes.

   _____

Important: *BE, HAVE,* and *DO* are the most common helping verbs in English.

BASE FORM	present-tense forms	past-tense forms
BE	am, is, are	was, were
HAVE	have, has	had
DO	do, does	did

Exercise 5.19 Underline each verb phrase, and double underline the main verb. Then fill in the blanks.

1.   Geraldine's father has enrolled at his daughter's college.

  a.   The **base form of the helping verb** in this sentence is _____ .

  b.   The **base form of the main verb** in this sentence is _____ .

2.   He and his daughter both are studying ancient Greek literature.

  a.   The **base form of the helping verb** in this sentence is _____ .

  b.   The **base form of the main verb** in this sentence is _____ .

3.   Even before this semester, they always did enjoy works by the great authors of antiquity.

  a.   The **base form of the helping verb** in this sentence is _____ .

  b.   The **base form of the main verb** in this sentence is _____ .

||| **4.   Do not confuse a one-word verb with the helping verb in a verb phrase.**

If the word that can change tense is a form of *BE* or *HAVE* or *DO*, it might be either a one-word verb or a helping verb in a verb phrase.

HAVE	Jud <u>has</u> a talent for mathematics.
STUDY	Jud <u>has studied</u> mathematics for ten years.

> In the first sentence, *has* is a one-word verb, and the sentence is about **having**.
> In the second sentence, *has* is a helping verb in the verb phrase *has studied*,
> and the sentence is about **studying**.

Exercise 5.20 Underline each one-word verb and verb phrase. Double underline the main verb in each verb phrase.

1.   Many households have two or more television sets.

  Most children have watched many hours of TV before entering kindergarten.

2.   We certainly did try to file our taxes on time.

  We did most of the paperwork last weekend.

3.   Swimming is a relaxing form of exercise.

  The motel guests were relaxing beside the pool.

▌▌▌▌ **5.**   **Do not confuse an *ING* word by itself with the main verb in a verb phrase.**

An *ING* word is often the **main verb in a verb phrase** after a form of *BE* (any one of these helping verbs: *am, is, are, was,* or *were*).

COOK   Leonard <u>is cooking</u> dinner right now.
                  Leonard <u>was cooking</u> dinner for hours.
                      Cooking is the main verb in the verb phrases *is cooking* and *was cooking*.

But an *ING* word by itself is not a verb.

PREFER   Leonard <u>prefers</u> cooking healthy meals.
                      Cooking is not part of a verb phrase in this sentence, so it is not a verb.

Exercise 5.21 Some of the *ING* words are main verbs in verb phrases, and some are not. (1) Underline each one-word verb and verb phrase. Double underline the main verb in each verb phrase. (2) Circle each *ING* word that is not part of a verb phrase.

1.   Mariko is studying in the library.

2.   Some people like studying late at night.

3.   Studying history demands a good memory for dates.

4.   The whole class was studying hard for the mid-term examination.

5.   We made a date to begin studying at 9 PM.

▌▌▌▌▌ **5F.**   **Some verb phrases have more than one helping verb.**

One special group of helping verbs is called **modals.** Modals are very often used along with other helping verbs.

will	can	shall	may	must
would	could	should	might	

PREPARE   Paula <u>will be preparing</u> dinner soon.
                  Paula <u>might have been preparing</u> dinner at that time.
                      Will and *be* are helping verbs in the verb phrase *will be preparing*.
                      Might, have, and *been* are helping verbs in the verb phrase *might have been preparing*.

Exercise 5.22 Underline each verb phrase, and double underline the main verb. Follow this model:

Andrea <u>will be <u>calling</u></u> about the assignment.

She <u>will <u>call</u></u> before noon.

1.   Peter will buy the newspaper.

Peter might have bought the newspaper this morning.

2.   More American companies are conducting business overseas.

International business is being conducted by fax machine and telephone.

3.   A Senate staff member had released the information.

No information should have been released without authorization.

5G.   The first helping verb in a verb phrase is often contracted.

KNIT   Deborah'<u>s knitting</u> a scarf.
                  Deborah <u>is knitting</u> a scarf.
                       The contraction *Deborah's* contains the helping verb *is* in the verb phrase *is knitting*.

Exercise 5.23 (1) Rewrite each sentence, changing the contraction into two words. (3) In your rewritten sentences, underline each verb phrase, and double underline the main verb. Follow this model:

Soon we'll leave for the lecture.

<u>Soon we will <u>leave</u> for the lecture.</u>

1.   Bill's leaving at noon.

_____

2.   On the last trip he'd driven all night.

_____

3.   Usually he'd have gone by the expressway.

_____

4.   But this time he'll be traveling on Route 22.

5H.   One or more words may interrupt a verb phrase, especially in a negative sentence or a question.

PERFORM   Juan <u>was</u> not <u><u>performing</u></u> with the group last year.
             Juan <u>wasn't</u> <u><u>performing</u></u> with the group last year.
             Not (or the contracted form *n't*) interrupts the verb phrase *was performing*.

SHOW   <u>Will</u> you please <u><u>show</u></u> us the most direct route?
             You and *please* interrupt the verb phrase *will show*.

Exercise 5.24 Underline each verb phrase, and double underline the main verb. Don't underline any interrupting words.

1.   Is anybody else from your college planning to attend the conference?

2.   I will not forget to bring the registration form.

3.   Did the cost of food rise because of the drought?

4.   Some people are always worrying about their health but are still eating junk food.

5.   Vanessa was already writing the first draft of her paper, even though she hadn't finished her research.

Remember: A verb may be either a one-word verb or a verb phrase.

Exercise 5.25 To review, underline each one-word verb and verb phrase. Double underline the main verb in each verb phrase. Don't underline any interrupting words. Remember that a sentence may have more than one verb.

1.   Yuri likes his new job and is already earning a good salary.

2.   Eating healthy foods is becoming increasingly expensive.

3.   The survey is being conducted by a marketing firm.

4.   Somebody always starts to leave before the performance has ended.

5.   I will not call you until I finish the letter that I'm writing.

6.   The lights dimmed and the curtain slowly rose as the orchestra began to play.

7.   We haven't been receiving all of our mail.

Important: If you made more than one mistake in Exercise 5.25, get help before going on.

RULES SUMMARY, Part 2

In the longer one-page exercises that follow, you'll practice applying all the rules which you've learned or reviewed in this module. Before you go on to the longer exercises, check your understanding by filling in the blanks in the Rules Summary below. Fill in the blanks from memory, thinking carefully about what each rule means. If you need help, look back again at the Rules.

1.   A verb that is more than one word is called a _____

      _____ .

2.   Every verb phrase contains at least one _____ verb, and a

      _____ verb.

3.   The _____ _____ tells what a verb phrase is

      about.

4.   The _____ verb or verbs in a verb phrase express various time relationships.

5.   The helping verb, not the main verb, shows the _____ .

6.   The first _____ _____ in a verb phrase is

      often contracted.

7.   One or more words may _____ a verb phrase, especially in a negative

      sentence or a question.

Now turn to the Answers to check your work. Use the Rules and your dictionary as you go on to do the longer exercises that follow.

Module 5: *Verbs and Verb Phrases*

PRACTICE, Part 2

Exercise 5.26   **Number of Mistakes** _____

Underline each one-word verb and verb phrase. Double underline the main verb in each verb phrase. Don't underline any interrupting words. The first sentence has been marked for you.

This year as usual, especially when she <u>begins</u> to run short of cash for Christmas presents,

my sister Cynthia <u>will</u> probably <u>go</u> to the outdoor market to look for bargains. Once I went with

her, but I will never go again. At any time of year, the place is full of jostling crowds, but at

Christmas time it's a madhouse. Excited vendors are shouting at customers, and frustrated

shoppers are screaming at cashiers. Merchandise is lying around in messy heaps on outdoor

counters. Racks of clothing clutter up the sidewalks, so people walk in the street and block

traffic. The sound of honking horns adds to the noise and confusion. Sometimes a guard chases

a shoplifter through the crowds. While he is away, a customer quietly switches the price tags.

But that is the only thing that happens quietly there. Last year Cynthia came home with a

headache along with her purchases. Still, she loves bargains, so no doubt she will go back to the

market again this December.

Important: This paragraph contained 5 verb phrases, not counting the one that was marked for you. How many did you find? _____ If you did not find all 5, try again before you check your work.
This paragraph also contained 14 one-word verbs, not counting the one that was marked for you. How many did you find? _____ If you did not find all 14, try again before you check your work.

Exercise 5.27   **Number of Mistakes** _____

This paragraph is in the past tense. (1) Underline each one-word verb and verb phrase. Double underline the main verb in each verb phrase. Don't underline any interrupting words.

Even ten years ago, Americans were beginning to shift their view of alcoholic

beverages. Many people, anxious about their health, were drinking less. In restaurants,

they were ordering white wine instead of martinis. Others had stopped drinking liquor

entirely. Equally important, attitudes were changing. Intoxicated people no longer

seemed so funny. Comedians made fewer jokes about the antics of drunks. The police

were arresting drunk drivers, and in more and more states, the courts were giving them

stiff fines and were even sending them to prison. Abuse of alcohol was being

recognized as a threat to health, to life, and to society.

(2) Rewrite the paragraph in the present tense, changing *Even ten years ago* to *These days*, and changing each one-word verb and helping verb to its present-tense form. (Hint: Change *was* to *is*, and *were* to *are*.) (3) In your rewritten paragraph, underline each one-word verb and verb phrase. Double underline the main verb in each verb phrase. Your first sentence will begin like this: *These days, Americans are beginning to . . .*

_____

_____

_____

_____

_____

_____

_____

_____

_____

_____

_____

_____

_____

Module 5: *Verbs and Verb Phrases*

WRITING TEST

NAME _____

PURPOSE	To show that you can recognize both one-word verbs and verb phrases in your own writing, and that you can continue to apply what you have learned in previous modules.

ASSIGNMENT	Write a short autobiography, introducing yourself and telling about some of your activities, accomplishments, and goals that might come as a surprise to your teacher and classmates.

Check off each step in the writing process as you complete it.

DRAFT On scratch paper, write a rough draft of your autobiography. Try to write sentences that sound natural but aren't too complicated.

❏ In the first paragraph, **write at least four sentences in the present tense**, telling things that are true about you, and things that you usually do or are doing now.

❏ In the second paragraph, **write at least four sentences in the past tense**, telling some of your past experiences or activities.

❏ In the third paragraph, **write at least four sentences in the future tense**, telling your plans for the future.

REVISE ❏ Read over the draft of your autobiography to make sure that your ideas are clear and sound real. Try to anticipate what a reader will need to know in order to understand and believe what you have written. Add, take out, or change ideas, words, and sentences as necessary. Remember, it's good for a draft to become messy.

EDIT Review the Rules for this module. Mark the one-word verbs and verb phrases in your draft like this:

❏ Underline each one-word verb and verb phrase. Double underline the main verb in each verb phrase.

❏ As you do this, make sure that each verb is in the appropriate tense.

Use your dictionary and the Rules for previous modules to find and correct any mistakes in:

❏ Nouns: Singular and Plural Forms
❏ Spelling
❏ Writing Conventions
❏ Wrong Words

FINAL COPY ❏ Write the final copy of your autobiography carefully, using blue or black ink and standard-sized (8½ by 11 inch) paper. Better yet, type or use a word processor. Write your name in the upper right-hand corner or use whatever heading your instructor requires. Remember that you are now preparing your writing for a reader.

❏ Underline every one-word verb and verb phrase in your final copy just as you did in your draft.

PROOFREAD ❏ Read your final copy **out loud**. If you find any mistakes, it's OK to correct them neatly by hand. Or if you have used a word processor, go back and correct your mistakes, and then print out a clean final copy.

Attach your final copy to these instructions, and hand them both in.

6 Understanding Sentences I

NAME _____

As you complete each exercise, record your number of mistakes below.

PART 1

6.1 _____	6.8 _____	6.15 _____
6.2 _____	6.9 _____	6.16 _____
6.3 _____	6.10 _____	6.17 _____
6.4 _____	6.11 _____	Summary ____
6.5 _____	6.12 _____	6.18 _____
6.6 _____	6.13 _____	6.19 _____
6.7 _____	6.14 _____	6.20 _____

PART 2

6.21 _____	6.26 _____	6.30 _____
6.22 _____	6.27 _____	6.31 _____
6.23 _____	6.28 _____	6.32 _____
6.24 _____	Summary _____	6.33 _____
6.25 _____	6.29 _____	

INSTRUCTOR'S COMMENTS

Instructions:

❑ Followed carefully
❑ Not followed carefully enough

Checking:

❑ Careful
❑ Not careful enough to catch all your mistakes
❑ Green pen not used for checking
❑ Entire correct answer not always written in

Writing Test:

❑ Excellent
❑ Good
❑ Acceptable
❑ Not yet satisfactory

Other:

Module 6: *Understanding Sentences I*

RULES, Part 1: Sentence Structure

6A. Every sentence has two parts, a <u>subject</u> part and a <u>verb</u> part.

Remember: A verb may be either a one-word verb or a verb phrase.
A verb changes form to show different tenses.

The subject answers the question WHO? or WHAT? **in front of** the verb.

       S
Children / <u>play</u> games.

> *Play* is the verb. *Children* is the subject because it answers the question *WHO play games?*

To analyze a sentence, follow these steps:

First, find the **verb,** and underline it.

       Children <u>play</u> games.

Second, find the **subject,** and mark it with an S.

       S
Children <u>play</u> games.

Third, draw a **slash** between the subject part and the verb part.

       S
Children / <u>play</u> games.

Exercise 6.1 Analyze each sentence like this: (1) Underline the verb (remember that a verb may be either a one-word verb or a verb phrase). (2) Mark the subject with an S. (3) Draw a slash between the subject part and the verb part. Follow this model:

       S
The announcer / <u>has dropped</u> the microphone.

1. Dogs bark.

2. Somebody cheated me.

3. The helicopter will land over there.

4. Those songs were popular in the 1950s.

118

5.   The children were telling ghost stories.

Remember: Check your work as you go along, using the Answers in the back of the book.

6B.   Some sentences contain a <u>complement</u>, a word that completes the meaning of the verb.

A complement answers the question WHO? (WHOM?) or WHAT? **after** the verb.

      S
Children / <u>play</u>.

        This sentence has no complement.

      S   C
Children / <u>play</u> games.

        Games is a complement after the verb *play*, because it answers the question *Children play WHAT?*

    S   C
We / <u>like</u> Sybil.

        Sybil is a complement after the verb *like*, because it answers the question *We like WHOM?*

Important: As you do the following exercises, be sure to follow the steps in the instructions in order. **Always look for the verb first.** Remember that a verb may be either a one-word verb or a verb phrase.

Exercise 6.2 (1) Underline the verb. (2) Mark the subject with an S. (3) Mark the complement with a C. (4) Draw a slash between the subject part and the verb part. Follow this model:

          S   C
    The cat / <u>scratched</u> my hand.

1.   Someone destroyed the evidence.

2.   Jason seems unhappy.

3.   Pamela has an older sister.

4.   Their explanation was incredible.

5.   Nobody will answer the question.

Important: Don't confuse the main verb in a verb phrase with a complement.

       S
Sybil / <u>is teaching</u>.

> This sentence has no complement. *Teaching* is the main verb in the verb phrase *is teaching*.

       S   C
Sybil / <u>is</u> a teacher.

> *Teacher* is a complement after the verb *is*. It answers the question *Sybil is WHAT?*

Exercise 6.3 (1) Underline each one-word verb and verb phrase. Double underline the main verb in each verb phrase. (2) Mark the subject with an S. (3) If there is a complement, mark it with a C. (4) Draw a slash between the subject part and the verb part. Follow this model:

           S   C
Our class / <u>is</u> large.
           S   C
Our class / <u>is <u>reading</u> a play.

1.   The audience was noisy.

       The audience was applauding.

2.   Keisha is writing the minutes.

       Keisha is the secretary.

3.   The assignment has confused the students.

       They have many questions.

6C.   A sentence can have several verbs, or subjects, or complements.

1.   A sentence can have more than one verb.

Exercise 6.4 (1) Underline each verb. (2) Mark the subject with an S. (3) If there is a complement, mark it with a C. (4) Draw a slash between the subject part and the verb part. Follow this model:

        S   C
The dog / <u>chased</u> and <u>killed</u> a bird.

1.   Esther was driving and had an accident.

2.   The cliffs will erode and eventually will crumble.

3.   I wrote, stamped, and mailed the letters immediately.

||| **2.**   **One verb can have more than one subject.**

Exercise 6.5 (1) Underline the verb. (2) Mark each subject with an S. (3) If there is a complement, mark it with a C. (4) Draw a slash between the subject part and the verb part. Follow this model:

         The dog and cat / destroyed the upholstery.

1.   Some flowers and insects eat animals.

2.   Your friends and family will help.

3.   Cars, trucks, and buses jammed the intersection.

||| **3.**   **One verb can have more than one complement.**

Exercise 6.6 (1) Underline the verb. (2) Mark the subject with an S. (3) Mark each complement with a C. (4) Draw a slash between the subject part and the verb part. Follow this model:

         My cat / eats only liver and fish.

1.   That shop sells newspapers, magazines, and paperback books.

2.   Few people are both active and fat.

3.   Most sophomores will take history and science.

Exercise 6.7 To review the Rules so far, do this: (1) Underline each verb. (2) Mark each subject with an S. (3) Mark each complement with a C. (4) Draw a slash between the subject part and the verb part. Follow this model:

         McNeil and Lehrer / discuss and analyze the news and current events.

1.   Next year my brother will visit China, Taiwan, and Japan.

2.   Old movie heroes smoke, drink, and drive fast cars.

3.   Crabs, shrimp, and other shellfish are delicious but expensive.

Important: A series is a list of three or more items. The items in a series should be separated by commas.

<pre>
            S
The audience / <u>clapped</u>, <u>stamped</u>, and <u>cheered</u>.
</pre>

> *Clapped, stamped,* and *cheered* is a series of three verbs, separated by commas. Don't forget the comma before *and*.

Exercise 6.8 (1) Rewrite each group of sentences as one sentence, without repeating words. **Use commas as necessary.** (2) In your rewritten sentence, do this: (a) Underline each verb. (b) Mark each subject with an S. (c) Mark each complement with a C. (d) Draw a slash between the subject part and the verb part. Follow this model:

I bought pencils.
I bought pens.
I bought paper.

(handwritten) I / bought pencils, pens, and paper.

1.   Women boarded the bus.
     Men boarded the bus.
     Children boarded the bus.

     _____

     _____

2.   Kareem drinks soda pop.
     Kareem drinks seltzer water.
     Kareem drinks nonalcoholic beer.

     _____

     _____

3.   Lovingly Stacy washed her new car.
     Lovingly Stacy waxed her new car.
     Lovingly Stacy polished her new car.

     _____

     _____

6D.   The parts of a sentence are often expanded.

Some words tell more about other words in a sentence. In this book, words that tell more about subjects, verbs, and complements are called **expansion**. Expansion is marked with parentheses. Arrows show which word is expanded.

S
Cats / <u>purr</u>.

> This sentence has no expansion.

S
(My)→cats / <u>purr</u> (when I scratch their ears).

> *My* is expansion telling WHOSE cats.
> *When I scratch their ears* is expansion telling WHEN they purr.

1.   The subject of a sentence is often expanded by a word or group of words telling more about it.

S   C
(Many)→children / <u>play</u> games.

> *Many* is expansion telling HOW MANY children.

S   C
(Happy)→children / <u>play</u> games.

> *Happy* is expansion telling WHAT KIND of children.

S   C
Children←(in large families) / <u>play</u> games.

> *In large families* is expansion telling WHAT KIND of children.

Exercise 6.9 (1) Mark the subject with an S. (2) Put parentheses around expansion of the subject, and draw an arrow from the expansion to the subject. Follow this model:

$$\left(\text{Some}\right)^{\curvearrowright}\overset{S}{\text{parents}} / \underline{\text{worry}}.$$

1.   Most women / <u>work</u>.

2.   Women of all ages / <u>work</u>.

3.   Several women in the office / <u>were preparing</u> the report.

Important: Don't confuse the subject with words that expand it.

S   C
(A)→parent←(with young children) / <u>has</u> little free time.

> *Parent* is the subject because it answers the question *WHO has little free time?*
> *With young children* is expansion telling WHAT KIND of parent.

Exercise 6.10 (1) Underline the verb. (2) Mark the subject with an S. (3) Put parentheses around expansion of the subject, and draw an arrow from the expansion to the subject. (4) Draw a slash between the subject part and the verb part. Follow this model:

$$\left(A\right)\overset{\curvearrowright\;S\curvearrowleft}{man}\left(\text{in tattered clothes}\right)\Big/\underline{stood}\text{ on the corner.}$$

1. The visitors from the central office will arrive soon.

2. Several teachers in the gerontology program are working together on a research project.

3. Some catalogs for winter clothing appear in the middle of summer.

||| **2.**   **Just like the subject, the complement can be expanded.**

          S   C
Hortense / <u>sees</u> (many)→movies.

> *Movies* is a complement because it answers the question *Hortense sees WHAT?*
> *Many* is expansion telling HOW MANY movies.

          S   C
Hortense / <u>likes</u> movies←(with happy endings).

> *Movies* is a complement.
> *With happy endings* is expansion telling WHAT KIND of movies.

Exercise 6.11 (1) Mark the complement with a C. (2) Put parentheses around expansion of the complement, and draw an arrow from the expansion to the complement. Follow this model:

       S   C
Matt / <u>prefers</u> (classical)↷music.

     S
1. People / <u>have</u> different problems.

     S
2. People / <u>have</u> problems of many different kinds.

     S
3. People / <u>have</u> many problems in their everyday lives.

||| **3.**   **The verb (or the entire verb part) of a sentence can be expanded.**

Verb expansion adds information that answers questions like WHEN? or WHERE? or HOW? Verb expansion can come either **before** the verb or **after** the verb.

S
My cousins / (often) <u>traveled</u>.

> *Often* is expansion telling WHEN my cousins traveled.

S
My cousins / <u>traveled</u> (in the Southwest).

> *In the Southwest* is expansion telling WHERE they traveled.

S
My cousins / <u>traveled</u> (by car).

> *By car* is expansion telling HOW they traveled.

Exercise 6.12 (1) Underline the verb. (2) Put parentheses around verb expansion. Follow this model:

S
Winners / (never) <u>quit</u>.

S
1. Mary Ellen / quietly collapsed.

S
2. Jerome / always tries hard.

S
3. Someone / usually will respond after the deadline.

4. Don't confuse verb expansion with a complement.

Important: A complement answers the question WHO? or WHAT? after the verb. Complements are
often **nouns**.
Verb expansion works differently: It tells WHEN? or WHERE? or HOW?

S   C
The team / <u>lost</u> the game.

> *Game* is a complement because it answers the question *The team lost WHAT?*

S
The team / <u>lost</u> (last night).

> *Last night* is verb expansion telling WHEN the team lost.

S   C
The team / <u>lost</u> the game (last night).

> This sentence has both a complement *(game)* and verb expansion *(last night)*.

125

Exercise 6.13 (1) Underline the verb, and draw a slash between the subject part and the verb part. (2) If there is a complement, mark it with a C. (3) If there is verb expansion, put parentheses around it.

1.   Mr. Sokoloff walks slowly.

     Mr. Sokoloff walked his dog.

2.   Clarissa writes with a fountain pen.

     Clarissa writes many letters.

3.   The speeding driver stopped suddenly.

     The speeding driver suddenly stopped his car.

Important: Expansion often contains an important part of the **meaning** of a sentence, but the **structure** of the sentence consists of the verb(s), subject(s), and complement(s).

S   C

(Evening) students / (sometimes) <u>study</u> (their college) assignments (at their desks) (at work).

> This sentence has the pattern **subject-verb-complement**. Expansion is important to the meaning of the sentence, but it is not part of the sentence's basic structure.

S   C

Students / <u>study</u> assignments.

> This is the basic structure of the sentence. The verb is *study*. *Students* is the subject because it answers the question *WHO study? Assignments* is the complement because it answers the question *Students study WHAT?*

Remember: When you analyze the structure of a sentence, always look for the verb(s) first.

Exercise 6.14 To review the Rules so far, do this: (1) Underline each verb. (2) Mark each subject with an S. (3) Mark each complement with a C. (4) Put parentheses around all expansion. (5) Draw a slash between the subject part and the verb part. Follow this model:

$\left(\text{A}\right) \overset{S}{\text{storm}} \left(\text{in the tropics}\right) \Big/ \left(\text{sometimes}\right) \underline{\text{strikes}} \left(\text{without warning}\right).$

1.   Stu will send a map of the route and a letter with detailed driving instructions.

2.   A kettle of water and a pot of spaghetti sauce were simmering on the stove.

3.   One member of the audience finally went to the stage.

6E.   **Two sentences are sometimes connected by a joining word like *and* or *but*. We call this kind of sentence a <u>compound sentence</u>.**

||| 1.   Because a compound sentence consists of two sentences connected by a joining word, it can be rewritten as two separate sentences.

Jamal / <u>arrived</u> at the theater early, **but** all the seats / <u>had been sold</u>.
> This is a compound sentence with the joining word *but*.

Jamal / <u>arrived</u> at the theater early. All the seats / <u>had been sold</u>.
> The compound sentence has been rewritten as two separate sentences.

Exercise 6.15 (1) Draw a box around the joining word. (2) Rewrite the compound sentence as two separate sentences. (3) In your rewritten sentence, underline the verb, and draw a slash between the subject part and the verb part. Follow this model:

The stock market was recovering, [but] the public was uneasy about the future.

The stock market/was recovering. The public/was uneasy about the future.

1.   Most middle-class families had money, but they weren't spending it on luxuries.

_____

_____

2.   Taxes were rising, and voters were demanding new economy in government.

_____

_____

||| 2.   In a compound sentence, always use a comma <u>in front of</u> the joining word.

Yumiko / finally <u>finished</u> her paper**, but** she / still <u>is studying</u> for the test.
> In this compound sentence, a comma is used in front of the joining word *but*.

Important: Never use a comma **after** the joining word. Always use a comma **in front of** the joining word.

✗
I / <u>like</u> to eat lunch at noon **but,** my boss / always <u>eats</u> later.
> This punctuation is incorrect.

I / <u>like</u> to eat lunch at noon**, but** my boss / always <u>eats</u> later.
> This punctuation is correct. The comma comes in front of the joining word.

Important: Because a compound sentence consists of two sentences connected by a joining word, we draw two slashes when we analyze it.

Exercise 6.16 (1) Underline the verb, and draw a slash between the subject part and the verb part. (2) Rewrite the two sentences as a compound sentence, using the given joining word. (3) In your rewritten sentence, do this: (a) Draw a box around the comma + joining word. (b) Underline each verb, and draw a slash between each subject part and verb part. Follow this model:

> Lev/ <u>is</u> lazy.
> **but**   His brother / <u>is</u> energetic.
>
> <u>Lev/<u>is</u> lazy ⎡, but⎤ his brother / <u>is</u> energetic.</u>

1.   The rain fell in the wrong places.

   and   The reservoirs remained empty.

   _____

   _____

2.   Forecasters predicted a shortage.

   but   Agriculture and business continued to waste water.

   _____

   _____

|||| **3.**   **Do not confuse a compound sentence with a sentence that has more than one verb.**

Lex / <u>bought</u> a hot dog, and Lisa / <u>ordered</u> a beer.
> This is a compound sentence.

Lex / <u>bought</u> a hot dog and <u>ordered</u> a beer.
> This simple sentence has one subject and two verbs.

Remember: We draw two slashes when we analyze a compound sentence.

Exercise 6.17 (1) In the compound sentence, put a comma in front of the joining word, and draw a box around the comma + the joining word. (2) Underline each verb, and draw a slash between each subject part and verb part. Follow this model:

Computers / <u>were</u> on sale, and Wendy / <u>decided</u> to buy one.

Wendy / <u>bought</u> a computer system and <u>assembled</u> it herself.

1. The umpire blew his whistle and stopped the play.

    The umpire made a bad call and the manager became angry.

2. The latecomers took their seats and the professor began her lecture.

    The professor closed the door and began her lecture.

3. We started for the airport on time but the heavy traffic delayed us.

    We started for the airport on time but missed our flight.

RULES SUMMARY, Part 1

In the longer one-page exercises that follow, you'll practice applying all the rules which you've learned or reviewed in this module. Before you go on to the longer exercises, check your understanding by filling in the blanks in the Rules Summary below. Fill in the blanks from memory, thinking carefully about what each rule means. If you need help, look back again at the Rules.

1. Every sentence has two parts, a _____ part and a

    _____ part.

2. A subject answers the question _____ or

    _____ **in front of** the verb.

3. A complement answers the question _____ or

    _____ **after** the verb.

4. In this book, words that tell more about other words in a sentence are called

    _____ .

5.   Analyze the structure of a sentence like this:

    a.   First, find the _____ and _____ it.

          Always look for the _____ first.

    b.   Second, find the _____ and mark it with an S.

    c.   Third, find the _____ (if there is one) and mark it with a C.

    d.   Finally, draw a _____ between the subject part and the

          _____ part.

6.   A compound sentence consists of two sentences connected by a joining word like

    _____ or _____ .

7.   In a compound sentence, always use a _____ in front of the joining word.

8.   When we analyze a compound sentence, we draw _____ slashes.

Now turn to the Answers to check your work. Use these Rules and your dictionary as you go on to do the longer exercises that follow.

Module 6: *Understanding Sentences I*

PRACTICE, Part 1

Exercise 6.18   **Number of Mistakes** _____

Remember: Analyze the structure of a sentence like this:
First, find the **verb** by looking for a word that shows different tenses.
Then, find the **subject** by asking WHO? or WHAT? in front of the verb.
Next, find the **complement** by asking WHO? (WHOM?) or WHAT? after the verb.
Finally, draw a **slash** between the subject part and the verb part.

(1) Underline each verb. (2) Mark each subject with an S, and each complement with a C. You might find it helpful to put parentheses around expansion. (3) In each compound sentence, draw a box around the comma + joining word. (4) Draw a slash between each subject part and verb part. There will be two slashes in a compound sentence. Follow this model:

                S   C
A German swimmer / <u>won</u> four gold medals in the Olympics.

1.   The Olympic decathlon includes javelin-throwing, running, pole-vaulting, long-jumping, and six other

      events.

2.   People by the hundreds report sightings of UFOs every year.

3.   The Democratic committee produced an expensive television campaign, but their candidates for the city

      council lost the election.

4.   The lab technicians will order several boxes of computer disks and new ribbons for the printers.

5.   Women in the Old West cooked, sewed, scrubbed, plowed the land, and fired rifles from the barricades

      beside their men.

6.   Many new immigrants from Spanish-speaking countries now are entering the United States, and

      bilingual education programs are expanding.

Exercise 6.19   **Number of Mistakes** _____

(1) Underline each verb. (2) In each compound sentence, draw a box around the comma + joining word. (3) Draw a slash between each subject part and verb part. There will be two slashes in a compound sentence. The first sentence has been marked for you.

Henry / often <u>recalls</u> his first day of driving lessons. His instructor smiled encouragingly

and pointed to the ignition key and the accelerator. Henry hesitantly turned the key, and then he

stepped on the gas. The motor actually started to run. He looked at his instructor with

amazement. Next, the instructor taught him how to shift gears. Henry shifted into "Drive" and

held on tight to the wheel. His father's Chevrolet gave a familiar shudder and then slowly edged

forward. Henry anxiously looked ahead. A truck and a car with a "Wide Load" sign were

creeping toward him at 20 miles an hour. Quickly he slammed on the brakes, and his instructor

almost went through the windshield. Telling Henry to stop, the instructor began to open the car

door. Henry tried to obey, but he stepped on the accelerator instead of the brake. Henry had a

new instructor for his next lesson.

Exercise 6.20   **Number of Mistakes** _____

Remember: The items in a series should be separated by commas.

Many students in that pre-law program / <u>are</u> Asian, African-American, or Hispanic.

> *Asian, African-American, or Hispanic* is a series of three complements, with the joining word *or*. Don't forget the comma in front of the joining word.

Here are some sentences about a famous disaster. (1) Use the given joining word to rewrite each group of sentences as one sentence, without repeating words. (2) In your rewritten sentence, underline each verb, and draw a slash between the subject part and the verb part. (3) Put your rewritten sentences into paragraph form. Finish this exercise on a sheet of your own paper.

1. **or**   People worked on the night shift.
              People drank in all-night bars.
              People slept soundly in their beds.

2. **and**   Faint tremors startled them.
              Louder thumps startled them.
              Ominous rumbles startled them.

3. **and**   Seconds later, the ground shook.
              Seconds later, the ground heaved.
              Seconds later, the ground split open.

4. **and**   Within minutes, factories were mountains of loose bricks and blazing timbers.
              Within minutes, stores were mountains of loose bricks and blazing timbers.
              Within minutes, homes were mountains of loose bricks and blazing timbers.

5. **and**   For days, a lurid tower of flame and smoke reddened the sky.
              For days, a lurid tower of flame and smoke darkened the sky.
              For days, a lurid tower of flame and smoke blotted out the sky.

6. **or**   The San Francisco earthquake was a greater disaster than the sinking of the Titanic.
              The San Francisco earthquake was a greater disaster than the collapse of the Johnstown Dam.
              The San Francisco earthquake was a greater disaster than the Great Chicago Fire.

_____

_____

_____

_____

_____

_____

_____

Module 6: *Understanding Sentences I*

RULES, Part 2: Correcting Fragments and Run-ons

|||||| **6F.   Check your writing for <u>fragments</u>.**

Important: A sentence must have a subject and a verb. If a group of words doesn't have both a subject and a verb, it is not a sentence. It is a **fragment**.

              S
Many city people / <u>enjoy</u> vacations in the country.
> This group of words is a sentence. It has both a verb and a subject.

✗ Many city people on vacation in the country.
> This group of words has no verb, so it's a fragment.

✗ And enjoy vacations in the country.
> This group of words has no subject, so it's a fragment.

Exercise 6.21 (1) If a group of words is a sentence, do this: (a) Underline the verb. (b) Mark the subject with an S. (c) Draw a slash between the subject part and the verb part. (d) Write in SENT. (2) If a group of words is a fragment, put an ✗ in front of it, and write in FRAG.

1.   Information from both books and magazines.   _____

       Information from both books and magazines is helpful.   _____

2.   People in the middle-income bracket pay higher taxes.   _____

       People in the middle-income bracket.   _____

3.   A used car with a good engine and low mileage.   _____

       A used car with a good engine and low mileage is worth a lot.   _____

Remember: Check your work as you go along, using the Answers in the back of the book.

Exercise 6.22 (1) If a group of words is a sentence, do this: (a) Underline the verb. (b) Mark the subject with an S. (c) Draw a slash between the subject part and the verb part. (d) Write in SENT. (2) If a group of words is a fragment, put an ✗ in front of it, and write in FRAG.

1.   My cousin lives in Oakland.   _____

       And commutes to work in San Francisco.   _____

2.   For example, worry about the future of their children.   _____

      For example, parents worry about the future of their children.   _____

3.   Some students never study in the library.   _____

      And never study at home, either.   _____

Exercise 6.23 (1) If a group of words is a sentence, do this: (a) Underline the verb, and draw a slash between the subject part and the verb part. (b) Write in SENT. (2) If a group of words is a fragment, put an **✗** in front of it, and write in FRAG.

[1]Lawrence used to eat at a local diner.   1 _____

[2]Really enjoyed the great tasting food.   2 _____

[3]Not to mention the low prices. [4]Then he   3 _____

read a Health Department report on   4 _____

the kitchen. [5]Roaches, greasy pots, filthy   5 _____

refrigerator. [6]It was hard to believe.   6 _____

[7]But better not to take chances. [8]He   7 _____

found another place to have lunch.   8 _____

6G.   Correct most fragments by connecting them to a sentence.

The players / were ready. **✗** And wanted to win.
The players / were ready and wanted to win.
    The fragment has been corrected by connecting it to the sentence.

Exercise 6.24 (1) Put an **✗** in front of each fragment. (2) Correct the fragment by connecting it to the sentence. (3) In your rewritten sentence, underline each verb, and draw a slash between the subject part and the verb part.

1.   People facing religious persecution emigrated. To the New World.

_____

2.   They farmed the land. And established new communities.

_____

3.   The native inhabitants taught them to grow new crops. Such as corn and squash.

_____

‖‖‖ 6H.   Check your writing for <u>run-ons</u>.

If two (or more) sentences are written as if they are one, the result is a **run-on**.

✗

The climate in Cuernavaca is wonderful the sun always shines.

This run-on is incorrect.

A run-on in which a comma is used between the two sentences is sometimes called a **comma splice**.

✗

The climate in Cuernavaca is wonderful, the sun always shines.

This run-on is also incorrect. A comma cannot join sentences.

The punctuation mark between complete sentences is usually a period—**but never a comma.**

The climate in Cuernavaca / <u>is</u> wonderful. The sun / always <u>shines</u>.

These two sentences are correct.

Exercise 6.25 (1) If a group of words is a sentence, do this: (a) Underline each verb. (b) Draw a slash between the subject part and the verb part. (c) Write in SENT. (2) If a group of words is a run-on, put an **✗** where the second sentence begins, and write in RUN-ON.

1.   The station canceled its regular programs, it was holding a

     fund-raising drive.   _____

2.   The volunteers were answering phone calls, they were taking

     pledges for donations.   _____

3.   With telephones ringing in the background, the announcer looked

     into the camera and pleaded for funds.   _____

||||| **6I.**   **One way to correct a run-on is to rewrite it as two sentences.**

✗

She drinks coffee I prefer tea.
She / <u>drinks</u> coffee. I / <u>prefer</u> tea.

> The run-on has been corrected by rewriting it as two sentences.

Important: Many run-ons occur when a new sentence begins with a pronoun.

✗

The noise goes on for days, it makes me hate the 4th of July.
The noise / <u>goes</u> on for days. It / <u>makes</u> me hate the 4th of July.

> The run-on has been corrected by rewriting it as two sentences.
> The pronoun *it* is the subject of the second sentence.

Here are some pronouns that often cause run-ons:

I he she it	we you they	this that

Exercise 6.26 (1) Put an **✗** where the second sentence begins. Then circle the pronoun that begins the second sentence. (2) Correct the run-on by rewriting it as two sentences. (3) In your rewritten sentences, underline the verb, and draw a slash between the subject part and the verb part. Follow this model:

Brad kept his New Year's resolution, ⓗe quit smoking.

Brad / <u>kept</u> his New Year's resolution. He / <u>quit</u> smoking.

1.   Mrs. White rented a cottage for the summer she loves it.

_____

2.   Owning a house is a lot of trouble, it is better to rent.

_____

3.   In the 1980s, the price of housing rose sharply, that hurt middle-income families.

_____

Important: Many run-ons also occur when a new sentence begins with words like *then* or *next*. Transitional words like these cannot join sentences.

X
Georgina strained a ligament, then she broke her toe.
Georgina / <u>strained</u> a ligament. Then she / <u>broke</u> her toe.

> The run-on has been corrected by rewriting it as two sentences.
> *Then* cannot be used to join sentences.

Exercise 6.27 (1) Put an **X** where the second sentence begins. Then circle the word that begins the second sentence. (2) Correct the run-on by rewriting it as two sentences. (3) In your rewritten sentences, underline the verb, and draw a slash between the subject part and the verb part.

1.   She cried for a while, then she got mad.

      _____

2.   Mr. Gordon reviewed his insurance policy next he called the police.

      _____

3.   At the end of the first set, Jennifer seemed tired, then she recovered and won the tennis match.

      _____

6J.   A second way to correct a run-on is to rewrite it as a compound sentence.

Remember: To make a compound sentence, insert a comma + a joining word like *and* or *but* between the sentences.

X
She drinks coffee I prefer tea.
She / <u>drinks</u> coffee**, but** I / <u>prefer</u> tea.

> The run-on has been corrected by rewriting it as a compound sentence.

Remember: Never use a comma **after** the joining word. Always use a comma **in front of** the joining word.

X
The package / <u>was</u> especially heavy **and,** we / <u>wanted</u> to wrap it securely.

> This punctuation is incorrect.

The package / <u>was</u> especially heavy**, and** we / <u>wanted</u> to wrap it securely.

> This punctuation is correct. The comma comes in front of the joining word.

Remember: When we analyze a compound sentence, we draw two slashes.

Exercise 6.28 (1) Put an ✗ where the second sentence begins. (2) Correct the run-on by rewriting it as a compound sentence, using the given joining word. **Don't forget the comma.** (3) In your rewritten sentence, do this: (a) Draw a box around the comma + joining word. (b) Underline each verb, and draw a slash between each subject part and verb part. Follow this model:

but   Nylon cord is thin, ✗ it is very strong.

Nylon cord / is thin [, but] it / is very strong.

1. **and**   We waited until 4 PM then we called again.

                 _____

                 _____

2. **but**   Express mail is faster than first class, it costs nearly $10.

                 _____

                 _____

3. **and**   Wallis finished the letters, then he hurried to the Post Office.

                 _____

                 _____

RULES SUMMARY, Part 2

In the longer one-page exercises that follow, you'll practice applying all the rules which you've learned or reviewed in this module. Before you go on to the longer exercises, check your understanding by filling in the blanks in the Rules Summary below. Fill in the blanks from memory, thinking carefully about what each rule means. If you need help, look back again at the Rules.

1. If a group of words doesn't have both a subject and a verb, it is not a sentence but a

              _____ .

2. Correct most fragments by connecting them to a _____ .

3. If two (or more) sentences are written as if they are one, the result is a _____ .

4. Many run-ons occur when a new sentence begins with a _____ , or with a

        word like *then* or _____ .

5.   One way to correct a run-on is to rewrite it as _____ sentences.

6.   Another way to correct a run-on is to insert a comma plus a joining word like _____ or

_____ to make a _____ sentence.

Now turn to the Answers to check your work. Use these Rules and your dictionary as you go on to do the longer exercises that follow.

Module 6: *Understanding Sentences I*

PRACTICE, Part 2

Exercise 6.29   **Number of Mistakes** _____

Some of the following groups of words are sentences, some are fragments, and some are run-ons. (1) If a group of words is a sentence, do this: (a) Underline each verb. (b) Mark each subject with an S. (c) Draw a slash between each subject part and verb part. Remember to draw two slashes in a compound sentence. (d) Write in SENT. (2) If a group of words is a fragment, write in FRAG. (3) If a group of words is a run-on, write in RUN-ON.

1. Car insurance is going up every year it now often costs $1000.   _____

2. Our business manager wasn't friendly, but she was never rude, either.   _____

3. By checking the ads every day, dialing hundreds of numbers, and never giving up.   _____

4. Jacqueline is confident about getting this job, her interview went very well.   _____

5. The meeting began at seven o'clock and ran smoothly, it ended at ten.   _____

6. To fly halfway across the country, spend a thousand dollars on hotel rooms, meals, and plane tickets, and return without a contract.   _____

7. It's hard to change old habits.   _____

8. For example, to watch less TV.   _____

9. Vitamin C with breakfast, vitamin E at bedtime.   _____

10. Getting up early, eating healthy food, and drinking lots of water.   _____

11. The space shuttle gently touched the ground, and the waiting crowd cheered.   _____

12. The crew members were smiling, they waved at the crowd.   _____

13. Everyone applauded.   _____

14. They made it, they're American heroes.   _____

Exercise 6.30   **Number of Mistakes** _____

This paragraph contains both sentences and fragments. (1) Rewrite the paragraph, correcting each fragment by connecting it to the appropriate sentence. **Make no other changes.** (2) In your rewritten paragraph, underline every verb, and draw a slash between the subject part and the verb part.

> Many famous persons encountered incredible obstacles. But continued to pursue their goals. The composer Beethoven lost his hearing. And then wrote some of his greatest musical masterpieces. Including his most powerful symphonies. The artist and writer James Thurber became almost completely blind but continued his career. By drawing his famous cartoons on huge canvases under bright lights. The great actress Sarah Bernhardt became lame in 1905. Lost her leg to gangrene in 1914. And went on to play the most famous roles of her career. Before her death in 1923.

_____

_____

_____

_____

_____

_____

_____

_____

_____

_____

_____

_____

_____

_____

_____

_____

_____

_____

Exercise 6.31   **Number of Mistakes** _____

Important: Use *but* to join two sentences that are contrasted. Use *and* to join two sentences that are not contrasted.

---

(1) Correct the run-on by rewriting it as a compound sentence, using a comma + *and* or *but*. (2) In your rewritten sentence, do this: (a) Draw a box around the comma + joining word. (b) Underline each verb, and draw a slash between each subject part and verb part. Follow this model:

> Boris likes cats, he is allergic to them.
>
> Boris/likes cats [, but] he/is allergic to them,

1. Fei-chen won the boxing match, he was disqualified.

   _____

2. Beverly Sills was a great singer her fans adored her.

   _____

3. Luis loved children, he planned to have a large family.

   _____

4. Ross seldom receives mail, today he got three letters from old friends.

   _____

5. The snow is already 15 inches deep it still is falling.

   _____

6. Savings bonds are a popular investment they don't pay good interest.

   _____

7. Kiyoko won a prize in mathematics, she prefers to major in history.

   _____

8. Angelo received the pre-medical science prize, he is going to medical school next year.

   _____

Exercise 6.32

This paragraph contains both sentences and run-ons. (1) Rewrite the paragraph, correcting each run-on by rewriting it as two sentences. **Make no other changes.** You might find it helpful to read the paragraph out loud. (2) In your rewritten paragraph, underline every verb, and draw a slash between the subject part and the verb part. If you need more space, continue on a sheet of your own paper.

       Computerized telephones are becoming more and more popular in homes and offices, they save people time and trouble. Busy people are often away from home, while away, they're anxious not to miss important calls from friends and relatives. In the office, these people have the opposite problem, at the worst possible moment, a phone call will interrupt their work. With computerized attachments, modern phones solve these problems easily. After a few rings, a recording comes on and invites the caller to leave a message. Sometimes this recording will answer the caller's main question, then there's no need to call back. Many smart phones allow users to dial a single digit to transfer a call, in fact, some phones even transfer calls automatically to another number. In these and in many other ways, computerized phones help people to do their jobs with less stress.

_____

_____

_____

_____

_____

_____

_____

_____

_____

_____

_____

_____

_____

_____

_____

Exercise 6.33   **Number of Mistakes** _____

Read the following paragraph.

> Annie owned a car, but it was a wreck. The roof leaked. The engine sputtered, choked, and started slowly on cold mornings. The radio received only one station. The transmission and windshield wipers made strange noises. Her car got low gas mileage and burned oil. However, that old Ford was her first car, and she loved it.

(1) Copy the specified kind of sentence from the paragraph. (2) Mark your copied sentence like this: (a) Underline each verb. (b) Mark each subject with an S. (c) Mark each complement (if there is one) with a C. (d) Draw a slash between each subject part and verb part. Remember to put two slashes in a compound sentence. (e) Draw a box around the comma + the joining word in each compound sentence. Follow this model:

A sentence with one subject, one verb, and one complement:

The ràdio/received only one station.

1. A sentence with two subjects and one verb:

    _____

2. A sentence with one subject and two verbs:

    _____

3. A sentence with one subject and three verbs:

    _____

4. A sentence with one subject and one verb, but no complement:

    _____

5. A compound sentence, using a comma + *but*:

    _____

6. A compound sentence, using a comma + *and*:

    _____

Caution: This exercise prepares you for the Writing Test, so check it with special care. If you made more than one mistake, get help before going on.

Module 6: *Understanding Sentences I*

WRITING TEST

NAME _____

PURPOSE   To show that you can recognize the structure of your own sentences, and that you can continue to apply what you have learned in previous modules.

ASSIGNMENT   Choose an older relative or friend. Write that person's name and relationship to you here:

NAME: _____

RELATIONSHIP: _____

Write a series of seven sentences about your subject, using these sentence patterns:

❏   1.   a sentence with one subject, one verb, and one complement

❏   2.   a sentence with two subjects and one verb

❏   3.   a sentence with one subject and two verbs

❏   4.   a sentence with one subject and three verbs

❏   5.   a sentence with one subject and one verb, but no complement

❏   6.   a compound sentence, using a comma + *but*

❏   7.   a compound sentence, using a comma + *and*

Check off each step in the writing process as you complete it.

GET READY   ❏   On scratch paper, write as many interesting and significant facts about your relative or friend as you can think of. Make sure you have plenty of ideas to show why you chose this person.

DRAFT   ❏   On scratch paper, write a rough draft of your seven sentences. Try to write sentences that sound natural but aren't too complicated.

Write your sentences in the seven patterns above. Check off each pattern as you use it. Number each sentence to show which of the seven patterns it follows.

REVISE   ❏   Read over your draft sentences to make sure that each sentence tells something interesting about your subject and is in the pattern that is called for. Make whatever changes are necessary. Remember, it's good for a draft to become messy.

EDIT ❏ Review Exercise 6.33 and the Rules for this module. Make sure that your seven sentences follow the seven patterns above.

❏ Analyze each of your seven sentences like this:

■ Underline each verb. Remember that a verb can be a one-word verb or a verb phrase.

■ Mark each subject with an S.

■ Mark each complement with a C.

■ Draw a slash between each subject part and verb part. Remember to draw two slashes in a compound sentence.

■ Draw a box around the comma + joining word in each compound sentence.

Use your dictionary and the Rules for previous modules to find and correct any mistakes in:

❏ Nouns: Singular and Plural Forms
❏ Verbs: Tense
❏ Spelling
❏ Writing Conventions
❏ Wrong Words

FINAL COPY ❏ Write the final copy of your sentences carefully, using blue or black ink and standard-sized (8½ by 11 inch) paper. Better yet, type or use a word processor. Write your name in the upper right-hand corner or use whatever heading your instructor requires. Remember that you are now preparing your writing for a reader.

❏ Number and mark each sentence in your final copy just as you did in your draft.

PROOFREAD ❏ Read your final copy **out loud**. If you find any mistakes, it's OK to correct them neatly by hand. Or if you have used a word processor, go back and correct your mistakes, and then print out a clean final copy.

Attach your final copy to these instructions, and hand them both in.

7 Verb Agreement

NAME _____

As you complete each exercise, record your number of mistakes below.

PART 1

7.1 ____	7.9 ____	Summary ____
7.2 ____	7.10 ____	7.17 ____
7.3 ____	7.11 ____	7.18 ____
7.4 ____	7.12 ____	7.19 ____
7.5 ____	7.13 ____	7.20 ____
7.6 ____	7.14 ____	7.21 ____
7.7 ____	7.15 ____	
7.8 ____	7.16 ____	

PART 2

7.22 ____	7.27 ____	7.31 ____
7.23 ____	7.28 ____	7.32 ____
7.24 ____	7.29 ____	7.33 ____
7.25 ____	7.30 ____	7.34 ____
7.26 ____	Summary ____	7.35 ____

Review Exercise C ____

INSTRUCTOR'S COMMENTS

Instructions:

- ❑ Followed carefully
- ❑ Not followed carefully enough

Checking:

- ❑ Careful
- ❑ Not careful enough to catch all your mistakes
- ❑ Green pen not used for checking
- ❑ Entire correct answer not always written in

Writing Test:

- ❑ Excellent
- ❑ Good
- ❑ Acceptable
- ❑ Not yet satisfactory

Other:

Module 7: *Verb Agreement*

RULES, Part 1: Present-tense Verbs

Verb agreement means: A present-tense verb has different forms, depending on whether its subject is **singular** or **plural**.

TRAVEL   The Petersons / <u>travel</u> every summer.
                Ms. Peterson / <u>travels</u> every summer.

> *TRAVEL* has two different forms because the subject *Petersons* in the first sentence is **plural**, and the subject *Ms. Peterson* in the second sentence is **singular**.

7A.   Check your writing for <u>verb agreement</u>.

Exercise 7.1 The following paragraphs are written in the present tense. The paragraph in the **left** column has **plural** subjects, so the verbs have **no endings**. The paragraph in the **right** column has **singular** subjects, so the verbs have *S* **endings**.

(1) Underline each verb. (2) Write S over each subject, and draw a slash between the subject part and the verb part. (3) In the paragraph on the right, draw a box around the *S* ending on each verb. The first sentence in each paragraph has been marked for you.

Every day some very fast planes / <u>leave</u>
Heathrow Airport in London. They arrive in New
York only three hours later. The seats cost a lot.
But some business people need to meet deadlines.
So they take these planes to save time. They
complete their business in New York quickly.
Often they return home the same day.

Every day a very fast plane / <u>leave</u>[s]
Heathrow Airport in London. It arrives in New
York only three hours later. A seat costs a lot.
But Colin Walker needs to meet deadlines. So he
takes this plane to save time. He completes his
business in New York quickly. Often he returns
home the same day.

Remember: Check your work as you go along, using the Answers in the back of the book.

1.   To make a present-tense verb agree with a <u>plural</u> subject or with *I* or *you*, add no ending.

To find out whether a subject is plural, try replacing it with the plural pronoun *they* or *we*.

LEARN   The girls / <u>learn</u> things quickly.
                     They / <u>learn</u> things quickly.

> The plural pronoun *they* can replace the plural subject *girls*.
> *Learn* has no ending to agree with a plural subject.

                     My friend and I / <u>learn</u> things quickly.
                     We / <u>learn</u> things quickly.

> The plural pronoun *we* can replace the plural subject *my friend and I*.
> *Learn* has no ending to agree with a plural subject.

The pronouns *I* and *you* may not be plural, but add no ending to make a present-tense verb agree with them.

LEARN   I / <u>learn</u> things quickly.
                     You / <u>learn</u> things quickly.

> *Learn* has no ending to agree with *I* and *you*.

Exercise 7.2 Fill in the appropriate present-tense form of the given verb.

1.   EAT   Americans / _____ too much red meat.

2.   COUNT   I / _____ fat grams, not calories.

3.   LOSE   You / _____ weight by eating fruit.

4.   KILL   Salt and animal fat / _____ millions.

5.   STUDY   We / _____ food labels carefully.

2.   To make a present-tense verb agree with a <u>singular</u> subject (but not *I* or *you*), add S.

To find out whether a subject is singular, try replacing it with the singular pronoun *he*, *she*, or *it*.

LEARN   My friend / <u>learns</u> things quickly.
                     She / <u>learns</u> things quickly.

> The singular pronoun *she* can replace the singular subject *my friend*.
> *Learns* has an *S* ending to agree with a singular subject.

Exercise 7.3 Fill in the appropriate present-tense form of the given verb.

1.   LIKE   Marietta / _____ studying statistics.

                   She / _____ studying statistics.

2.   APPOINT   The President / _____ ambassadors.

                      He / _____ ambassadors.

3.   HELP   A college diploma / _____ you to get a job.

                      It / _____ you to get a job.

Exercise 7.4 To review the Rules so far, fill in the appropriate present-tense form of the given verb.

1.   NEED   You / _____ a sense of humor in hard times.

2.   SEE   My grandmother / _____ almost perfectly since her

                      cataract operation.

3.   DISCOURAGE   A dictatorship / _____ creative thinking.

4.   BEGIN   In their fifties and sixties, couples / _____ to look

                      forward to retirement.

5.   BUY   I / _____ special paper for my computer printer.

6.   REQUIRE   A medical career / _____ a lot of training.

7.   DEMAND   Most professions / _____ at least one graduate-school

                      degree.

3.   When a verb agrees with a singular subject, sometimes it has an extra syllable. In this case, add *ES*, not *S*.

     PASS   That car / <u>passes</u> everything but the gas station.
                          Passes has two syllables, so it has an *ES* ending to agree with a singular subject.

Exercise 7.5 Fill in the appropriate present-tense form of the given verb. Say each answer out loud as you write it, listening carefully for the sound of the extra syllable.

1.   MARCH   The mayor of any big city / _____ in many parades.

2.   MISS   This answer / _____ the point of the question.

3.   MASH   That chef / sometimes _____ 50 pounds of potatoes at

                      once.

4.   WAX   The museum / never _____ its antique wooden

furniture.

5.   PREACH   A good teacher / never _____ at his students.

| | 4. | **To make a verb ending in *SK* or *SP* or *ST* agree with a singular subject, add *S*.** |

Verbs ending in *SK* or *SP* or *ST* may be hard to pronounce, but never add *ES* to these verbs.

    ASK   He / <u>asks</u> too many questions.
                         Asks doesn't have two syllables, so it has an *S* ending to agree with a singular subject.

Exercise 7.6 Fill in the appropriate present-tense form of the given verb. Say each answer out loud as you write it, listening carefully to make sure that you don't add an extra syllable.

1.   RISK   A bad driver / _____ other people's lives, as well as his own.

2.   TEST   Going to college / _____ your time-management skills.

3.   GASP   A person with heat stroke / <u>turns</u> red and _____ for breath.

Remember: An *ES* ending adds an extra syllable.
                Never add an *ES* ending to a verb ending in *SK* or *SP* or *ST*.

Exercise 7.7 Fill in the appropriate present-tense form of the given verb. Say each answer out loud as you write it.

1.   CATCH   When a parent lies, a child / _____ on quickly.

2.   ASK   My English teacher / _____ us to do a long writing

assignment every week.

3.   DISMISS   This judge / _____ charges against most first-time

defendants.

4.   TRUST   A smart parent / _____ her children most of the time.

5.   CONSIST   A basketball team / _____ of a center, two forwards,

and two guards.

6.   RUSH   The shop manager / usually _____ to leave on Friday.

| | | | | | 7B.   Pronoun subjects like *everyone* are singular.

Singular subjects like *everyone* can be confusing, because they have general, plural meanings.

     NEED   All people / <u>need</u> oxygen.
                  Because *all people* is plural, *need* has no ending.

                 Everyone / <u>needs</u> oxygen.
                  Because *everyone* is singular, *needs* has an *S* ending.

Here are six words that are always singular:

| everyone | anyone | no one |
| everybody | anybody | nobody |

Write these six singular words here to help you remember them:

_____   _____   _____

_____   _____   _____

Exercise 7.8 Fill in the appropriate subject for each verb.

1.   Everyone/Most people   _____ / <u>tries</u> to pass the buck.

                                 _____ / <u>try</u> to pass the buck.

2.   Everybody/All of us   _____ / <u>like</u> to win.

                                 _____ / <u>likes</u> to win.

3.   Few people/No one   _____ / <u>want</u> taxes to rise.

                                 _____ / <u>wants</u> taxes to rise.

4.   Anybody/We all   _____ / <u>appreciates</u> a sincere compliment.

                                 _____ / <u>appreciate</u> a sincere compliment.

5.   Not many of us/Nobody   _____ / <u>enjoy</u> working all the time.

                                 _____ / <u>enjoys</u> working all the time.

7C.   Some verbs need spelling changes when adding an ending to show agreement.

1.   If a verb ends in a <u>consonant</u> + Y, change the Y to I and add *ES*.

TRY   My neighbor / <u>tries</u> to keep his yard neat.
CARRY   This plane / <u>carries</u> nearly three hundred passengers.
                        Tries and *carries* are spelled with *I*, not *Y*.

This is Spelling Rule A2.1 in Appendix A.

Exercise 7.9 Fill in the appropriate present-tense form of the given verb.

1.   CRY   Someone / always _____ at a wedding.

2.   WORRY   That intersection / _____ every parent in the neighborhood.

3.   TERRIFY   The entrance examination / _____ most students.

2.   If a verb ends in a <u>vowel</u> + Y, do not change the Y to I.

PLAY   My sister's son / <u>plays</u> with his food at mealtime.
                        Plays is spelled with *Y*, not *I*.

This is Spelling Rule A2.2 in Appendix A.

Exercise 7.10 Fill in the appropriate present-tense form of the given verb.

1.   LAY   That chicken / _____ brown eggs.

2.   REMARRY   A widower / almost always _____ within two years.

3.   ANNOY   My sister / often _____ me with her nosy remarks.

4.   TRY   Nobody / _____ to be unsuccessful.

5.   SAY   Everyone / _____ that love is blind.

Exercise 7.11 To review the Rules so far, fill in the appropriate subject for each verb.

1.   child / children   The _____ / <u>seem</u> quiet.

2.   I / She   _____ / always <u>reads</u> as much as possible.

3. shadow / shadows   The _____ / <u>fall</u> at dusk.

4. You / She   _____ / <u>looks</u> uncomfortable.

5. Jo and Amy / Jo   _____ / seldom <u>arrives</u> on time.

6. Nobody / Few people   _____ / <u>know</u> how to pronounce the word

    mischievous.

7. Everybody / People   _____ / <u>says</u> that inflation may become a

    problem again.

Exercise 7.12 To review the Rules so far, fill in the appropriate present-tense form of the given verb. Say each answer out loud as you write it.

1. PASS   A safe driver / never _____ without signaling first.

2. SEEM   A new style / usually _____ strange at first.

3. DRIVE   I / never _____ in the passing lane.

4. RELY   An older athlete / _____ on experience instead of

                 speed.

5. HUSK   You / always _____ the corn too soon, before the water

                 starts to boil.

6. EMPHASIZE   Southern customs / _____ good manners and

                 hospitality.

7. COAST   An incumbent official / usually _____ to easy victory.

8. MARRY   Today young people / usually _____ in their twenties.

9. TRUST   Everybody / _____ a respectable-looking older woman.

||||| 7D.   Don't confuse verbs with infinitives.

Remember: An infinitive isn't a verb. It doesn't change to show different tenses.

> LIKE   My son / <u>likes</u> to swim.
>   My son / <u>liked</u> to swim.
>> *Likes* and *liked* are verbs in the present and past tenses.
>> *To swim* is an infinitive.

Because an infinitive isn't a verb, it doesn't show agreement.

> LIKE   They / <u>like</u> to swim.
>   He / <u>likes</u> to swim.
>> *Like* and *likes* are present-tense verbs, and agree with their subjects.
>> *To swim* is an infinitive and doesn't show agreement.

Exercise 7.13 (1) Underline the verb, circle the infinitive, and draw a slash between the subject part and the verb part. (2) Rewrite each sentence in the **present** tense. (3) In your rewritten sentence, underline the verb, circle the infinitive, and draw a slash between the subject part and the verb part. Follow this model:

My daughter / <u>wanted</u> (to play) racquetball.

My daughter / <u>wants</u> (to play) racquetball.

1. The committee wanted to require more liberal arts courses.

   _____

2. The university planned to lobby for funds.

   _____

3. The study group helped students to improve their grades.

   _____

4. Three professors intended to retire.

   _____

5. Nobody wanted to go to the library.

   _____

7E.   In a sentence with more than one verb, each present-tense verb must agree with its subject.

✗

A campaign worker / <u>calls</u> people at home and <u>ask</u> for contributions.
A campaign worker / <u>calls</u> people at home and <u>asks</u> for contributions.

Both *calls* and *asks* must agree with the singular subject *worker*.

Exercise 7.14 (1) Write one sentence to answer each group of questions below. Don't use *does* or *do* in your answer. (2) In your answer, underline each verb, and draw a slash between the subject part and the verb part. Follow this model:

Does Lisa sing folk songs? Does she play the guitar?

Yes, she / *sings folk songs and plays the guitar.*

1.   Does the coach skate well? Does he ski even better?

Yes, he _____

2.   Does the new teacher worry too much? Does she work too hard?

Yes, she _____

3.   Do the trainees exercise in the morning? Do they study in the afternoon?

Yes, they _____

7F.   Every present-tense verb must agree with its subject, even if other words come between the subject and the verb.

Remember: Don't confuse **expansion** with the **subject**. To find the subject, ask the question WHO? or WHAT? in front of the verb.

                                     S
PLAY   (The)→children←(on my block) / <u>play</u> games.

> *Children* is the subject because it answers the question *WHO play games?*
> *On my block* is expansion telling more about *children*.
> *Play* agrees with its plural subject *children*, not with *block*.

Exercise 7.15 (1) Mark the subject with an S. (2) Put parentheses around expansion of the subject. (3) Fill in the appropriate present-tense form of the given verb. Follow this model:

OPEN   (The) sch**S**ools (in this neighborhood) / __*open*__ tomorrow.

(The) sch**S**ool (in this neighborhood) / __*opens*__ tomorrow.

1. INTEREST   The discovery of those scientists / _____ me.

The discoveries of that scientist / _____ me.

2. INTIMIDATE   Women with confidence / _____ some men.

A woman with confidence / _____ some men.

3. WIN   The programs on that TV channel / _____ awards every

year.

One program on that TV channel / _____ an award every

year.

Important: Expansion of the subject beginning with *of* and *of the* can be confusing, because it often contains an important part of the meaning.

BORROW   One**S**←(of my friends) / always <u>borrows</u> my math textbook.

> *One* is the subject, not *friends*, even though *friends* is essential to the meaning. The sentence is about what **one friend** does.
> *Borrows* agrees with its singular subject.

Exercise 7.16 (1) Mark the subject with an S. (2) Put parentheses around expansion of the subject. (3) Fill in the appropriate present-tense form of the given verb. Follow this model:

ASSIGN   (Only) o**S**ne (of my professors) / __*assigns*__ oral reports.

1. PLAN   Several occupants of that building / _____ to move soon.

2. UNLOCK   One of those keys / _____ this door.

3. SHARE   Two members of the department / _____ the corner office.

4. NEED   Some of those bottles / _____ to be washed.

5. UNDERSTAND   One of the interpreters / _____ Swahili.

RULES SUMMARY, Part 1

In the longer one-page exercises that follow, you'll practice applying all the rules which you've learned or reviewed in this module. Before you go on to the longer exercises, check your understanding by filling in the blanks in the Rules Summary below. Fill in the blanks from memory, thinking carefully about what each rule means. If you need help, look back again at the Rules.

1. In the _____ tense, a verb must agree with its subject.

2. To make a present-tense verb agree with a _____ subject or *I* or *you*, add no

   ending.

3. To make a present-tense verb agree with a singular subject (but not *I* or *you*), add *S* or _____ .

4. When the verb needs an extra syllable, add _____ to show agreement with a singular subject.

5. When the verb ends in *SK* or _____ or _____ , add _____ to show

   agreement with a singular subject.

6. These subjects are always singular:

   everyone _____ _____

   _____ _____ _____

Now turn to the Answers to check your work. Use these Rules and your dictionary as you go on to do the longer exercises that follow.

Module 7: *Verb Agreement*

PRACTICE, Part 1

(1) Rewrite each sentence as two sentences. (2) In your rewritten sentences, underline each verb, and draw a slash between the subject part and the verb part. Follow this model:

A yellow Nissan and two taxis park here every day.

A yellow Nissan / parks here every day.
Two taxis / park here every day.

1. The delivery men and the janitor use the service entrance.

    _____

    _____

2. Jesse and his partner design toys.

    _____

    _____

3. That Congressman and his supporters deny the charges.

    _____

    _____

4. Two planes and one train leave for Minneapolis daily.

    _____

    _____

5. Harvey and I ask many questions in class.

    _____

    _____

Exercise 7.18

Number of Mistakes _____

This paragraph contains base forms of verbs in capital letters. (1) Rewrite the paragraph in the present tense. **Use one-word verbs only.** (2) In your rewritten paragraph, underline each verb. Your first sentence will begin like this: *My friend Milagros loves* . . .

My friend Milagros LOVE sewing. She BUY beautiful fabric in a shop near where she LIVE. She and her mother carefully LAY out the pattern for her dress. Then Milagros CUT it out, BASTE it, and SEW it together. She USE her iron as she FINISH each seam. Her brother and her mother HELP her with some of the work. For example, they ADJUST the hem and FIT the waist. Milagros SAY that she ENJOY sewing. She not only SAVE money by making her own clothes, but she always LOOK better than the other women in her office.

_____

_____

_____

_____

_____

_____

_____

_____

_____

_____

_____

_____

_____

_____

_____

_____

_____

Exercise 7.19   **Number of Mistakes** _____

Remember: Every present-tense verb must agree with its subject, even if other words come between the subject and the verb.

(1) Mark the subject with an **S**. (2) Put parentheses around expansion of the subject. (3) Fill in the appropriate present-tense form of the given verb. Follow this model:

TWIST   (The) road (through the mountains) / ___twists___ dangerously.

1. LEAK   One of the faucets / _____ slightly.

2. PLAY   Four members of this orchestra / sometimes _____

                together in a string quartet.

3. SEEM   An increase in income taxes / _____ inevitable.

4. TEST   One of the exercises / _____ your sense of balance.

5. CONFUSE   The instructions on this test / _____ many students.

6. NEED   The manager of these stores / _____ some part-time

                Christmas employees.

7. LOOK   All of those textbooks / _____ difficult.

8. ARRIVE   Only one out of all these employees / ever _____ early.

9. SAY   The leader of those workshops / _____ that no prior

                experience with computers is necessary.

10. ACT   Everybody in most families / _____ irrational at one

                time or another.

Exercise 7.20   **Number of Mistakes** _____

Remember: An infinitive isn't a verb; it doesn't show agreement.

This passage contains errors in verb agreement and in infinitives. (1) Underline each verb and circle each infinitive. (2) Correct each error in the space above the line. The first sentence has been done for you.

(To pay) his bills, Ngo Nhu has have to drive his taxi up to 16 hours a day. Even so, he hardly

make enough to put nourishing food on the table for his wife and three small children. To get

through his long day behind the wheel, he dream the American dream. As he creeps through the

downtown traffic, he imagine relaxing with his family after supper in the backyard of their

suburban home—the home he plans to buys some day. These thoughts keep him going until the

restaurants and theaters close and the streets grows dark and empty. But when he get home after

midnight, he finds his wife in bed and his children fast asleep.

So as each week drag on, Ngo Nhu become impatient with distant hopes and dreams. He

try to make an extra buck by racing ahead of other taxis to picks up fares. As he drive faster and

faster, his passengers cringe. When he switch lanes without signaling, nervous passengers often

asks to get out. The cops chase him when he rush through stop signs, and just one traffic ticket

costs him a full day's pay.

When Ngo Nhu finally take a day off, however, life once more seem good and the future

bright. He plays with his children, talk to his wife about the week's adventures, and study his

manual of English verbs. Then the next morning, he drives away at dawn, and the cycle of

dreams and frustrations start all over again for Ngo Nhu.

Important: This paragraph contained 19 errors, not counting the one that was corrected for you. How many did you find? _____ If you didn't find all 19, try again before you check your work.

Exercise 7.21

Number of Mistakes _____

This paragraph is written in the past tense. (1) Underline each verb.

When Lila went to Europe, she admired the wonderful subways there. The cleanliness of the Paris Metro and the Vienna U-Bahn amazed her. Maintenance people polished the brass railings and washed down the walls. Gratefully, she sank into the soft seats and enjoyed the smooth ride. Excellent maps and clear signs on every wall guided her efficiently from one unfamiliar station to another. She remembered the sweltering cars, dirty stations, and confusing signs in the subways back home. Certainly, Lila never got homesick when she rode in European subway trains.

(2) Rewrite the paragraph in the present tense. **Use one-word verbs only.** (3) In your rewritten paragraph, underline each verb. Your first sentence will begin like this: *When Lila goes to Europe . . .*

_____

_____

_____

_____

_____

_____

_____

_____

_____

_____

_____

_____

_____

_____

_____

_____

Module 7: *Verb Agreement*

RULES, Part 2: Special Problems

7G. Two important verbs are <u>irregular</u> in the present tense.

1. *HAVE* is irregular.
The present-tense form that agrees with a singular subject is *has*.

HAVE   My sister / <u>has</u> three children.
> *Has* agrees with the singular subject *sister*.

Remember: To make a present-tense verb agree with a plural subject or with *I* or *you*, add no ending.

HAVE   My brothers / <u>have</u> no children.
I / <u>have</u> no children.
You / <u>have</u> no children.
> *HAVE* does not change to agree with a plural subject or with *I* or *you*.

Exercise 7.22 Fill in the appropriate present-tense form of *HAVE*.

1. Lolita / _____ a new pair of sunglasses.

2. These banks / now _____ evening hours.

3. Coolidge / always _____ the best answer.

4. The Harrises / _____ nineteen grandchildren.

5. Abby / never _____ enough money.

6. You / _____ a large apartment, don't you?

Remember: Check your work as you go along, using the Answers in the back of the book.

2. *DO* is irregular.
The present-tense form that agrees with a singular subject is *does*.

DO   Those plasterers / <u>do</u> sloppy work.
That plasterer / <u>does</u> sloppy work.
> *Do* agrees with the plural subject *plasterers*.
> *Does* agrees with the singular subject *plasterer*.

Exercise 7.23 Fill in the appropriate present-tense form of *DO*.

1.   Shaheed / _____ his math problems carefully.

2.   I / _____ the best I can.

3.   Some people / _____ their best work under pressure.

7H.   *DO* can be either a <u>one-word verb</u> or a <u>helping verb</u> in a verb phrase.

DO	Vincent / <u>does</u> a good job.
LIKE	Vincent / really <u>does like</u> rock music.

> In the first sentence, *does* is a one-word verb, and the sentence is about **doing**.
> In the second sentence, *does* is a helping verb, and *like* is a main verb. The sentence
> is about **liking**.

Exercise 7.24 (1) Underline each one-word verb and verb phrase. Double underline the main verb in each verb phrase. (2) Draw a slash between the subject part and the verb part.

1.   Aurelia usually does very nice work.

     Of course, Kristie sometimes does earn higher job ratings.

2.   First I did the dishes.

     I always do try to finish all my chores before watching TV.

3.   Those two skaters do perform beautifully together.

     They do the spins in perfect unison.

Remember: Only the helping verb shows agreement. The main verb doesn't agree.

1.   Make the helping verb *DO* agree with its subject.

SING	Ophelia / <u>does sing</u> in the chorus.
	Ophelia and Ethel / <u>do sing</u> in the chorus.

> The helping verbs *does* and *do* agree with their subjects.
> The main verb *sing* doesn't show agreement.

Exercise 7.25 Fill in the appropriate present-tense form of the helping verb *DO*.

1.   Rena / really _____ <u>like</u> Hiroshi.

     Both Rena and her sister / really _____ <u>like</u> Hiroshi.

2. These chairs / _____ not <u>need</u> repairs.

    That chair / _____ not <u>need</u> repairs.

3. _____ that store still <u>offer</u> discounts?

    _____ those stores still <u>offer</u> discounts?

||| **2. Use a verb phrase with the helping verb *DO* and the word *not* to make a statement <u>negative</u>.**

The word *not* always interrupts a negative verb phrase.

      LIKE   Vincent / <u>does</u> not <u>like</u> country music.
                         Does like is a verb phrase, interrupted by *not.*

Exercise 7.26 (1) Underline each one-word verb and verb phrase. Double underline the main verb in each verb phrase. Don't underline any interrupting words. (2) Draw a slash between the subject part and the verb part.

1. Sally often eats fish and chicken.

    Sally does not eat red meat.

2. Angus does not want a pet.

    Angus's wife wants a little dog.

3. That night watchman does not sleep on the job.

    This night watchman sleeps on the job.

Exercise 7.27 (1) Underline each verb, and draw a slash between the subject part and verb part. (2) Rewrite each sentence, making it negative. (3) In your rewritten sentence, underline each verb phrase, and double underline the main verb. Draw a slash between the subject part and the verb part. Follow this model:

    Her husband / <u>travels</u> a lot.

    Her husband / does not travel a lot.

1. Those new shirts look good on you.

    _____

2.   This typewriter works well.

_____

3.   That teacher tries to help.

_____

Remember: In contractions, apostrophes show where letters have been omitted.

     LIKE   Vincent / <u>doesn</u>'t <u>like</u> that new rock band.
                              Does like is a verb phrase, interrupted by the contraction *n't*.

Exercise 7.28 (1) Underline each verb, and draw a slash between the subject part and verb part. (2) Rewrite each sentence, making it negative and contracting *not* with the helping verb *DO*. (3) In your rewritten sentence, underline each verb phrase, and double underline the main verb. Draw a slash between the subject part and the verb part. Follow this model:

    Her husband / <u>travels</u> a lot.

    Her husband / doesn't travel a lot.
_____

1.   Those new shirts look good on you.

_____

2.   This typewriter works well.

_____

3.   That teacher tries to help.

_____

    3.   **Use a verb phrase with the helping verb *DO* to ask a <u>question</u> that can be answered *yes* or *no*.**

In questions that can be answered *yes* or *no*, the helping verb is **in front of** the subject. Because of this, you can't draw a slash in a question.

     LIKE   <u>Does</u> Vincent <u><u>like</u></u> that new rock band?
                                Does like is a verb phrase, interrupted by the subject *Vincent*.

Exercise 7.29 Underline each one-word verb and verb phrase. Double underline the main verb in each verb phrase. Don't underline any interrupting words.

1.　She wants me to call her back.

　　Does she want me to call her back?

2.　You need a receipt.

　　Do you really need a receipt?

3.　Do their parents ever return their calls?

　　Their parents never return their calls.

Exercise 7.30 (1) Underline each verb, and draw a slash between the subject part and verb part. (2) Rewrite each sentence, turning it into a question. (3) In your rewritten sentence, underline each verb phrase, and double underline the main verb. Follow this model:

> Her husband / travels a lot.
>
> *Does her husband travel a lot?*

1.　Those new shirts look good on you.

　　_____

2.　This typewriter works well.

　　_____

3.　That teacher tries to help.

　　_____

RULES SUMMARY, Part 2

In the longer one-page exercises that follow, you'll practice applying all the rules which you've learned or reviewed in this module. Before you go on to the longer exercises, check your understanding by filling in the blanks in the Rules Summary below. Fill in the blanks from memory, thinking carefully about what each rule means. If you need help, look back again at the Rules.

1.　The verbs *HAVE* and _____ are irregular.

　　a.　The present-tense form of *HAVE* that agrees with a singular subject is _____ .

b.   The present-tense form of *DO* that agrees with a singular subject is _____ .

2.   *DO* can be a one-word verb or a _____ verb in a verb phrase.

3.   The helping verb *DO* must _____ with its subject.

Now turn to the Answers to check your work. Use these Rules and your dictionary as you go on to do the longer exercises that follow.

Module 7: *Verb Agreement*

PRACTICE, Part 2

Exercise 7.31   **Number of Mistakes** _____

(1) Underline each verb phrase, and double underline the main verb. Don't underline any interrupting words.
(2) Write one sentence to answer each group of questions, using one-word verbs in the **present** tense. (3) In your rewritten sentence, underline each verb. Follow this model:

Does Woody have a difficult job? Does he work long hours? Does he get up early?

Yes, he / has a difficult job, works long hours, and gets up early.

1. Does Wolfgang want a new piano? Does he have one picked out? Does he expect to get a discount?

    Yes, he _____

    _____

2. Does Wanda watch her weight? Does she do exercises every day? Does she go to the gym twice a week?

    Yes, she _____

    _____

3. Do the twins ask a lot of questions? Do they get into mischief? Do they keep their parents busy?

    Yes, they _____

    _____

4. Does the lab contain twenty computers? Does it have lots of work space? Does it stay open on

    weekends?

    Yes, it _____

    _____

Exercise 7.32   **Number of Mistakes** _____

(1) Underline each verb.

    After leaving Chicago, Andy and Oscar now live on a farm. They say they want a
quiet life in the fresh air. They get up every morning at dawn. Before they have
breakfast, they pick their way through the cow dung, open the smelly chicken coop, and
hold their noses as they snatch the eggs. While they make a fire in their woodburning
stove, they choke on the smoke. Then Andy and Oscar drive a deafening tractor out to
the field. As they breathe in the blowing dust, they sneeze furiously. Until late in the
evening, they do chores in the barn. Exhausted, they go to sleep and dream of a
soundproof office and an air-conditioned apartment.

(2) Rewrite the paragraph, changing *Andy and Oscar* to *Oscar*, and making whatever other changes are
necessary. (3) In your rewritten paragraph, underline each change. Your first sentence will begin like this:
After leaving Chicago, Oscar now lives on a . . .

_____

_____

_____

_____

_____

_____

_____

_____

_____

_____

_____

_____

_____

_____

Exercise 7.33

Number of Mistakes _____

Remember: (1) Because an infinitive isn't a verb, it doesn't show agreement. (2) In a verb phrase, the helping verb, not the main verb, shows agreement.

This paragraph contains base forms of verbs in capital letters. (1) Rewrite the paragraph, using the appropriate present-tense or infinitive form. **Make no other changes.** (2) In your rewritten paragraph, underline each one-word verb and verb phrase. Double underline the main verb in each verb phrase. Circle each infinitive. Your first sentence will begin like this: *Somebody makes plans (to break) most...*

Somebody MAKE plans to BREAK most world records as soon as someone else SET them. When an athlete RUN the mile in under four minutes, his rival immediately START training to BEAT his time. When a woman SWIM around Manhattan in the summer, another HAVE to DO it in the winter. It SEEM heroic to TRY to BREAK records like these, but some other attempts DO not MAKE sense. We GRIEVE if someone DIE trying to FLY fast, but it DO LOOK silly for a person to EAT or to DANCE himself to death. In contests like these, foolish people often REFUSE to STOP. If a person HAVE to KILL himself to WIN, he KILL himself. At that moment he just WANT to DO one thing—to DANCE longer, or to EAT more, or to SCREAM louder than anyone else in the world.

_____

_____

_____

_____

_____

_____

_____

_____

_____

_____

_____

_____

_____

_____

_____

_____

Exercise 7.34

Number of Mistakes _____

(1) Underline each verb.

Marjorie impresses me with her skill at tennis. She certainly understands how to keep her opponents off balance. Her drop shots, for example, often catch them off guard. And after a drop shot, she hits long. Her serves usually land deep in the court, and her opponents find it hard to return them. Her friends want her as a partner and fear her as an opponent. All in all, Marjorie's skill on the tennis court really overwhelms me.

(2) Rewrite the paragraph, making it negative and contracting *not* with the helping verb *DO*. (3) In your rewritten paragraph, underline each verb phrase, and double underline the main verb. Don't underline any interrupting words. Your first sentence will begin like this: *Marjorie doesn't impress me . . .*

Exercise 7.35   Number of Mistakes _____

Remember: Every present-tense verb must agree with its subject, even if other words come between the subject and the verb.

This paragraph contains errors in verb agreement. (1) Underline each one-word verb and verb phrase. Double underline the main verb in each verb phrase. (2) Correct each error in the space above the line. The first sentence has been marked for you.

       Recent medical research <u>shows</u> that our emotional reaction to life's ups and downs <u>have</u> a *has*

profound effect on our health. The fifteen billion nerve cells in our brains constantly change our

hopes and fears into chemical substances, and those substances in turn either heals or harm our

bodies. Many people accepts these facts but insist that this information don't help them.

Depression run in their family, they say. But researchers again have an answer: If a person act

cheerful, then he begins to feel cheerful. When something unexpected wreck his plans, a smart

person looks for a hidden advantage instead of moaning over it. When he gets a chance to say

something positive, he don't hesitate to say it. When a sensible person see something beautiful,

she takes time out to enjoy it. When a small misfortune happen, she turns it around in her head

until she find the funny side. (Everything do have a funny side.) This positive behavior produce

positive feelings. Most of the time we has the power to do what makes life more enjoyable—to

see the bright side, or, if that don't exist, to remember that sooner or later things will change.

This makes sense, and often mean the difference between sickness and health.

Important: This paragraph contained 15 errors, not counting the one that was corrected for you. How many did you find? _____ If you didn't find all 15, try again before you check your work.

Exercise 7.36   **Number of Mistakes** _____

Review Exercise C: Nouns, Verb Agreement

This passage contains errors in nouns and verb agreement. Underline each error, and correct it in the space above the line. For help, use your Rules and your dictionary. You may also find it helpful to underline each verb and mark its subject. The first error has been corrected for you.

                     owners
       All cat <u>owner</u> know that domestic cats belong to the same family of mammals as lions.

When a pet cat pounce on an insect or licks its paws and wash its face, it look just like a lion in

the zoo. But in one important way, cats and lion are completely different. Outdoors, in pursuit

of birds or mouses, a domestic cat act very independent. Aloof and solitary, it don't seek help

from other cats, but stalk its victims alone. But lions, especially the females, tend to live and to

hunt in groups. The lions travel together and brings down their victims in a coordinated attack.

They treat every member of the group, even a cub, as an equal. If a weak or injured lion don't

keep up with the group, the others prod and push him. If one lion by accident hurt another as

they scramble over a carcass, the others lick her wounds and comforts her. In this cooperative

behavior, lions doesn't resemble domestic cats at all—and in fact, they differ from all other

members of the cat family.

Important: This paragraph contained 13 errors, not counting the one that was corrected for you. How many did you find? _____ If you didn't find all 13, try again before you check your work.

Module 7: *Verb Agreement*

WRITING TEST

NAME _____

PURPOSE   To show that you can make present-tense verbs agree with their subjects, and that you can continue to apply what you have learned in previous modules.

ASSIGNMENT   Choose a person (not yourself) who has an interesting job. Write that person's name and job here:

NAME: _____

JOB: _____

Describe a typical day at work for this person, telling why you think his or her job is interesting.

Check off each step in the writing process as you complete it.

GET READY   ❑   On scratch paper, write down as many details about the person's job as you can think of. Make sure you have plenty of ideas to show why you chose this person.

DRAFT   ❑   On scratch paper, write a rough draft of your description. Try to write sentences that sound natural but aren't too complicated. Write about what this person does that is interesting. Write also a few negative sentences, telling what this person doesn't do or doesn't have to worry about. Your first sentence will begin like this: *Every day [your subject]* . . .

In every sentence, use either a one-word present-tense verb or a present-tense verb phrase with *DO*. (For example, write *she looks* or *she doesn't look*, not *she would look*.) **Write at least 12 sentences.**

REVISE   ❑   Read over the draft of your description to make sure that your ideas are clear and sound real. Try to anticipate what a reader will need to know in order to understand and believe what you have written. Add, take out, or change ideas, words, and sentences as necessary. Remember, it's good for a draft to become messy.

Make sure that you have written only about what your subject does (or doesn't do) on a typical day.

    ❑   After you have finished revising your ideas, underline each one-word verb and verb phrase. Double underline the main verb in each verb phrase. Count the present-tense verbs that you used, and write the number here: _____ .

EDIT   ❑   Review the Rules for this module. Find and correct any mistakes in present-tense verb forms. Make sure that every verb is in the present tense and agrees with its subject.

Use your dictionary and the Rules for previous modules to find and correct any mistakes in:

❑   Nouns: Singular and Plural Forms
❑   Sentences: Fragments and Run-Ons
❑   Spelling
❑   Writing Conventions
❑   Wrong Words

FINAL COPY   ❑   Write the final copy of your description carefully, using blue or black ink and standard-sized (8½ by 11 inch) paper. Better yet, type or use a word processor. Write your name in the upper right-hand corner, or use whatever heading your instructor requires. Remember that you are now preparing your writing for a reader.

❑   Underline every verb in your final copy just as you did in your draft.

PROOFREAD   ❑   Read your final copy **out loud**. If you find any mistakes, it's OK to correct them neatly by hand. Or if you have used a word processor, go back and correct your mistakes, and then print out a clean final copy.

Attach your final copy to these instructions, and hand them both in.

8 The Verb BE

NAME _____

As you complete each exercise, record your number of mistakes below.

PART 1

8.1 ____	8.7 ____	8.13 ____
8.2 ____	8.8 ____	8.14 ____
8.3 ____	8.9 ____	Summary ____
8.4 ____	8.10 ____	8.15 ____
8.5 ____	8.11 ____	8.16 ____
8.6 ____	8.12 ____	

PART 2

8.17 ____	8.21 ____	8.24 ____
8.18 ____	8.22 ____	8.25 ____
8.19 ____	8.23 ____	8.26 ____
8.20 ____	Summary ____	

Review Exercise D ____

INSTRUCTOR'S COMMENTS

Instructions:

- ❏ Followed carefully
- ❏ Not followed carefully enough

Checking:

- ❏ Careful
- ❏ Not careful enough to catch all your mistakes
- ❏ Green pen not used for checking
- ❏ Entire correct answer not always written in

Writing Test:

- ❏ Excellent
- ❏ Good
- ❏ Acceptable
- ❏ Not yet satisfactory

Other:

Module 8: *The Verb BE*

RULES, Part 1: *BE* as a One-word Verb

8A. **The verb *BE* has three present-tense forms to agree with different subjects: *am*, *is*, and *are*.**

The verb *BE* is the most irregular verb in English. Its forms don't even look or sound like *BE*, except in the infinitive *to be* and the future tense *will be*.

1. In the present tense use *am* to agree with *I*.

BE   I / <u>am</u> at home.
            Am agrees with the subject *I*.

2. In the present tense use *is* to agree with a <u>singular</u> subject (not *I* or *you*).

BE   She / <u>is</u> at home.
            Is agrees with the subject *she*.

3. In the present tense use *are* to agree with a <u>plural</u> subject or with *you*.

BE   The girls / <u>are</u> at home.
            You / <u>are</u> at home.
            Are agrees with the subject *the girls*, and with the subject *you*.

Whether the subject *you* is singular or plural, use *are* to agree with it in the present tense.

BE   You / <u>are</u> my friend.
            You both / <u>are</u> my friends.
            Are agrees with both singular *you* and plural *you both*.

Exercise 8.1 Fill in the appropriate **present-tense** form of *BE*.

My wife and I _____ trying to raise our children in a non-sexist way, but

we _____ unable to control the way other people talk to our four-year olds.

The children _____ twins, but Emma _____ much more

aggressive than her brother Dominick. The neighbors _____ quick to praise

Emma as "a little lady," but then they lift an eyebrow when she _____ too

boisterous. At the same time, they _____ apt to look at Dominick and ask,

"Why _____ you so quiet today? Did the cat get your tongue?" I

_____ not happy to see that sexual stereotyping _____ still

alive and well, at least on our block.

Remember: Check your work as you go along, using the Answers in the back of the book.

4.   Never write *be* instead of *am*, *is*, or *are*.

✗

BE   She be late.

                 Sentences with *be* are incorrect in writing, although they sometimes occur in speech.

            She / <u>is</u> late.

                 This sentence is correct.

Exercise 8.2 These sentences contain base forms of the verb *BE*, in capital letters. (1) Rewrite each sentence, using the appropriate **present-tense** form. (2) Mark your rewritten sentence like this:

The plane BE on schedule.

The plane / is on schedule. _____

1.   We BE brothers.

_____

2.   They BE good athletes.

_____

3.   I BE crazy about her.

_____

4.   That boy BE too lazy to tie his shoes.

_____

5.　　**Never leave out the verbs *am*, *is*, and *are*.**

✗

BE　　　　　　They late.

> Sentences with omitted verbs are incorrect in writing, although they sometimes occur in speech.

They / <u>are</u> late.

> This sentence is correct.

Exercise 8.3 The verb *BE* has been left out of these sentences. (1) Rewrite each sentence, using the appropriate **present-tense** form. (2) Mark your rewritten sentence like this:

We early.

We / <u>are</u> early.

1.　Herby my hairdresser.

_____

2.　Those teachers smart.

_____

3.　I hungry already.

_____

6.　　***Am*, *is*, and *are* are often contracted.**

Are and *is* can be contracted with their subjects, and with *not*.

<u>They are</u> my friends.　　　<u>They're</u> my friends.
<u>Carol is</u> my sister.　　　　<u>Carol's</u> my sister.

> The apostrophes show where the letters *A* and *I* have been omitted.

You <u>are not</u> my friends.　　You <u>aren't</u> my friends.
Lee <u>is not</u> my sister.　　　Lee <u>isn't</u> my sister.

> The apostrophes show where the letter *O* has been omitted.

Am can be contracted with its subject *I*.

<u>I am</u> lucky.   <u>I'm</u> lucky.
> The apostrophe shows where the letter *A* has been omitted.

Because the apostrophe shows an omitted letter, it is **never correct** to write *I'am*.

Contracted forms are more informal than uncontracted forms, but they're usually acceptable in writing.

Exercise 8.4 (1) Underline the verb, and draw a slash between the subject part and the verb part. (2) Rewrite each sentence, using the contracted form of the verb. (3) In your rewritten sentence, underline the verb, and draw a slash between the subject part and the verb part. Follow this model:

Somebody / <u>is</u> at the door.

Somebody'/s at the door.

1.   You are rather short-tempered these days.

_____

2.   I am eager to hear from you.

_____

3.   Nobody is perfect.

_____

4.   They are members of the Latin Club.

_____

8B.   A present-tense verb must always agree with its subject, even when the subject follows the verb.

In sentences beginning with *here* and *there*, the verb is usually a form of *BE*, and the subject **follows** the verb. Be especially careful to make the verb agree with its subject in this case.

                                                    S
BE   There <u>are</u> / many good stories in this book.
> *Stories* is the subject because it answers the question *WHAT are in this book?* *Are* agrees with *stories*.

                                                    S
BE   Here <u>is</u> / one good story.
> *Is* agrees with *story*.

Exercise 8.5 Fill in the appropriate **present-tense** form of the verb *BE*.

1. There _____ / only one answer.

    There _____ / several possible answers.

2. Here _____ / three examples.

    Here _____ / the best example I can think of.

3. There _____ / a big oak table in the dining room.

    There _____ / five pieces of furniture in the living room.

8C.   The verb *BE* has two past-tense forms to agree with different subjects: *was* and *were*.

The verb *BE* is the only verb that must agree with its subject in the past tense as well as the present tense.

1.   In the past tense use *was* to agree with a <u>singular</u> subject or with *I*.

BE   One student / <u>was</u> absent yesterday.
                I / <u>was</u> absent yesterday.
                   Was agrees with *student* and with *I*.

2.   In the past tense use *were* to agree with a <u>plural</u> subject or with *you*.

BE   The boys / <u>were</u> absent yesterday.
                You / <u>were</u> absent yesterday.
                   Were agrees with *boys* and with *you*.

Whether the subject *you* is singular or plural, use *were* to agree with it in the past tense.

BE   You / <u>were</u> my friend.
                You both / <u>were</u> my friends.
                   Were agrees with both singular *you* and plural *you both*.

Exercise 8.6 Fill in the appropriate **past-tense** form of *BE*.

"Where _____ you when Kennedy was shot?" This

_____ a familiar question when I _____ a child, and the

answers _____ always interesting. We _____ at my parents'

house last November 22nd, and a replay of the shocking events in Dallas _____

on TV again. My small daughter suddenly looked up and asked, "Who _____

Jack Kennedy?"

3. *Was* and *were* can be contracted with *not*.

He <u>was not</u> ready.   He <u>wasn't</u> ready.
They <u>were not</u> ready.   They <u>weren't</u> ready.
      Apostrophes show where the letter *O* has been omitted.

Exercise 8.7 Fill in the contracted form of the underlined words.

1.   We / <u>were not</u> sure of the answer.

     We / _____ sure of the answer.

2.   My mother / <u>was not</u> able to finish college.

     My mother / _____ able to finish college.

3.   You / <u>were not</u> there when we called.

     You / _____ there when we called.

Remember: The verb *BE* must agree with its subject, even if the subject follows the verb.

Exercise 8.8 Fill in the appropriate **past-tense** form of the verb *BE*.

1.   There _____ / two terrible bus accidents in South America last year.

     There _____ / a major train accident last year, also.

2.   There _____ / a large celebration for the United States Bicentennial in 1976.

     There _____ / many Bicentennial festivals across the country.

3.   There _____ / a scratch on that table before I refinished it.

     There _____ / many scratches on that table before I refinished it.

Exercise 8.9 (1) Underline each verb in this **present** tense paragraph:

> We are new at our jobs as bank tellers, so a counterfeit bill is hard for us to detect. But there are older tellers in this bank whose index fingers are as sensitive as lie detectors. To their sharp eyes, a presidential face on a large bill is as familiar as their own. Presidents with crooked noses or bent ears are as obvious to them as the false smiles on the faces of thieves.

(2) Rewrite the paragraph in the **past** tense. (3) In your rewritten paragraph, underline each verb.

_____

_____

_____

_____

_____

_____

8D. Use the appropriate tense of the verb.

Many sentences signal what tense they are in.

BE   Dinner / <u>is</u> ready **now**.
> The time word *now* and the verb *is* show that this sentence is in the present tense.

BE   Alma / <u>was</u> late **last week**.
> The time words *last week* and the verb *was* show that this sentence is in the past tense.

Exercise 8.10 (1) Underline each verb, and draw a slash between the subject part and the verb part. (2) Circle the time word or words. (3) Write in PRESENT or PAST to tell the tense of the sentence. Follow this model:

(At this moment) I / <u>am</u> very sleepy.   PRESENT

1. Life was hard in the twelfth century.   _____

2. Life is more complex today.   _____

3. Last year, Mr. Coleman was the chairman.   _____

4. Caterina is away from her desk right now.   _____

5.   In the past, it was a disgrace for a man to have a working wife.   _____

Exercise 8.11 Fill in the appropriate present-tense and past-tense forms of *BE*. You might find it helpful to circle any time words and underline any other verbs.

1.   Reatha / _____ at her sister's right now.

     Reatha / _____ at her mother's last week.

2.   You / never _____ wrong before.

     But you / _____ wrong now, believe me!

3.   My brother and I / _____ good friends when we were in high school.

     We / _____ still good friends now that we attend college together.

Important: The tense depends upon the meaning of the sentence.

> I remember the day when I received the good news.
>> *Remember* is a present-tense verb because I'm remembering now in the present.
>> *Received* is a past-tense verb because I received the good news in the past.

Exercise 8.12 (1) Underline each verb. (2) Fill in the appropriate present-tense or past-tense form of *BE*. You might find it helpful to circle any time words. Follow this model:

> I remember when my dog Raymond _____was_____ a puppy.

1.   Julian wonders why he _____ so shy when he was a child.

2.   My grandparents seldom talk about the days when they _____ young.

3.   Do you remember the time when we _____ almost late for the plane?

Remember: A verb must always agree with its subject, even though other words may come between the subject and the verb.

>   S
> (The)→children←(on my block) / are all under six years old.
>> *On my block* is expansion telling more about *children*.
>> *Are* agrees with its plural subject *children*, not with *block*.

189

Exercise 8.13 (1) Mark the subject with an S. (2) Put parentheses around expansion of the subject. (3) Fill in the appropriate **present-tense** form of *BE*.

1.   The author of those new books / _____ from Argentina.

2.   The pressures of the modern world / _____ a threat to health.

3.   The center of most people's lives / _____ still their family.

4.   A channel through reefs and sandbars / _____ often hard for a ship's pilot

     to find.

5.   The number of violent crimes in our area / _____ relatively low.

6.   The point of many jokes / _____ basically cruel.

7.   The targets of much masculine humor / _____ wives and mothers-in-law.

Exercise 8.14 (1) Mark the subject with an S. (2) Put parentheses around expansion of the subject. (3) Fill in the appropriate **past-tense** form of *BE*.

1.   The best skiers in yesterday's race / _____ from Switzerland.

2.   Each delegate to any of the two most recent conventions / _____ at least 18

     years old.

3.   Several books from that set / _____ on the table last night.

4.   Nobody from either of the classes / _____ able to attend the lecture.

5.   The monasteries of Ireland / _____ centers of Christian learning in the

     early Middle Ages.

6.   The first Christian missionary to the Germans / _____ an English monk.

7.   Before the Revolution, the principal religion of the Chinese people / _____

     Confucianism.

RULES SUMMARY, Part 1

In the longer one-page exercises that follow, you'll practice applying all the rules which you've learned or reviewed in this module. Before you go on to the longer exercises, check your understanding by filling in the blanks in the Rules Summary below. Fill in the blanks from memory, thinking carefully about what each rule means. If you need help, look back again at the Rules.

1. The verb *BE* has three _____ -tense forms: *I* _____ ; *he/she/it*

    _____ ; *we / you / they* _____ .

2. Forms of the verb *BE* are often _____ with their subjects or with the word

    _____ . Use an _____ to show where letters are omitted. The

    contracted form of *I am* is _____ .

3. A verb must agree with its _____ even if the subject follows the verb.

    Sentences like this often begin with the words *here* or _____ .

4. The verb *BE* has two _____ -tense forms: *I / he / she / it* _____ ;

    we / you / they _____ .

Now turn to the Answers to check your work. Use these Rules and your dictionary as you go on to do the
longer exercises that follow.

Module 8: *The Verb BE*

PRACTICE, Part 1

Exercise 8.15   **Number of Mistakes** _____

(1) Rewrite each sentence as two sentences. **Be sure not to change the tense.** (2) In your rewritten sentences, underline each verb, and draw a slash between the subject part and the verb part. Follow this model:

> Both Elaine and her parents are choir members.
>
> Elaine / is a choir member.
> Her parents / are choir members.

Caution: Be sure to check for correct singular and plural noun forms as well as correct verb forms.

1. The city and its suburbs are smoggy.

    _____

    _____

2. Both my father and I are policemen.

    _____

    _____

3. My friends and I were active children.

    _____

    _____

4. A T-square and a set of pens were ready on the architect's table.

    _____

    _____

5. There are some Indian carpets and a beautiful Persian rug in that museum.

    _____

    _____

Exercise 8.16 **Number of Mistakes** _____

Remember: An infinitive isn't a verb; it doesn't show agreement.

This paragraph contains base forms of verbs, in capital letters. (1) Rewrite the paragraph, using the appropriate present-tense or infinitive form. **Make no other changes.** (2) In your rewritten paragraph, underline each verb, and circle each infinitive. Your first sentence will begin like this: *Parents often like (to imagine) that . . .*

Parents often LIKE to IMAGINE that their children BE very talented. Sometimes a father WANT his son to BE a movie star, and so he TEACH the boy how to SING and to DANCE almost before he KNOW how to WALK or to TALK. A mother THINK her daughter BE sure to BE another Pavlova, so she SEND the child to school to LEARN ballet before she BE able to READ. It BE true that every now and then a Shirley Temple TURN up and MAKE a million dollars before she BE four years old; and once every four or five centuries a Mozart WRITE a symphony when he BE only nine. But much more often, these children BE remarkable only to their parents. And when a so-called child prodigy GROW up, he never WANT to SEE a piano or to DANCE a step. He BECOME a plumber or a policeman, which BE just what he wanted to BE from the start.

_____

_____

_____

_____

_____

_____

_____

_____

_____

_____

_____

_____

_____

_____

_____

_____

Module 8: *The Verb BE*

RULES, Part 2: *BE* as a Helping Verb

|||||| **8E.** **BE can be either a <u>one-word verb</u> or a <u>helping verb</u> in a verb phrase.**

BE   Shelley / <u>is</u> happy.
<u>Was</u> Shelley happy?

> *Is* and *was* are one-word verbs, and the sentences are about **being**.

SING   Shelley / <u>is <u>singing</u></u> a folk song.
Shelley / <u>was <u>singing</u></u> a folk song.

> *Is* and *was* are helping verbs, and *singing* is the main verb.
> The sentences are about **singing**.

Exercise 8.17 (1) Underline each one-word verb and verb phrase. Double underline the main verb in each verb phrase. (2) Draw a slash between the subject part and the verb part.

1. Charlotte is an excellent pianist.

   Charlotte is playing the piano in the studio.

2. I am ready to leave.

   I am going to the store.

3. It was snowing last night.

   The temperature was less than 32 degrees.

Remember: Check your work as you go along, using the Answers in the back of the book.

|||||| **8F.** **Use the helping verb *BE* + the *ING* form of a main verb to tell what <u>is happening right now</u> or what <u>was happening in the past</u>.**

BAKE   Freddy / <u>is baking</u> a cake.

> The helping verb *is* is in the present tense.
> This sentence tells what is happening right now.

BAKE   Freddy / <u>was baking</u> a cake.

> The helping verb *was* is in the past tense.
> This sentence tells what was happening in the past.

An *ING* verb phrase can also tell what is going to happen in the future.

TAKE   Les / <u>is taking</u> the train at six o'clock.

> The helping verb *is* is in the present tense, but the time words *at six o'clock* make this sentence tell what is going to happen in the future.

Exercise 8.18 (1) Underline each one-word verb and verb phrase. Double underline the main verb in each verb phrase. (2) Draw a slash between the subject part and the verb part.

1. SING   We sang well last night.

    We were singing Handel's *Messiah* for the first time.

2. WORK   I always work hard.

    I am working harder than ever these days.

3. RUN   That show first ran on Broadway forty years ago.

    Now it is running again.

Remember: Some verbs need spelling changes before you add an *ING* ending.

Exercise 8.19 Fill in the *ING* form of the given main verb.

1. ROB   The defendant / <u>was_____</u> the store when the police

    walked in.

2. PLAN   Bertram / <u>is_____</u> to go to Trinidad for a vacation this

    winter.

3. FILE   Those clerks / <u>are_____</u> our computer output.

4. WRITE   Jordana / <u>was_____</u> a poem.

5. BAT   Since the rookie / <u>is_____</u> .300, he plays in almost every

    game.

‖‖‖ **8G.   The helping verb** *BE* **must** <u>agree</u> **with its subject and show the appropriate** <u>tense</u>.

Remember: Only the helping verb shows agreement.

    RUN   Lillian / <u>is running</u> in the park.
                             Lillian and Rodney / <u>are running</u> in the park.

> The helping verb *is* agrees with *Lillian*, and the helping verb *are* agrees with *Lillian and Rodney*.
> The main verb *running* doesn't show agreement.

Remember: The verb *BE* must agree with its subject in both the past tense and the present tense.

    RUN   Lillian / <u>was running</u> in the park.
                             Lillian and Rodney / <u>were running</u> in the park.

> The helping verb *was* agrees with *Lillian*, and the helping verb *were* agrees with *Lillian and Rodney*.
> The main verb *running* doesn't show agreement.

Exercise 8.20 Fill in the appropriate **present-tense** form of the helping verb *BE*, and the *ING* form of the given verb. Follow this model:

    LOSE   We / ___*are*___ ___*losing*___ time.

1.   WORK   I / _____ _____ for a computer software

                       company now.

2.   CUT   Those departments / _____ _____ down on

                       their staff.

3.   TRY   Irina / _____ _____ to start her own

                       business.

Exercise 8.21 Fill in the appropriate **past-tense** form of the helping verb *BE*, and the *ING* form of the given verb.

1.   DECLINE   Until recently, unemployment / _____ _____ .

2.   HURRY   I / _____ _____ to catch the bus when I

                       twisted my ankle.

3.   HOPE   _____ you _____ for a raise?

Exercise 8.22 These sentences contain base forms of the helping verb *BE* in capital letters, and base forms of the main verbs. (1) Rewrite each sentence with the appropriate present-tense or past-tense form of *BE* and the *ING* form of the main verb. (2) Mark your rewritten sentence like this:

I BE GO skiing today.

I / am going skiing today.

1.   We BE TRY right now to get this job finished.

_____

2.   They BE PAY too much for car insurance last year.

_____

3.   My two sisters BE PLAN to go skating yesterday.

_____

Important: Often a helping verb is not repeated before a second main verb.

The engine / was vibrating and was making strange noises.
> This sentence is correct but seems slightly unnatural.

The engine / was vibrating and making strange noises.
> This sentence is more natural. *Was* is understood as the helping verb for the second main verb *making*.

Exercise 8.23 Underline each verb phrase, and double underline the main verb. Draw a slash between the subject part and the verb part.

1.   Often school-aged brothers and sisters will quarrel and compete with each other.

2.   My friend Jewel is studying Spanish and hoping to make a career as a bilingual secretary.

3.   The oncoming drivers were slowing their cars and staring at the accident.

4.   The student government is preparing petitions, collecting signatures, and organizing a campaign to

establish a daycare center on campus.

5.   A volunteer will answer the phone and accept your donation.

RULES SUMMARY, Part 2

In the longer one-page exercises that follow, you'll practice applying all the rules which you've learned or reviewed in this module. Before you go on to the longer exercises, check your understanding by filling in the blanks in the Rules Summary below. Fill in the blanks from memory, thinking carefully about what each rule means. If you need help, look back again at the Rules.

1. The verb *BE* can be either a one-word verb or a _____ verb in a verb

   phrase.

2. Use the helping verb *BE* + the _____ form of a main verb to tell what _____

   _____ right now or _____ _____

   in the past.

3. The helping verb *BE* must _____ with its subject and show the appropriate

   _____ .

4. Often a helping verb is not repeated before a second _____ verb.

Now turn to the **Answers** to check your work. Use these **Rules** and your dictionary as you go on to do the longer exercises that follow.

Module 8: *The Verb BE*

PRACTICE, Part 2

Exercise 8.24　　　　　　　　　　　　　　　**Number of Mistakes** _____

Remember: Forms of the verb *BE* are often contracted.

Forms of the verb *BE* have been left out of this paragraph. (1) Rewrite the paragraph in the present tense, including the missing verbs, and contracting each verb. (For help, insert the missing verbs into this paragraph before you rewrite it with contractions.) (2) In your rewritten paragraph, underline each one-word verb and verb phrase. Double underline the main verb in each verb phrase. Your first sentence will begin like this: *Hello, Josie, I'm calling from the . . .*

　　　　Hello, Josie, I calling from the union hall. They going to take a strike vote soon. They telling us to accept the contract, but we going to turn it down. It just no good. It cutting back our benefits, and there no more money in it anywhere, except for the managers. . . . Yes, that right. I afraid that it going to be a long strike. We probably not going to get that new refrigerator, after all. . . . I sorry, Josie, but I glad that you so understanding. You the best wife in the world.

_____

_____

_____

_____

_____

_____

_____

_____

_____

_____

_____

Exercise 8.25

Number of Mistakes _____

This paragraph contains errors in verbs, verb phrases, and infinitives. (1) Underline each one-word verb and helping verb, double underline each main verb, and circle each infinitive. (2) Correct each error in the space above the line. The first line has been marked for you.

thinks   *know*

Aunt Mattie, like many people over sixty, <u>think</u> all her young relatives <u>need</u> (to knows)

how great the good old days was—before TV, when she and her sisters was growing up. Every

Sunday, my brother Jake watch her coming up the block, frowns, and mutters that trouble be on

the way. She always rush into our kitchen with a big hello, but then she act like a lady preacher.

There is a thousand things she like to criticize. While we are eating dinner, Auntie M. tries

to gets our attention, and if she don't, she thumps the table, demands silence, and begin

to preach a sermon against modern times. She says it be a scandal that girls these days is wearing

sexy jeans and that boys are kissing girls they don't even know. And there is those loud radios all

over the place! When she was a girl, she declare, things was a lot different. She say life was

better when times was harder. And then she asks what I'am doing with all the money that I

earns. We tries to be polite, but she really test our patience. Jake usually jumps up and leave the

room at some point long before Aunt Mattie's final amen. The next time she wants to visit, we

are ready to tell her that we has to goes out!

Important: This paragraph contained 25 errors, not counting the two that were corrected for you. How many did you find? _____ If you didn't find all 25, try again before you check your work.

Exercise 8.26   **Number of Mistakes** _____

This paragraph contains base forms of the verb *BE* in capital letters. (1) Rewrite the paragraph with the appropriate present-tense or past-tense form of *BE*. **Make no other changes.** (2) In your rewritten paragraph, underline each one-word verb and verb phrase. Double underline the main verb in each verb phrase. Your first sentence will begin like this: *Who __am__ I? Well, sonny, . . .*

Who BE I? Well, sonny, my name BE Bill Williams, and I BE 97 years old. In World War I, I BE a fighter pilot. The Red Baron and I BE stalking each other up there in the clouds. Fragments of shrapnel BE flying all around me, but I BE not one bit scared. Here BE an old photograph of me in my uniform. I BE twenty years old at the time. Those campaign ribbons on my chest BE my pride and joy then, and they still BE now. And here on this table BE some more souvenirs—a couple of old brass artillery shells that now BE lamps. It BE hard to believe, but these shells BE once in a German cannon. And now they BE decorating my living room. I BE one high flyer in the Great War, child, and I still BE.

_____

_____

_____

_____

_____

_____

_____

_____

_____

_____

_____

_____

_____

_____

_____

Exercise 8.27   **Number of Mistakes** _____

Review Exercise D: Verb Agreement, The Verb BE

This passage contains errors in verb agreement and the verb *BE*. Underline each one-word verb and verb phrase. Double underline the main verb in each verb phrase. Correct each error in the space above the line. For help, use your **Rules** and your dictionary. The first line has been marked for you.

                               are

      These days, baby toys <u>is <u>selling</u></u> briskly, and toy manufacturing <u>is</u> big business. In the past,

toys for infants was mostly simple plastic rattles and terry-cloth balls. Now toy makers is

constantly trying to come up with new gimmicks that will appeal to parents and expectant

parents. In fact, they're turning for inspiration to research on babies, even on unborn babies.

Investigators recently discovered that soft music was able to soothe not only a pregnant woman

but also her unborn child. So an ingenious manufacturer is now selling "Babyphones,"

lightweight stereo speakers that a mother-to-be wears around her waist. A cassette player hook

onto her pocket or purse. If the fetus starts kicking, the expectant mother switch on "womb

tunes" (as the maker call these tapes). What else do the fetus hear besides violins or guitars?

One favorite be a home-made tape of Mom and Dad singing lullabies. Then to help the newborn

to make the transition from the familiar womb to the scary outside world, toy makers has yet

another helpful invention. For nine months the baby was listening to the sounds of its mother's

body and the beat of her heart. After birth, the parents is able to buy a tape player to put in the

baby's bed, where it play the same comforting rhythms. Toy manufacturers is also publicizing the

discovery that babies enjoys the high contrast of black and white. Now zebras, pandas, and other

black-and-white animals is making big bucks for them. They're also promoting black-and-white

mobiles to hang on the crib. In this age of the consumer, the manufacturers exploits the idea

that nobody be too young for an expensive toy.

Important: This paragraph contained 15 errors, not counting the one that was corrected for you. How many did you find? _____ If you didn't find all 15, try again before you check your work.

Module 8: *The Verb BE*

WRITING TEST

NAME _____

PURPOSE   To show that you can use the verb *BE* in both the present and past tenses, and that you can continue to apply what you have learned in previous modules.

ASSIGNMENT   Think of a room that you've known for many years, one that has changed over time. Or think of a room (bedroom, living room, porch, *etc.*) you have now which is different from one you had in the past. Write a comparison of the old room and the new room.

Check off each step in the writing process as you complete it.

GET READY   ❑   On scratch paper, write as many details about the old and new rooms as you can. Make sure you have plenty of ideas to show why you chose this room.

DRAFT   On scratch paper, write a rough draft of your comparison. Try to write sentences that sound natural but aren't too complicated.

      ❑   Write one paragraph beginning *I remember*... that describes how the room looked in the past. Tell what objects were in the room, how many of them there were, and where they were. In every sentence, use a past-tense form of *BE*. Write at least one sentence beginning with *There was* and another beginning with *There were*. **Write at least six sentences.**

      ❑   Write another paragraph that describes how the room looks now. Tell what objects are in the room, how many of them there are, and where they are. In every sentence, use a present-tense form of *BE*. Write at least one sentence beginning with *There is* and another beginning with *There are*. **Write at least six sentences.** Be sure to end with a sentence that tells how you feel about the changes you have described.

REVISE   ❑   Read over the draft of your comparison to make sure that your ideas are clear and sound real. Try to anticipate what a reader will need to know in order to understand and believe what you have written. Add, take out, or change ideas, words, and sentences as necessary. Remember, it's good for a draft to become messy.

      ❑   After you have finished revising your ideas, underline each one-word verb and verb phrase. Double underline the main verb in each verb phrase.

      ❑   Count the forms of *BE* that you used and underlined, and write the number here: _____ .

EDIT   ❑   Review the Rules for this module. Find and correct any mistakes in forms of the verb *BE*. Make sure that every verb is in the appropriate tense and agrees (if necessary) with its subject.

Use your dictionary and the Rules for previous modules to find and correct any mistakes in:

❑   Nouns: Singular and Plural Forms
❑   Verbs: Tense and Agreement
❑   Sentences: Fragments and Run-Ons
❑   Spelling
❑   Writing Conventions
❑   Wrong Words

FINAL COPY   ❑   Write the final copy of your comparison carefully, using blue or black ink and standard-sized (8½ by 11 inch) paper. Better yet, type or use a word processor. Write your name in the upper right-hand corner, or use whatever heading your instructor requires. Remember that you are now preparing your writing for a reader.

                 ❑   Underline every verb in your final copy just as you did in your draft.

PROOFREAD   ❑   Read your final copy **out loud**. If you find any mistakes, it's OK to correct them neatly by hand. Or if you have used a word processor, go back and correct your mistakes, and then print out a clean final copy.

Attach your final copy to these instructions, and hand them both in.

9 Past-Tense Verbs

NAME _____

As you complete each exercise, record your number of mistakes below.

9.1 ____	9.8 ____	9.14 ____
9.2 ____	9.9 ____	9.15 ____
9.3 ____	9.10 ____	9.16 ____
9.4 ____	9.11 ____	9.17 ____
9.5 ____	Summary ____	9.18 ____
9.6 ____	9.12 ____	9.19 ____
9.7 ____	9.13 ____	9.20 ____

Review Exercise E ____

INSTRUCTOR'S COMMENTS

Instructions:

☐ Followed carefully
☐ Not followed carefully enough

Checking:

☐ Careful
☐ Not careful enough to catch all your mistakes
☐ Green pen not used for checking
☐ Entire correct answer not always written in

Writing Test:

☐ Excellent
☐ Good
☐ Acceptable
☐ Not yet satisfactory

Other:

Module 9: *Past-Tense Verbs*

RULES

Important: All verbs are either **regular** or **irregular**. Regular verbs form their past tense in one way, and irregular verbs form their past tense in another way.

> Last night Nicole / <u>ate</u> dinner and then <u>watched</u> TV.
> > *Ate* is an irregular past-tense form.
> > *Watched* is a regular past-tense form.

9A. To form the past tense of most <u>irregular</u> verbs, change the whole word.

> TEACH Sean / <u>taught</u> aerobics last year.
> > *Taught* is the past-tense form of the irregular verb *TEACH*.

If you don't already know the past-tense form of an irregular verb, you'll have to look it up in the dictionary.

❑ Look up the irregular verb *SING* in your dictionary. **If you don't have your dictionary, don't go on until you do have it.** Be sure to find the word with the label *v* for *verb*.

❑ How many other forms are listed? _____

Usually three or four other forms are listed. *Sings* may be listed also, to remind you that verbs must agree with their subjects in the present tense.

❑ Write in the three other forms of *SING* (ignore *sings* if it's listed):

SING _____ _____ _____

The 1st form *sing* (or *sings*) is used in the **present** tense.
The 2nd form *sang* is used in the **past** tense.
The 3rd form *sung* is the **past participle**.
The 4th form *singing* is the *ING* **form**.

For some irregular verbs, the past-tense form and the past participle are the same. For others, they're different.

> BRING I / <u>brought</u>. I / have <u>brought</u>.
> SWIM I / <u>swam</u>. I / have <u>swum</u>.
> > *BRING* has the same past-tense and past participle forms.
> > *SWIM* has different past-tense and past participle forms.

Exercise 9.1 Look up the following verbs in your dictionary, and write in the verb forms you find there. Ignore the form that ends in *S* if it's listed. **If you don't have your dictionary, don't go on until you do have it.**

		past tense	past participle	*ING* form
1.	SAY	_____	_____	_____
2.	GO	_____	_____	_____
3.	SEE	_____	_____	_____
4.	LEAVE	_____	_____	_____
5.	BRING	_____	_____	_____
6.	BUY	_____	_____	_____
7.	PAY	_____	_____	_____
8.	HAVE	_____	_____	_____
9.	BE	_____	_____	_____
10.	PUT	_____	_____	_____

Remember: Check your work as you go along, using the Answers in the back of the book.

Exercise 9.2 Fill in the past-tense form of the given verb. For help, use your dictionary.

1. GET   On September 30, 1829, George Worsham, a Virginia farmer,

   _____ his tax bill in the mail.

2. PAY   He _____ forty cents per slave, ten cents per horse, and

   one cent per two-wheel carriage.

3. BUY   On May 1, 1862, he _____ his grandson Henry a new

   horse for $120.

4. BRING   Henry's mother _____ a box of cornbread to the

   PUT   verandah and _____ it in his knapsack.

5. SAY   Henry _____ goodbye and _____

   RIDE   away to join the First Virginia Cavalry in the Shenandoah Valley.

6. SEND   On February 27, 1865, the Confederate States of America

              _____ Mr. Worsham $2965 in worthless currency for

              his dead horse, and nothing for his dead grandson.

7. LEAVE   One by one, the freed blacks _____ the farm, and

    SELL   Worsham _____ his livestock.

8. SPEAK   On June 1, 1870, Worsham and his sons _____ to their

    TELL   lawyer and _____ him to file for bankruptcy.

Important: Don't confuse the past participle of a verb with its past-tense form.

                    ✗
    SEE   I / <u>seen</u> the Florida Keys last year.
               I / <u>saw</u> the Florida Keys last year.

               Seen is the past participle of *SEE*. Although this verb is sometimes used like this
                   in speech, *seen* isn't a correct past-tense form in writing.
               Saw is the correct past-tense form of *SEE*.

Exercise 9.3 Fill in the past-tense form of the given verb. For help, use your dictionary.

1. BEGIN   In 1861, the Civil War _____ with Confederate

              victories at Fort Sumter and Bull Run.

2. RUN   For many months after that, the timid Northern generals _____

    DO   away or _____ nothing.

3. COME   Early in 1862, Ulysses S. Grant _____ to Lincoln's

              attention as the first Northern general to win a battle.

4. BE   The subsequent battles at Shiloh and Antietam _____

              bloody but indecisive.

5. SEE   The following year, Grant _____ a chance to win

              control of the Mississippi Valley.

6. DRINK   On July 4, 1863, Grant _____ a victory toast at

    SING   Vicksburg, and his troops _____ *Yankee Doodle* on the

              banks of the Mississippi.

7.   SWING   After this triumph, the tide of the war _____ in favor of

                     the North.

‖‖‖ 9B.   To form the past tense of <u>regular</u> verbs, add *D* or *ED*.

WALK   They / <u>walked</u> to work during the strike.
LIVE   My friends / <u>lived</u> in Greece last year.
> *Walked* and *lived* are the past-tense forms of the regular verbs *WALK* and *LIVE*.

Passed, the past-tense form of *PASS*, causes special problems. Don't confuse *passed* with *past*, which means something like "an earlier time" or "beyond."

PASS   We / **passed** the courthouse.
WALK   We / <u>walked</u> **past** the courthouse.

Write *passed* in this sentence: We _ _ _ _ _ _ the library.

Write *past* in this sentence: We walked _ _ _ _ the library.

Exercise 9.4 Fill in the past-tense form of the given verb.

1.   PRESENT   According to Joseph Smith, in 1829 a heavenly messenger

     CALL   _____ him with a Bible-like book which he

                     _____ the Book of Mormon.

2.   PRACTICE   Because he and his followers _____ polygamy, an angry

     LYNCH   mob _____ him in 1844.

3.   PASS   The leadership of the Mormon Church _____ to

                     Brigham Young.

4.   FOLLOW   Thousands of Mormon converts _____ Young to Salt

     ESTABLISH   Lake City where they _____ a new community.

Important: Don't get confused and add *ED* to make the past-tense form of an **irregular** verb. Whenever you're not sure of a past-tense form, use your dictionary.

✗   **✗**

BEGIN   The band / <u>beginned</u> to play as the team <u>ranned</u> onto the field.
RUN   The band / <u>began</u> to play as the team <u>ran</u> onto the field.

> *BEGIN* and *RUN* are irregular verbs. Past-tense forms with *ED* endings are incorrect.

Exercise 9.5 Fill in the past-tense form of the given verb.

1. PLANT   Grace / _____ a garden and

    GROW   _____ tomatoes.

2. STEAL   The shortstop / _____ third base and then

    SCORE   _____ .

3. TEACH   Mr. Erickson / _____ my high school Spanish class

    PASS   and _____ all his students with a B.

4. CATCH   The child / _____ chicken pox and

    DEVELOP   _____ a high fever.

5. SIT   Everybody / _____ in his seat and

    PRETEND   _____ to be working.

9C.   Some regular verbs need spelling changes before adding an ending to make a past-tense form.

1.   If a verb ends in a <u>consonant</u> + *Y*, change the *Y* to *I* before adding *ED*.

FRY   We / <u>fried</u> the onions.

> *Fried* is spelled with *I*, not *Y*.

This is Spelling Rule A2.1 in Appendix A.

||| **2.**   **If a verb ends in a <u>vowel</u> + *Y*, do not change the *Y* to *I*.**

PLAY   My son / <u>played</u> with those little cars when he was younger.
                      Played is spelled with *Y*, not *I*.

This is Spelling Rule A2.2 in Appendix A.

Exercise 9.6 Fill in the past-tense form of the given verb.

1.   RELY   During the 1940s, American factories _____ on

     CARRY   millions of women workers while their men _____

                      arms in World War II.

2.   ENJOY   Most of these women _____ their earning power and

     BURY   independence, but _____ these feelings when their

                      husbands and sweethearts returned.

3.   STAY   Then throughout the 1950s, most wives _____ home

     PLAY   and once again _____ a traditional role.

4.   DELAY   The post-war "baby boom" and sentimentalization of family life

                      _____ modern feminism for an entire generation.

Important: Don't confuse **regular** verbs ending in a vowel + *Y* with these three irregular verbs: *LAY, PAY,* and *SAY*.

      LAY   I / <u>laid</u> the envelope down.
      PAY   I / <u>paid</u> the bill.
      SAY   I / <u>said</u> nothing to her.
                   Laid, paid, and *said* are the past-tense forms of the irregular verbs *LAY, PAY,* and *SAY*.

Never use the regular *ED* ending to make the past-tense form of the irregular verbs *LAY, PAY,* and *SAY*.

                  ✗
      PAY   I / <u>payed</u> the bill.
                  I / <u>paid</u> the bill.
                   Paid is the correct past-tense form of the irregular verb *PAY*.

Exercise 9.7 (1) Rewrite this paragraph, using the appropriate past-tense forms of the given verbs. (2) In your rewritten paragraph, underline each verb.

> After the bank COLLAPSE, the investigators LAY the entire blame on the bank officials. They SAY that the officers RELY on inside information about stock investments and DELAY paying interest on loans. As usual, the officers DENY the charges, but the depositors PAY dearly for these illegal practices.

_____

_____

_____

_____

_____

3.　　If a verb ends in a <u>single vowel</u> + a <u>single consonant</u>, double the consonant before adding *ED*.

DROP　　　　　　　Matilda / <u>dropped</u> her keys while opening the door.
　　　　　　　　　　　Dropped is spelled with a double *P*.

This is Spelling Rule A3.1 in Appendix A.

Important: Failing to double the consonant can cause a wrong-word mistake.

✗

ROB　　　　　　　Bonnie and Clyde / <u>robed</u> banks.
　　　　　　　　　　Bonnie and Clyde / <u>robbed</u> banks.
　　　　　　　　　　　　Robed is the past-tense form of *ROBE*, not of *ROB*.
　　　　　　　　　　　　The correct past-tense form of *ROB* is *robbed*, with a double *B*.

Exercise 9.8 Fill in the past-tense form of the given verb.

1.　HOPE　　　　　I / _____ to get a B in my philosophy course last

　　　　　　　　　　semester, but I didn't really expect to.

　　HOP　　　　　Edmund / _____ four miles last year to win a bet.

2.　ROB　　　　　Somebody / _____ the liquor store on the corner last week.

　　ROBE　　　　The graduates / _____ in the hall before the ceremony.

3.　RAP　　　　　Who / _____ on my door a minute ago?

　　RAPE　　　　The Romans / _____ the Sabines.

4.   PLAN   That group / _____ the conference two years in

                   advance.

     PLANE   The carpenter / _____ the door so it would fit better.

5.   STARE   We / _____ at each other in disbelief.

     STAR   The film / _____ William Hurt and Glenn Close.

||||| **9D.**   **In most sentences with more than one verb,
                  every verb must be in the same tense.**

Whenever the doorbell <u>rings</u>, the Doberman <u>dashes</u> to the door and <u>barks</u> furiously.

> Because the verbs in this sentence tell what usually happens, *RING*, *DASH*, and *BARK* are in the present tense.

When the doorbell <u>rang</u>, the Doberman <u>dashed</u> to the door and <u>barked</u> furiously.

> Because the verbs in this sentence tell what happened in the past, *RING*, *DASH* and *BARK* are in the past tense.

Remember: A present-tense verb must agree with its subject.

Exercise 9.9 (1) Underline each verb. (2) Fill in the appropriate present-tense and past-tense form of the given verb. You might find it helpful to circle any time words.

1.   JUMP   Every morning when the alarm clock rings, they / _____
                   out of bed.

                   Every morning when the alarm clock rings, she / _____
                   out of bed.

                   When the alarm rang yesterday, they / _____ out of
                   bed.

                   When the alarm rang yesterday, she / _____ out of bed.

2.   HAVE   Cassie and her husband / always _____ a miserable
                   time when they go camping.

                   Cassie / always _____ fun when she goes to the beach.

                   Last year in California, Cassie and her husband / _____
                   a wonderful vacation.

                   Cassie / <u>was</u> sorry when she _____ to come back home.

Important: When telling about events that happened in the past, check your writing carefully for the *ED* ending on all regular verbs.

Exercise 9.10 This passage contains errors in past-tense verbs. (1) Underline each verb. (2) Correct each error in the space above the line.

As the storm battered the coast, the men on board the small fishing boat grasp the ropes

and furled their sails. Desperately, they flash distress signals to the shore. But the waves surge

savagely, overturned their boat, and threaten to drown them. All night, they clutch the hull of

their craft with aching fingers. At dawn, while the storm still raged, helicopter pilots risk their

lives when they hovered over the fishermen, dropped ladders, and pluck them out of the sea.

Important: Check carefully for the *D* ending in the past-tense expression *used to*.

      USE   We / <u>used</u> to go to the beach every summer.
                            This expression tells about something we were in the habit of doing in the past.

Be careful not to leave off the *D* ending on *used*. When a past-tense form is followed by the word *to*, you often won't hear the past-tense ending pronounced. But it's incorrect to write a regular past-tense verb without the *D* ending.

                      ✗
      USE   I / <u>use</u> to play second base.
                        Use is incorrect.

                    I / <u>used</u> to play baseball.
                        The past-tense verb *used* is correct.

Exercise 9.11 Fill in the past-tense form of *USE* + the infinitive of the given verb. Follow this model:

      GROW   Ahmed / _*used*_ _*to grow*_ tomatoes in the back yard.

1.   DIE   Millions / _____ _____ of smallpox.

2.   HAVE   Some middle-income folks / _____ _____

                  cooks and chauffeurs.

3.   SAVE   Some retired Americans / _____ _____

                  money by living abroad.

RULES SUMMARY

In the longer one-page exercises that follow, you'll practice applying all the rules which you've learned or reviewed in this module. Before you go on to the longer exercises, check your understanding by filling in the blanks in the Rules Summary below. Fill in the blanks from memory, thinking carefully about what each rule means. If you need help, look back again at the Rules.

1. All verbs are either _____ or irregular.

2. To form the past tense of most irregular verbs, _____ the whole word.

3. The past-tense forms of the irregular verbs *LAY*, *PAY*, and *SAY* are _____ , _____ ,

   and _____ .

4. To form the past tense of regular verbs, add _____ or _____ .

5. Some regular verbs need _____ changes before adding a past-tense ending.

   a. If a verb ends in a **consonant** + *Y*, change the *Y* to _____ before adding *ED*.

   b. If a verb ends in a _____ + *Y*, don't change the *Y* to *I*.

   c. If a verb ends in a single vowel + a single consonant, _____ the final

      consonant before adding *ED*.

6. In most sentences with more than one verb, every verb must be in the _____

   tense.

7. Be careful not to leave off the _____ ending in the expression *used to*.

Now turn to the Answers to check your work. Use these Rules and your dictionary as you go on to do the longer exercises that follow.

Module 9: *Past-Tense Verbs*

PRACTICE

Exercise 9.12   **Number of Mistakes** _____

To help you learn which **irregular** verbs cause you trouble, fill in the past-tense form of each verb, and then write in the letter (or letters) that each past-tense form is spelled with.

They buy.   They _____

They bring.   They _____

They catch.   They _____

They teach.   They _____

Spell all these verbs with <u>A</u> _ _ _ _ or with

<u>O</u> _ _ _ _ in the past tense.

They throw.   They _____

They know.   They _____

They grow.   They _____

Spell all these verbs with _ _ in the past tense.

_____

They steal.   They _____

They rise.   They _____

They freeze.   They _____

They choose.   They _____

Spell all these verbs with an _ in the past tense.

_____

They say.   They _____

They lay.   They _____

They pay.   They _____

Spell all these verbs with _ _ _ in the past

tense.

They ring.   They _____

They swim.   They _____

They begin.   They _____

They drink.   They _____

They sing.   They _____

Spell all these verbs with an _ in the past tense.

They send.   They _____

They lose.   They _____

They spend.   They _____

They keep.   They _____

They feel.   They _____

They sleep.   They _____

They leave.   They _____

Spell all these verbs with a _ in the past tense.

_____

They quit.   They _____

They cut.   They _____

They hit.   They _____

They hurt.   They _____

They put.   They _____

These verbs all have _____ change in

the past tense.

216

Exercise 9.13   **Number of Mistakes** _____

Remember: The items in a series should be separated by commas.

(1) Write one sentence to answer each group of questions, using past-tense verbs. (2) In your answer, underline each verb, and draw a slash between the subject part and the verb part. Follow this model:

Did Olaf stand up? Did he start an argument? Did he stalk away?

<u>Yes, he</u> / <u>stood up</u>, <u>started</u> an argument, and <u>stalked</u> away.

1. Did Cesar wash the dishes? Did he dry them? Did he put them away?

    <u>Yes, he</u> _____

    _____

2. Did the phone ring? Did it stop? Did it begin ringing again?

    <u>Yes, it</u> _____

    _____

3. Did Colette worry about money? Did she shop very carefully? Did she pay all her bills?

    <u>Yes, she</u> _____

    _____

4. Did Consuelo attend school? Did she keep house for her family? Did she study every weekend?

    <u>Yes, she</u> _____

    _____

5. Did I wake up at 9 AM? Did I have breakfast? Did I listen to the morning news? Did I go back to bed?

    <u>Yes, I</u> _____

    _____

6. Did the preacher pray? Did he read from the Bible? Did he lead a hymn? Did he say the benediction?

    <u>Yes, he</u> _____

    _____

Exercise 9.14   **Number of Mistakes** _____

Remember: In most sentences with more than one verb, every verb must be in the same tense.

Fill in the appropriate present-tense or past-tense form of the given verb. You might find it helpful to circle any time words and underline any other verbs.

1. GO   Whenever she finishes early, Muriel / _____ straight home.

                  When she finished early last night, Muriel / _____ straight home.

2. BUY   Before my brother moved to Chicago last year, he / _____ a new car.

                  Every time my brother makes a big change in his life, he / _____ a new car.

3. BE   Whenever their parents disapprove of something, Maggie and Joan / _____ eager to do it.

                  Although their parents disapproved, Maggie and Joan / _____ eager to become models.

4. DO   If a person is ambitious, he or she / _____ the best job possible.

                  Because Latrelle was ambitious, she always / _____ her best work.

5. ASK   Every night, when Edith's husband comes home, she / _____

    FEEL   him how he _____ .

                  Last night, when Edith's husband came home, she / _____

                  him how he _____ .

6. STOP   Whenever she had time, Mrs. Franklin / _____ and

    BUY   _____ a newspaper to read on her way to work.

                  Whenever she has time, Mrs. Franklin / _____ and

                  _____ a newspaper to read on her way to work.

Exercise 9.15   **Number of Mistakes** _____

Fill in the appropriate present-tense or past-tense form of the given verb.

1. DROP   Last year, a number of people _____ their senile

    DRIVE   parents at the door of an emergency room and _____ away.

2. PASS   If Congress _____ that controversial bill, the President

    REACH   will veto it when it _____ his desk.

3. FLY   When I'm writing at my computer, time _____ , and I

    LOSE   _____ myself in whatever I am doing.

4. SHOP   A working mother often _____ for groceries on the

    RUSH   way home and _____ to start dinner before her

              husband arrives.

5. WASH   While he _____ the dishes, she lies down on the sofa

    WATCH   and _____ TV.

6. HIDE   Recently, a deranged man _____ a hammer under his

    CHIP   coat, and then attacked the famous statue of David and

              _____ its toe.

7. RING   When the doorbell _____ , Brenda looked to see who

    UNLOCK   was there before she _____ the door.

8. ASK   A young child is hard to live with because she _____

    GET   questions constantly and _____ into a lot of mischief.

9. BE   There _____ several drugs which prolong the lives of

    FIND   AIDS victims, but until doctors _____ a cure, the

              disease will continue to spread.

10. SING   Before the game started, Roseanne _____ *The Star-*

    CAUSE   *Spangled Banner* off key and almost _____ a riot.

Exercise 9.16   **Number of Mistakes** _____

Remember: An infinitive isn't a verb. It never changes form.

(1) Underline each verb, circle each infinitive, and draw a slash between the subject part and the verb part.
(2) Rewrite each sentence in the past tense. (3) In your rewritten sentence, underline each verb, circle each infinitive, and draw a slash between the subject part and the verb part. Follow this model:

> My brother / wants (to buy) a house.
>
> My brother / wanted (to buy) a house.

1.   Some people drink to forget their problems.

     _____

2.   Stocks begin to rise when interest rates fall.

     _____

3.   AIDS victims try to obtain this experimental drug.

     _____

4.   It costs too much to travel abroad.

     _____

5.   A close call teaches us to drive more carefully.

     _____

6.   These immigrants are always happy to help their friends.

     _____

7.   We have to run fast to stay in the same place.

     _____

8.   It is dangerous to accept his favors.

     _____

9.   He plans to demand repayment.

     _____

Exercise 9.17   **Number of Mistakes** _____

Remember: In most sentences with more than one verb, every verb must be in the same tense.

This passage contains errors in regular past-tense verbs. (1) Underline each verb. (2) Correct each error in the space above the line. The first sentence has been done for you.

The 14 leading cars *carried* carry tents and equipment, and the next seven transported the animals. In the fading light of June 22, 1918, the crew hitch the four sleeping cars to the end of the train. The flagman signaled to the engineer, and the Hagenbeck-Wallace Circus clatter out of Michigan City. In the wooden sleepers, 300 circus people chatted and play cards, or climbed into their bunks and dream of the next day's opening performance in Hammond, Indiana.

Near the town of Ivanhoe, the circus train pulled into a side track while the crew try to fix an overheated brake box. The Pullman cars extended out onto the main track, so Ernest Trimm, the flagman, propped up emergency flares and check to make sure that the signal lights were flashing warnings. Suddenly, an unscheduled troop train thunder down the track, hurtling toward the circus cars. Asleep at the throttle, Engineer Alonso Sargent never slow down. As the oncoming train pass through the yellow caution lights, Trimm waved his lantern frantically and then hurl it through the engineer's window. But the speeding locomotive rip past the red stop lights and plowed into the fragile wooden sleeping cars, crushing and killing most of the performers. Gas lights started fires in the wreckage, and the animals bellowed in terror as the flames lick toward them. Trapped in their cages, some burn to death. Their roars terrify the townspeople, and hysterical reports traveled from house to house. According to so-called eye witnesses, lions and tigers jumped from the train and roam the streets.

On the evening after the wreck, the circus open on schedule. Performers and acts from all over the country rush to Indiana and substituted for the victims of the crash. For years afterwards, the people of Ivanhoe use to sit around on summer evenings, talking about that terrible night when one exhausted man destroy almost an entire circus.

Important: This passage contained 19 errors, not counting the one that was corrected for you. How many did you find? _____ If you didn't find all 19, try again before you check your work.

Exercise 9.18

This paragraph contains base forms of verbs in capital letters. (1) Rewrite the paragraph, using the appropriate past-tense or infinitive form. **Make no other changes.** (2) In your rewritten paragraph, underline each verb, and circle each infinitive. Your first sentence will begin like this: *In the Middle Ages, marriage customs used (to be) strange . . .*

In the Middle Ages, marriage customs USE to BE strange and cruel, especially for women. While brides BE still in their cradles, their parents USE to ARRANGE their weddings. Sometimes a girl never SEE her husband until they MEET at the altar rail, and all too often this meeting TURN out to BE quite a shock. But no matter how she FEEL about him, the marriage contract MAKE it clear that he HAVE to HAVE an heir. If the wife FAIL to DELIVER a child within a year or two, her husband often USE to GET an annulment, and then he MARRY someone else. The man BE free to TAKE a mistress, but if his wife even LOOK at another man, he BEAT her. Some women THINK that it BE better not to MARRY at all, and CHOOSE to ENTER the convent instead.

_____

_____

_____

_____

_____

_____

_____

_____

_____

_____

_____

_____

_____

_____

Exercise 9.19   **Number of Mistakes** _____

This paragraph contains errors in verbs and infinitives. (1) Underline each verb, and circle each infinitive. (2) Correct each error in the space above the line. The first sentence has been marked for you.

                      got   *warned*

Last week when I get out of the elevator in my apartment building, my neighbor Sam warn

me (to be) careful. He remind me about the rise in street crime during this past year. I just

laughed as I pushed open the front door. After I stepped onto the sidewalk, I stoped, buttoned

up my coat, pulled on my gloves, and pick up all my packages again. It never occured to me to

see if I had everything. I entered the bank on the corner and ask to apply for a credit card. The

guard open the gate into the office area. I wented inside and get an application to fill out. But

when I reached for my purse to get a pen, my purse wasn't there. I started to screamed. I shook

the gate and yell, "Somebody stole my purse! Somebody rob me!" The guard told me to stopped

for a minute and to try to think. I admitted to him, "Yes, maybe I left it on the street when I

stopped and put my gloves on." In a panic, I ran all the way home. There I seen Sam, just inside

the door, with my purse in his hand. He say, with a look of astonishment, "Some stranger found

your purse by the door and give it to me." This week Sam switch the topic of his conversation

from crime to the weather.

Important: This paragraph contained 16 errors, not counting the ones that were corrected for you. How many did you find? _____ If you didn't find all 16, try again before you check your work.

Exercise 9.20   **Number of Mistakes** _____

(1) Underline each verb.

      I am not a suspicious person, but I know something is wrong. Whenever I leave the house, someone follows me. I never see him, but I know that he is there. I hear the sound of feet behind me when I walk. As I stop to glance into shop windows, I catch a glimpse of someone who stands off to one side, but when I turn around, he is not there. I feel his presence in crowds. As I choose a magazine, he looks over my shoulder. As I buy toothpaste or pay for my groceries, he passes near and counts my change. As I hurry home, I feel his eyes on my back. I go out less and less. He watches me through my windows. When the phone rings, I never answer. I sleep very little. My friends think that I am paranoid, but I wonder if they are in league with him.

(2) Rewrite the paragraph in the past tense. (3) In your rewritten paragraph, underline each change. Your first sentence will begin like this: *I was not a suspicious person, . . .*

_____

_____

_____

_____

_____

_____

_____

_____

_____

_____

_____

_____

_____

Exercise 9.21   **Number of Mistakes** _____

Review Exercise E: Verb Agreement, Past-Tense Verbs

This passage contains errors in present-tense verbs, past-tense verbs, and infinitives. (1) Underline each one-word verb and verb phrase. Double underline the main verb in each verb phrase. Circle each infinitive. (2) Correct each error in the space above the line. For help, use your Rules and your dictionary. The first sentence has been marked for you.

My grandmother grew up in the Great Depression of the 1930s, when it ~~costed~~ *cost* just eight

cents (to buy) a loaf of bread. Even with such low prices, her parents was too poor to put a

good meal on the table every day. She and her family seen some really hard times. Since almost

everybody were in the same boat, though, they laugh off their troubles, and waited for the

economy to recovered. They and their neighbors was right to believe what President Roosevelt

always said on his weekly radio broadcasts, that prosperity was just around the corner.

Compared to the Great Depression, recent years seem prosperous to most people. Parts of

the economy is thriving, and one of my own neighbors have two BMWs and a vacation home.

But the lives of many working people today aren't much different from my grandmother's. For

example, my nephew, a recent high school graduate, is having a hard time finding a decent job,

and not one of his friends own a car. There is people in the middle, like me and my husband.

We pay our bills and drive an old station wagon, but our dream of owning our own home get

dimmer and dimmer. Our future seem just as likely to get worse as it is to get better, as America

move toward the year 2000.

Important: This passage contained 13 errors in verbs, verb phrases, and infinitives, not counting the one that was corrected for you. How many did you find? _____ If you didn't find all 13, try again before you check your work.

Module 9: *Past-Tense Verbs*

WRITING TEST

NAME _____

PURPOSE   To show that you can write correct past-tense verbs, and that you can continue to apply what you have learned in previous modules.

ASSIGNMENT   Think of an unusual event or person that you once saw, perhaps on the street or in a bus or some other public place. Describe the event or person, and tell how you felt as you saw it.

Check off each step in the writing process as you complete it.

GET READY   ❑   On scratch paper, write down as many details about the event or person as you can think of. Make sure you have plenty of ideas to show why you chose this event or person.

DRAFT   ❑   On scratch paper, write a rough draft of your description. Try to write sentences that sound natural but aren't too complicated.

        In every sentence, use a one-word past-tense verb. (For example, write *she looked*, not *she would look*.) **Write at least 12 sentences.**

REVISE   ❑   Read over the draft of your description to make sure that your ideas are clear and sound real. Try to anticipate what a reader will need to know in order to understand and believe what you have written. Add, take out, or change ideas, words, and sentences as necessary. Remember, it's good for a draft to become messy.

       ❑   After you have finished revising your ideas, underline each one-word verb and verb phrase. Double underline the main verb in each verb phrase.

       ❑   Count the past-tense verbs that you used, and write the number here: _____ .

EDIT   ❑   Review the Rules for this module. Find and correct any mistakes in past-tense verb forms.

       Use your dictionary and the Rules for previous modules to find and correct any mistakes in:

       ❑   Nouns: Singular and Plural Forms
       ❑   Verbs: Tense and Agreement
       ❑   Sentences: Fragments and Run-Ons
       ❑   Spelling
       ❑   Writing Conventions
       ❑   Wrong Words

FINAL COPY   ❑   Write the final copy of your description carefully, using blue or black ink and standard-sized (8½ by 11 inch) paper. Better yet, type or use a word processor. Write your name in the upper right-hand corner, or use whatever heading your instructor requires. Remember that you are now preparing your writing for a reader.

❑   Underline every verb in your final copy just as you did in your draft.

PROOFREAD   ❑   Read your final copy **out loud**. If you find any mistakes, it's OK to correct them neatly by hand. Or if you have used a word processor, go back and correct your mistakes, and then print out a clean final copy.

Attach your final copy to these instructions, and hand them both in.

10 Understanding Sentences II

NAME _____

As you complete each exercise, record your number of mistakes below.

PART 1

10.1 ____	10.5 ____	Summary ____
10.2 ____	10.6 ____	10.8 ____
10.3 ____	10.7 ____	10.9 ____
10.4 ____		

PART 2

10.10 ____	10.13 ____	10.15 ____
10.11 ____	Summary ____	10.16 ____
10.12 ____	10.14 ____	10.17 ____

Review Exercise F ____

Module 10: *Understanding Sentences II*

RULES, Part 1: Verb Expansion

Remember: The verb (or the entire verb part of a sentence) can be expanded by words telling WHEN? or WHERE? or HOW?

> Accidents / <u>happen</u> (in bad weather).
> Accidents / <u>happen</u> (on highways).
> Accidents / <u>happen</u> (unexpectedly).
>> *In bad weather* is expansion telling WHEN accidents happen.
>> *On highways* is expansion telling WHERE accidents happen.
>> *Unexpectedly* is expansion telling HOW accidents happen.

10A. **A special kind of verb expansion begins with <u>expansion words</u> like *when*, *because*, and *if*.**

This kind of expansion usually tells more about whole sentences. It tells things like WHEN? or WHERE? or HOW? or WHY? or UNDER WHAT CONDITION?

> Accidents / sometimes <u>happen</u> (**when** roads are slippery).
> Accidents / sometimes <u>happen</u> (**because** people are careless).
> Accidents / sometimes <u>happen</u> (**if** drivers are reckless).
>> *When roads are slippery* is expansion telling WHEN accidents sometimes happen.
>> *Because people are careless* is expansion telling WHY accidents sometimes happen.
>> *If drivers are reckless* is expansion telling UNDER WHAT CONDITION accidents sometimes happen.

Exercise 10.1 (1) Circle the expansion word *when*, *because*, or *if*. (2) Put parentheses around the entire expansion beginning with that expansion word. Follow this model:

> Ernest / never <u>studies</u> ((when) the baby is awake) .

1. Ms. Montoya / <u>will teach</u> a Saturday morning section if enough students register for it.

2. People / sometimes <u>tell</u> lies when they're under pressure.

3. Children / sometimes <u>become</u> angry because their parents neglect them.

Remember: Check your work as you go along, using the Answers in the back of the book.

||| **1.**   **Sentences with this kind of expansion have two parts:**
              a <u>base sentence</u> part and an <u>expansion</u> part.

Roseanne / <u>left</u> early (**because** she had an appointment).

     Roseanne left early is the base sentence.
     Because she had an appointment is expansion telling WHY she left early.

Exercise 10.2 (1) Circle the expansion word, and put parentheses around the expansion. (2) In the base sentence, underline the verb, and draw a slash between the subject part and verb part. (3) Write in what the expansion tells about the base sentence. Follow this model:

Leah / <u>lost</u> her temper (ⓦⓗⓔⓝ Thomas lied to her) .

The expansion tells _____*when*_____ Leah lost her temper.

1.   Wendell bought a bicycle when he moved to Palo Alto.

    The expansion tells _____ Wendell bought a bicycle.

2.   Most people will lose weight if they exercise.

    The expansion tells under what _____ most people will lose weight.

3.   Many elderly people have difficulties because they live on fixed incomes.

    The expansion tells _____ many elderly people have difficulties.

So far you have worked with three common verb expansion words: *when*, *because*, and *if*. Here are seven more:

after	before	until	while
although	unless	so that	

Memorize all ten of these verb expansion words, and then test your memory by writing them here:

_____   _____   _____

_____   _____   _____

_____   _____   _____

_____

||| **2.** **This kind of verb expansion <u>combines</u> sentences by changing one sentence into expansion of the other.**

Moira / <u>is</u> upset. Her car / <u>has</u> a flat tire.
Moira / <u>is</u> upset (**because** her car has a flat tire).

> The expansion word *because* combines the two sentences by changing *Her car has a flat tire* into expansion telling WHY Moira is upset.

Exercise 10.3 (1) Combine each pair of sentences, using the given expansion word to change the **second** sentence into expansion of the **first**. (2) Mark your rewritten sentence like this:

when   We began to worry. The lights went out.

We/ began to worry ((when) the lights went out).

1. **unless**   You will not get that job. You're willing to travel.

_____

2. **after**   Minneapolis held a tickertape parade. The Twins won the World Series.

_____

_____

3. **before**   Coast-to-coast trips were a rare event. Plane travel became common.

_____

_____

4. **while**   Mr. Liang will repair your shoes. You wait.

_____

_____

5. **so that**   Jo Beth stopped watching TV. She would have more time to read.

_____

_____

6. **unless**   Children become confused. Parents agree about discipline.

_____

_____

||| **3.   This kind of verb expansion always contains a subject and a verb.**

                                 S V

The telephone / never <u>rang</u> (**because** it was off the hook).

      The verb expansion Because it was off the hook *contains a subject and a verb.*

Exercise 10.4 (1) Circle the expansion word, and put parentheses around the expansion. (2) Write S and V above the subject and verb of the expansion. Follow this model:

                                      S V

Wood / <u>burns</u> easily ((when) it is dry) .

1.   Mr. Reyes / <u>was traveling</u> in Mexico when he met his future wife.

2.   You / <u>will see</u> a small explosion if the experiment succeeds.

3.   Many older students / <u>attend</u> college because they want a career, not just a job.

|||||| **10B.   Verb expansion by itself is a <u>fragment</u>, even when it contains a subject and a verb.**

                      S   V

✗ (**When** Marjorie snaps her fingers.)

      When Marjorie snaps her fingers is expansion used by itself, without a base sentence. So it's a fragment, even though it contains a subject and a verb.

                      S   V

Lamont / <u>jumps</u> (**when** Marjorie snaps her fingers).

      This sentence is correct because the expansion when Marjorie snaps her fingers is used with the base sentence Lamont jumps.

Exercise 10.5 (1) Circle the expansion word, and put parentheses around the expansion. Then write S and V above the subject and verb of the expansion. (2) If a group of words is a sentence, do this: (a) In the base sentence, underline the verb, and draw a slash between the subject part and the verb part. (b) Write in SENT. (3) If a group of words is a fragment, put an ✗ in front of it, and write in FRAG. Follow this model:

                     S V

✗ ((When) my car needs repairs) .   <u>FRAG</u>

                                    S V

I / <u>take</u> my car to Joe's Garage ((when) it needs repairs) .   <u>SENT</u>

1.   When times are good.   _____

     People spend money when times are good.   _____

2.   Robin is cooperative if people treat her politely.   _____

     If people treat Robin politely.   _____

3.   Because the weather was bad and only four people attended. _____

     The meeting ended early because only four people attended. _____

10C.   This kind of verb expansion can come at the <u>end</u> of a base sentence or at the <u>beginning</u>.

Saturday classes / <u>are</u> popular (**because** many students work during the week).
(**Because** many students work during the week), Saturday classes / <u>are</u> popular.

> *Saturday classes are popular* is the base sentence.
> *Because many students work during the week* is expansion telling WHY Saturday classes are popular.
> These two sentences mean the same thing.

1.   When this kind of verb expansion comes at the <u>beginning</u> of a sentence, a comma is needed to separate the expansion from the base sentence.

(**If it rains**), we / <u>will move</u> the picnic to the gym.

> The expansion *if it rains* comes at the beginning of the sentence, so a comma is needed.

Exercise 10.6 (1) Circle the expansion word, and put parentheses around the expansion. (2) In the base sentence, underline the verb, and draw a slash between the subject part and the verb part. (3) Rewrite the sentence, moving the expansion to the beginning. Be sure to punctuate your rewritten sentence correctly. (4) Mark your rewritten sentence like this:

Someone / <u>went</u> for help ((when) the fire spread) .

((when) the fire spread), someone / went for help.

1.   Putting money in the bank doesn't make sense if the inflation rate is high.

     _____

     _____

2.   The leaves turn red when there is an early frost.

     _____

     _____

3.   Most Japanese children are taller than their parents because their diet contains more protein than in the past.

_____

_____

||| **2.   A sentence may have more than one expansion of this kind.**

(**When** the weather was hot), we / <u>moved</u> the children's mattresses onto the fire escape (**so that** they could sleep).

> *We moved the children's mattresses onto the fire escape* is the base sentence.
> *When the weather was hot* is expansion telling WHEN we moved the children's mattresses.
> *So that they could sleep* is expansion telling WHY we moved the mattresses.

Exercise 10.7 (1) Circle each expansion word, and put parentheses around the expansion. (2) In the base sentence, underline the verb, and draw a slash between the subject part and the verb part. Follow this model:

((After) the picnic was over) , the parents / <u>talked</u> ((while) their children played softball) .

1.   Few people like to speak before somebody else breaks the ice, unless they have something important

on their minds.

2.   When someone teaches us something before we are ready to learn it, we will not understand it.

3.   After Marco dealt out the cards, he repeated the rules so that everyone would understand.

RULES SUMMARY, Part 1

In the longer one-page exercises that follow, you'll practice applying all the rules which you've learned or reviewed in this module. Before you go on to the longer exercises, check your understanding by filling in the blanks in the Rules Summary below. Fill in the blanks from memory, thinking carefully about what each rule means. If you need help, look back again at the Rules.

1.   A special kind of verb expansion begins with _____ _____

like *when*, *because*, and *if*.

2.   A sentence that is expanded in this way has two parts: a _____

_____ part and an _____ part.

3. Verb expansion words can _____ sentences by changing one sentence into

_____ of the other.

4. This special kind of expansion contains a _____ and a

_____ .

5. Verb expansion by itself is a _____ , even when it contains a subject and a verb.

6. This kind of verb expansion can come either at the _____ of a base sentence

or at the _____ .

7. When this kind of verb expansion comes at the beginning of a sentence, a _____

is needed to separate it from the base sentence.

Now turn to the **Answers** to check your work. Use these **Rules** and your dictionary as you go on to do the longer exercises that follow.

Module 10: *Understanding Sentences II*

PRACTICE, Part 1

Exercise 10.8   **Number of Mistakes** _____

All sentences in this paragraph are correct. (1) Put parentheses around expansion beginning with verb expansion words. You might find it helpful to circle the expansion words. (2) In the base sentence, or in any sentence without verb expansion, underline the verb, and draw a slash between the subject part and the verb part. Follow this model:

I / will write a letter (if I have time) .

People and information continue to hurtle through space at higher and higher speeds.

When John Adams traveled from Boston to Williamsburg in the 1770s, he was on the road for

more than a week. Today the trip takes 90 minutes by plane. After Andrew Jackson was elected

President in 1828, a month went by before some voters heard the news. Today most people

know the new President's name before the polls close. However, one notable exception to this

law of progress is the daily mail. The pony express was faster in the 19th century than some

modern mail trucks. Back in the 1930s, the postman came to my grandmother's house twice a

day unless the snow was more than three feet deep. When she mailed a letter in the late

afternoon, it usually arrived the next morning at a friend's house fifty miles away. If her friend

wrote back that morning, Grandmother sometimes got her reply the same day. This kind of

service used to cost just two cents. Today I pay over $9 for Express Mail so that an important

letter will get to its destination overnight. In fact, although it runs up my phone bill, I often

phone long distance instead of writing because the mails are so undependable. Today's postal

service seems to be an example of progress in reverse.

Exercise 10.9   **Number of Mistakes** _____

This paragraph contains both sentences and fragments. (1) Put parentheses around expansion beginning with verb expansion words. (2) If a group of words is a sentence, do this: (a) In the base sentence, or in any sentence without verb expansion, underline each verb and draw a slash between the subject part and the verb part. (b) Write in SENT. (3) If a group of words is a fragment, put an X in front of it, and write in FRAG.

[1] In 1492, while Spain was still a great European power, Christopher   1 _____

Columbus set sail with three ships from a port near Seville. [2] After the   2 _____

Spanish monarchs Ferdinand and Isabella had financed his voyage. [3] Columbus   3 _____

sailed west to find new lands. [4] Although he told a different story later.   4 _____

[5] According to this later story, because he was seeking another route to   5 _____

Cathay or "the Indies." [6] If that story was true, Columbus organized   6 _____

a strange expedition. [7] There were no diplomats or soldiers on his ships.   7 _____

[8] Although Europeans well knew the wealth and power of those eastern lands.   8 _____

[9] After Columbus and his crew had sailed for 64 days. [10] Until they landed   9 _____

on an island in the Caribbean. [11] When they returned to Spain, their   10 _____

ships carried some gold and a number of captive "Indians," but no news   11 _____

of eastern civilizations. [12] However, because the strange tale of sailing   12 _____

west to India persisted. [13] We still call those islands the West Indies and   13 _____

refer to the native inhabitants of the American continent as Indians.

Module 10: *Understanding Sentences II*

RULES, Part 2: More About Correcting Fragments and Run-ons

10D. **Correct most fragments which begin with verb expansion words by connecting them to a base sentence.**

Harlan / usually <u>studies</u> in the library. ✗ Because it's quiet there.
Harlan / usually <u>studies</u> in the library (**because** it's quiet there).

The fragment has been corrected by connecting it to the base sentence.

Exercise 10.10 (1) Circle the expansion word, and put parentheses around the fragment it creates. Put an ✗ in front of the fragment. (2) Correct the fragment by connecting it to the sentence. (3) Mark your rewritten sentence like this:

Laverne got a B in math. ✗ (Because) she studied hard) .

<u>Laverne</u> / got a B in math ((because) she studied hard).

1. Everyone will be able to hear. If the audio system operates properly.

    _____

    _____

2. Customers were growing irritated. Because the lines were very long.

    _____

    _____

3. When their children become teenagers and begin to do things on their own. Parents worry.

    _____

    _____

10E.   Correct many run-ons by using an expansion word to change one sentence into expansion of the other.

✗
Jeanette budgets her time carefully, she is taking six classes.
Jeanette / budgets her time carefully (**because** she is taking six classes).

> The run-on has been corrected by using the verb expansion word *because* to change the second sentence into expansion of the first.

Exercise 10.11 (1) Put an **✗** where the second sentence begins. (2) Correct the run-on by using the given expansion word to change the **second** sentence into expansion of the first. (3) Mark your rewritten sentence like this:

when   Seth found his glasses,[✗] he looked under the car.

Seth/ found his glasses ((when) he looked under the car).

1.   **because**   Sarah is nervous, she has a job interview tomorrow.

_____

2.   **so that**   Many people look forward to retirement, they will be able to travel.

_____

3.   **after**   The tenants ended their strike, they received a rent reduction.

_____

Important: When changing a sentence into expansion to correct a run-on, be careful that your corrected sentence makes sense.

✗
We were cold, we wore heavy jackets.

> This is a run-on.

✗ We were cold (**because** we wore heavy jackets).

> This sentence seems correct, but it doesn't make sense. *Because we wore heavy jackets* isn't the reason why we were cold.

(**Because** we were cold), we / <u>wore</u> heavy jackets.

> This sentence is correct and makes sense. *Because we were cold* is the reason why we wore heavy jackets.

Exercise 10.12 (1) Put an **✗** where the second sentence begins. (2) Correct the run-on by using the given expansion word to change one of the sentences into expansion of the other. **Be sure that your sentence makes sense.** (3) Mark your rewritten sentence like this:

$$X$$

when   Vito gets sulky, it rains.

Vito / gets sulky ((when) it rains).

1. **after**   Ursula lost her voice, she won the speech contest.

_____

2. **until**   I practiced the piano sonata, I played it perfectly.

_____

3. **unless**   The bus arrives soon, we will be late.

_____

4. **because**   People eat out more frequently, they have more money.

_____

5. **before**   Josephine goes shopping, she always looks in the newspaper for sales.

_____

Remember: You can correct a run-on in three ways:

1. Rewrite the run-on as two sentences.

    ✗
    Gus liked his job, he didn't feel appreciated by his manager.
    > This is a run-on.

    Gus / liked his job. He / didn't feel appreciated by his manager.
    > The run-on has been corrected by rewriting it as two sentences.

2. Rewrite the run-on as a compound sentence with a comma + a joining word like *and* or *but*. When we analyze a compound sentence, we draw two slashes, one in each of the sentences that are joined.

    Gus / liked his job, **but** he / didn't feel appreciated by his manager.
    > The run-on has been corrected by rewriting it as a compound sentence with a comma + *but*.

3. Rewrite the run-on by changing one sentence into expansion of the other. When we analyze a sentence like this, we draw a slash only in the base sentence.

    (Although Gus liked his job), he / didn't feel appreciated by his manager.
    > The run-on has been corrected by using the expansion word *although* to change one sentence into expansion of the other.

Exercise 10.13 Put an ✗ where the second sentence begins, and correct each run-on in three ways: (a) Rewrite it as two sentences. (b) Rewrite it as a compound sentence, using the given joining word. (c) Rewrite it using the given expansion word to change one sentence into expansion of the other. Mark your sentences like this:

✗

I needed more time, the report was due.

a.   I/needed more time. The report /was due.

b.   but   I/needed more time |, but| the report/was due.

c.   although   (Although) I needed more time), the report/was due.

1.   Martinique was 21 years old, she filed papers to become a citizen.

    a.   _____

    b.   **and**   _____

    c.   **when**   _____

2.   Social services like education are suffering, the public resists raising taxes.

    a.   _____

    b.   **but**   _____

    c.   **although**   _____

RULES SUMMARY, Part 2

In the longer one-page exercises that follow, you'll practice applying all the rules which you've learned or reviewed in this module. Before you go on to the longer exercises, check your understanding by filling in the blanks in the Rules Summary below. Fill in the blanks from memory, thinking carefully about what each rule means. If you need help, look back again at the Rules.

1.   Most fragments which begin with verb expansion words can be corrected by

    _____ them to a base sentence.

2.   There are at least three ways to correct a run-on:

    a.   Rewrite it as _____ sentences.

b.   Rewrite it as a _____ sentence, using a comma + a joining word like

_____ or _____.

c.   Rewrite it by changing one of the sentences into _____ of the other.

Now turn to the Answers to check your work. Use these Rules and your dictionary as you go on to do the longer exercises that follow.

Module 10: *Understanding Sentences II*

PRACTICE, Part 2

Exercise 10.14   **Number of Mistakes** _____

Remember: Verb expansion by itself isn't a sentence. It's a fragment.

(1) Put parentheses around expansion beginning with verb expansion words. (2) Put an ✗ in front of each fragment. (3) Correct each fragment by connecting it to the sentence that it expands. (4) Mark your rewritten sentence like this:

✗ (When a deadline is near.) People often work long hours, (until they're too tired to sleep.)

(when a deadline is near), people / often work long hours, (until they're too tired to sleep).

1. While Claire prepared for her examinations, her husband did the shopping. So that she was free to study.

   _____

   _____

2. Before the cost of living became so expensive. Most women stayed at home while their husbands worked.

   _____

   _____

3. Before Bertha arrived. They hid the presents. Because they wanted to surprise her.

   _____

   _____

4. Although everyone feels angry at times, anger is a dangerous emotion. If we don't control it.

   _____

   _____

Exercise 10.15   **Number of Mistakes** _____

Remember: When expansion comes at the **beginning** of a sentence, a comma is needed to separate the expansion from the base sentence.

This paragraph contains both sentences and fragments. (1) Rewrite the paragraph, correcting each fragment by connecting it to the appropriate base sentence. **Make no other changes.** (2) In your rewritten paragraph, do this: (a) Put parentheses around expansion beginning with verb expansion words. (b) In the base sentence, or in any sentence without expansion, underline the verb, and draw a slash between the subject part and the verb part. Your paragraph will begin like this: (*When the brutal emperor Caligula ruled Rome*) , *he* / *had complete power to do anything, no matter how inhuman.*

When the brutal emperor Caligula ruled Rome. He had complete power to do anything, no matter how inhuman. On the hottest days, he often removed the canopies at the outdoor theater. Then he refused to let anyone leave. So that the spectators collapsed from sunstroke. When Caligula was sick once. A friend promised to commit suicide. If the gods spared the emperor's life. Later after Caligula got well. He compelled his friend to keep that promise. He forced important administrators to trot beside his chariot. Because he enjoyed making them look ridiculous. When two officials failed to announce his birthday. He removed them from office and sent them into exile. If he liked the looks of a woman, he took her home with him. Even if she was unwilling. Until he died at the hands of an assassin. Caligula continued to brutalize others. Because other people's suffering was, for him, the best entertainment.

_____

_____

_____

_____

_____

_____

_____

_____

_____

_____

_____

_____

_____

_____

Exercise 10.16   **Number of Mistakes** _____

Each group of words is a run-on. Some commas are correct, because they separate expansion from a base sentence. Other commas are incorrect, because they cause run-ons. (1) Put parentheses around expansion beginning with verb expansion words. (2) Put an ✗ above each incorrect comma. (3) Correct each run-on by rewriting it as two sentences. Mark your rewritten sentences like this:

> Many people are basically dishonest, ✗ (if they have a chance to cheat) , they will take it.
>
> *Many people / are basically dishonest. (If they have a chance to cheat), they / will take it.*

1.   I am taking typing lessons now, when I go to graduate school, I will type all of my papers.

   _____

   _____

2.   If you want the best coffee, you will grind the beans yourself, whole beans stay fresh longer.

   _____

   _____

3.   The babysitter lived twelve blocks away, before I went to work, I had to take my son to her house.

   _____

   _____

4.   Although Marie is dedicated to her job, she also makes time for her family, she is always there when they

   need her.

   _____

   _____

5.   When I left the store, I waited on the corner for the light to change, while I waited, I thought about all my

   chores.

   _____

   _____

Exercise 10.17   **Number of Mistakes** _____

Remember: A run-on can be corrected by changing one sentence into expansion of the other. Be careful that your corrected sentence makes sense.

Correct each run-on by using the given expansion word (or words) to change one of the sentences in the run-on into expansion of the other. Write your sentences first on scratch paper, and then put your corrected sentences into paragraph form. If you need more space, continue on a sheet of your own paper. Your paragraph will begin like this: *Although Albert Einstein was perhaps the greatest scientist of all time, he was a very simple . . . .*

1. **although**   Albert Einstein was perhaps the greatest scientist of all time, he was a very simple human being.

2. **when**   He joined the faculty of the Institute for Advanced Study at Princeton, he had to name his own salary.

3. **because**   The director had to plead with him to accept more money, he asked for such an impossibly small amount.

4. **so that**   As a child, he was slow in learning new things, his teachers saw no special talent in him.

5. **after**   He became a renowned physicist, his colleagues at Princeton smiled in disbelief,
    when   he asked them to pause and repeat their statements again, his mind understood new
    because   things so slowly.

6. **if**   Famous scientists and world leaders visited him, he greeted them wearing his usual outfit, an old sweater, baggy pants, and a pair of sandals.

7. **when**   Some children came knocking on his door one Christmas Eve, he followed them
    while   through the streets of Princeton, he accompanied their carols on his violin.

_____

_____

_____

_____

_____

_____

_____

_____

_____

Exercise 10.18

Number of Mistakes _____

Review Exercise F: Fragments and Run-ons

This paragraph contains fragments and run-ons. Rewrite the paragraph, correcting the errors like this:
(1) Connect each fragment to the appropriate sentence. (2) Rewrite each run-on as two sentences. **Make no other changes**. For help, use your Rules and your dictionary. If you need more space, continue on a sheet of your own paper. Your first sentence will begin like this: *In 1935, a scientist named Charles Richter developed a scale using numbers to measure the intensity of . . .*

In 1935, a scientist named Charles Richter developed a scale. Using numbers to measure the intensity of earthquakes. Few people feel an earthquake rated 1 unless they're very sensitive to faint tremors. Most people do notice a number 2. Although nothing seems to move. Almost everyone sees and feels the effects of a number 3 earthquake because it makes hanging objects swing. Beginning with number 4, an earthquake makes sounds, dishes rattle. Glasses clink, sometimes they even tumble from the shelf. A number 5 earthquake is frightening. Because it's strong enough to break windows and to crack walls. A number 6 injures people. And even kills them when loose bricks and weak chimneys come crashing down. A number 7 destroys whole buildings. And often buries thousands in the rubble. A number 8 shakes the earth strongly. So that even hills move. Although more violent earthquakes are theoretically possible, none stronger than an 8 is presently on record.

_____

_____

_____

_____

_____

_____

_____

_____

_____

_____

_____

Important: There should be 13 sentences in your corrected paragraph. How many did you write? _____ If you did not write 13 sentences, try again before you check your work.

Module 10: *Understanding Sentences II*

WRITING TEST

NAME _____

PURPOSE   To show that you can write correct sentences with verb expansion words, and that you can continue to apply what you have learned in previous modules.

ASSIGNMENT   Think about an accident in which more than one person was involved. Choose an accident that happened to you or to someone you know well, or an accident that was in the news. Describe the accident and tell how it affected the lives of the persons involved.

Check off each step in the writing process as you complete it.

GET READY   ❑   On scratch paper, write down as many details about the accident as you can think of. Make sure you have plenty of ideas to show why you chose this accident.

DRAFT   ❑   On scratch paper, write a rough draft of your description. Try to write sentences that sound natural but aren't too complicated.

Use at least eight of these verb expansion words:

❑   *after*
❑   *before*
❑   *until*
❑   *when*
❑   *while*
❑   *because*
❑   *so that*
❑   *although*
❑   *if*
❑   *unless*

❑   Write one paragraph describing exactly what happened. **Write at least six sentences.**

❑   Write another paragraph telling how the accident affected the lives of the people involved. **Write at least six sentences.**

❑   Put an **X** in the box next to each verb expansion word as you use it, and underline it in your description.

REVISE   ❑   Read over the draft of your description to make sure that your ideas are clear and sound real. Try to anticipate what a reader will need to know in order to understand and believe what you have written. Add, take out, or change ideas, words, and sentences as necessary. Remember, it's good for a draft to become messy.

❏   After you have finished revising your ideas, count the verb expansion words that you used and underlined, and write the number here: _____ .

EDIT   ❏   Review the Rules for this module. Find and correct any fragments and run-ons.

       Use your dictionary and the Rules for previous modules to find and correct any mistakes in:

          ❏   Nouns: Singular and Plural Forms
          ❏   Verbs: Tense and Agreement
          ❏   Spelling
          ❏   Writing Conventions
          ❏   Wrong Words

FINAL COPY   ❏   Write the final copy of your description carefully, using blue or black ink and standard-sized (8½ by 11 inch) paper. Better yet, type or use a word processor. Write your name in the upper right-hand corner or use whatever heading your instructor requires. Remember that you are now preparing your writing for a reader.

       ❏   Underline every verb expansion word in your final copy just as you did in your draft.

PROOFREAD   ❏   Read your final copy **out loud**. If you find any mistakes, it's OK to correct them neatly by hand. Or if you have used a word processor, go back and correct your mistakes, and then print out a clean final copy.

Attach your final copy to these instructions, and hand them both in.

11 More about Verb Phrases

NAME _____

As you complete each exercise, record your number of mistakes below.

PART 1

11.1 ____	11.7 ____	11.12 ____
11.2 ____	11.8 ____	Summary ____
11.3 ____	11.9 ____	11.13 ____
11.4 ____	11.10 ____	11.14 ____
11.5 ____	11.11 ____	11.15 ____
11.6 ____		

PART 2

11.16 ____	11.21 ____	11.24 ____
11.17 ____	11.22 ____	11.25 ____
11.18 ____	Summary ____	11.26 ____
11.19 ____	11.23 ____	11.27 ____
11.20 ____		

PART 3

11.28 ____	11.32 ____	11.35 ____
11.29 ____	11.33 ____	11.36 ____
11.30 ____	11.34 ____	11.37 ____
11.31 ____	Summary ____	11.38 ____

Review Exercise G ____

INSTRUCTOR'S COMMENTS

Instructions:

☐ Followed carefully
☐ Not followed carefully enough

Checking:

☐ Careful
☐ Not careful enough to catch all your mistakes
☐ Green pen not used for checking
☐ Entire correct answer not always written in

Writing Test:

☐ Excellent
☐ Good
☐ Acceptable
☐ Not yet satisfactory

Other:

Module 11: *More about Verb Phrases*

RULES, Part 1: Verb Phrases with *HAVE*

11A. ***HAVE* can be either a <u>one-word verb</u> or a <u>helping verb</u> in a verb phrase.**

HAVE	Priscilla / <u>has</u> ten dollars. Priscilla / <u>had</u> a good time. *Has* and *had* are one-word verbs, and the sentences are about **having**.
SPEND	Priscilla / <u>has <u>spent</u></u> all her money. Priscilla / <u>had <u>spent</u></u> all her money before she left. *Has* and *had* are helping verbs, and *spent* is the main verb. The sentences are about **spending**.

Exercise 11.1 (1) Underline each one-word verb and verb phrase. Double underline the main verb in each verb phrase. (2) Draw a slash between the subject part and the verb part. Follow this model:

Sim / <u>had</u> good luck at the car races.

Sim / <u>had <u>gone</u></u> to the races for the first time.

1. Someone has my notebook.

   Someone has taken my notebook by mistake.

2. No one had the answer.

   No one had answered the last question.

3. Many cities have financial problems.

   Many cities have grown smaller in population in the last ten years.

Remember: Check your work as you go along, using the Answers in the back of the book.

Remember: Only the helping verb shows agreement. The main verb doesn't agree.

WRITE	They / <u>have <u>written</u></u> their paper already. She / <u>has <u>written</u></u> her paper already. *Have* and *has* agree with their subjects. The main verb *written* doesn't show agreement.

Remember: *HAVE* is irregular. The present-tense form that agrees with a singular subject is *has*.

FORGET   They / <u>have forgotten</u> my telephone number.
She / <u>has forgotten</u> my telephone number.
Have agrees with plural *they*, and *has* agrees with singular *she*.

Exercise 11.2 Fill in the appropriate present-tense form of the helping verb *HAVE*.

1. BEGIN   Poland / _____ <u>begun</u> to trade with the West.

Poland and Czechoslovakia / _____ <u>begun</u> to trade with

the West.

2. BEAT   _____ you <u>beaten</u> the computer at chess?

The computer / _____ <u>beaten</u> me at chess.

3. HAVE   My brother / _____ <u>had</u> to borrow money.

I / _____ <u>had</u> to borrow money.

11B.   With the helping verb *HAVE*, use the <u>past participle</u> of the main verb.

1.   To form the past participle of most <u>irregular</u> verbs, change the whole word.

GO   We / <u>have gone</u> to the movies twice this week.
Gone is the past participle of the main verb *GO*.

If you don't already know the past participle of an irregular verb, you'll have to look it up in the dictionary.

❑ Look up the irregular verb *DRINK* in your dictionary. **If you don't have your dictionary, don't go on until you do have it.** Be sure to find the word with the label *v* for *verb*.

❑ Write in the three other forms of *DRINK* (ignore *drinks* if it's listed):

DRINK   _____   _____   _____

The 1st form *drink* (or *drinks*) is used in the **present** tense.
The 2nd form *drank* is used in the **past** tense.
The 3rd form *drunk* is the **past participle**.
The 4th form *drinking* is the *ING* form.

Remember: For some irregular verbs, the past-tense form and the past participle are the same. For others, they're different.

Exercise 11.3 Look up these verbs in your dictionary, and write in the verb forms you find there. **Do not guess.** If you don't have your dictionary, don't go on until you do have it.

		past tense	past participle	*ING* form
1.	SEE	_____	_____	_____
2.	GO	_____	_____	_____
3.	BUY	_____	_____	_____
4.	PAY	_____	_____	_____
5.	HAVE	_____	_____	_____

Exercise 11.4 Fill in the past participle of the given main verb. For help, use your dictionary.

1. GO   By the end of the 1970s, sales of American cars / <u>had</u>

                  _____ down.

2. TAKE   Before we knew it, Japan / <u>had</u> _____ the lead.

3. CHOOSE   For years, American companies / <u>had</u> _____ to ignore

                  the problem.

4. DO   Congress / still <u>hasn't</u> _____ much about it.

5. RISE   Prices / <u>have</u> _____ , and profits / <u>have</u>

    SHRINK   _____ .

6. TEACH   This shift in the balance of trade / <u>has</u> _____ us some

                  harsh lessons.

7. HAVE   We / <u>have</u> _____ to change our ways.

Remember: Don't confuse the past participle of a verb with its past-tense form.

Exercise 11.5 Fill in the past-tense form and the past participle of the given verb. For help, use your dictionary.

1. SEE   In the early 1990s, we / _____ big changes in Eastern

                  Europe.

                  We / <u>have</u> _____ more big changes recently.

2.   BECOME   In 1990, the two Germanys / once more _____ one

nation.

Before that, several countries with Communist governments / <u>had</u>

_____ democracies.

3.   BREAK   Soon the Baltic States / _____ away from the Soviet

Union.

By the end of 1991, the Soviet Union / <u>had</u> _____ up.

2.   To form the past participle of <u>regular</u> verbs, add *D* or *ED*.

WALK   I / <u>walked</u> to work today.
              I / <u>have walked</u> to work every day this week.
                  Walked is both the past-tense form and the past participle of *WALK*.

Exercise 11.6 Write in the appropriate forms of these verbs.

	past tense	past participle	*ING* form
1. TALK	_____	_____	_____
2. SMILE	_____	_____	_____
3. EXPECT	_____	_____	_____

Exercise 11.7 Fill in the past participle form of the given main verb.

1.   LEARN   Doctors / <u>have</u> _____ how to save premature babies.

2.   PREVENT   Modern medicine / <u>has</u> _____ many childhood diseases.

3.   DECREASE   Infant mortality / <u>has</u> dramatically _____ .

Exercise 11.8 This paragraph contains errors in verb phrases with *HAVE*. (1) Underline each verb phrase, and double underline the main verb. (2) Correct each error in the space above the line. The first sentence has been done for you.

                                                       terrorized

Over the centuries, triskaidekaphobia—the fear of the number 13—<u>has terrorize</u> many

people and caused them to act in strange ways. In all ages and in all countries, people have refuse to hold celebrations on the 13th of the month, and in some societies, they have even

drown children born on this evil day. Recently, architects have learn to deal with

triskaidekaphobia by giving the number 14 to the floor after 12. In this way, also, hospitals have

trick patients into accepting beds on the 13th floor. Yet despite this superstition, for almost two

centuries Americans have saluted a flag with 13 stripes, and immigrants have flock to pledge

allegiance to it from all over the world.

3. **Some verb forms need spelling changes before adding an ending to form a past participle.**

If a verb ends in a <u>consonant</u> + *Y*, change the *Y* to *I* before adding *ED*.

If a verb ends in a <u>single vowel</u> + a <u>single consonant</u>, double the consonant before adding *ED*.

Exercise 11.9 Fill in the appropriate form of the given main verb.

1. OCCUR   Some serious accidents / <u>have</u> _____ in my apartment

building this winter.

2. SLIP   Several elderly tenants / <u>have</u> _____ on icy sidewalks.

3. APPLY   They / <u>have</u> _____ to the landlord for compensation.

4. DENY   He / <u>has</u> _____ any responsibility.

5. PLAN   The tenants organization / <u>has</u> _____ a protest meeting

for next week.

Remember: In verb phrases, the helping verb, not the main verb, shows the tense.

11C. **Use verb phrases with the <u>present tense</u> of *HAVE* along with other present-tense verbs.**

Use verb phrases with the <u>past tense</u> of *HAVE* along with other past-tense verbs.

Verb phrases with the **present tense** of *HAVE* mean that something began in the past and is still happening or is still true in the present.

DRIVE   We / <u>are driving</u> to San Diego.
               We / <u>have driven</u> 2,000 miles already.

> *Have driven* is a verb phrase with the present tense of the helping verb *HAVE*.
> This means that we started driving in the past, and now we are still driving.

Verb phrases with the **past tense** of *HAVE* mean that something happened or was true in the past, before something else happened.

DRIVE   Last month, we / <u>were driving</u> to San Diego.
               We / <u>had driven</u> 2,000 miles before the car <u>broke</u> down.

> *Had driven* is a verb phrase with the past tense of *HAVE*.
> This means that we drove that far in the past up until the time that the car broke down.

Exercise 11.10 Fill in the appropriate present-tense or past-tense forms of the helping verb *HAVE*. You might find it helpful to circle any time words and underline any other verbs.

1.   LIKE   Pilar / _____ <u>liked</u> Rafael for six months, and she still does.

                   Pilar / _____ <u>liked</u> Tomas, until she saw him with Emilia.

2.   BE   Ruby and Dee / _____ <u>been</u> friends for years; they live

                   next door to one another.

                   Ruby and Vikki / _____ <u>been</u> best friends until Vikki

                   married Ruby's brother.

3.   TAKE   Stavros / _____ <u>taken</u> the bus to work every day this week.

                   Stavros / _____ <u>taken</u> his bicycle to work, until the

                   weather became colder.

Exercise 11.11 (1) Underline each one-word verb and verb phrase. Double underline the main verb in each verb phrase:

     My sister is in the kitchen. She has been there for less than an hour. She has
     baked two pies already. She plans to make two more.

(2) Rewrite the paragraph, changing *My sister is* to *My sister was*, and making whatever other changes are necessary. (3) Mark your rewritten paragraph in the same way.

_____

_____

_____

Exercise 11.12 (1) Underline each one-word verb and verb phrase. Double underline the main verb in each verb phrase:

> Russ was in the garage. He had been there all afternoon. He had changed only one snow tire. He was too tired to finish the job.

(2) Rewrite the paragraph, changing *Russ was* to *Russ is*, and making whatever other changes are necessary.
(3) Mark your rewritten paragraph in the same way.

_____

_____

_____

RULES SUMMARY, Part 1

In the longer one-page exercises that follow, you'll practice applying all the rules which you've learned or reviewed in this module. Before you go on to the longer exercises, check your understanding by filling in the blanks in the **Rules Summary** below. Fill in the blanks from memory, thinking carefully about what each rule means. If you need help, look back again at the **Rules**.

1. *HAVE* can be either a _____ verb or a _____

    verb in a verb phrase.

2. The present-tense form of *HAVE* that agrees with a singular subject is _____ .

3. With the helping verb *HAVE*, use the _____ _____

    of the main verb.

4. To form the past participle of most _____ verbs, change the whole word.

5. To form the past participle of regular verbs, add _____ or _____ .

6. In verb phrases, the _____ verb, not the main verb, shows **tense**.

7. Use verb phrases with the _____ tense of *HAVE* to mean that something

    began in the past and is still happening or is still true in the present.

8. Use verb phrases with the _____ tense of *HAVE* to mean that something

    happened or was true in the past, before something else happened.

Now turn to the **Answers** to check your work. Use these **Rules** and your dictionary as you go on to do the longer exercises that follow.

Module 11: *More about Verb Phrases*

PRACTICE, Part 1

Exercise 11.13   **Number of Mistakes** _____

(1) Rewrite each sentence, using the given time words, and changing each verb as appropriate. (2) In your rewritten sentences, underline each one-word verb and verb phrase. Double underline the main verb in each verb phrase. Draw a slash between the subject part and the verb part of every sentence. Follow this model:

Now, Charles acts on Broadway.

Last year, <u>Charles/ acted on Broadway.</u>

For the past year, <u>Charles / has acted on Broadway.</u>

Until he broke his arm, <u>Charles / had acted on Broadway.</u>

1.   Every day, Minnie drives to work.

Last week, _____

For the past month, _____

Until she wrecked her car, _____

2.   This year, Pedro is the store manager.

Last year, _____

For the last five years, _____

Before the store was closed, _____

3.   Noreen reads romance magazines and writes in her diary.

Last month, _____

For the last six months, _____

Until she eloped, _____

Exercise 11.14   **Number of Mistakes** _____

(1) Underline each verb:

> Every day Charlene makes her rounds as a traffic patrol officer. She checks
> parking meters, and she writes tickets for violators. Drivers often are angry with her. But
> Charlene never relents, for she is proud of her reputation as a heartless meter maid.

(2) Rewrite the paragraph, using the given time words, and changing each verb as appropriate. For help, look back at Exercise 11.13. (3) In your rewritten paragraphs, underline each one-word verb and verb phrase. Double underline the main verb in each verb phrase. Draw a slash between the subject part and the verb part of every sentence.

1. <u>Last week,</u> _____

   _____

   _____

   _____

   _____

2. <u>For the last six months,</u> _____

   _____

   _____

   _____

   _____

3. <u>Until a driver attacked her,</u> _____

   _____

   _____

   _____

   _____

Exercise 11.15   **Number of Mistakes** _____

(1) Underline each verb:

Every morning at 11 AM, Heinrich Count von Schlegel visits the west bank of the
blue Danube. His neighbors notice that, at almost the same hour, Frau Hilde
Hindenberg, the banker's widow, goes to the same spot. Behind their shuttered
windows these nosy neighbors whisper about the count and the widow. But all this
gossip is nonsense. Each time these two go to the embankment, they sit about three
meters apart. The widow closes her eyes for a snooze. The count waits for her first
snore before he rolls up his pants to the knee for a sunbath. Then he buries his head in
a book, while she snores gently on. If he feels the slightest interest in her plump form,
he certainly never gives any sign of it.

(2) Rewrite the paragraph, using the time words *For the last seven years*, and changing the verbs into
verb phrases with the helping verb *HAVE*. For help, look back at Exercise 11.13 and Exercise 11.14.
(3) In your rewritten paragraph, underline each one-word verb and verb phrase. Double underline the main
verb in each verb phrase. Your first sentence will begin like this: *For the last seven years, every morning at 11
AM, Heinrich Count von Schlegel has visited* . . . .

_____

_____

_____

_____

_____

_____

_____

_____

_____

_____

_____

_____

Module 11: *More about Verb Phrases*

RULES, Part 2: Verb Phrases with *DO* and Modals

11D. With the helping verb *DO*, use the <u>base form</u> of the main verb.

GO   Daryl / <u>did</u> not <u>go</u> out last night.
                   Go is the base form of the main verb *GO*.

Remember: In verb phrases, helping verbs show agreement and tense.

            Use verb phrases with the helping verb *DO* to make a statement **negative**, or to **ask a question**.

Exercise 11.16 Fill in the appropriate forms of the helping verb *DO* and the given main verb. Be sure to make the helping verb agree with its subject and show the correct tense. You might find it helpful to circle any time words and underline any other verbs. Follow this model:

     WATCH   When Ignatius stays home, he / __*does*__ not __*watch*__
                         sports on television.

1. TRY   _____ they _____ to find summer jobs last year?

2. HAVE   After Delma pays her bills, she / usually _____ not

                   _____ enough money left to buy lunch.

3. FEEL   _____n't most people _____ nervous when they see a black cat?

Remember: Check your work as you go along, using the Answers in the back of the book.

Important: Never use a past participle in a verb phrase with *DO*.

                                ✗
     WASH   Bette / <u>did</u> not <u>washed</u> the dishes.
                Bette / <u>did</u> not <u>wash</u> the dishes.
                     Using a past participle with the helping verb *DO* is incorrect.

Exercise 11.17 Fill in the appropriate form of the given main verb.

1. LIVE   My uncle / <u>had</u> _____ in this neighborhood for years.

                  He / <u>doesn't</u> _____ here any more.

2. TRY   I / <u>have</u> _____ to be reasonable.

                  But you / <u>don't</u> even _____ .

3. USE   Daisy still / <u>doesn't</u> _____ a typewriter.

                  Her sister / <u>has</u> _____ a word processor for two years now.

4. BOTHER   Nothing / <u>had</u> ever _____ Marsha except her husband's

                  smoking.

                  It / <u>didn't</u> even _____ her that he left his wet towels on

                  the bathroom floor.

5. STOP   I / <u>have</u> always carefully _____ for a yellow light.

                  One time I / <u>didn't</u> _____ , and of course I got a ticket.

11E.   Nine special helping verbs are called <u>modals</u>.

Here are the nine modal helping verbs which you learned in Module 5:

will	can	shall	may	must
would	could	should	might	

The most common modal helping verb is *will*, which is used for the future tense.

WATCH   They / <u>will watch</u> the game next Monday night.
                 Will watch is a verb phrase in the future tense.

The other modal helping verbs show various shades of meaning.

FIX   Don / <u>can fix</u> your car for you.
                 Can suggests **ability**.

FINISH   I / <u>must finish</u> this job by tonight.
                 Must suggests **obligation**.

Memorize the nine modal helping verbs, and then test your memory by writing them here:

_____   _____   _____   _____   _____

_____   _____   _____   _____

Exercise 11.18 Notice how modal verb phrases are used. (1) Underline each verb phrase, and double underline the main verb. Don't underline any interrupting words. (2) Draw a slash between the subject part and the verb part. Follow this model:

HELP	The mechanic / would not <u>help</u> me.

1. SEE   You will see us tomorrow.

2. ACCEPT   Alvin may not accept your nomination.

3. PAINT   I might not paint my house until spring.

4. MEET   You simply must meet Mr. Fowler.

5. REMEMBER   We shall always remember this occasion.

6. FIND   Deitra couldn't ever find that committee list.

7. FORGET   Felix can never forget the past.

8. LEAVE   You should not leave the scissors on that table.

||| **1.   Modal helping verbs do not have different forms to agree with their subjects.**

STOP   He / <u>must stop</u> now.
                     They / <u>must stop</u> now.
> *Must* is used with both singular and plural subjects.

Exercise 11.19 Fill in the appropriate form of the given modal helping verb.

1. CAN   Your brother / _____ <u>borrow</u> my motorcycle.

                    Your brothers / _____ <u>borrow</u> my motorcycle.

2. WOULD   They / _____ <u>appreciate</u> a card or a letter.

                    She / _____ <u>appreciate</u> a card or a letter.

3.   MIGHT   Alice / _____ <u>need</u> more time.

Alice and Ray / _____ <u>need</u> more time.

||| **2.   With modal helping verbs, use the <u>base form</u> of the main verb.**

LIKE   I / <u>would like</u> some more fruit.
GO   Luz / <u>should go</u> to the eye doctor.
                      Like and *go* are base forms of *LIKE* and *GO*.

Exercise 11.20 Fill in the appropriate form of the given modal helping verb and main verb.

1.   CAN   COMPLETE   You / _____ _____ this form at your convenience.

2.   WILL   ANSWER   No one / _____ _____ my question.

3.   SHOULD STAY   Aaron / _____ _____ until two o'clock.

4.   SHALL   OVERCOME   We / _____ _____ all obstacles in our path.

5.   MIGHT   ARRIVE   Raul / _____ _____ early.

||| **3.   Modal helping verbs do not have past-tense forms. But *could* is often used as the past tense of *can*, and *would* is often used as the past tense of *will*.**

THINK   I / <u>think</u> that he <u>can do</u> it if he <u>will try</u>.
                      These verbs suggest the present tense.

I / <u>thought</u> that he <u>could do</u> it if he <u>would try</u>.
                      These verbs suggest the past tense.

Exercise 11.21 Fill in the appropriate modal helping verb. You might find it helpful to circle any time words and underline any other verbs.

1.   can / could   I think that I _____ do it.

I thought that I _____ do it.

2.   will / would   By this afternoon we _____ be ready to go.

We promised an hour ago that we _____ be ready to go by 3 PM.

3.   can / could   Last year, students _____ not major in business at that school.

                          This year, they _____ major in business or computers.

||| **4.   Be careful not to leave out the modal helping verbs *will* and *would*.**

                          ✗
BE   I be home for Christmas.
                          ✗
HAVE   I rather have Ms. Goldfarb for my teacher.
                              These sentences are incorrect because the helping verbs have been left out.

BE   I / <u>will be</u> home for Christmas.
                          I / <u>'ll be</u> home for Christmas.
HAVE   I / <u>would</u> rather <u>have</u> Ms. Goldfarb for my teacher.
                          I / <u>'d</u> rather <u>have</u> Ms. Goldfarb for my teacher.
                              These sentences are correct.

Exercise 11.22 These sentences are incorrect. (1) Rewrite each sentence, correcting it by including the missing helping verb *will* or *would*. (2) Rewrite each sentence a second time, contracting the verb phrase. (3) Mark your rewritten sentences like this:

She rather go shopping.

She / would rather go shopping.

She'/d rather go shopping.

1.   She prefer not to talk about that.

_____

_____

2.   He be there before midnight.

_____

_____

3.   They rather fight than switch.

_____

_____

4.   I be home soon.

_____

_____

5.   We rather take our time.

_____

_____

RULES SUMMARY, Part 2

In the longer one-page exercises that follow, you'll practice applying all the rules which you've learned or reviewed in this module. Before you go on to the longer exercises, check your understanding by filling in the blanks in the Rules Summary below. Fill in the blanks from memory, thinking carefully about what each rule means. If you need help, look back again at the Rules.

1.   With the helping verb *DO*, use the _____ form of the main verb.

2.   Never use a _____ _____ in a verb phrase

      with *DO*.

3.   The nine special helping verbs called modals are:

      _____   _____   _____   _____   _____

      _____   _____   _____   _____

4.   Modals don't have different forms to _____ with their subjects.

5.   With modal helping verbs, use the _____ - _____

      of the main verb.

6.   Modal helping verbs don't have _____ -tense forms. But *could* is often used

      as the past tense of _____ , and *would* is often used as the past tense of

      _____ .

Now turn to the Answers to check your work. Use these Rules and your dictionary as you go on to do the longer exercises that follow.

Module 11: *More about Verb Phrases*

PRACTICE, Part 2

Exercise 11.23   **Number of Mistakes** _____

(1) Underline each verb:

> On the first of the month, Kim always balances her checkbook. She pays all her
> bills, and she plans her budget. Then she writes a letter to her father and asks him for
> money.

(2) Rewrite the paragraph, using the given time words, and changing each verb as appropriate. (3) In your rewritten paragraphs, underline each one-word verb and verb phrase. Double underline the main verb in each verb phrase.

1. <u>On last October 1, Kim balanced her checkbook.</u> _____

     _____

     _____

     _____

2. <u>On the first of the month ever since she left home, Kim has balanced her checkbook.</u> ____

     _____

     _____

     _____

3. <u>Every month until she lost her job, Kim had balanced her checkbook.</u> _____

     _____

     _____

     _____

4. <u>Tomorrow, Kim should balance her checkbook.</u> _____

     _____

     _____

     _____

Exercise 11.24   **Number of Mistakes** _____

(1) Underline each one-word verb and verb phrase:

> Mickey has been a very satisfactory child. As an infant, he would eat his cereal. At two, he could feed himself. At four, he could tie his shoelaces. Now at six, Mickey is the star pupil in the first grade. He reads well and is very good at arithmetic. His teacher pastes gold stars on his papers. Furthermore, he can draw, he can sing, and he knows when to keep quiet. Mickey is a winner, and he even seems to know it. His parents are proud of him. Mention his name. They will beam with delight.

(2) Rewrite the paragraph in the negative, contracting *not* with the one-word verb or helping verb.
(3) In your rewritten paragraph, underline each one-word verb and verb phrase. Double underline the main verb in each verb phrase. Don't underline any interrupting words. Your first sentence will begin like this: *Mickey hasn't been a very. . . .*

_____

_____

_____

_____

_____

_____

_____

_____

_____

_____

_____

_____

_____

_____

_____

Exercise 11.25   **Number of Mistakes** _____

(1) Underline each one-word verb and verb phrase:

> Geraldine wanted to lose weight. She planned exactly what food she would buy,
> and how much of it. She had even memorized the layout of the supermarket, because
> she knew that if she could stay away from the ice cream and candy, she would lose five
> pounds in one week. She said that she was going to stick to her diet until she could get
> into every outfit which was hanging in her closet, especially those velvet slacks which
> she hadn't been able to wear for years. But, of course, Geraldine had made these plans
> before. Her friends didn't think that she would actually lose a pound.

(2) Rewrite the paragraph in the present tense, changing *Geraldine wanted* to *Geraldine wants*, and making whatever other changes are necessary. (3) In your rewritten paragraph, underline each one-word verb and verb phrase. Double underline the main verb in each verb phrase. Don't underline any interrupting words. Your first sentence will begin like this: *Geraldine <u>wants</u> to lose weight. She <u>plans</u> . . . .*

_____

_____

_____

_____

_____

_____

_____

_____

_____

_____

_____

_____

_____

_____

Exercise 11.26   **Number of Mistakes** _____

These sentences contain errors in verb phrases. (1) Underline each one-word verb and verb phrase. Double underline the main verb in each verb phrase. Don't underline any interrupting words. (2) Correct each error in the space above the line. (3) Put a caret (^) if a helping verb has been omitted, and write the missing word in the space above the line. Follow this model:

> Rocco doesn't needs help; he rather rely on himself.

1. We knew that last year Einar had hope to get a larger apartment, but now he has gave up on it.

2. We have did this so often that it have almost become a habit.

3. Old Mrs. Benson had went to the play, but she did not stayed for the second act.

4. Homer don't ever drink alcoholic beverages; he rather have soda pop.

5. Several students in this course have taking journalism before, or have work for the student newspaper.

6. After deregulation, the price of plane tickets didn't dropped as much as the airlines had promise.

7. Our deadline for filing applications have now been extended.

8. The Governor have asked the State Assembly to cut the budget because he had solemnly promise in his

   campaign never to raise taxes.

9. We must remembers to turn out the lights before we leave; Irma didn't remembered, and she has recently

   receive an enormous electric bill.

10. My father has study Chinese history in a local college ever since he returned from his trip to China.

11. He rather study the Chinese language, but the college doesn't offered it.

Exercise 11.27   **Number of Mistakes** _____

This paragraph contains errors in one-word verbs and in verb phrases with *HAVE*. (1) Underline each one-word verb and verb phrase. Double underline the main verb in each verb phrase. (2) Correct each error in the space above the line. The first sentence has been done for you.

In 1981, President Reagan chose Dr. C. Everett Koop as Surgeon General of the United States

because he had openly oppose [*opposed*] abortion. But once the Senate had confirm his appointment, this

conservative doctor astonish everyone. The President had ask him to write a report showing that

abortion was harmful to women's health. Koop believe that abortion was morally wrong, but, when

he study the evidence, he seen that it failed to prove that abortion necessarily caused physical or

psychological damage to women. So he explain to the President that he, as an honest scientist,

could not write this report. Then he turn his attention to smoking and AIDS. The Administration

had not express much interest in these problems, but, according to Koop, they was health hazards

which the Surgeon General's office could and should do something about. Within a few years, his

warnings on cigarette packages had catched the attention of every smoker, and many had kick the

habit. Next, his report on AIDS show that for the first time someone in the government had taken

the deadly virus seriously. He strongly encourage early sex education and the use of condoms. The

Administration was angry, and the liberals was happy. Both said that he had change. Koop

answered mildly that he had not budge from his original position on any issue. By the time he leave

office in 1989, many of his early opponents had turned into supporters, and some of his former

supporters claim that he had betray them. In TV interviews after his retirement, Dr. Koop insisted

that his views had never altered. The problem, he said, was that no one had bother to learn what his

convictions really was in the first place.

Important: This paragraph contained 22 errors, not counting the one that was corrected for you. How many did you find? _____ If you did not find all 22, try again before you check your work.

Module 11: *More about Verb Phrases*

RULES, Part 3: Passive Verb Phrases

||||| **11F.**   Sentences may be either <u>active</u> or <u>passive</u>.

A sentence is **active** when the subject is doing the action of the verb. Most sentences are active.

EAT

           S
Eva / <u>eats</u> apples.
           S
Eva / <u>ate</u> an apple.
           S
Eva / <u>is eating</u> an apple.
           S
Eva / <u>will eat</u> an apple.

> Eva is doing the eating in these active sentences.

A sentence is **passive** when the action of the verb is happening to the subject. Usually a group of words with *by* tells who is doing or was doing the action.

EAT

           S
The apple / <u>was eaten</u> by Eva.

> The eating happened to the apple in this passive sentence.
> *By Eva* tells who did the eating.

Exercise 11.28 Write in ACTIVE if the sentence is active (and the subject is doing the action) or PASSIVE if the sentence is passive (and the action is happening to the subject).

1.   A small committee / <u>planned</u> the conference.   _____

     The conference / <u>was planned</u> by a small committee.   _____

2.   Dr. Hermann / <u>will teach</u> the Business 400 seminar.   _____

     The Business 400 seminar / <u>is taught</u> by Dr. Hermann.   _____

3.   George / <u>decorated</u> that cake.   _____

     That cake / <u>was decorated</u> by George.   _____

4.   The shortstop / <u>was throwing</u> the ball.   _____

     The ball / <u>was thrown</u> too late.   _____

5. Those packages / usually <u>are</u> <u>delivered</u> by UPS.   _____

    UPS / <u>has</u> not <u>delivered</u> those packages yet.   _____

Remember: Check your work as you go along, using the Answers in the back of the book.

1. For an <u>active</u> sentence with the helping verb *BE*, use the *ING* form of the main verb.

> CHECK   An immigration official / <u>is checking</u> our luggage.
> > *Checking* is the *ING* form of *CHECK*.

2. For <u>passive</u> sentences, use the helping verb *BE* with the past participle of the main verb.

Passive verb phrases with the **present** tense of the helping verb *BE* tell what is usually happening or true.

> CHECK   Our luggage / <u>is</u> usually <u>checked</u> by an immigration official.
> > This is a passive sentence with the present tense of the helping verb *BE*.
> > *Checked* is the past participle of *CHECK*.

Passive verb phrases with the **past** tense of the helping verb *BE* tell what happened or was true in the past.

> CHECK   Our luggage / <u>was checked</u> by an immigration official.
> > This is a passive sentence with the past tense of the helping verb *BE*.
> > *Checked* is the past participle of *CHECK*.

Remember: To make the past participle of most **irregular** verbs, change the whole word.

> STRIKE   The house / <u>was struck</u> by lightning.
> > *Struck* is the past participle of the irregular verb *STRIKE*.

Exercise 11.29 Fill in the appropriate form of the given main verb in these passive sentences.

1. LOSE   Lots of money / <u>is</u> _____ on Wall Street every day.

2. CATCH   Sardines / <u>are</u> _____ in nets.

3. BREAK   His windshield / <u>was</u> _____ by a rock.

Remember: To make the past participle of **regular** verbs, add *D* or *ED*.

> PRESENT   The play / <u>was presented</u> Off-Broadway.
> > *Presented* is the past participle of regular *PRESENT*.

Exercise 11.30 Fill in the appropriate form of the given main verb in these passive sentences.

1. PERFORM   Every day the same routine tasks / <u>are</u> _____ by dozens

                   of workers.

2. USE   That old trunk / <u>is</u> now _____ as a coffee table.

3. ANNOY   Emily / <u>was</u> _____ by that remark.

Remember: The helping verb *BE* must agree with its subject in both the present tense and the past tense.

> DESIGN   Those dresses / <u>are designed</u> by Ellis.
> Those dresses / <u>were designed</u> by Ellis.
> *Are* and *were* agree with the plural subject *dresses*.

Exercise 11.31 Fill in the appropriate form of the helping verb *BE* and of the given main verb in these passive sentences. You might find it helpful to circle any time words and underline any other verbs.

1. CARRY   Nowadays the supplies / _____ usually _____

                  by trucks.

                  Ten years ago the supplies / _____ _____

                  by trains.

2. FASCINATE   When I was a child, I / _____ _____ by

                  complicated puzzles.

                  I / _____ still _____ by puzzles that are

                  hard to solve.

3. INFLUENCE   These days teenagers / _____ often _____

                  by peer pressure.

                  In the past, teenagers / _____ _____ by their

                  families as much as by their friends.

Important: Don't confuse **active** sentences and **passive** sentences.

In an **active** sentence, the subject is doing the action. In active sentences with the helping verb *BE*, use the *ING* form of the main verb.

In a **passive** sentence, the action is happening to the subject. In passive sentences, use the past participle of the main verb with the helping verb *BE*. Often a group of words with *by* tells who is doing the action.

Exercise 11.32 Fill in the appropriate form of the given main verb in these active and passive sentences.

1.   DRIVE   We / <u>were</u> _____ our cars to the airport.

   My mother / <u>was</u> _____ to the airport by my cousin.

2.   EAT   Iris / <u>is</u> _____ the last crumb of pie.

   That entire pie / <u>was</u> _____ by just two people.

3.   TAKE   We / <u>are</u> _____ our places now.

   This seat / <u>is</u> already _____ by my wife.

4.   GROW   All these vegetables / <u>were</u> _____ by my husband.

   This summer my husband / <u>is</u> _____ corn and peas.

5.   SHAKE   The trees / <u>were</u> _____ in the wind.

   The trees / <u>were</u> _____ by the wind.

Important: Sometimes the helping verb *GET* is used instead of *BE* in a passive sentence. *GET* is more informal than *BE* but is usually acceptable in writing.

   SNATCH   Many purses / <u>are snatched</u> in crowded streets during the holidays.
   Many purses / <u>get snatched</u> in crowded streets during the holidays.
   These two passive sentences both mean the same thing.

Exercise 11.33 Fill in the appropriate form of the helping verb *GET* and of the given main verb in these passive sentences. You might find it helpful to circle any time words and underline any other verbs.

1.   INJURE   Somebody / _____ _____ seriously every

   season playing football.

2.   PROMOTE   Benita / _____ _____ last month, so her

   friends gave her a party.

3.   ROB   Last night, Ali / _____ _____ in front of his

                     own house.

4.   PAY   Miss Ecklestein / _____ _____ much less

                     than she deserves.

5.   SENTENCE   The arsonists / _____ _____ to a long

                     prison term after a very short trial.

6.   DIVORCE   Basil and Vera / _____ _____ just two

     MARRY   months after they _____ _____ .

Important: Be careful not to leave the *D* ending off the past participles *used* and *supposed*. When a regular past participle is followed by the word *to*, you won't hear the past participle ending pronounced. But it's incorrect to write a regular past participle without the *D* ending.

                                      ✗
     USE   I / <u>am use</u> to the noise.
                      I / <u>am used</u> to the noise.
                          Used is the correct past participle of *USE*.

Exercise 11.34 Fill in the appropriate form of the helping verb *BE* and of the given main verb in these passive sentences. You might find it helpful to circle any time words and underline any other verbs.

1.   USE   Now that they have lived in the tropics for ten years, they /

                      _____ _____ to the heat.

2.   SUPPOSE   Next year, food prices / _____

                      _____ to rise again.

3.   USE   Cordelia / _____ _____

                      to her father's bad temper, so she hardly notices it any more.

4.   SUPPOSE   The painter / _____

                      _____ to finish this job yesterday.

5.   USE   We / _____ _____ to

                      getting our own way when we were young.

RULES SUMMARY, Part 3

In the longer one-page exercises that follow, you'll practice applying all the rules which you've learned or reviewed in this module. Before you go on to the longer exercises, check your understanding by filling in the blanks in the Rules Summary below. Fill in the blanks from memory, thinking carefully about what each rule means. If you need help, look back again at the Rules.

1. A sentence is _____ when the subject is doing the action of the verb. A

    sentence is _____ when the action of the verb is happening to the subject.

2. For an **active** sentence with the helping verb *BE*, use the _____ form of the

    main verb.

3. For **passive** sentences, use the helping verb *BE* with the _____

    _____ of the main verb.

4. The helping verb *BE* must _____ with its subject in both the present tense

    and the _____ tense.

5. Sometimes the helping verb _____ is used instead of *BE* in passive

    sentences.

6. Be careful not to leave the _____ ending off the past participles *used* and

    _____ .

Now turn to the Answers to check your work. Use these Rules and your dictionary as you go on to do the longer exercises that follow.

Module 11: *More about Verb Phrases*

PRACTICE, Part 3

Exercise 11.35   **Number of Mistakes** _____

Remember: In an **active** sentence, the subject is doing the action. The *ING* form of the main verb is used with the helping verb *BE*. In a **passive** sentence, the action is happening to the subject. Use the past participle of the main verb with the helping verb *BE*. Often a group of words with *by* tells who is doing the action.

Fill in the appropriate form of the given main verb in these active and passive sentences.

1. BEAT   Rosita / is _____ eggs for the meringue.

2. BEAT   The eggs / aren't yet _____ stiffly enough to add the sugar.

3. FRIGHTEN   Something / was _____ the animals.

4. FRIGHTEN   The animals / were _____ by something outside the house.

5. BE   Those children / are _____ suspiciously quiet.

6. SELECT   The leader / is _____ a date for the workshop.

7. GROW   The grass / was _____ so quickly that we had to mow
              the lawn twice a week.

8. FREEZE   The cold temperature / was _____ the road surfaces
              throughout a three-state area.

9. CHOOSE   All those candidates / were _____ for interviews by the
              committee.

10. MARRY   That couple / was _____ by a ship's captain.

11. WRITE   The students / were _____ essays about the book they
              had just discussed.

12. WRITE   This novel / was _____ by James Baldwin.

Exercise 11.36   **Number of Mistakes** _____

Remember: With the helping verb *HAVE*, use the past participle of the main verb.

These sentences contain errors in verb phrases. (1) Underline each one-word verb and verb phrase. Double underline the main verb in each verb phrase. Don't underline any interrupting words. (2) Correct each error in the space above the line. Follow this model:

              has   *taking*

    Horace <u>have told</u> June that she is <u>taken</u> too much time to get ready.

1. Last week, when Monique was driven her car through town at 50 miles an hour, she was overtaking by a

    patrol car and given a ticket.

2. Silver is tarnish by exposure to air, so Heloise has store all her silverware in plastic bags.

3. I'm not yet use to digital clocks and watches, even though they have been common for more than a

    decade.

4. My sister was suppose to go back to work on Monday, but instead she is taken another week off.

5. During the winter the pipes had froze, and the floor was ruin by the water.

6. Professor Parnell was talking to each of his students while they was writing their papers.

7. Kip is being difficult these days, and his parents are annoy by his attitude.

8. When Cecil and Jerilyn got marry last May, they was given a large check by his parents.

9. Chadwick has being sick for several weeks, so he has not did as much work as he was suppose to.

10. Too many couples get divorce before they has really tried to solve their problems.

Exercise 11.37   **Number of Mistakes** _____

This paragraph contains the base forms of verbs in capital letters. (1) Rewrite the paragraph, changing each base form into the appropriate form. **Make no other changes.** (2) In your rewritten paragraph, underline each one-word verb and verb phrase. Double underline the main verb in each verb phrase. Circle each infinitive. Your paragraph will begin like this: *Every culture <u>forbids</u> people ⟨to perform⟩ certain acts which <u>are</u> <u>called</u> . . .*

      Every culture FORBID people to PERFORM certain acts which BE CALL taboos. Some modern taboos BE not always CONSIDER evil in the past. In ancient Egypt, royal siblings often GET MARRY to each other. American Indian warriors USE to EAT the hearts of enemies that they HAVE KILL, to SHOW respect for their courage. Now both incest and cannibalism HAVE BECOME almost universal taboos. We BE HORRIFY by incest. And if anyone EAT human flesh today, that person BE CONDEMN as a monster. In 1972 a famous plane crash in the Andes ILLUSTRATE how strongly this taboo BE FEEL in modern times. Although some survivors KEEP themselves alive by eating the bodies of the passengers who HAVE PERISH in the crash, the taboo against cannibalism BE too strong for most of them. Instead they CHOOSE to DIE of starvation.

_____

_____

_____

_____

_____

_____

_____

_____

_____

_____

_____

_____

_____

_____

Exercise 11.38

This paragraph contains errors in verbs and verb phrases. (1) Underline each one-word verb and verb phrase. Double underline the main verb in each verb phrase. Don't underline any interrupting words. (2) Correct each error in the space above the line. The first sentence has been done for you.

began

Since my wife and I <u>begun</u> to do crossword puzzles together, we <u>have <u>bought</u></u> a lot of reference

books, including a new edition of *The Guinness Book of World Records*. This book has certainly help

us with our puzzles, but it have also been a source of fascinating information. It don't just tell about

recent sports records. Each edition try to include every amazing and amusing feat of the human

race. Here are some we will always remember: (1) Although Strombo the Maniac has establish the

longest official record of 65 hours for lying on a bed of nails, that record was totally demolish by

Silki the Fakir, who done the same thing for 111 days—but only his followers saw him do it. (2)

Lightning has strucked one living man seven times—Roy Sullivan, a Shenandoah park ranger. His

body was hit in five different places, and twice his head was burn bald. (3) Steve Weldon of Texas

has ate the longest meal in the shortest time: 100 yards of spaghetti in 28 seconds. (4) By the time

he died in 597 AD, St. Simon Stylites had chalk up the all-time pole-sitting record: 45 years on top

of a stone pillar. (5) And what book has selled the most copies in the past 25 years? *The Guinness*

Book of World Records, of course!

Important: This paragraph contained 12 errors, not counting the one that was corrected for you. How many did you find? _____ If you didn't find all 12, try again before you check your work.

Exercise 11.39   Number of Mistakes _____

Review Exercise G: Verb Agreement, Past-Tense Verbs, Verb Phrases

This paragraph contains errors in verbs and verb phrases. (1) Underline each one-word verb and verb phrase. Double underline the main verb in each verb phrase. Don't underline any interrupting words. (2) Correct each error in the space above the line. The first sentence has been marked for you.

My mother has often tried to tell me that crime do not pay. But then, my mother have never

run for office. I have never told her about what happen when I was a sophomore in high school. I

had campaign hard to be class president, and election day had finally arrive. Just before the vote was

taking, the teacher remind us, "Don't vote for yourself. Each student must writes down somebody

else's name on the ballot." But I was scare that I might lose the election by one vote. I knew that I

should not have did it, but when the slips was passed around, I voted for myself. I has never

forgotten the moment when the votes was all counted and the teacher said, "There are 31 votes for

Mary Williams and one vote for Ted Collins." As soon as the teacher announce the results, Ted

jumped up to say that I had not cast my vote for him. But then he sat down even more quickly. It

tooked me a day to figure out that Ted had voted for himself, too. He could not accuse me without

accusing himself. So even if I did committed a crime, on that occasion I wasn't punish. In fact, the

teacher even praise me because I had gave my vote to my opponent.

Important: This paragraph contained 18 errors, not counting the one that was corrected for you. How many did you find? _____   If you didn't find all 18, try again before you check your work.

Module 11: *More About Verb Phrases*

WRITING TEST

NAME _____

PURPOSE   To show that you can use verb phrases correctly, and that you can continue to apply what you have learned in previous modules.

ASSIGNMENT   Think of someone like a parent or grandparent, or another older person who has worked hard or has helped others all his or her life. Write that person's name here:

NAME: _____

Write a brief biography of that person, telling the effect he or she has had on others.

Check off each step in the writing process as you complete it.

GET READY   ❏   On scratch paper, write down as many details about the person as you can think of. Make sure you have plenty of ideas to show why you chose this person.

DRAFT   ❏   On scratch paper, write a rough draft of your biography. Try to write sentences that sound natural but aren't too complicated.

❏   Write one paragraph telling what the person has done over the years. In every sentence, use a verb phrase with *HAVE* (for example, *She has successfully raised three children*). **Write at least six sentences.**

❏   Write another paragraph telling how things are going for the person now. In every sentence, use a verb phrase with *BE* (for example, *She is now living in Florida* or *He was robbed on the street last month*). **Write at least six sentences.**

REVISE   ❏   Read over the draft of your biography to make sure that your ideas are clear and sound real. Try to anticipate what a reader will need to know in order to understand and believe what you have written. Add, take out, or change ideas, words, and sentences as necessary. Remember, it's good for a draft to become messy.

❏   After you have finished revising your ideas, underline each one-word verb and verb phrase. Double underline the main verb in each verb phrase.

❏   Count the verb phrases that you used, and write the number here: _____ .

EDIT   ❏   Review the Rules for this module. Find and correct any mistakes in verb phrases. Make sure that every verb is in the correct form and agrees (if necessary) with its subject.

Use your dictionary and the Rules for previous modules to find and correct any mistakes in:

❑   Nouns: Singular and Plural Forms
❑   Verbs: Tense and Agreement
❑   Sentences: Fragments and Run-Ons
❑   Spelling
❑   Writing Conventions
❑   Wrong Words

FINAL COPY   ❑   Write the final copy of your biography carefully, using blue or black ink and standard-sized (8½ by 11 inch) paper. Better yet, type or use a word processor. Write your name in the upper right-hand corner, or use whatever heading your instructor requires. Remember that you are now preparing your writing for a reader.

❑   Underline every verb in your final copy just as you did in your draft.

PROOFREAD   ❑   Read your final copy **out loud**. If you find any mistakes, it's OK to correct them neatly by hand. Or if you have used a word processor, go back and correct your mistakes, and then print out a clean final copy.

Attach your final copy to these instructions, and hand them both in.

12 Understanding Sentences III

NAME _____

As you complete each exercise, record your number of mistakes below.

PART 1

12.1 _____   12.7 _____   12.12 _____

12.2 _____   12.8 _____   Summary _____

12.3 _____   12.9 _____   12.13 _____

12.4 _____   12.10 _____   12.14 _____

12.5 _____   12.11 _____   12.15 _____

12.6 _____

PART 2

12.16 _____   12.20 _____   Summary _____

12.17 _____   12.21 _____   12.24 _____

12.18 _____   12.22 _____   12.25 _____

12.19 _____   12.23 _____

Review Exercise H _____

INSTRUCTOR'S COMMENTS

Instructions:

☐ Followed carefully
☐ Not followed carefully enough

Checking:

☐ Careful
☐ Not careful enough to catch all your mistakes
☐ Green pen not used for checking
☐ Entire correct answer not always written in

Writing Test:

☐ Excellent
☐ Good
☐ Acceptable
☐ Not yet satisfactory

Other:

Module 12: *Understanding Sentences III*

RULES, Part 1: Noun Expansion

Remember: Subjects and complements (and other nouns) can be expanded by words telling more about them, like WHICH? or WHAT KIND?

S   C

(Most)→students←(at this college) / <u>want</u> a (daycare)→center←(on campus).

> The noun *students* is the subject because it answers the question *WHO wants a daycare center?*
> *Most* and *at this college* are expansion telling WHICH students.
> The noun *center* is the complement because it answers the question *Students want WHAT?*
> *Daycare* and *on campus* are expansion telling WHAT KIND of center they want.

Exercise 12.1 (1) Put parentheses around expansion of the subject and around expansion of the complement. (2) Draw an arrow from the expansion to the word it expands. Follow this model:

(One) convenience (of modern life) / <u>is</u> (telephone) service.

1.   S   C

   Most families in the United States / <u>own</u> several television sets.

2.   S   C

   Inhabitants of large cities / <u>receive</u> many channels carried by cable networks.

3.   S   C

   People living in rural areas / <u>need</u> special equipment for TV reception.

Remember: Check your work as you go along, using the Answers in the back of the book.

12A. A special kind of noun expansion begins with the <u>expansion words</u> *who*, *which*, and *that*.

S   C

Most women / <u>like</u> men←(**who** are courteous).

> *Who are courteous* is expansion of the complement *men* in the base sentence. The expansion tells WHICH men.

Exercise 12.2 (1) Circle the expansion word *who*, *which*, or *that*, and put parentheses around the expansion. (2) Draw an arrow from the expansion to the noun it expands. Follow this model:

S   C

Vladimir / <u>has</u> a friend ((who) is studying law) .

1.   S   C

   I / <u>met</u> a woman who knew you in high school.

2.   S   C

   Coleen / <u>needs</u> an apartment which has at least two bedrooms.

3.   S   C

   Racism / <u>is</u> a problem that concerns us all.

Important: Expansion of the subject can be confusing because it interrupts a base sentence.

              S

Agencies ⟵(**which** provide free pre-natal care) / <u>save</u> lives and money.

        Agencies save lives and money is the base sentence.
        Which provide free pre-natal care is expansion telling WHICH agencies.

Exercise 12.3 (1) Circle the expansion word *who*, *which*, or *that*, and put parentheses around the expansion. (2) Draw an arrow from the expansion to the noun it expands. Follow this model:

                   S   C

   An athlete ⟵((who)takes steroids) / <u>is risking</u> his health.

1.   S

   New courses that explore cultural diversity / <u>are being offered</u>.

2.   S   C

   A subject which too many women students avoid / <u>is</u> mathematics.

3.   S   C

   People who learn to think optimistically / <u>may</u> actually <u>add</u> years to their lives.

Exercise 12.4 (1) Circle the expansion word, put parentheses around the expansion, and draw an arrow from the expansion to the noun it expands. (2) In the base sentence, do this: (a) Underline the verb. (b) Mark the subject with an S and the complement (if any) with a C. (c) Draw a slash between the subject part and the verb part. (3) Write in the base sentence. Then underline the verb, and draw a slash between the subject part and the verb part. Follow this model:

        S ⟵

Houses ((which) are priced right)/<u>sell</u> quickly.

Houses / <u>sell quickly</u>.

1.   A person who expects good results makes better decisions.

   _____

2.   The newspaper interviewed the community leaders who organized the boycott.

   _____

3.   The children told a story that their parents could hardly believe.

   _____

4.   Senior citizens who need long-term health care often become penniless.

_____

5.   A car which has special safety features gets a reduction on insurance.

_____

III   1.   This kind of noun expansion always contains a subject and a verb.

                                                   S   V

After a long search, Susan / finally <u>found</u> a job←(**which** she really loves).

> *Which she really loves* is expansion telling WHAT KIND of job Susan found.
> The expansion contains a subject, *she*, and a verb, *loves*.

Exercise 12.5 (1) Circle the expansion word, put parentheses around the expansion, and draw an arrow from the expansion to the noun it expands. (2) In the expansion, write S above the subject and V above the verb. Follow this model:

                                                          S   V

Hattie / <u>lost</u> the tape cassette ((that) she borrowed from Kevin) .

1.   My younger brother / <u>bought</u> a computer which he uses nearly every day.

2.   Gladys / <u>has</u> a nephew whom the whole family calls *Bubba*.

3.   The owl species that the scientists discovered / <u>was</u> nearly extinct.

III   2.   Noun expansion words are often subjects in the expansion they create.

                      S   V

Travelers←(**who** take charter flights) / <u>risk</u> delays or cancellations.

> *Who* is the subject of the verb *take* in the expansion *who take charter flights*.

                                               S   V

Since deregulation, the airlines / <u>have</u> new fares←(**which** are considerably more expensive).

> *Which* is the subject of the verb *are* in the expansion *which are considerably more expensive*.

Exercise 12.6 (1) Circle the expansion word, put parentheses around the expansion, and draw an arrow from the expansion to the noun it expands. (2) In the expansion, write S above the subject and V above the verb.

1.   The people who arrived late / <u>didn't</u> <u>seem</u> at all embarrassed.

2.   Dorcas's biology teacher / <u>assigned</u> two textbooks which cost at least $45 each.

3.   The only books that interest many teen-aged boys / <u>are</u> science fiction fantasies.

> ║║║║ **12B.   Noun expansion by itself is a <u>fragment</u>,
> even when it contains a subject and a verb.**

               S   V

✗ **(Which** helped her to figure out her taxes).

> *Which helped her to figure out her taxes* is expansion used by itself, without a base sentence. So it's a fragment, even though it contains a subject and a verb.

                              S   V

✗ A computer program◄─(**which** helped her to figure out her taxes).

> *Which helped her to figure out her taxes* is expansion used with a group of words that isn't a base sentence. So this is also a fragment, even though the expansion contains a subject and a verb.

                            S   V

Essie / <u>bought</u> a computer program◄─(**which** helped her to figure out her taxes).

> This sentence is correct because the expansion *which helped her to figure out her taxes* is used with the base sentence *Essie bought a computer program.*

Exercise 12.7 (1) Circle the expansion word, put parentheses around the expansion, and draw an arrow from the expansion to the noun it expands. (2) Write S and V above the subject and verb in the expansion. (3) If the group of words is a sentence, do this: (a) In the base sentence, underline the verb, and draw a slash between the subject part and the verb part. (b) Write in SENT. (4) If a group of words is a fragment, put an ✗ in front of it, and write in FRAG. Follow this model:

✗ People ((who)) drive too slowly) .   <u>FRAG</u>

People ((who)) drive too slowly)/<u>cause</u> accidents.   <u>SENT</u>

1.   An old Harley-Davidson motorcycle which Jake inherited

    from his uncle.   _____

    Jake drives an old Harley-Davidson motorcycle which he inherited

    from his uncle.   _____

2.   Neighbors avoid the young men who loiter in the hallways.   _____

    The young men who loiter in the hallways smoking and drinking beer.   _____

3.   Some children who cause trouble and demand attention.   _____

Some children who always cause trouble only want attention.   _____

Important: When *who* and *which* are expansion words, they can't start a sentence. A statement that starts with *who* or *which* is always a fragment.

✗ (**Who** had taught the course only once before).
✗ (**Which** I decided there and then to study).
These fragments are incorrect. *Who* and *which* are expansion words.

Who and *which* can start a sentence only when the sentence is a question.

Who is teaching accounting?
Which course did you want?
These questions are correct. *Who* and *which* are not expansion words.

Exercise 12.8 (1) Circle the expansion words *who* and *which* and put parentheses around the expansion. (2) If a group of words is a sentence, do this: (a) In the base sentence, or in any sentence without noun expansion, underline the verb. (b) In every sentence that is a statement, draw a slash between the subject part and the verb part. You cannot draw a slash in a question. (c) Write in SENT. (3) If a group of words is a fragment, put an ✗ in front of it and write in FRAG.

[1]Pattie is planning a surprise party for her   1 _____

husband. [2]Who is having a birthday next week.   2 _____

[3]All their friends will meet on Friday night at a   3 _____

local restaurant. [4]She's also inviting some   4 _____

of the people who work with him. [5]There are   5 _____

several restaurants in the neighborhood. [6]Which   6 _____

serve large parties. [7]Which one has she chosen?   7 _____

12C. Correct most fragments which begin with noun expansion words by connecting them to a base sentence.

The worker / <u>dropped</u> a rock. ✗ Which broke his toe.
The worker / <u>dropped</u> a rock⬑(**which** broke his toe).
> The fragment has been corrected by connecting it to the base sentence.

Exercise 12.9 (1) Circle the expansion word, put parentheses around the fragment it creates, and put an ✗ in front of the fragment. (2) Correct the fragment by connecting it to the appropriate noun in the base sentence. (3) Mark your rewritten sentence like this:

I lost the directions. ✗ (Ⓦhich) came with the invitation) .

I / lost the directions ((which) came with the invitation).

1.   This is a fact. Which almost everyone recognizes.

_____

2.   We all trust a person. Who tells the truth.

_____

3.   The two teenagers discovered a cave. That contained broken pottery and arrowheads.

_____

12D. Noun expansion words <u>combine</u> sentences by changing one sentence into expansion of the other.

Monroe / <u>scored</u> the point. It / <u>put</u> his team ahead.
Monroe / <u>scored</u> the point⬑(**which** put his team ahead).
> The expansion word *which* combines the two sentences by changing *It put his team ahead* into expansion telling WHICH point Monroe scored.

Important: Use noun expansion beginning with *who* to refer to **people**. Use noun expansion beginning with *which* or *that* to refer to **things**.

The surgeon⬑(**who** is performing my father's operation) / <u>asked</u> for a second opinion.
> *Who* is used here because the surgeon is a person.

He / <u>doesn't want</u> to perform an operation⬑(**which** isn't really necessary).
> *Which* is used here because an operation is a thing, not a person.

Important: In speech, we often hear noun expansion with *that* used to refer to a person as well as to a thing. However, in writing, it's better to use *who* to refer to a person.

✗

My father / <u>is</u> the person←(**that** always took care of me).
My father / <u>is</u> the person←(**who** always took care of me).
> Use *who* to refer to a person.

Exercise 12.10 (1) Combine each pair of sentences, using *who* or *which* to change the **second** sentence into expansion of the **first**. (2) Mark your rewritten sentence like this:

Janice comforted the child. He was hurt.

> Janice / comforted the child←((who) was hurt).

1. Donald did something. It bothered me.

   _____

2. Kalliope married a man. He was old enough to be her father.

   _____

3. The director made a film. It shocked the public.

   _____

Important: Noun expansion must directly follow the noun it expands. Sentences in which expansion doesn't directly follow the noun it expands are confusing and sometimes ridiculous.

✗

The man / <u>was driving</u> a truck←(**who** saw the accident).
> This sentence makes no sense, because *who saw the accident* incorrectly follows *truck*. The truck did not see the accident.

The man←(**who** saw the accident) / <u>was driving</u> a truck.
> This sentence makes sense, because *who saw the accident* correctly follows *man*, the noun it expands.

Exercise 12.11 These sentences are incorrect. (1) Circle the expansion word, put parentheses around the expansion, and draw an arrow from the expansion to the noun it expands. (2) Rewrite the sentence correctly. (3) Mark your rewritten sentence like this:

The bike had faulty brakes ((that) we borrowed) .

> The bike←((that) we borrowed) / had faulty brakes.

1. The canoe capsized in the rapids that Dudley repaired.

    _____

2. The cat brought home a dead bird which Luci adopted.

    _____

3. The doctor saved many patients who developed the new surgical procedure.

    _____

    _____

Exercise 12.12 (1) Combine each group of sentences, using *who* or *which* to change the **second and third** sentences into expansion of the first. (2) Mark your rewritten sentence like this:

> The woman received a trophy. She won the speed-skating race. The trophy was three feet tall.
>
> *The woman ((who) won the speed-skating race) / received a trophy ((which) was three feet tall).*

1. The police officer wore a bullet-proof vest. The officer was shot in the robbery. The vest saved his life.

    _____

    _____

2. Someone hates people. He loves movies. The people talk during the show.

    _____

    _____

3. The readings always treated controversial subjects. Our teacher assigned the readings. The subjects were

    in the news.

    _____

    _____

RULES SUMMARY, Part 1

In the longer one-page exercises that follow, you'll practice applying all the rules which you've learned or reviewed in this module. Before you go on to the longer exercises, check your understanding by filling in the blanks in the Rules Summary below. Fill in the blanks from memory, thinking carefully about what each rule means. If you need help, look back again at the Rules.

1. A special kind of noun expansion begins with the expansion words _____ , _____ ,

    and *that*.

2. Noun expansion beginning with *who*, *which*, and *that* always contains a

    _____ and a _____ .

3. The noun expansion words *who*, *which*, and *that* are often _____ in the

    expansion they create.

4. Even when noun expansion contains a subject and a verb, expansion by itself is a

    _____ .

5. Most fragments caused by noun expansion words can be corrected by _____

    them to a base sentence.

6. Noun expansion words _____ sentences by changing one sentence into

    _____ of the other.

7. Noun expansion must directly _____ the noun it expands.

Now turn to the Answers to check your work. Use these Rules and your dictionary as you go on to do the longer exercises that follow.

Module 12: *Understanding Sentences III*

PRACTICE, Part 1

Exercise 12.13   **Number of Mistakes** _____

This paragraph contains all correct sentences. (1) Put parentheses around expansion beginning with *who*, *which*, or *that*, and draw an arrow from the expansion to the noun it expands. (2) In the base sentence, or in any sentence without noun expansion, underline the verb, and draw a slash between the subject part and the verb part. Follow this model:

People (who do research)/<u>make</u> interesting discoveries.

Modern medicine now approves some of the folk remedies which our ancestors swore by.

In the past, doctors warned against old women who treated fever with willow bark. They merely

laughed at country druggists who recommended chicken soup for colds. But today many doctors

prescribe these remedies, which recent research shows to be effective. For centuries, people who

had heart trouble chewed foxglove. Digitalis, a modern drug which is widely used for heart

disease, comes from this herb. However, not all folk remedies are helpful. Movie cowboys who

gulp down a bottle of whiskey for snakebite get up and ride away. But in real life, anyone who

drinks whiskey for snakebite helps to spread the poison by dilating the blood vessels. Putting

cobwebs on open wounds only multiplies the germs. Some so-called cures which are still

popular are actually killers. A heatstroke victim who climbs into an ice-cold bath is likely to

have a heart attack. A folk remedy that sometimes causes tetanus is manure on a bee sting. So

folk medicine still deserves skepticism. Your doctor's advice is best.

Exercise 12.14   **Number of Mistakes** _____

Remember: Expansion by itself, or a noun plus expansion, is a **fragment**.

(1) Put parentheses around expansion beginning with *who*, *which*, or *that*, and draw an arrow from the expansion to the noun it expands. (2) If the group of words is a sentence, do this: (a) In the base sentence, underline the verb, and draw a slash between the subject part and the verb part. (b) Write in SENT. (3) If a group of words is a fragment, put an **X** in front of it, and write in FRAG. Follow this model:

   X The poem (which was selected by the editors) .   *FRAG*

   The poem / <u>was selected</u> by the editors.   *SENT*

   The poem (which was selected by the editors) / <u>was written</u>
   by a high school student.   *SENT*

1.   The new accountant who was hired last week.   _____

    A new accountant was hired last week.   _____

    The new accountant who was hired last week seems very competent.   _____

2.   The accident which Mrs. Antoine witnessed involved three cars.   _____

    The accident which was witnessed by Mrs. Antoine.   _____

    The accident involved three cars.   _____

3.   Students who attend college at night often have trouble budgeting their time.   _____

    Students who work all day and attend college at night.   _____

    Some students work all day and attend college at night.   _____

4.   A fact which almost everyone recognized.   _____

    That was a fact which almost everyone recognized.   _____

    Almost everyone recognized that fact.   _____

5.   Anyone who considers the risks will not try hang gliding.   _____

    Anyone who considers the risks.   _____

    Only a foolhardy person will try a dangerous sport like hang gliding.   _____

Exercise 12.15   **Number of Mistakes** _____

This paragraph contains both sentences and fragments. (1) Put parentheses around expansion beginning with *who*, *which*, or *that*, and draw an arrow from the expansion to the noun it expands. (2) If the group of words is a sentence, do this: (a) In the base sentence, or in any sentence without noun expansion, underline the verb, and draw a slash between the subject part and the verb part. (b) Write in SENT. (3) If a group of words is a fragment, put an ✗ in front of it, and write in FRAG.

¹Animals have elaborate systems of movements and sounds which resemble human communication. ²Systems which some people describe as language. ³Certainly most animals, in one way or another, communicate fear, pleasure, or sexual desire. ⁴For example, the songs that birds sing. ⁵Which have some of the qualities of human speech. ⁶Each melody which we hear signals food, danger, or a sense of territory. ⁷There are studies of the sounds which dolphins make. ⁸Curious underwater vibrations which are like the pulses of Navy sonar equipment. ⁹One scientist considers these sounds to be the equivalent of human speech. ¹⁰And the complicated dances which bees perform. ¹¹These intricate movements tell other bees about sources of nectar. ¹²Scientists are now studying animals which seem to be able to learn human language. ¹³A woman who invented a signal system which resembles the finger talk of the deaf. ¹⁴She taught it to a chimpanzee which now has a vocabulary of over 100 words. ¹⁵But not even this smart monkey uses sounds or signals which are exactly like human language. ¹⁶Sounds that express general and original ideas.

1 _____

2 _____

3 _____

4 _____

5 _____

6 _____

7 _____

8 _____

9 _____

10 _____

11 _____

12 _____

13 _____

14 _____

15 _____

16 _____

Module 12: *Understanding Sentences III*

RULES, Part 2: Punctuating Sentences

Commas prevent confusion by separating the different parts of a sentence.

| | **Rule 1.** | **Use commas to separate the items in a series.** |

Remember: A series is a list of three or more items.

> The French flag is blue**,** white**,** and red.
>> *Blue*, *white*, and *red* is a series of three colors, separated by commas. Notice the comma before *and*.

> The children refused to eat dinner**,** quarreled with one another**,** and insisted on staying up until midnight.
>> *Refused to eat dinner*, *quarreled with one another*, and *insisted on staying up until midnight* is a series of three things the children did. Notice the comma before *and*.

You first learned this rule in Module 6.

Exercise 12.16 Rewrite each group of sentences as one sentence. Be sure to punctuate your rewritten sentence correctly. Mark your rewritten sentence like this:

> Pia dug clams.
> Pia scrubbed them.
> Pia made a sauce for the linguini.

Pia / dug clams, scrubbed them, and made a sauce for the linguini.

1. Americans value democracy.
    Americans value education.
    Americans value economic opportunity.

    _____

    _____

2. For centuries, the Vikings attacked England.
    For centuries, the Vikings stole its treasures.
    For centuries, the Vikings returned to their homeland to enjoy their loot.

    _____

    _____

3. Food is a basic need for every child.
    Shelter is a basic need for every child.
    Love is a basic need for every child.

    _____

    _____

||||| **Rule 2.**   **In a compound sentence with a joining word like *and*, *but*, or *or*, use a comma in front of the joining word.**

Anita / <u>had forgotten</u> the meeting. Maybe she / <u>had been delayed</u>.
Anita / <u>had forgotten</u> the meeting, **or** maybe she / <u>had been delayed</u>.
        The sentences have been joined with a comma + *or*.

You first learned this rule in Module 6.

Exercise 12.17 Rewrite each pair of sentences as a compound sentence, using the given joining word. Mark your rewritten sentence like this:

and   I had my father's undivided attention. He pampered me.

I / had my father's undivided attention [, and] he / pampered me.

1. **but**   There is no proof of visitors from outer space. Many people believe in them.

    _____

    _____

2. **and**   Tania will work in June. Then she will go to summer school.

    _____

    _____

3. **or**   Elderly people may become difficult to please. They may mellow with age.

    _____

    _____

|||||| **Rule 3.** **When verb expansion comes at the beginning of a sentence, use a comma to separate it from the base sentence.**

(If you start late)**,** you / <u>will be caught</u> in traffic.

> The verb expansion *if you start late* comes at the beginning of the sentence, so a comma is needed after it.

You first learned this rule in Module 10.

Remember: You learned ten verb expansion words in Module 10:

when	because	if	after	before
until	while	although	so that	unless

Write all ten of these verb expansion words here:

_____   _____   _____

_____   _____   _____

_____   _____   _____

_____

Exercise 12.18 Combine the sentences, using the given expansion word. Be sure to punctuate your rewritten sentence correctly. Mark your rewritten sentence like this:

    unless   I find more information. My paper will be very short.

(Unless I find more information), my paper / <u>will be</u> very short.

1. **because**   Latex paint is soluble in water. It is easy to use.

_____

2. **until**   The barbarians invaded from the east. Rome ruled the world.

_____

3. **after**   The Civil War ended. Many Confederate soldiers returned to ruined homes and farms.

_____

||||| **Rule 4.** **Use commas to separate transitional words from the rest of a sentence.**

There are many common transitional words, like *first*, *second*, and *third*, or *then*, *next*, and *finally*. Transitional words are used to show the relationship between sentences in a paragraph.

Children need food and shelter. <u>Next</u>, they need a sense of security.

> The transitional word *next* shows the logical relationship of the two sentences. It is followed by a comma.

Here are five important transitional words:

however	therefore	furthermore	nevertheless	also

Memorize these five transitional words and write them here:

_____   _____   _____

_____   _____

Exercise 12.19 Rewrite each pair of sentences, using the given transitional word at the beginning of the second sentence. Be sure to punctuate your rewritten sentences correctly. Mark your rewritten sentences like this:

therefore   Our time was short. We made the most of it.

Our time/was short. Therefore, we/made the most of it.

1. **however**   Parents worry about their children's safety. They must permit their children to experiment and explore.

_____

_____

2. **also**   The candidate was highly qualified. He had the backing of the local newspaper.

_____

_____

3. **nevertheless**   The wedding was held right after Grandfather died. It was a joyous occasion.

_____

_____

Important: Don't confuse **transitional** words with **joining** words. Transitional words cannot join sentences.

> Ian likes English**, but** he plans to major in accounting.
>> This compound sentence is correct.

> **✗**
> Ian likes English**, however**, he plans to major in accounting.
>> This run-on is incorrect. The transitional word *however* cannot join sentences.

> Ian likes English. **However,** he plans to major in accounting.
>> These two sentences are correct. *However* is a transitional word, and is separated from the rest of the sentence with a comma.

Exercise 12.20 Put an **✗** where the second sentence begins, and correct the run-on by rewriting it as two sentences. Be sure to punctuate your rewritten sentence correctly. Mark your rewritten sentence like this:

> ✗
> Pollution kills animals and plants, furthermore, it causes health problems.

Pollution /kills animals and plants. Furthermore, it / causes health problems.

1.   Most young people are in college to prepare for a career, however, they often shortchange themselves.

_____

_____

2.   Many students do not study history, also, they seldom take a foreign language beyond the basics.

_____

_____

3.   The global economy is becoming interdependent, therefore, the ability to speak a foreign language will often translate into higher pay.

_____

_____

Exercise 12.21 You have learned about punctuation with **joining**, **expansion**, and **transitional** words. To review, fill in the appropriate answer:

1. and   but   or

    These are _____ words, which are used to create compound sentences.

2. when   because   if   after   before
    until   while   although   so that   unless
    who   which   that

    These are _____ words, which turn one sentence into expansion of another.

3. however   therefore   furthermore   nevertheless   also

    These are _____ words, which show logical relationships, but never join sentences.

Exercise 12.22 Rewrite each pair of sentences in three ways: (a) Rewrite them as a compound sentence, using the given **joining** word. (b) Rewrite them using the given **expansion** word to change one sentence into expansion of the other. Be sure that your sentence makes sense. (c) Rewrite them as two sentences using the given **transitional** word. Be sure to punctuate your rewritten sentence correctly. Mark your rewritten sentence like this:

Zora is slow. She is competent.

a. but   Zora / is slow , but she / is competent.

b. although   (Although Zora is slow), she / is competent.

c. however   Zora / is slow. However, she / is competent.

1. Women need more iron than men. Many women take mineral supplements.

    a. **and**   _____

        _____

    b. **because**   _____

        _____

    c. **therefore**   _____

        _____

2.   Americans are very health-conscious. Most of us eat diets rich in sugar and fat.

    a.   **but**   _____

                  _____

    b.   **although**   _____

                  _____

    c.   **nevertheless** _____

                  _____

Exercise 12.23 Look closely at the punctuation in each sentence below. Then fill in the appropriate **joining, expansion,** or **transitional** word.

1. also / and   Cholesterol can damage your heart. _____ ,
                        most foods rich in cholesterol are fattening.

2. but / however   Exercising regularly takes discipline. _____ ,
                        it pays off in many ways.

3. however / although Being well organized saves time. _____ , it
                        also takes time.

4. and / also   The idea was truly brilliant, _____ she thought
                        of it all by herself.

5. but / however   During the Great Depression of the 1930s bread cost only eight cents,

                        _____ some people didn't have eight cents.

6. so that / therefore Los Angeles is located in a valley surrounded by mountains.

                        _____ , the air is often polluted.

7. and / therefore   People are marrying later, _____ they are
                        having smaller families.

8. however / although _____ Eubie was well prepared, he seemed
                        nervous.

RULES SUMMARY, Part 2

In the longer one-page exercises that follow, you'll practice applying all the rules which you've learned or reviewed in this module. Before you go on to the longer exercises, check your understanding by filling in the blanks in the Rules Summary below. Fill in the blanks from memory, thinking carefully about what each rule means. If you need help, look back again at the Rules.

1. Use commas to separate the items in a _____.

2. In a compound sentence, use a _____ in front of a joining word like _____

    or _____ or *or*.

3. When verb expansion comes at the beginning of a sentence, use a comma to separate it from the

    _____ _____.

4. Use commas to separate _____ words from the rest of a sentence.

5. Transitional words like *however*, *therefore*, and *furthermore* cannot _____

    _____ .

Now turn to the Answers to check your work. Use these Rules and your dictionary as you go on to do the longer exercises that follow.

Module 12: *Understanding Sentences III*

PRACTICE, Part 2

Exercise 12.24   **Number of Mistakes** _____

Remember: Noun expansion must follow the noun it expands.

---

(1) Combine each group of sentences, using the given expansion words. Be sure that your sentence makes sense, and that you punctuate your rewritten sentence correctly. (2) Mark your rewritten sentence like this:

when	She heard the news.
	The girl laughed.
who	She won the prize.

(When she heard the news), the girl ⟵(who won the prize)/ laughed .

1. **when**   The list of contributors reaches one thousand.
                    The woman will make a large donation.
    who   She organized this drive.

    _____

    _____

2. **because**   Beauregard wants to be fashionable.
                    He wears fancy boots.
    which   They hurt his feet.

    _____

    _____

3.   The antique table collapsed.
    which   It was standing in the hall.
    when   Amos put the package on it.

    _____

    _____

4. **unless**   You send it by Express Mail.
                    A letter will not arrive by Thursday.
    which   It is mailed this afternoon.

    _____

    _____

Exercise 12.25   **Number of Mistakes** _____

Combine each group of sentences, using the given expansion and joining words. Be sure that your rewritten sentence makes sense, and that you punctuate it correctly. Put your rewritten sentences into paragraph form. Write the final copy of your paragraph on a sheet of your own paper, and attach it to this page.

1.   Michelangelo was a 16th century sculptor.
    who   He also painted.

2.   His huge paintings on the ceiling of the Sistine Chapel in Rome are in every art history book.
    but   His marble statues are perhaps even more famous.

3. **because** Marble was plentiful in the hills near Florence.
           He always used this beautiful stone.

4. **while**   He was planning his statues.
           He seemed to hear voices speaking from inside the uncarved marble.

5.   One day he was painting a prince's portrait.
    which   He wanted to finish it before sunset.
    when   His helpers carried in a large chunk of marble.

6. **after**   They left.
           Michelangelo sensed the presence of an invisible person in the room.
    but   He continued to paint.

7.   He turned and saw the marble.
    and   Then he understood.

8. **when**   He touched the rough surface.
           Michelangelo felt a figure.
    which   It moved in the marble.

9.   It was Moses, the prophet.
    who   He was waiting for Michelangelo to set him free.

10.   The prince would have to wait.
    who   He had ordered the painting.
    because At this moment a more important person was giving Michelangelo orders.

11.   With a shout of joy, he lifted his hammer and struck the first of the ten thousand blows.
    which   They would free the prophet from his marble prison.

Exercise 12.26   **Number of Mistakes** _____

Review Exercise H: Fragments and Run-ons

This paragraph contains fragments and run-ons. Rewrite the paragraph, correcting the errors like this: (1) Connect each fragment to the appropriate sentence. (2) Rewrite each run-on as two sentences. **Make no other changes.** For help, use your Rules and your dictionary.

> Our ancestors died of many diseases. Which the modern world knows little about. Like bubonic plague and smallpox. In the Middle Ages, bubonic plague killed thousands, in fact, the populations of entire cities died of this scourge. Which recurred every few generations. Doctors could only lock the city gates, they had no cures. People shuddered when anyone mentioned its name, they called it the Black Death. Up to the 18th century, smallpox was another killer. Even if the victims recovered, the pockmarks which it left on their faces disfigured them for life, this was particularly dreadful for women. However, because of the miracles of modern medicine. Smallpox, like bubonic plague, has become merely a memory. Past success in eliminating these diseases encourages researchers. Who are now seeking cures for AIDS and cancer.

_____

_____

_____

_____

_____

_____

_____

_____

_____

_____

_____

_____

Important: There should be 12 sentences in your corrected paragraph. How many did you write? _____ If you did not write 12 sentences, try again before you check your work.

Module 12: *Understanding Sentences III*

WRITING TEST

NAME _____

PURPOSE   To show that you can write correct sentences with expansion, joining, and transitional words; that you can punctuate your sentences correctly; and that you can continue to apply what you have learned in previous modules.

ASSIGNMENT   Write a short history of the past term or semester, explaining the people and events that have been important to you in your college work and/or your personal life. What did you expect? What actually happened? What good or bad effects have these people and events had upon you?

Check off each step in the writing process as you complete it.

GET READY ❑   On scratch paper, write down as many details about the past term or semester as you can think of. Make sure you have plenty of ideas about the important things that happened.

DRAFT ❑   On scratch paper, write a rough draft of your account. Try to write sentences that sound natural but aren't too complicated. Write at least 12 sentences.

In every sentence, use at least one of these expansion, joining, or transitional words:

❑ *who*	❑ *after*	❑ *and*	❑ *however*
❑ *which*	❑ *before*	❑ *but*	❑ *therefore*
	❑ *until*	❑ *or*	❑ *furthermore*
	❑ *when*		❑ *nevertheless*
	❑ *while*		❑ *also*
	❑ *because*		
	❑ *so that*		
	❑ *although*		
	❑ *if*		
	❑ *unless*		

❑   Put an **✗** in the box next to each word as you use it, and underline it in your history.

REVISE ❑   Read over the draft of your account to make sure that your ideas are clear and sound real. Try to anticipate what a reader will need to know in order to understand and believe what you have written. Add, take out, or change ideas, words, and sentences as necessary. Remember, it's good for a draft to become messy.

❑   After you have finished revising your ideas, count the words from the list that you used and underlined, and write the number here: _____ .

EDIT   ❑   Review the Rules for Part 1 of this module, Part 2 of Module 6, and Module 10. Find and correct any fragments and run-ons.

                   ❑   Review the Rules for Part 2 of this module. Make sure that every sentence is punctuated correctly.

                        Use your dictionary and the Rules for previous modules to find and correct any mistakes in:

                        ❑   Nouns: Singular and Plural Forms
                        ❑   Verbs: Tense and Agreement
                        ❑   Spelling
                        ❑   Writing Conventions
                        ❑   Wrong Words

FINAL COPY   ❑   Write the final copy of your account carefully, using blue or black ink and standard-sized (8½ by 11 inch) paper. Better yet, type or use a word processor. Write your name in the upper right-hand corner or use whatever heading your instructor requires. Remember that you are now preparing your writing for a reader.

                   ❑   Underline words from the list in your final copy just as you did in your draft.

PROOFREAD   ❑   Read your final copy **out loud**. If you find any mistakes, it's OK to correct them neatly by hand. Or if you have used a word processor, go back and correct your mistakes, and then print out a clean final copy.

Attach your final copy to these instructions, and hand them both in.

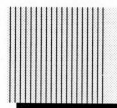

Appendix A: Spelling

NAME _____

As you complete each exercise, record your number of mistakes below.

A.1 ____   A.5 ____   A.9 ____

A.2 ____   A.6 ____   A.10 ____

A.3 ____   A.7 ____

A.4 ____   A.8 ____

INSTRUCTOR'S COMMENTS

Instructions:

☐ Followed carefully
☐ Not followed carefully enough

Checking:

☐ Careful
☐ Not careful enough to catch all your mistakes
☐ Green pen not used for checking
☐ Entire correct answer not always written in

Writing Test:

☐ Excellent
☐ Good
☐ Acceptable
☐ Not yet satisfactory

Other:

Appendix A: *Spelling*

Spelling is an important writing convention. There is usually only one correct way to spell a word, and of course you can find it in the dictionary. However, in this Appendix you'll learn four useful spelling rules that will help you spell hundreds of common words without having to look them up.

A1.   **Use *I* before *E*, with two exceptions:**
            use *EI* after *C*, and
            use *EI* to sound like *A*.

We <u>believe</u> the package contains books.
> Use *IE* to spell *believe*. This word follows the basic rule.

We <u>received</u> it today.
> Use *EI* after *C* to spell *received*.

Its <u>weight</u> surprised us.
> Use *EI* to spell *weight* because it sounds like *A*.

This rhyme will help you remember the rule. Memorize it, if you don't know it already:

I before E,
Except after C,
Or when sounded like A (as in <u>neighbor</u> and <u>weigh</u>).

Write the rhyme here to help you remember it:

_____

_____

_____

Exercise A.1 (1) Fill in IE or EI to spell each word correctly. (2) Write in 1, 2, or 3 to tell which line of the rhyme explains the word's spelling: 1 - I before E,
                                                                                                  2 - Except after C,
                                                                                                  3 - Or when sounded like A (as in <u>neighbor</u> and <u>weigh</u>).

Follow this model:

     a tribal leader: ch í e f   1

1.   a piece of open land: f __ __ ld   _____

2.   the top of a room: c __ __ ling   _____

3. the number after seven: _ _ ght   _____

4. the paper that proves you paid for something: rec _ _ pt   _____

5. a close companion: fr _ _ nd   _____

6. to look at something, usually from far off: v _ _ w   _____

7. they carry blood: v _ _ ns   _____

Remember: Check your work as you go along, using the Answers in the back of the book.

Here are four common exceptions to this spelling rule:

       either   neither   weird   height

Write each of these four words here, and memorize its spelling:

     _____   _____

     _____   _____

One word that causes many people trouble is *their*, meaning *belonging to them*.

     Write *their* here: _____

Exercise A.2 This paragraph contains many words spelled with *IE* and *EI*. Some of them are correct and some are misspelled. Underline each misspelled word and correct it in the space above the line. For help, use your dictionary. The first error has been corrected for you.

        believe

Do you <u>beleive</u> in magic? When people play the lottery or enter a sweepstakes, they always

beleive in their hearts that they're going to win. It's hard to conceive that the odds against

winning a sweepstakes are millions to one. Did you ever have a freind who won a big state

lottery? Probably not. But most of us have friends and neighbors who consistently play their

lucky number and lose. These people might not spend a dime without a receipt, and they would

be outraged if a theif took thier hard-earned dollars. However, again and again they decieve

themselves and squander money that never can be retreived, all on a brief fantasy of magical

gains. (Do you believe that you have a lucky number?)

Important: The letters *A, E, I, O,* and *U* are vowels. All other letters are consonants.

Write the five vowels here: ___ ___ ___ ___ ___

Exercise A.3

1. Circle every vowel in these words:

    s t r a p   h a v e   t o u c h e d   e e r i e

2. Put a box around every consonant in these words:

    s t r a p   h a v e   t o u c h e d   e e r i e

A2.   Sometimes *Y* must be changed to *I* before adding *ES* or *ED*.

**1.   If a word ends in a <u>consonant</u> + *Y*,
         change the *Y* to *I* before adding *ES* or *ED*.**

PENNY   Those <u>pennies</u> won't buy much these days.
TRY   Nobody ever <u>tried</u> to do that before.

> The words *penny* and *try* end in a consonant + *Y*. So change *Y* to *I* before adding an ending beginning with *E*.

**2.   If a word ends in a <u>vowel</u> + *Y*,
         do not change the *Y* to *I* before adding an ending.**

PRAY   The farmers <u>prayed</u> for rain.
TOY   The factory makes wooden <u>toys</u>.

> The words *pray* and *toy* end in a vowel + *Y*. So do not change *Y* to *I* before adding an ending.

Exercise A.4 Add first an *S* or *ES* ending, and then an *ED* ending, to each word. Follow these models:

annoy   *annoys*   *annoyed*

rely   *relies*   *relied*

1. play   _____   _____

2. marry   _____   _____

3. enjoy   _____   _____

4. reply   _____   _____

5. terrify   _____   _____

6. X-ray   _____   _____

| | **A3.** | Sometimes a final consonant must be doubled before adding an ending. |

1. If a word ends in a <u>single vowel</u> + a <u>single consonant</u>, double the consonant before adding an ending beginning with a vowel.

SAD   sadder, sadden
FORGET   forgetting
PATROL   patrolled, patrolling

> Each word ends in a single vowel + a single consonant, so the consonant is doubled before adding an ending beginning with a vowel.

2. If a word ends in a <u>double vowel</u> + a <u>single consonant</u>, do not double the consonant.

FEAR   feared, fearing
PEEL   peeled, peeling

> Each word ends in a double vowel + a single consonant, so the consonant is not doubled.

3. If a word has more than one syllable and the last syllable is <u>not accented</u>, usually do not double the final consonant. Most of these words end in *ER*.

DIFFER   different, differed
GATHER   gathered, gathering

> Each word has more than one syllable and the last syllable of each word is not accented, so the final consonant is not doubled.

Exercise A.5 Add the given ending to each word. Follow this model:

run + ER   *runner* _____

1. grin + ING   _____

2. rain + ED   _____

3. star + ING   _____

4. matter + ED   _____

5. repel + ENT   _____

6. repeal + ING _____

7. shop + ED   _____

8. swim + ER   _____

9. prefer + ED   _____

10. cover + ED   _____

A4.   Be especially careful with *ING* endings.

**1.   If a word ends in a consonant + *E*,
drop the *E* before adding *ING*.**

HOPE   Emma was <u>hoping</u> for a letter.
WRITE   She was <u>writing</u> a note to her sister.

> Each word ends in a consonant + *E*, so the *E* is dropped before adding *ING*.

Remember: If a word ends in a **single vowel** + a **single consonant**, double the consonant before adding *ING*.

HOP   A robin was <u>hopping</u> about under my window.
SIT   A wren was <u>sitting</u> on a nearby tree.

> Each word ends in a single vowel + a single consonant, so the final consonant is doubled before adding *ING*.

This was Rule A3.

Exercise A.6 Fill in the *ING* form of the given word.

1. ROBE   The choir members were _____ in the vestry.

   ROB   The gang has been _____ small shops in the

   neighborhood.

2. PLAN   _____ next year's schedule is the chairman's

   responsibility.

   PLANE   The carpenter is _____ the boards.

318

3. STARE   In American society, _____ at strangers is considered

                to be impolite.

      STAR   Many actors who have _____ roles on television never

                work in motion pictures.

2. Never drop Y before adding *ING*.

WORRY   <u>Worrying</u> won't help.
STUDY   <u>Studying</u> might help.
                    Each word ends in *Y*, so the *Y* isn't dropped before adding *ING*.

Important: Do not become confused about words ending in *Y*. Remember the rules you have learned:

Rule A2 says: **Do** change *Y* to *I* when adding *ES* or *ED*.
Rule A4 says: **Do not** change *Y* to *I* when adding *ING*.

WORRY   Linda <u>worries</u> about every deadline.
                Linda is <u>worrying</u> about the deadline next week.
                    In *worries*, *Y* is changed to *I* because the ending is *ES*.
                    In *worrying*, *Y* is not changed to *I* because the ending is *ING*.

Exercise A.7 Add an *ES* ending, an *ED* ending, and an *ING* ending to each word. Follow this model:

HURRY   <u>hurries</u>   <u>hurried</u>   <u>hurrying</u>

             + ES   + ED   + ING

1. CARRY _____   _____   _____

2. WORRY _____   _____   _____

3. TRY   _____   _____   _____

4. REPLY   _____   _____   _____

5. STUDY   _____   _____   _____

DIE and *LIE* have irregular *ING* forms.

       DIE   The <u>dying</u> embers glowed.
       LIE   <u>Lying</u> under oath is a serious crime.

> *Dying* is the irregular *ING* form of *DIE*.
> *Lying* is the irregular *ING* form of *LIE*.

STUDY and *WRITE* have *ING* forms that cause more trouble than any others.

       STUDY   <u>Studying</u> is necessary to pass that course.
       WRITE   <u>Writing</u> papers is easier on a computer.

> *Y* is not dropped from *studying* because *Y* is never dropped before *ING*.
> *E* is dropped from *writing* before *ING*.

Write each of these irregular or troublesome words here, and memorize its spelling:

    lying   _____   dying   _____

    studying   _____   writing   _____

Exercise A.8 Fill in the *ING* form of the given word.

1. OCCUR   Incidents involving guns are _____ with alarming

                        frequency.

2. MARRY   People these days are _____ at a later age.

3. SAY   There is an old _____ : "Handsome is as handsome

                        does."

4. LIE   The senators believed that the witness was _____ .

5. WRITE   To children, _____ is a lot like drawing pictures.

6. HIT   The missile did not succeed in _____ its target.

7. SMILE   People in photographs are usually _____ .

8. STUDY   Few students who get low grades really enjoy _____ .

9. DIE   Many Native Americans are striving to keep the old ways of their people from

                        _____ out.

10. WORRY   _____ about problems seldom helps us to solve them.

Exercise A.9 (1) Rewrite this paragraph, adding the given ending to each word. (2) In your rewritten paragraph, underline every change. Your first sentence will begin like this: *Reading, 'riting, and 'rithmetic have been called the three R's....*

> READ + ING, 'RITE + ING, and 'rithmetic have been called the three R's of education, the basics that every child should have STUDY + ED and MASTER + ED by the end of elementary school. Now some educators are SAY + ING that the new basics will be READ + ING, WRITE + ING, and COMPUTE + ING. But the computer should not be IDENTIFY + ED only with STUDY + ING arithmetic and numbers. For example, word PROCESS + ING is much more than just TYPE + ING. Young children have TRY + ED USE + ING a word processor before they have even STUDY + ED the alphabet, and their teachers are SAY + ING that WRITE + ING on the computer has HELP + ED them to read sooner and with more UNDERSTAND + ING. A special computer language called <u>LOGO</u> APPLY + ES REASON + ING skills by HAVE + ING children draw pictures on the screen. Some people are WORRY + ED that children will become too dependent on machines, but the ones who are WORRY + ING the most are usually not the ones who have TRY + ED to teach in this new way.

_____

_____

_____

_____

_____

_____

_____

_____

_____

_____

_____

_____

_____

_____

_____

Important: You can catch many spelling mistakes if you count the number of syllables when you write a long word or a word with repeated letters.

> **Mis-sis-sip-pi**
>
> Noticing that *Mississippi* has four syllables helps to spell it correctly.

Exercise A.10 (1) Say each word out loud and write in its number of syllables. (2) Use your dictionary to check your answer, and then to write the word in syllables, using hyphens between syllables. Follow this model:

beginning	_3_	_be - gin - ning_

1. commercial _____ _____

2. environment _____ _____

3. studying _____ _____

4. athletic _____ _____

5. representative _____ _____

6. vehicle _____ _____

Appendix A: *Spelling*

WRITING TEST

NAME _____

PURPOSE   To show that you can use words that are hard to spell correctly, and that you can continue to apply what you have learned in previous modules.

ASSIGNMENT   Write a short story about something very important, either based on real life or drawn from your imagination.

In your story, use and underline at least 16 of the following hard-to-spell words:

❑ *either*	❑ *studying*	❑ *government*
❑ *brief*	❑ *shopping*	❑ *commercial*
❑ *view*	❑ *dying*	❑ *separate*
❑ *their*	❑ *writing*	❑ *environment*
❑ *believe*	❑ *worrying*	❑ *marital*
❑ *review*	❑ *hoping*	❑ *definitely*
❑ *neighbor*	❑ *lying*	❑ *consistent*
❑ *belief*		❑ *occurred*
❑ *receive*		

Write here six words that you often have trouble spelling:

❑ _____   ❑ _____   ❑ _____

❑ _____   ❑ _____   ❑ _____

In your story, use and underline all six of these words.

Check off each step in the writing process as you complete it.

GET READY   ❑   On scratch paper, write down as many details for your story as you can think of. Make sure you have plenty of ideas about the important things that happened.

DRAFT   ❑   On scratch paper, write a rough draft of your story. Try to write sentences that sound natural but aren't too complicated. Keep writing until you've used at least 16 of the words from the first list, and all six of the words from your own list.

❑   As you use each word, put an **✗** in the box next to it, and underline it in your story.

REVISE   ❑   Read over the draft of your account to make sure that your ideas are clear and sound real. Try to anticipate what a reader will need to know in order to understand and believe what you have written. Add, take out, or change ideas, words, and sentences as necessary. Remember, it's good for a draft to become messy.

❑ After you have finished revising your ideas, count the words from the two lists that you used and underlined, and write the number here: _____ . If you did not use at least 22 words, write more.

EDIT ❑ Review the Rules for this Appendix. Find and correct any mistakes in spelling.

Use your dictionary and the Rules for previous modules to find and correct any mistakes in:

❑ Nouns: Singular and Plural Forms
❑ Verbs: Tense and Agreement
❑ Sentences: Fragments and Run-Ons
❑ Writing Conventions
❑ Wrong Words

FINAL COPY ❑ Write the final copy of your story carefully, using blue or black ink and standard-sized (8½ by 11 inch) paper. Better yet, type or use a word processor. Write your name in the upper right-hand corner or use whatever heading your instructor requires. Remember that you are now preparing your writing for a reader.

❑ Underline words from the lists in your final copy just as you did in your draft.

PROOFREAD ❑ Read your final copy **out loud**. If you find any mistakes, it's OK to correct them neatly by hand. Or if you have used a word processor, go back and correct your mistakes, and then print out a clean final copy.

Attach your final copy to these instructions, and hand them both in.

Appendix B: Possessives

NAME _____

As you complete each exercise, record your number of mistakes below.

B.1 ____	B.6 ____	B.11 ____
B.2 ____	B.7 ____	B.12 ____
B.3 ____	B.8 ____	B.13 ____
B.4 ____	B.9 ____	B.14 ____
B.5 ____	B.10 ____	B.15 ____

INSTRUCTOR'S COMMENTS

Instructions:

❑ Followed carefully
❑ Not followed carefully enough

Checking:

❑ Careful
❑ Not careful enough to catch all your mistakes
❑ Green pen not used for checking
❑ Entire correct answer not always written in

Writing Test:

❑ Excellent
❑ Good
❑ Acceptable
❑ Not yet satisfactory

Other:

Appendix B: *Possessives*

B1. **To write the possessive form of most nouns, add <u>apostrophe + S</u>.**

That is <u>Patrick's</u> book.

> The possessive form *Patrick's* means that the book belongs to Patrick. He owns it.

The possessive form often indicates **ownership** or possession. It also can indicate other relationships between two people or things, all of them having something to do with **belonging**.

The class is reading <u>Alice Walker's</u> novels.

> The possessive form *Alice Walker's* means that the novels belong to Alice Walker in the sense that she wrote them.

The store sold <u>men's</u> clothing.

> The possessive form *men's* means that the clothing belongs to men in the sense that it was made for men.

They did <u>a full day's</u> work.

> The possessive form *a full day's* means that the work was enough to fill a day.

Exercise B.1 (1) In each sentence, circle the noun that the possessive form describes. (2) Draw an arrow from the possessive to the noun. Follow this model:

Dad's (taxi) finally arrived.

1. We sent a thank-you note to grandfather's friends.

2. The government's new policy was announced at a press conference.

3. An old union motto is, "A day's work for a day's pay."

Remember: Check your work as you go along, using the Answers in the back of the book.

Exercise B.2 Rewrite each phrase, changing the base form of the noun into a possessive form. Say each answer out loud as you write it, and underline the possessive form. Follow this model:

BOB answer

<u>Bob's</u> answer

1. JENNIFER scarf

2. ONE MONTH pay

3. ROBERT FROST poems

Important: Even when a singular noun ends in *S* or *Z*, it is still correct to add **apostrophe + S** to write the possessive form. The possessive ending adds an extra syllable.

That is <u>Lois's</u> book.

    The possessive form *Lois's* is correct. The book belongs to Lois.

Exercise B.3 Rewrite each phrase, changing the base form of the noun into a possessive form. Say each answer out loud as you write it, and underline the possessive form. Follow this model:

TESS computer

<u>Tess's</u> computer

1. JAMES new pen

2. ONE CLASS assignments

3. GARCIA MARQUEZ novels

B2. When a <u>plural</u> noun ends in S, add an <u>apostrophe only</u> to write the possessive form.

Those are the <u>boys'</u> hockey sticks.

> The possessive form *boys'* means that the hockey sticks belong to more than one boy.

Most plural nouns end in *S*. When a plural noun that ends in *S* is made possessive, no sound is added. That's why we write the possessive form with an apostrophe only.

✗

The <u>boys's</u> soccer team won the playoffs.

> This possessive form is incorrect.

The <u>boys'</u> soccer team won the playoffs.

> The plural *boys* ends in *S*. The possessive form *boys'* (with an apostrophe only) is correct.

Exercise B.4 Rewrite each phrase, changing the base form of the noun into a possessive form. Say each answer out loud as you write it, and underline the possessive form. Follow this model:

GIRLS coats

<u>*girls'*</u> *coats* _____

1. SOME COOKS equipment

_____

2. THREE DAYS time

_____

3. the DOCTORS offices

_____

Remember: Ask yourself "Who (or what) does the item belong to?" The answer is the word that needs a possessive ending.

The <u>boy's</u> hockey sticks.

> This possessive form (*boy* + apostrophe + *S*) is correct if the hockey sticks belong to one boy.

The <u>boys'</u> hockey sticks.

> This possessive form (*boys* + apostrophe only) is correct if the hockey sticks belong to more than one boy.

Appendix B: *Possessives*

Exercise B.5 Each underlined possessive form is correct. Circle the ending. Then write in who or what the item belongs to. Follow this model:

      our class ('s) final examination

      The examination belongs to _our class_____ .

1. society's problems

   The problems belong to _____ .

2. the mothers' group

   The group belongs to _____ .

3. his parents' income

   The income belongs to _____ .

4. my teachers' advice

   The advice belongs to _____ .

5. one city's budget

   The budget belongs to _____ .

Important: Irregular plurals do **not** end in *S*. When an irregular plural is made possessive, an S sound is added. We write the possessive form with an apostrophe + *S*.

     The men's bowling team got new uniforms.
        Men is an irregular plural, ending in *N*, not *S*. The possessive form *men's* (with apostrophe + *S*) is correct.

Exercise B.6 Fill in the appropriate possessive form. Say each answer out loud as you write it. Follow this model:

     The car belongs to my two sisters.

     _my two sisters'_____ car

1. The tools belong to my brother.

   _____ tools

   The tools belong to my brothers.

   _____ tools

2.   The career belongs to one woman.

_____ career

The careers belong to many women.

_____ careers

3.   The opinion belongs to one person.

_____ opinion

The opinions belong to many people.

_____ opinions

4.   The schedule belongs to my boss.

_____ schedule

The schedule belongs to our bosses.

_____ schedule

5.   The responsibilities belong to a man.

_____ responsibilities

The responsibilities belong to men.

_____ responsibilities

Exercise B.7 To review the rules about noun possessives, look over your work so far and write in APOSTROPHE + S or APOSTROPHE ONLY.

1.   To make most nouns possessive, add _____ .

2.   Most plural nouns end in *S*. To make most plural nouns possessive, add _____ .

3.   Irregular plural nouns (for example, *men*, *women*, and *children*) do not end in *S*. To make irregular plural nouns possessive, add _____ .

Exercise B.8 Rewrite each phrase, changing the expansion into a possessive form. Say each answer out loud as you write it, and underline the possessive form. Follow this model:

    the correct answer ← (given by Bob)

    <u>Bob's correct answer</u>

1.   the parents ← (of Jean-Luc)

2.   the lectures ← (presented by our professor)

3.   the tests ← (given by our professors)

4.   the enormous hat ← (worn by that woman)

5.   the hard work ← (that took ten years)

6.   the oral reports ← (presented by the students)

7.   the new policy ← (introduced by the government)

8.   the skinned knees and stubbed toes ← (typical of my little sister)

Exercise B.9 Rewrite this paragraph, changing the expansion into a possessive form. Say each sentence out loud as you write it, and underline the possessive form. Your first sentence will begin like this: *Our grandparents' house was . . .*

        The house←(owned by our grandparents) was crowded. In the recreation room, the stereo←(belonging to Tasha) was blaring rap music while the cousins checked out the new dance steps←(of one another). In the kitchen, the wonderful aroma of roast turkey wafted from the oven←(belonging to Grandma) while the yam casserole←(made by Uncle Joe) and the mince pies←(made by Aunt Betty) were displayed for the approval←(of the assembled guests). In the living room, the photo albums←(belonging to our grandparents) were being passed around, to the amusement←(of everyone). "Look at the miniskirts←(of our aunts)! Get a load of the haircut←(on Joe)!" From the den, where the television←(belonging to Grandad) was tuned to a football game, came the occasional roar of voices←(of men). The yearly Thanksgiving Day reunion←(of the family) was in full swing.

_____

_____

_____

_____

_____

_____

_____

_____

_____

_____

_____

_____

_____

_____

_____

_____

Exercise B.10 Rewrite each group of sentences as one sentence, changing the **second** sentence into a possessive form. Underline the possessive form in your answer. Follow this model:

Edward usually borrows a bicycle. The bicycle belongs to Augusta.

Edward usually borrows Augusta's bicycle.

1. Penelope was surprised by the plan. The plan belonged to her husband.

_____

2. The young woman stole the money from the account. The account belonged to her employers.

_____

3. Many parents know little about the friends. The friends belong to their children.

_____

B3. **Don't confuse possessive <u>nouns</u> (which have an apostrophe) with possessive <u>pronouns</u> (which do not have an apostrophe).**

If the pen is <u>Maria's</u> and that is <u>her</u> dictionary, then the notebook must also be <u>hers</u>.

The possessive noun *Maria's* has an apostrophe. The possessive pronouns *her* and *hers* do not.

There are two different possessive **pronoun** forms. Use the first form before a noun (*her dictionary*), and the second form by itself, without a noun (*hers*). These possessive pronoun forms **never** have apostrophes.

pronouns	possessive forms	
I	my	mine
you	your	yours
he	his	his
she	her	hers
it	its	its
we	our	ours
they	their	theirs

Important: **Never** write the possessive pronoun *mine* with an *S* ending.

✗

That seat is <u>mines</u>.

> The word *mines* is incorrect in writing, although it sometimes occurs in speech.

That seat is <u>mine</u>.

> This sentence is correct.

Exercise B.11 Underline each word in which an apostrophe is used incorrectly, and correct the word in the space above the line. Follow this model:

> *yours*
> Is this key <u>your's</u>?

1. Valerie says that her sister's cooking is better than her's and even better than mine.

2. The jury asked it's foreman to request a copy of the judge's instructions.

3. Sid's brother and sister-in-law were both married for the second time, and the couple always joked that

   their children were "his, her's and our's."

Remember: Apostrophes are used in contractions to show where letters have been omitted.

<u>Here's</u> a dictionary. <u>Don't</u> forget to check for spelling mistakes.

> These apostrophes are correct. *Here's* is a contraction for *Here is*. *Don't* is a contraction for *do not*.

Exercise B.12 These sentences contain errors in possessive forms and contractions. Underline each error, and correct it in the space above the line. Be careful not to correct any word that doesn't need an apostrophe. Follow this model:

> *Isn't Marcie's   its*
> <u>Isnt</u> this <u>Marcies</u> scarf? Alvin thinks <u>its</u> hers.

1. Whos the person who wanted to borrow Melvins notebook?

2. We havent seen any apartment as attractive as ours, except perhaps yours.

3. Its been predicted that the finance committee will deliver its report only after the Senates last meeting of

   the year.

Important: **Never** use apostrophes to make nouns plural.

> **✗**
>
> Luanne's two <u>sister's</u> moved to Phoenix.
>> An apostrophe is correct in the possessive *Luanne's*. It is incorrect in the plural *sisters*.

> Luanne's two <u>sisters</u> moved to Phoenix.
>> This sentence is correct.

Exercise B.13 Rewrite each sentence, changing the base forms of nouns into the appropriate plural or plural possessive forms. **Make no other changes.** In your rewritten sentences, underline every change. Follow this model:

> The CHILD ignored their PARENT WARNING.
>
> <u>The children ignored their parents' warnings.</u>

1. Both WOMAN waited for the LETTER to arrive.

    _____

2. TEACHER SALARY were raised last year.

    _____

3. Many CUSTOMER objected to the SALESMAN high-pressure TACTIC.

    _____

Remember: Do use apostrophes in **possessive nouns** and in **contractions**.
Do not use apostrophes in **possessive pronouns**.

Exercise B.14 This paragraph contains errors in possessive forms and contractions. Underline each error, and correct it in the space above the line. Be careful not to correct any word that doesn't need an apostrophe. The first error has been corrected for you.

> It's
> <u>Its</u> becoming almost a habit: The University raises its tuition nearly every year, and when it
>
> does, its certain that a small group of students will protest against the administrators decision.
>
> They lock themselves into the Presidents office and hang banners out the windows. After a
>
> weeks delay and negotiation, the administrators call the police. They always say that the decision
>
> hasnt been easy, but that the students whove gone on strike are interfering with other students
>
> right to an education.

Exercise B.15 (1) Rewrite this paragraph, changing the base forms of nouns into the appropriate plural or possessive or plural possessive forms. **Make no other changes.** (2) In your rewritten paragraph, underline every change. Your first sentence will begin like this: *My two sisters' babies were born . . .*

My two SISTER BABY were born just two WEEK apart, so the CHILD grew up together. ROSA little girl and CHITA little boy were both healthy INFANT, but their MOTHER often wondered why the CHILD PERSONALITY were so very different. Little ROBERT temperament was sunny, but his cousin ESTELLA TANTRUM became famous in the family. Still, the two CHILD got along together very well. Perhaps OPPOSITE attract. At any rate, they never fought over EACH OTHER TOY, and they happily shared their COOKY and TREAT. In fact, their RELATIVE always called them "the TWIN."

Appendix B: *Possessives*

WRITING TEST

NAME _____

PURPOSE   To show that you can write sentences using a variety of possessive forms correctly.

ASSIGNMENT   Write six sentences, using these possessive forms:

❑   1.   a sentence about someone or something that belongs to or is related to **Mr. Brown** in some way

❑   2.   a sentence about something **written by [a well-known author]**

❑   3.   a sentence comparing something **designed for men** with something **designed for women**

❑   4.   a sentence with one noun possessive form using apostrophe + *S*, and one noun possessive form using apostrophe only

❑   5.   a sentence with one noun possessive form (with an apostrophe) and one pronoun possessive form (with no apostrophe)

❑   6.   a sentence with three possessive forms referring to things belonging to various members of a family

Check off each step in the writing process as you complete it.

DRAFT   ❑   On scratch paper, write a rough draft of your six sentences. Try to write sentences that sound natural but aren't too complicated.

Number your sentences from 1 to 6, according to the six possessive forms above. Put an **X** in the box next to each possessive form as you use it, and underline the possessive form in your sentence.

REVISE   ❑   Read over the draft of your sentences to make sure that your sentences are clear and sound real. Make whatever changes are necessary. Remember, it's good for a draft to become messy.

Make sure that your six sentences use the six possessive forms above.

EDIT   ❑   Review the Rules for this appendix. Find and correct any mistakes in possessive forms.

❑   Use your dictionary and the Rules for previous modules as you find and correct any other mistakes.

FINAL COPY   ❏   Write the final copy of your sentences carefully, using blue or black ink and standard-sized (8½ by 11 inch) paper. Better yet, type or use a word processor. Write your name in the upper right-hand corner or use whatever heading your instructor requires. Remember that you are now preparing your writing for a reader.

                  ❏   Number and mark each sentence in your final copy just as you did in your draft.

PROOFREAD   ❏   Read your final copy **out loud**. If you find any mistakes, it's OK to correct them neatly by hand. Or if you have used a word processor, go back and correct your mistakes, and then print out a clean final copy.

Attach your final copy to these instructions, and hand them both in.

Answers

How to Use This Book

Exercise 0.1

1. past-tense verbs
2. instructor / teacher / professor
3. Rules
4. letter
5. check
6. passed
7. Rules Summary
8. mistakes
9. Review Exercise E
10. Writing Test
11. boxes

Exercise 0.2

1. confused
2. note
3. 21   once
4. underline
5. count
6. instructions

Exercise 0.3

often a writing mistake is just ∧ slip of the <u>pin</u>, but it <u>my</u> badly confuse a reader.

Module 1: *Three Essential Skills*

Exercise 1.1 [Check to see that all letters and symbols are correctly written, and in the correct order. If you have any blank lines left over at the end of any name or formula that you copied, or if you ran out of lines, you have made a mistake. Keep checking your work until you find the mistake. Then write in the entire item again above the line, using your green pen.]

Exercise 1.2

1. A girl with three younger **<u>brothers</u>** often has a difficult childhood.
2. In the early evening, the fireworks factory was rocked by a **<u>powerful</u>** explosion.
3. When his mother walked in with a tiny bundle in her arms, Gerald rushed up to get a good look at his new baby **<u>sister</u>**.
4. The **<u>best</u>** way to prepare this sauce is to beat it vigorously for three minutes.
5. Victor, an experienced **<u>electrician</u>** from Czechoslovakia, wants to join the local electricians' **<u>union</u>**.

Exercise 1.3 [The three mistakes that you cannot hear, but must actually see, are the word *sail*, the incorrect capital letter *P* in *Property*, and the missing capital letter *W* in *whatever*.]

      Buying property is ✗ **<u>even</u>** riskier than buying used **<u>cars</u>**. For example, a store **<u>by</u>** the library in my ✗y neighborhood is going to **<u>be</u>** put up for **<u>sale</u>** soon. The owner, Hank Dawson, **<u>may</u>** try to get $\underline{\$90,000}$ for **<u>it</u>**, but the value of the ✗e **<u>property</u>** is actually much less than that. A building inspector **was** in the basement recently and saw termites. He checked the beams and found **they** were completely rotten and ready to collapse. Buyers, beware! Dawson is a born liar. **Whatever** claims he makes about that building, you can bet **your** bottom dollar they're **not** true.

Exercise 1.4 [The writer omitted words.]

Today most people know that smoking is **a** health hazard. But **in** the motion pictures of the 1920s and 1930s, cigarette smoking appeared **to** be harmless and even glamorous. Film stars wearing tuxedos and evening gowns lighted **each** other's cigarettes in night club scenes. Screen detectives chain-smoked as **they** solved their cases. The children in "Our Gang" pictures sneaked their first puffs behind **the** barn. To modern audiences watching **old** movies, the constant presence of this dangerous habit **is** somewhat disturbing.

Exercise 1.5 [The writer omitted the endings on words.]

Today most people know that smoking is a health hazard. But in the motion **pictures** of the 1920s and 1930s, cigarette smoking **appeared** to be harmless and even glamorous. Film stars **wearing** tuxedos and evening **gowns** lighted each other's cigarettes in night club **scenes**. Screen detectives chain-smoked as they **solved** their cases. The children in "Our Gang" pictures sneaked their first puffs behind the barn. To modern audiences **watching** old movies, the constant presence of this **dangerous** habit is somewhat disturbing.

Exercise 1.6 [The writer misspelled words by reversing letters.]

Today most **people** know that smoking is a health hazard. But in the motion pictures of the 1920s and 1930s, cigarette smoking appeared to be harmless and even glamorous. **Film** stars wearing tuxedos and evening gowns **lighted** each other's cigarettes in night club scenes. Screen detectives chain-smoked as they solved their cases. The **children** in "Our Gang" pictures sneaked their **first** puffs behind the barn. To **modern audiences** watching old movies, the constant presence of this dangerous habit is somewhat **disturbing**.

Exercise 1.7 [Dictionaries may differ in the wording of definitions, and in the order in which they give items of information.]

1. The word *calorie* has **seven** letters and is spelled **c-a-l-o-r-i-e**.
2. Each part of a word that is pronounced separately is called a **syllable**. For example, the word *syl-la-ble* has three syllables. The dictionary shows that the word *calorie* has **three** syllables.
3. The dictionary shows that when you pronounce this word, the **first** syllable is stressed.
4. The dictionary gives the abbreviation **n.** to show that the word *calorie* is used as a noun.
5. The first meaning given for the word *calorie* is: **The amount of heat needed to raise the temperature of one gram of water one degree centigrade**.
6. To summarize, the five basic pieces of information which the dictionary gives about every word are:
    a. its **spelling**;
    b. how many **syllables** it has;
    c. its **pronunciation**;
    d. whether it is used as a verb, an adjective, a **noun**, or in some other way; and
    e. what it **means**.

Module 2: *Writing Conventions*

Exercise 2.1 [If you used commas, do not count them incorrect.]

Here layeth the body of Anne the wife of Bartholomew Gidly Esquire who was buried February 7th 1737. Elizabeth his daughter was buried December 2d 1713.

Exercise 2.2

Computers will probably change our old writing conventions and may have already introduced a few new ones.

Exercise 2.3

1. In the first part of this passage, the writer is focusing attention on the fact that the child Helen Keller **did not know** what words were.
2. In the second part of the passage, the writer is focusing attention on the moment when Helen first **understood** [OR, realized, etc.] that each thing had a name.
3.   The blind and deaf child, Helen Keller, stood by the pump. Water rushed from the spout. As she put one hand under the cold stream, her teacher, Annie Sullivan, spelled the word *water* into the other hand. Using a special code, Annie tapped out each letter of that word, just as she had done so many times before. But to Helen this was just a game. She didn't know that these taps meant words. She didn't know what words were. She only knew about things—hot and cold, wet and dry, soft and hard **things**. ¶ Suddenly the little girl became very still, with her whole attention concentrated on the sensation of those spelling fingers. At that moment the mystery of language was revealed to her. She understood that those taps meant the wonderful cool thing that was running over her hand. She understood that each thing had a name. Each thing in the world had its own special name—water, trees, flowers, her doll. She took her hand out of the water and tapped its name into the warm hand of her friend. She was almost seven years old and she had just "spoken" her first word.

Exercise 2.4

Anglo-Saxon, an old Germanic language, ranks first among many languages that contributed to our modern English vocabulary. This language, spoken by early inhabitants of England, gave us words like <u>cow</u>, <u>pig</u>, <u>plow</u>, <u>walk</u>—common words associated with outdoor life and the activities of farmers and workers.

The second most important source of modern English words is Norman French. This language, brought to England by a conquering army, gave us words like <u>beef</u>, <u>pork</u>, <u>study</u>, <u>dance</u>—more refined words associated with life indoors and the pastimes of a ruling class.

Exercise 2.5

1. **When Roberto** goes to college, he will study psychology and **Spanish**.
2. **Has** your mother made an appointment with the doctor?
3. **Today I** went to see **Dr. Alston**.
4. **My** youngest uncle is an engineer for the **Sperry Corporation**.
5. **The** house where **Aunt Sally** was born is on **Narcissus Street**.

Exercise 2.6

1. St. Mary's is the only **church** in the **neighborhood** that has a **raffle** every Friday night.
2. Our accounting **professor** owns stock in the **railroad** which was taken over by the Metropolitan Transit Authority.
3. The local **high school** improved its **curriculum** by offering new courses in **geography** and requiring four years of Spanish or another **foreign language**.

Exercise 2.7

1. **Is** it time to go**?**
2. **Did** he ask if it was time to go**?**
3. **He** asked if it was time to go**.**
4. **They** couldn't decide whether or not to write the letter**.**
5. **Did Loretta** write the letter**?**

Exercise 2.8

1. **Los Angeles** has the worst pollution problem in **California**, and perhaps the worst in the **United States**.

2.   Between Battery **Park and** Greenwich Village, most of the **streets** in **New York City** have names instead of numbers.
3.   [No changes are necessary. The title **Dr.** is always abbreviated. Abbreviations are acceptable in an address.]

Exercise 2.9

1.   I read only **three** chapters of the book Mrs. Duff lent me, **and** then I lost it.
2.   The **professor** in my **government** class assigned **133 pages** of homework for **Tuesday.**
3.   When I was **six years** old, we moved to a quiet **street** in **Philadelphia.**
4.   **Ninety** people began to picket in front of 10 Downing St., London, on March 9, 1968.
      [It would also be correct to spell out **Street.**]
5.   She told me to take **one** teaspoonful of cough medicine every four **hours** for the next 48 hours.

Exercise 2.10

1.   it's
2.   doesn't
3.   isn't
4.   I'm
5.   don't
6.   won't [The contraction **won't** is irregular.]

Exercise 2.11

It's amazing how much **we're** able to learn about the good old days from old mail order catalogues. **Here's** a sampling of their ads between 1912 and 1932:
       Model H Motor Car, $348: "**We'll** refund every penny if it **won't** go fifteen miles an hour."
       Baby Grand Piano, $118: "**She's** a beauty. Delivery? **It's** free!"
       Two-piece Bathing Suits, $1.63: "**They're** the latest — backless and skirtless." And a model says, "**Where's** your courage? **I'm** wearing one. **It's** the cat's pajamas."
       Bargains? **You're** wrong. A person **who's** making five dollars an hour today **wouldn't** have made five dollars a day when these ads were printed.

Exercise 2.12

If **you're** on a diet, **it's** likely that **you're** counting calories. However, nutritionists are now saying that calories **aren't** necessarily bad for a person **who's** trying to lose weight. **They've** discovered that carbohydrates like potatoes, bread, and cereals have lots of calories, but **they're** full of nutrition, so they **don't** add pounds quickly. On the other hand, fats like butter **aren't** nutritious at all, so **it's** easy to gain weight by eating them. Even worse, most people **don't** realize how much fat **they're** getting in cheese, meat, and ready-made foods. So if **you're** dieting, **you'd** do well to remember this: **Fat's** what makes you fat.

Exercise 2.13 [Different dictionaries may use different words in their definitions. Count your answer correct if you have chosen the right meaning, even if the words you have copied are somewhat different.]

1.   *Everyday* means "commonplace, usual."
      a.   **Every day** most people do their jobs and care for their families.
      b.   These **everyday** activities require commitment, even dedication.
2.   *Nobody* means "no person, no one."
      a.   The court declared Judge Crater dead even though **no body** was ever found.
      b.   Jane had nothing and **nobody** to call her own.
3.   *Sometimes* means "occasionally, now and then "
      a.   For criticizing your parents, **some times** are better than others.
      b.   You are **sometimes** exasperating.

Exercise 2.14

Health care costs so much nowadays that people worry **a lot** about taking care of **themselves**. **In fact,** everyday expenses are so heavy now that almost **nobody** (**myself** included) has any money put **aside** for health emergencies. **However**, I had a high fever **today** and decided that maybe I should see my doctor, who gave me an **antibiotic**. She said I **may be all right** by **tomorrow.** I certainly hope so, for I **do not** want to miss **another** day at work.

Exercise 2.15 [Different dictionaries may divide words into syllables differently.]

1.	carelessness	**care-less-ness**	**3** syllables
2.	revolution	**rev-o-lu-tion**	**4** syllables
3.	walked	**walked**	**1** syllable
4.	vehicle	**ve-hi-cle**	**3** syllables
5.	athlete	**ath-lete**	**2** syllables
6.	underlined	**un-der-lined**	**3** syllables

Exercise 2.16

When the ~~the~~ French sculptor Bartholdi offered **to** build **a** monumental statue in ~~a~~ New York Harbor to commemorate the first century **of** American independence, France promised to pay for constructing the statue, and America agreed to ~~to~~ finance the pedestal. Money poured in from thousands **of** French citizens. In contrast, Americans were **not** particularly enthusiastic about the project, and ~~and~~ journalists had to shame New York City millionaires into contributing even a few dollars from their fortunes. Recently, when Lady Liberty was about to celebrate her 100th birthday, Americans were much more ~~much~~ generous in contributing to the monument's restoration.

Exercise 2.17

Today I went to see **Dr. Alston**. She told me to take **one** teaspoonful of cough medicine every four **hours** for the next 48 hours. She said I **may be all right** by **tomorrow**.

Exercise 2.18

The **automobile** has changed the landscape and the way we live **dramatically** in less than a hundred years. **Cities** once were built on rivers, with stores clustered on Main Street. Now suburban **shopping** malls and parking lots sprawl for miles along the highways, and it's not **unusual** for families to own two or even three cars. Scientists who are **studying** the **environment** know that car **exhaust** fumes are a major cause of smog and acid rain. They even **believe** that our reliance on the internal **combustion** engine may be **contributing** to global warming. Yet many Americans still take **their** right to drive for granted, and the **average** person thinks commuting to work by car is far better than **riding** on the mass transit system.

RULES SUMMARY

A. Indent the first line of each **paragraph**.
B. Use capital letters for the first letter of each **sentence**; for the word **I**; for the first letter of a **name** or a word made from a **name**.
C. End every sentence with either a **period** or a question mark.
D. Avoid most **abbreviations**. Instead of & write **and**. Use abbreviations of titles like *Dr.* and *Mr.* with specific **names**.
E. Spell out the numbers **one** through **ten**. Don't spell out numbers in address, dates, or in most **scientific** or technical writing.
F. In contractions, use an **apostrophe** to show where letters have been omitted. [Check your spelling of *apostrophe*.]
G. Don't write **one** word as two words, or **two** words as one. Use your dictionary to find the meaning of the **one**-word form.

H.   If you divide a word at the end of a line, use a **hyphen** to divide it, between **syllables**. [Check your spelling of *hyphen*.]
I.   When proofreading, check carefully for **omitted** words and **repeated** words.
J.   When proofreading, use your **dictionary** to check spelling.

Exercise 2.19

1. Among many famous people who never graduated from **high school** are Alfred E. Smith, the politician, **and** Thomas Edison, the inventor.
2. Why **isn't Queen** Elizabeth coming to Toronto in **August ?**
3. **Everybody** in the congregation loves the **preacher** at Trinity **Church**.
4. Muhammad Ali earned $ **6,500,000** for **one** bout.
5. **Didn't** you lend that library **book** to **Uncle** Philip?
6. As **I** crossed the **avenue**, **someone** shouted my name.
7. In **three minutes**, **Megan's** going to be here.
8. George Patton, an **American general** in **World War** II, believed he had fought in **six** wars in previous incarnations.
9. This **summer I'm** [OR, **I am**] planning to enroll in Computer Science 101 in the **college** near my home.
10. The cassowary **and** the emu are **two** large **Australian** birds which **can't** fly.

Exercise 2.20   [Make sure that you indented the paragraph. ✗ marks where you should not leave a gap.]

_____ In our **history** class last week, I gave a report on the Golden Gate **Bridge** in California. I'd heard **a lot** about this bridge, but I **wasn't** really sure of all my facts. **When** I said the **bridge** was one of the **seven** wonders of the world, our **professor** asked me what the other wonders were. ✗ **In fact, I** didn't know, but I guessed the Rocky **Mountains**. No one else in the class even tried to guess. Our teacher laughed **and** said he'd give us a hint. **Every** single one of the seven wonders, he said, was built by man, and each was built at least 2,100 **years** ago. After a while, **someone** guessed **one** right answer, those huge stone pyramids in **Egypt**. But **nobody** could name even one of the other six wonders. Can you**?**

Exercise 2.21

The **public argument** between the big lighting **companies** and groups concerned about the **environment** has become quite **confusing** to a lot of people. The power companies claim that **their** experts are **studying** the **situation**. They say that by the year 2000 there will **probably** not be **enough** power if they can't build any more **nuclear** plants, and that **continuing** to use fossil **fuels** also adds to **environmental** problems. Big **business** is **generally prejudiced** in favor of the power companies. But many who are **interested** in the **future** of the planet oppose their plans because they **predict** that overreliance on **nuclear** power will **definitely** lead to more **tragedies** like the one at Chernobyl in the Soviet Union in 1986. The ordinary citizen **doesn't** know what to **believe**. Although blackouts and brownouts are **occurring regularly**, hardly any people are **writing** to their representatives in Congress about an energy policy, not **because** they're **indifferent**, but because they just don't know what all the **separate** issues are, let alone the answers.

Exercise 2.22   [You should have corrected only the words that you yourself missed or corrected wrongly in Exercise 2.21. Check your corrections against this list. Remember that dictionaries may differ in how they divide a word into syllables, so if your hyphens are different from those in the "syllables" column, check your answer against your own dictionary.]

	INCORRECT SPELLING	CORRECT SPELLING	SYLLABLES
1.	arguement	argument	ar-gu-ment
2.	companys	companies	com-pa-nies
3.	enviorment	environment	en-vi-ron-ment
4.	confussing	confusing	con-fus-ing
5.	thier	their	their
6.	studing	studying	stud-y-ing
7.	situtation	situation	sit-u-a-tion
8.	probaly	probably	prob-a-bly
9.	enought	enough	e-nough

10.	nuculear	nuclear	nu-cle-ar
11.	continueing	continuing	con-tin-u-ing
12.	feuls	fuels	fu-els
13.	enviromental	environmental	en-vi-ron-ment-al
14.	bussiness	business	bus-i-ness
15.	generaly	generally	gen-er-al-ly
16.	predjudiced	prejudiced	prej-u-diced
17.	intrested	interested	in-ter-est-ed
18.	furture	future	fu-ture
19.	perdict	predict	pre-dict
20.	nucular	nuclear	nu-cle-ar
21.	definately	definitely	def-i-nite-ly
22.	tradgedies	tragedies	tra-ge-dies
23.	dosen't	doesn't	does-n't
24.	beleive	believe	be-lieve
25.	occuring	occurring	oc-cur-ring
26.	regulerly	regularly	reg-u-lar-ly
27.	writting	writing	writ-ing
28.	becuase	because	be-cause
29.	indiffrent	indifferent	in-dif-fer-ent
30.	seperate	separate	se-par-ate

Module 3: *Spelling and Wrong Words*

Exercise 3.1 [[Different dictionaries may use different words in their definitions. Count your answer correct if you have chosen the right meaning, even if the words you have copied are somewhat different.]

1. *Compassion* means **a deep feeling of sharing the suffering of another; mercy**.
   The word that is needed in this sentence is **composition**, which means **a short school essay**.
2. *Hole* means **a cavity in a solid, . . . an opening through something**.
   The word that is needed in this sentence is **whole**, which means **containing all parts, complete, . . . constituting the full amount**.
3. *Accept* means **to receive something willingly or gladly, . . . to answer affirmatively**.
   The word that is needed in this sentence is **except**, which means **with the exclusion of, all but**.

Exercise 3.2

1.   WW   SP
   That is <u>know</u> big <u>promblem</u>.
2.   WW   SP
   She <u>brought</u> a ham <u>sanwitch</u> at the corner delicatessen.
3.   SP   WW
   <u>Thier</u> class was <u>to</u> large for the room.
4.   WW   SP
   <u>Their</u> is an important <u>diffrence</u> between spelling mistakes and wrong words.
5.   WW   SP
   His <u>mine</u> just wasn't focused on what he was <u>writting</u>.

Exercise 3.3 [Parentheses and italics mark the words that you should have circled.]

1. Lex bought <u>a computer</u> *(and)* <u>a printer</u>.
2. Then he <u>studied</u> *(and)* <u>practiced</u> with his word processing program.
3. After that, he <u>wrote</u> *(and)* <u>printed</u> a dozen letters in <u>an hour</u> *(and)* <u>a half.</u>

Exercise 3.4

1. **a** horse
    an hourglass
2. **a** service station
    an S-curve
3. **an** umbrella
    a university education

4. **a** once-in-a-lifetime-chance
    an ordinary example
5. **an** X-ray machine
    a xylophone
6. **a** C on the test
    an A on the test

Exercise 3.5

There is **an** American political party whose symbol is **a** donkey, **and** there is another whose symbol is **an** elephant.

Exercise 3.6

1. Sharon liked studying current events better **than** history.
2. **Then** she signed up for an archeology course.
3. Her class took a field trip to the Indian pueblos at Santa Clara and Taos in New Mexico; **then** they visited Mesa Verde National Monument.
4. They examined more **than** a dozen cliff dwellings of the ancient Anasazi culture which were abandoned mysteriously more **than** 600 years ago.
5. Now Sharon is thinking of majoring in Native American history rather **than** continuing her studies in journalism.

Exercise 3.7

When you spend more **than** you earn, **then** it's time to take out a loan.

Exercise 3.8

1. The celebrated orator Edward Everett spoke **to** the crowd at Gettysburg.
2. He spoke for **two** hours.
3. Abraham Lincoln spoke, **too** .
4. A photographer stood up **to** take Lincoln's picture.
5. By the time he had focused his camera, he was already **too** late.
6. After less than **two** minutes, Lincoln sat down.
7. It was **too** late **to** capture a great moment of history, the Gettysburg Address.

Exercise 3.9

Ramon goes **to** the school gym **to** swim because the health club is **too** expensive. **Two** of his friends go there, **too**.

Exercise 3.10

1. **It's** important to check the air pressure in your car's tires every week.
2. And **it's** a good idea to have your car serviced every 5,000 miles.
3. The garage crew should change **its** oil and oil filter.
4. Every 10,000 miles, your car should have **its** tires rotated.
5. Your car will last longer if **it's** not neglected.

Exercise 3.11

It's strange but true that an insect will often eat **its** mate, or even **its** offspring.

Exercise 3.12

1. Even if you don't believe in astrology, **you're** unusual if you don't know what sign of the Zodiac you were born under.

2.	Astrologers say that **your** sign in the stars influences **your** character and attitudes.
3.	For example, if **you're** a Leo, **your** temperament is domineering, like a lion's.
4.	And if **you're** a Gemini (born under the sign of the twins), **your** friends will notice that you have contradictory traits.
5.	To tell the truth, doesn't **your** sign of the Zodiac fit you?

Exercise 3.13

When **you're** anxious, **your** blood pressure sometimes rises.

Exercise 3.14

1.	Throughout the United States **there** are many young people who dream of a future in professional sports.
2.	**They're** interested in athletics, not **their** studies.
3.	**Their** minds are on news stories about huge salaries made by professional athletes.
4.	So every day **they're** out practicing instead of studying in the library.
5.	But **there** are few stories about college players who don't make the pros, or about high-paid athletes who lose all **their** money to bad investments.
6.	Students should be aware that **there** are few things more important than **their** college degrees.

Exercise 3.15

There are millions of men who support equal rights for women, and when the Equal Rights Amendment comes up for a vote again, **they're** going to be **there** at the polls to cast **their** votes for it.

Exercise 3.16

1.	**It's** the last decade of the 20th century.
2.	If these politicians are honest, **they're** unusual.
3.	It saves time if you admit it when **you're** wrong.
4.	The door slammed, and **then** he finally understood.
5.	The Belmont Sisters will appear on this program, **too**.
6.	The city is going to amend **its** charter.
7.	Communism collapsed in Russia sooner **than** anyone expected.
8.	**There** are three vacation days this month.
9.	**Your** reading level is a major ingredient of **your** success at most jobs.
10.	Shakespeare's most famous words are probably, " **To** be or not **to** be."

Exercise 3.17 [Dictionaries may differ in their definitions. No matter how your definitions are worded, make sure that you have picked definitions that make sense in the sentences.]

1.	*Passed* is the past-tense form of the verb **pass** .
	Past means **beyond in position**.
	Just **past** Rosie's bar, we **passed** a big accident.

2.	*Know* means **to possess knowledge, be aware**.
	No means **not any**.
	We **know** that you have **no** time to see us.

3.	*Here* means **to this place**.
	Hear means **to learn by hearing, to acquire, as news or information**.
	Here comes Joseph to **hear** the latest gossip.

4.	*Whose* is a possessive form meaning **belonging to *who* or *whom***.
	Who's is a contraction for **who is**.
	Who's the student **whose** papers are on the table?

5.	*Find* means **to come upon after a search**.
	Fine means **quite well, very well**.
	Harris felt **fine** after he was able to **find** the money.

6.	*Went* is the past-tense form of the verb **go**.
	When means **at the time that**.
	We were relieved **when** Aunt Julia finally **went** home.

Exercise 3.18

1. *Know* means **to possess knowledge**.
    Now means **at the present time**.
    No means **not any, not one**.
    Now , after years of research, doctors **know** how to prevent polio, but there is still **no** vaccine for the common cold.

2. *Bought* is the past-tense form of the verb **buy**.
    Brought is the past-tense form of the verb **bring**.
    My cousin **bought** a keg of beer and **brought** it to the party.

3. *Quit* means **to give up, to put something aside, to cease**.
    Quite means **to the greatest extent, completely, really**.
    Quiet means **making no noise, . . . free of turmoil and agitation**.
    Millie is usually a **quiet** person, but she has **quite** a temper, and once she gets started arguing, it's hard for her to **quit**.

4. *Who* is a pronoun referring to **a person or persons**.
    How means **in what way or manner, . . . a method of doing or performing**.
    Anyone **who** goes canoeing should know **how** to swim.

5. *Chance* means **an opportunity**.
    Change means **to make different, to alter**.
    Here's a **chance** to **change** your life: Take up hot air ballooning.

6. *Where* means **at or in what place**.
    Were is a past-tense form of the verb **be**.
    For a thousand miles, there **were** no mountains **where** it was possible to ski.

Exercise 3.19

1. I have complete **confidence** in you. I'm **confident** that you'll succeed.
2. Everyone values an **independent** person. However, sometimes it's hard to tell **independence** from stubbornness.
3. My father expects his children to be **obedient**. However, most parents today do not expect total **obedience**, although they do demand respect.
4. What's the **difference** between a calculator and a computer? A calculator is **different** from a computer mainly because it's used for only one purpose.
5. When choosing a career, you must consider what things are most **important** to you. Do not underestimate the **importance** of enjoying what you do.

RULES SUMMARY

1. *A* and *an* both mean **one**. Use **an** before words that start with a vowel sound, and use *a* before words that start with a **consonant** sound.
2. Do not confuse words that sound alike.
    a. Use *then* to mean **at that time** or **next**. Use *than* to **compare** two things or ideas.
    b. Use *to* to mean something like **in the direction of** and use *to* in an **infinitive**. Use *too* to mean **also**, or to mean **excessively** or *more than enough*. Use *two* to mean the **number** that comes after *one*.
    c. Use *its* to mean **belonging to it**. Use *it's* as a contraction of **it is** or **it has**.
    d. Use *your* to mean **belonging to you**. Use *you're* as a contraction of **you are**.
    e. Use *their* to mean **belonging to them**. Use *they're* as a contraction of **they are**. Use *there* to mean **at that place** or to start a **sentence**.
3. Do not confuse words that **look** alike or contain many of the same letters.
4. Do not confuse words that are **related** to each other.

Exercise 3.20

According to **an** old story, **an** astronomer claimed that he had **a** unique power. Whenever he gave **an** order, the sun, moon, **and** stars always obeyed. But he did not want to use his power in **an** irresponsible way, so he was careful to give commands only at **an** appropriate time. He explained that if he ordered the sun to rise **an** hour too soon, the crops would

burn up, **and** of course, **an** early moon would confuse the tides. But
on **a** certain evening, to celebrate **an** anniversary, the astronomer
ate **an** enormous meal, drank **an** entire bottle of wine,
and didn't wake up until noon the next day. He was amazed to see the disobedient
sun already shining in **a** cloudless sky. Broken-hearted, he retired to his cave
and never spoke to **a** heavenly body again.

Exercise 3.21

1. Where is **your** dictionary? **You're** sure to need it today.
2. This show has lost **its** popularity, and so **it's** time to take it off the air.
3. Diane struggled **to** the bus stop. She was carrying **two** big boxes, and had a full shopping bag, **too.** This luggage was almost **too** heavy for her to handle.
4. The passengers are picking up **their** luggage in the airport. Two friends are meeting them **there** to drive them home. **They're** all eager to get going.

Exercise 3.22

If **you're** not in the habit of writing down **your** ideas and then proofreading what is written there on the page, **it's** hard for you to see that, although some contractions and possessive pronouns sound exactly alike, **they're** very different. People who don't write much may not use apostrophes at all, because they don't realize their importance. **They're** simply not aware that every contraction must have its apostrophe to be correct. On the other hand, **there** are writers who treat apostrophes like confetti. They scatter them around in **their** writing like decorations. But **they're** guilty of confusing **their** readers even more than the writers who leave apostrophes out entirely. If **you're** ambitious to become a clear and correct writer, it's important for you to learn the following apostrophe rule and **its** application: "**There** is a group of words called possessive pronouns, which mean *belonging to*. These words are never written with apostrophes. When you use an apostrophe with a pronoun, **it's** always a contraction. Contractions can also be written as two words."

Exercise 3.23

It's an interesting fact that many people are much better at speaking **than** at writing. **There** are some people who can start a riot just by jumping up on **an** old crate and talking to **an** angry crowd. But **too** few of these born orators are able to write a **two**-line letter to the newspaper which **its** editor wouldn't find **too** awkward and ungrammatical to publish. Then there are those who would rather spend two hundred dollars on telephone calls **than** two dollars on stamps. When they pick up a telephone, **they're** chattering away in an instant. **And** yet when they pick up a pencil, **it's** likely that they'll chew it for twenty minutes before **they're** able to write a single word. You may be an excellent speaker, but unless you're able to write your ideas correctly and clearly, **you're** going to have problems.

Exercise 3.24

1. Even when two bottles of wine are made from grapes from the same vines, there is often a big **difference** between them if they're made in **different** years.
2. When teenagers see a lot of sex and **violence** on TV and in the movies, their behavior may become more **violent**.
3. **Independence** has its price; to become **independent**, you must learn to live alone.
4. I know that **patience** is a virtue, but I'm not very **patient** with a doctor who makes appointments with three **patients** in the same hour.
5. Is money **important**? Here's a clue: Only rich people say that money has no **importance**.
6. If you don't lose your **confidence**, you'll be OK. Act **confident**, and you'll get the job.
7. Not long ago, **obedience** was expected of every wife, but now few brides are willing to make a vow to be **obedient.**
8. The **silence** in the playroom is disturbing. Those children are never **silent** unless they're into mischief.

Exercise 3.25

An amazing number **of** people suffer from phobias, or strange fears. After a comet **passed** over Arizona, a woman **who** lived thousands of miles away in Maine refused to go out **of** her house for five years. She **thought** a falling **star** might land on her. A man in Detroit was terrified of elevators. He had to **find** a new doctor when his old one moved to an office on the 26th floor. A woman with a **violent** fear of lightning always hid under the bed during thunderstorms. That was the only place **where** she felt safe. A man became terrified of germs, so he **went** to a store and **bought** a surgical mask. He wore it night and day, **whether** at home or at work. Even **though** people with these phobias are often **quite** intelligent, they can't **accept** the evidence of facts about their fears. It's **no** use telling them how few people are killed by falling stars or elevators or lightning, or that you're not safe from germs even though you **breathe through** a mask. Their **minds** are full of irrational fears; they just can't **hear** you.

Exercise 3.27: Review Exercise A

You hear **a lot** about "the wonders of the world," but only a few people know that this phrase originally **referred** to seven wonders in the ancient world. Hardly anybody nowadays can name these monuments of early civilization. **There** is a good reason for this. Just one of these wonders is still standing, the huge stone pyramids in Egypt. A few people also **know** about the second wonder, the magnificent terraced gardens which a king of **Babylon** built to please his wife. The **third** wonder, a seated statue of Zeus in a temple at Olympia in **Greece**, was made of ivory **and** gold, with precious jewels in **its** eyes. (If this huge statue could have stood up, it would have hit **its** head on the **ceiling**.) Some fragments of the **fourth** wonder, a **temple** dedicated to the goddess Diana, were found in **Turkey** about a hundred **years** ago. Earthquakes destroyed all **three** of the other wonders: a beautiful tomb built for King Mausolus in Turkey, **an** enormous lighthouse near the coast of Egypt, and a giant statue of Apollo at Rhodes in Greece. The colossal statue at Rhodes must have been more spectacular **than** the Statue of Liberty. According to an old legend, it stood in the middle of **a** harbor with its legs spread **apart**, while ships **passed** between them.

Module 4: *Nouns*

Exercise 4.1 [Remember: Parentheses and italics mark the words that you should have circled.]

1. A *(bus)* finally arrived.
2. An empty *(bus)* finally arrived.
3. A completely empty *(bus)* finally arrived.
4. The *(computer)* has a *(printer)*.
5. The new *(computer)* has a broken *(printer)*.

Exercise 4.2

1.   S   P
   One oak *(tree)* may have 17,000 separate *(leaves)*.
2.   P   S
   Sixty-three young *(children)* crowded into one noisy *(room)*.
3.   S   P
   One important *(idea)* was discussed for seven long *(hours)*.

Exercise 4.3

1. two **trucks**
2. a few **kisses**
3. several dirty **dishes**

4.   four new **shirts**
5.   two sandy **beaches**

Exercise 4.4

1.   many loud **gasps**
2.   two bad **risks**
3.   three **toasts** to the bride

Exercise 4.5

1.   four computer **disks**
2.   some sharp **edges**
3.   three **buzzes** on the doorbell
4.   both broken **wrists**
5.   some big **boxes**
6.   three hard **tests**
7.   a few broken **sticks**
8.   several huge **losses**

Exercise 4.6

Austrians are fascinated by timepieces. In Vienna, many **streets** have two or three shops that sell fancy **watches** of all shapes and sizes, plus clocks made of gold, silver, porcelain, and many other precious **materials**. In Vienna's Clock Museum are two astronomical **clocks**, each as big as a room, and several **timepieces** so tiny that you can't read the **numbers** on their faces without a magnifying glass. The most famous Viennese timepiece is the Anker Clock. Three **floors** above the street, twelve life-sized **statues** of Austrian national heroes march out, and one by one, for sixty **minutes**, each moves across the clock's enormous face. When the clock strikes the hour, **melodies** by Vienna's many musical geniuses salute each of these historical **figures**.

Exercise 4.7

1.   some crying **babies**
2.   six sharp **knives**
3.   many green **leaves**
4.   those fond **memories**
5.   their religious **beliefs**
6.   my cousins' **wives**

Exercise 4.8

1.   four **feet**
2.   several **men**
3.   three crying **children**
4.   two loose **teeth**
5.   both young **women**
6.   all the news **media**

Exercise 4.9

1.   The →*(boat)* sank quickly.
2.   One →*(woman)* donated a →*(cake)*.
3.   That →*(messenger)* picked up this →*(package)* from the →*(store)*.

Exercise 4.10

1.
   These fresh *(peaches)* taste good.

2.
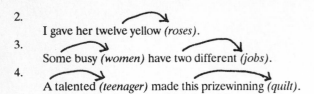
I gave her twelve yellow *(roses)*.
3.
Some busy *(women)* have two different *(jobs)*.
4.
A talented *(teenager)* made this prizewinning *(quilt)*.

Exercise 4.11

1.
    one picture *(frame)* S   many picture *(frames)* P
2.
    a political *(speech)* S   some political *(speeches)* P
3.
    that simple *(task)* S   those simple *(tasks)* P
4.
    this local *(library)* S   these local *(libraries)* P
5.
    an unusual *(child)* S   several unusual *(children)* P

Exercise 4.12 [Remember: Plural nouns can often be written with different plural determiners, or even with no determiner. Stars show where different plural determiners may be used. Be sure to check that both the determiner and the noun are plural.]

1.   these races
2.   the lists
3.   *two* men
4.   those tests
5.   *several* stitches
6.   *some* women

Exercise 4.13

1.   that patch
2.   one pony
3.   this knife
4.   the book
5.   a risk [or one risk]
6.   a push [or one push]

RULES SUMMARY, Part 1

1.   Nouns are words that **name** things.
2.   A noun that names one thing is **singular**. A noun that names more than one thing is **plural**.
3.   To make most nouns plural, add **S** or **ES** to the base form. A plural noun form
      with an *ES* ending always has an **extra** syllable. **Never** add *ES* to a noun
      ending in *SK* or **SP** or **ST**.
4.   To make the plural form of a noun ending in a consonant plus *Y*, change the *Y* to **I** and
      add *ES*. Some nouns ending in *IFE* or *F* change the *F* to **V** before adding *ES*.
5.   To make most irregular nouns plural, change the **whole word**.
6.   Nouns are usually used with **determiners** like *a* and *some*, that tell **which** or **how many**.
7.   In a noun phrase, both the determiner and the noun must be either **singular** or **plural**.

Exercise 4.14 [Remember: Parentheses and italics mark the words that you should have circled. Stars show where different plural determiners may be used.]

1.   The *(woman)* wrote a mystery *(story)*.
      The **women** wrote *some* mystery **stories**.

2. That *(man)* liked this *(scarf)*.
    Those **men** liked **these** **scarfs** [OR, **scarves**].
3. A *(girl)* fixed this broken *(shelf)*.
    Several **girls** fixed **these** broken **shelves**.
4. This *(child)* broke that *(dish)*.
    These **children** broke **those** **dishes**.
5. A *(neighbor)* planted a hickory *(tree)*.
    ** **Neighbors** planted **many** hickory **trees**.
6. The *(boy)* cut up one large *(pumpkin)* for a *(pie)*.
    The **boys** cut up **two** large **pumpkins** for **two** **pies**.

Exercise 4.15

1. The *(lawyer)* won her *(case)*.
    The **lawyers** won **their** **cases**.
2. One *(neighbor)* never mowed his *(lawn)*.
    Two **neighbors** never mowed **their** **lawns.**
3. That *(child)* caught a *(butterfly)* with his *(net)*.
    Those **children** caught ** **butterflies** with **their** **nets**.
4. The *(man)* made a phone *(call)*, and then he left.
    The **men** made **several** phone **calls**, and then **they** left.
5. This *(woman)* earned her master's *(degree)*.
    These **women** earned **their** master's **degrees**.
6. Because his *(wife)* had gone camping, that *(man)* ate out a lot.
    Because **their** **wives** had gone camping, **those** **men** ate out a lot.

Exercise 4.16

Both **parents** of the newborn quadruplets were returning home from the hospital. For the first 24 **hours**, two of their four tiny **babies** had struggled for their **lives**. Although still in incubators, now they all seemed to be doing well. So at this moment the parents were worrying more about the many huge **bills** that were piling up. The mother was asking herself why she had taken those fertility **pills**. And where, they both wondered, would they get the cash for all the **things** on their shopping list—diapers, **blankets**, **shirts**, pins, **bottles**, and countless other basic **items**? Approaching the front door, the couple saw that all the **lights** were shining in the three rooms of their small house. At first, they were afraid that burglars had been there, but as they looked around inside, their **eyes** widened with surprise. In the living room were four **boxes**, each filled with baby clothes, **toys**, and medical **supplies**. Among other **things** were four pairs of **booties**, matching sweaters and caps in four different **colors**, and even four little **hairbrushes**. When they picked up a big brown envelope, their **neighbors**, hiding in the backyard, all shouted at once through the kitchen window, "Open it!" More than fifty **checks** fell out on the table. For a few months, anyway, their **worries** about money were over.

Exercise 4.17

1. Leora broke one of her mother's favorite **dishes**.
    The handle of the **dish** broke off.
2. Another of those awful **tests** was given yesterday.
    Part of that **test** gave me a lot of trouble.
3. One of the **questions** was especially tricky.
    The first word of the **question** puzzled me.
4. Every one of those **knives** needs sharpening.
    The blade of the **knife** rusted in the rain.

Exercise 4.18

1. a lot of **ideas**
    a lot of **information**
2. a lot of **equipment**

a lot of **typewriters**
3.   a lot of **slices**
       a lot of **bread**
4.   a lot of **accidents**
       a lot of **luck**
5.   a lot of **leisure**
       a lot of **hobbies**
6.   a lot of **assignments**
       a lot of **homework**

Exercise 4.19

1.   Sophie has no **interest** in spelunking.
       Sophie has so many other **interests** that she hardly has time to sleep.
2.   Most of the **time** it is better to keep your temper.
       How many **times** must I tell you?
3.   **Experience** may be the best teacher.
       We usually can learn the most from our bad **experiences**.

RULES SUMMARY, Part 2

1.   Nouns following *of* or *of the* are often **plural**.
2.   Nouns naming things that can be **counted** have singular and plural forms.
3.   Nouns naming things that can't be **counted** have only one form.

Exercise 4.20

1.   Neither of the **apartments** was big enough for a family of four.
2.   A lot of the **steel** for the building had rusted.
3.   Each of the **women** thought that her child was the most intelligent in the class.
4.   How much of the **information** was useful for your paper?
5.   That is one of the best **comedies** the drama club has ever staged.
6.   Two quarts of whole **milk** daily is no longer recommended, even for adolescents.
7.   We bought a big bunch of **balloons**.
8.   There was a pile of broken **furniture** in the corner of the basement.
9.   Our teacher gave at least two assignments of **homework** every week.
10.   The roof of the **barn** was blown off in the storm.
11.   Happy coincidences are examples of good **luck**.
12.   Fresh vegetables are an excellent source of **vitamins**.

Exercise 4.21 [Remember: Parentheses and italics mark the words that you should have circled. Stars show where different plural determiners may be used. Be sure to check that both the determiner and the noun are plural.]

1.   This *(book)* contained that *(information)*.
       These books contained that information.
2.   The *(boy)* asked for hockey *(equipment)* for his *(birthday)*.
       The **boys** asked for hockey equipment for **their birthdays**.
3.   One *(piece)* of *(music)* will not be enough for that *(ceremony)*.
       ***Three* pieces** of music will not be enough for **those ceremonies**.
4.   The new *(tenant)* built some *(furniture)* for her *(apartment)*.
       The new **tenants** built some furniture for **their apartments**.
5.   This *(car)* stalled in *(traffic)*; its *(driver)* couldn't start it.
       These cars stalled in traffic; **their drivers** couldn't start **them**.
6.   That *(woman)* had much *(experience)* with *(carpentry)*.
       Those women had much experience with carpentry.

Exercise 4.22

       Joe and Gloria often switched **work-roles** before they had their first two **children**. About
three **times** a month, Gloria used to bring home several of her **friends** from work, and Joe would

prepare fancy **meals** for them. He specialized in **dishes** they could get their **teeth** into. One night
he served thick French onion soup to his two **guests**. As he mixed their **drinks**, he gave them some
advice about cooking: "When I sliced these **onions**, I used the sharpest of all my **knives**. Always
cut the cheese into small pieces. Three **dashes** of **salt** should be enough for a quart of soup. Keep
many different **spices** on your **shelves**." The women said that his soup was one of the best **feasts**
they had ever eaten. Gloria gave her husband two big **kisses** as a reward, and after dinner she
helped him clean up the mess. The other two **women** went home and told their **men** to make
onion soup for them. The next night stomping **feet**, several loud **crashes**, and excited **cries** were
heard in the kitchens of these **ladies**. Later they told Gloria that onion soup had turned their
happy marriages into complete **wrecks**.

Exercise 4.23 [Remember: Stars show where different plural determiners may be used.]

   Some rich local **citizens** recently bought *two* beautiful old **houses**, fixed **them** up, and opened
them to the public. *Some* teachers took **their** seventh-grade **classes** to visit **these** **mansions**.
Several **students** asked the **guides** to give **them** some information about the **families** who once lived there.
The **guides** told **them** all about the **men** and the **women** who had built **these houses** long ago.
Other **children** wanted to know more about the furniture, such as the tiny ornate **desks**, the huge **beds**,
the **cradles** made of jet black wood, and the six-foot **clocks** which still kept perfect time. Later on,
in **their** English **classes**, *many* **students** made up ** spooky **stories** about the **ghosts** who still sat
at **those** fancy **desks**, and rocked **those** black **cradles**, and slept in **those** big **beds**.

Exercise 4.24: Review Exercise B

   Three brown **bears** had frightened a troop of young **scouts** camping in the forest. When two
rangers arrived to get some **information** from the scout leaders about what had happened, some
of the little **campers** were still as pale as **ghosts**, and others were too **scared** to speak. The
children said that **three** huge bears had knocked over several **tables**, had torn one of their **tents**, and
then had run off into a clump of trees. **The** rangers knew that **an** adult female bear and **its** two
cubs were in the **neighborhood**, and they explained that female bears are even more ferocious
than males when **they're** protecting **their** cubs. One of the leaders **admitted** that the children had
left **a lot** of food out on **their** picnic tables, including an apple pie, several **loaves** of bread, and some
honey. "It's lucky you're not all dead," **one** ranger told all the campers angrily. "**There's** nothing
more dangerous **than** leaving food out when bears are **around**. You and your leaders can't be **too**
careful on these camping **trips**." The **men** left, shaking their heads. They were glad they **didn't**
have to kill a bear just because some of the **campers** had acted foolishly.

Module 5: *Verbs and Verb Phrases*

Exercise 5.1

1. PRESENT
    PAST
    FUTURE
2. FUTURE
    PAST
    PRESENT

Exercise 5.2

1. The flowers <u>bloomed</u>.   PAST
    The flowers <u>will bloom</u>.   FUTURE
    The base form of the verb is **BLOOM** .

2.   Acid rain <u>will destroy</u> living things.   FUTURE
      Acid rain <u>destroys</u> living things.   PRESENT
      The base form of the verb is **DESTROY** .
3.   These days many adults <u>attend</u> college.   PRESENT
      In the past few adults <u>attended</u> college.   PAST
      The base form of the verb is **ATTEND** .

Exercise 5.3

1.   Mr. Rafael <u>walks</u> fast.
      Mr. Rafael **walked** fast.
      Mr. Rafael **will walk** fast.
2.   The skies <u>cleared</u> gradually.
      The skies **clear** gradually.
      The skies **will clear** gradually.
3.   The bank tellers <u>will check</u> the total.
      The bank tellers **check** the total.
      The bank tellers **checked** the total.

Exercise 5.4

1.   The grass in the back yard three feet high.   X
      The grass in the back yard <u>grew</u> three feet high.   SENT
2.   Business English <u>is</u> a popular course.   SENT
      A popular course, Business English.   X
3.   The children in the playground.   X
      The children <u>are</u> in the playground.   SENT

Exercise 5.5

1.   Happy children.   X
2.   Children <u>play</u> games.   SENT
3.   Nobody <u>called</u>.   SENT
4.   It <u>is</u> late.   SENT
5.   Good evening.   X

Exercise 5.6

1.   Many students <u>work</u> slowly but eventually <u>succeed</u>.
      Many students **worked** slowly but eventually **succeeded**.
2.   When the twins <u>arrive</u> home late, their parents <u>complain</u>.
      When the twins **arrived** home late, their parents **complained**.
3.   Every Monday the managers <u>discuss</u> their plans and <u>decide</u> on a course of action for the week.
      Every Monday the managers **discussed** their plans and **decided** on a course of action for the week.

Exercise 5.7 [Remember: Parentheses and italics mark the words that you should have circled.]

1.   *(Where's)* Inez?
      Where **is** Inez?
2.   She *(wasn't)* at work today and *(isn't)* at home now.
      She **was** not at work today and **is** not at home now.
3.   *(There's)* a memo that *(I'm)* eager to get from her.
      There **is** a memo I **am** eager to get from her.

Exercise 5.8

1.   Sandra <u>plans</u> *(to type)* her paper.
      Sandra **planned** *(to type)* her paper.
      [You should have doubled the <u>n</u> in <u>planned</u>.]

2.   Alan <u>wants</u> *(to climb)* Mt. Hood.
     Alan **wanted** *(to climb)* Mt. Hood.
3.   Trump <u>hopes</u> *(to build)* the tallest skyscraper in the world.
     Trump **hoped** *(to build)* the tallest skyscraper in the world.

Exercise 5.9

1.   My boss <u>starts</u> *(working)* before breakfast.
     My boss **started** *(working)* before breakfast.
2.   *(Bicycling)* <u>requires</u> stamina.
     (Bicycling) **required** stamina.
3.   The Scouts <u>like</u> *(going)* on *(camping)* trips.
     The Scouts **liked** *(going)* on *(camping)* trips.

Exercise 5.10

1.   The jockeys <u>prefer</u> to ride at Hialeah Park.
     The jockeys **preferred** to ride at Hialeah Park.
     [You should have doubled the <u>r</u> in <u>preferred</u>.]
2.   Walking briskly <u>burns</u> calories.
     Walking briskly **burned** calories.
3.   Cooking and gardening <u>help</u> Yves to relax.
     Cooking and gardening **helped** Yves to relax.

Exercise 5.11

1.   A.   These tiny insects <u>fly</u> ten miles a day.
     B.   This tiny fly <u>travels</u> great distances.
          Fly is the verb in sentence **A**.
2.   A.   My aunt <u>cooks</u> gourmet dinners.
     B.   The best cooks <u>prepare</u> simple meals.
          Cooks is the verb in sentence **A**.
3.   A.   Many dances <u>demand</u> endurance.
     B.   Mary <u>dances</u> for the American Ballet Company.
          Dances is the verb in sentence **B**.
4.   A.   The priest <u>married</u> the couple.
     B.   The newly married couple <u>exchanged</u> rings.
          Married is the verb in sentence **A**.
5.   A.   Bike races <u>are</u> a new and popular sport in America.
     B.   The Portland bike team <u>races</u> every Tuesday evening.
          Races is the verb in sentence **B**.

Exercise 5.12

1.   The Lundbergs <u>need</u> to paint their house again.
2.   Skydiving <u>is</u> exciting to watch.
3.   Shouting and screaming, the children <u>rushed</u> into the playground.
4.   Because Miriam <u>hates</u> to hurt anyone's feelings, she <u>ends</u> up [OR, <u>ends up</u>] telling lies.
5.   Most guests <u>will enjoy</u> eating outdoors.
6.   There<u>'s</u> no place like home.

RULES SUMMARY, Part 1

1.   To find the verb in a sentence, find the word that can change form to show different **tenses** [OR, times].
2.   Every sentence must have at least one **verb**.
3.   *To* + the base form of a verb is an **infinitive**, which is never a verb.
4.   An **ING** word by itself is never a verb.
5.   Words that show **action** are not always verbs.

Exercise 5.13

Near the Italian town of Maranello, a blood-red car <u>rockets</u> around a twisting track. The speedometer <u>leaps</u> to 120 miles per hour. The driver <u>pumps</u> the brakes and <u>careens</u> into a hairpin turn. Skidding briefly, he <u>turns</u> the steering wheel sharply to regain his hold on the road. He <u>roars</u> around the track a few more times, and the car <u>screeches</u> to a stop. The driver <u>steps</u> out grinning. This Ferrari <u>passes</u>.

Enzo Ferrari <u>began</u> producing his racing cars in 1929. His trademark <u>was</u> a prancing black horse, the insignia of the Italian flying ace, Francesco Baracca. Ferrari cars <u>started</u> to win racing championships during the next decade. In 1945, Ferrari <u>designed</u> his first 12-cylinder model for everyday use. He <u>developed</u> a system of checks and controls to make certain that every part <u>was</u> perfect, and <u>hired</u> daring designers to create shovel-nosed hoods and swooping fenders. The result <u>was</u> a powerful and almost indestructible machine, so beautiful that thousands of car buffs <u>rushed</u> to buy it, even at extravagant prices.

The next Ferrari which <u>will come</u> out of Maranello <u>will cost</u> nearly $200,000, and it's likely to have a top speed of around 200 miles per hour. The Ferrari factory <u>will produce</u> no more than a few thousand of these cars, and they'<u>re</u> sure to disappear from the dealers' shops on the same day they <u>arrive</u>. Then most of them <u>will spend</u> their lives cruising over roads where the speed limit <u>is</u> 55 miles an hour—about one-fourth their capacity. Still, their proud drivers <u>will continue</u> to smile, and to smile again, as heads <u>turn</u> and eyes <u>stare</u> at these aristocrats of the road.

Exercise 5.14

This year Jan and Walter **are** intern doctors at Central Hospital. Medical facts **fill** their brains, but they **have** little experience in caring for critically ill people. They **work** 36-hour shifts. Just as they **tumble** into bed, too weary to shower, their beepers **sound** again. Their patients **need** transfusions. They **have** raging fevers. Jan and Walter **stagger** back to the intensive care unit. Their eyes **blur** as they **try** to read their patients' charts. They **worry** about making fatal errors. The resident doctors **check** Jan's prescriptions carefully, and the nurses **watch** closely as Walter's fingers **fumble** with the intravenous tubes. The patients just **pray** hard that no mistakes **slip** by.

Exercise 5.15

Last fall my friend Madeline **received** a summons to serve as a juror in civil court. Madeline **loved** to read about dramatic trials, but jury duty in civil court **was** quite a disappointment. Every day for two weeks, Madeline **listened** to lawyers as they **explained** their not very exciting cases. In one case, a man **collided** with a glass door. In another, a woman **slipped** on a rug. These people **wanted** compensation for minor bruises and nervous strain. The lawyers **asked** Madeline what she **did** for a living, what church she **attended**, what newspapers she **enjoyed** reading, etc. But they never **picked** her to be on a jury. They **seemed** to prefer people who **smiled** a lot when they **talked** and who **looked** at comic books while they **waited**. Madeline almost **died** of frustration and **hoped** to be called for jury duty in criminal court next time.

Exercise 5.16

1. Sasha <u>exercises</u> every night.   PRESENT
    Sasha <u>is exercising</u> right now.   PRESENT
    Sasha <u>will exercise</u> tomorrow.   FUTURE
2. William <u>was working</u> last night.   PAST
    William <u>is working</u> today.   PRESENT
    William <u>works</u> hard.   PRESENT

William <u>will work</u> for me next week.   FUTURE
William <u>worked</u> for me last week.   PAST

Exercise 5.17

1.   I <u>am planning</u> a trip to Canada.
      a.   The helping verb in this sentence is **am** .
      b.   The main verb in this sentence is **planning**.
      c.   The base form of the main verb is **PLAN**.
2.   The Economics Department <u>had planned</u> to install a new computer.
      a.   The helping verb in this sentence is **had**.
      b.   The main verb in this sentence is **planned**.
      c.   The base form of the main verb is **PLAN**.
3.   <u>Does</u> anybody ever <u>plan</u> to have an accident?
      a.   The helping verb in this sentence is **does**.
      b.   The main verb in this sentence is **plan**.
      c.   The base form of the main verb is **PLAN**.

Exercise 5.18

1.   Carl <u>is doing</u> research on the last primary election.
      Carl **was doing** research on the last primary election.
2.   Fewer Americans <u>are registering</u> to vote.
      Fewer Americans **were registering** to vote.
3.   The candidates <u>are worrying</u> about budget deficits while they <u>are promising</u> not to raise taxes.
      The candidates **were worrying** about budget deficits while they **were promising** not to raise taxes.

Exercise 5.19

1.   Geraldine's father **has enrolled** at his daughter's college.
      a.   The base form of the helping verb in this sentence is **HAVE** .
      b.   The base form of the main verb in this sentence is **ENROLL**.
2.   He and his daughter both **are studying** ancient Greek literature.
      a.   The base form of the helping verb in this sentence is **BE**.
      b.   The base form of the main verb in this sentence is **STUDY**.
3.   Even before this semester, they always **did enjoy** works by the great authors of antiquity.
      a.   The base form of the helping verb in this sentence is **DO**.
      b.   The base form of the main verb in this sentence is **ENJOY**.

Exercise 5.20

1.   Many households <u>have</u> two or more television sets.
      Most children <u>have watched</u> many hours of TV before entering kindergarten.
2.   We certainly <u>did try</u> to file our taxes on time.
      We <u>did</u> most of the paperwork last weekend.
3.   Swimming <u>is</u> a relaxing form of exercise.
      The motel guests <u>were relaxing</u> beside the pool.

Exercise 5.21 [Remember: Parentheses and italics mark the words that you should have circled.]

1.   Mariko <u>is studying</u> in the library.
2.   Some people <u>like</u> *(studying)* late at night.
3.   *(Studying)* history <u>demands</u> a good memory for dates.
4.   The whole class <u>was studying</u> hard for the mid-term examination.
5.   We <u>made</u> a date to begin *(studying)* at 9 PM.

Exercise 5.22

1.   Peter <u>will buy</u> the newspaper.
     Peter <u>might have bought</u> the newspaper this morning.
2.   More American companies <u>are conducting</u> business overseas.
     International business <u>is being conducted</u> by fax machine and telephone.
3.   A Senate staff member <u>had released</u> the information.
     No information <u>should have been released</u> without authorization.

Exercise 5.23

1.   Bill **is leaving** at noon.
2.   On the last trip he **had driven** all night.
3.   Usually he **would have gone** by the expressway.
4.   But this time he **will be traveling** on Route 22.

Exercise 5.24

1.   <u>Is</u> anybody else from your college <u>planning</u> to attend the conference?
2.   I <u>will</u> not <u>forget</u> to bring the registration form.
3.   <u>Did</u> the cost of food <u>rise</u> because of the drought?
4.   Some people <u>are</u> always <u>worrying</u> about their health but <u>are</u> still <u>eating</u> junk food.
5.   Vanessa <u>was</u> already <u>writing</u> the first draft of her paper, even though she <u>hadn't finished</u> her research.

Exercise 5.25

1.   Yuri <u>likes</u> his new job and <u>is</u> already <u>earning</u> a good salary.
2.   Eating healthy foods <u>is becoming</u> increasingly expensive.
3.   The survey <u>is being conducted</u> by a marketing firm.
4.   Somebody always <u>starts</u> to leave before the performance <u>has ended</u>.
5.   I <u>will</u> not <u>call</u> you until I <u>finish</u> the letter that <u>I'm writing</u>.
6.   The lights <u>dimmed</u> and the curtain slowly <u>rose</u> as the orchestra <u>began</u> to play.
7.   We <u>haven't been receiving</u> all of our mail.

RULES SUMMARY, Part 2

1.   A verb that is more than one word is called a **verb phrase**.
2.   Every verb phrase contains at least one **helping** verb, and a **main** verb.
3.   The **main verb** tells what a verb phrase is about.
4.   The **helping** verb or verbs in a verb phrase express various time relationships.
5.   The helping verb, not the main verb, shows the **tense**.
6.   The first **helping verb** in a verb phrase is often contracted.
7.   One or more words may **interrupt** a verb phrase, especially in a negative sentence or a question.

Exercise 5.26

      This year as usual, especially when she <u>begins</u> to run short of cash for Christmas presents,
my sister Cynthia <u>will</u> probably <u>go</u> to the outdoor market to look for bargains. Once I <u>went</u>
with her, but I <u>will</u> never <u>go</u> again. At any time of year, the place <u>is</u> full of jostling crowds, but at
Christmas time <u>it's</u> a madhouse. Excited vendors <u>are shouting</u> at customers, and frustrated
shoppers <u>are screaming</u> at cashiers. Merchandise <u>is lying</u> around in messy heaps on outdoor
counters. Racks of clothing <u>clutter</u> up the sidewalks, so people <u>walk</u> in the street and <u>block</u>
traffic. The sound of honking horns <u>adds</u> to the noise and confusion. Sometimes a guard <u>chases</u>
a shoplifter through the crowds. While he <u>is</u> away, a customer quietly <u>switches</u> the price tags.
But that <u>is</u> the only thing that <u>happens</u> quietly there. Last year Cynthia <u>came</u> home with a
headache along with her purchases. Still, she <u>loves</u> bargains, so no doubt she <u>will go</u> back to the
market again this December.

Exercise 5.27

These days, Americans **are beginning** to shift their view of alcoholic beverages. Many people, anxious about their health, **are drinking** less. In restaurants, they **are** now **ordering** white wine instead of martinis. Others **have stopped** drinking liquor entirely. Equally important, attitudes **are changing.** Intoxicated people no longer **seem** so funny. Comedians **make** fewer jokes about the antics of drunks. The police **are arresting** drunk drivers, and in more and more states, the courts **are giving** them stiff fines and **are** even **sending** them to prison. Abuse of alcohol **is being recognized** as a threat to health, to life, and to society.

Module 6: *Understanding Sentences I*

Exercise 6.1

1.   S
   Dogs / <u>bark</u>.
2.   S
   Somebody / <u>cheated</u> me.
3.   S
   The helicopter / <u>will land</u> over there.
4.   S
   Those songs / <u>were</u> popular in the 1950s.
5.   S
   The children / <u>were telling</u> ghost stories.

Exercise 6.2

1.   S   C
   Someone / <u>destroyed</u> the evidence.
2.   S   C
   Jason / <u>seems</u> unhappy.
3.   S   C
   Pamela / <u>has</u> an older sister.
4.   S   C
   Their explanation / <u>was</u> incredible.
5.   S   C
   Nobody / <u>will answer</u> the question.

Exercise 6.3

1.   S   C
   The audience / <u>was</u> noisy.
           S
   The audience / <u>was applauding.</u>
2.   S   C
   Keisha / <u>is writing</u> the minutes.
         S   C
   Keisha / <u>is</u> the secretary.
3.   S   C
   The assignment / <u>has confused</u> the students.
       S   C
   They / <u>have</u> many questions.

Exercise 6.4

1.   S   C
   Esther / <u>was driving</u> and <u>had</u> an accident.

2.   S
        The cliffs / will erode and eventually will crumble.
3.   S   C
        I / wrote, stamped, and mailed the letters immediately.

Exercise 6.5

1.   S   S   C
        Some flowers and insects / eat animals.
2.   S   S
        Your friends and family / will help.
3.   S   S   S   C
        Cars, trucks, and buses / jammed the intersection.

Exercise 6.6

1.   S   C   C   C
        That shop / sells newspapers, magazines, and paperback books.
2.   S   C   C
        Few people / are both active and fat.
3.   S   C   C
        Most sophomores / will take history and science.

Exercise 6.7

1.   S   C   C   C
        Next year my brother / will visit China, Taiwan, and Japan.
2.   S   C
        Old movie heroes / smoke, drink, and drive fast cars.
3.   S   S   S   C   C
        Crabs, shrimp, and other shellfish / are delicious but expensive.

Exercise 6.8

1.   S   S   S   C
        Women, men, and children / boarded the bus.
2.   S   C   C   C
        Kareem / drinks soda pop, seltzer water, and nonalcoholic beer.
3.   S   C
        Lovingly Stacy / washed, waxed, and polished her new car.

Exercise 6.9

1.   S
        (Most)→women / work.
2.   S
        Women←(of all ages) / work.
3.   S   C
        (Several)→women←(in the office) / were preparing the report.

Exercise 6.10

1.   S
        (The)→visitors←(from the central office) / will arrive soon.
2.   S
        (Several)→teachers←(in the gerontology program) / are working together on a research project.
3.   S
        (Some)→catalogs←(for winter clothing) / appear in the middle of summer.

Exercise 6.11

1.   S   C
    People / <u>have</u> (different) → problems.
2.   S   C
    People / <u>have</u> problems ← (of many different kinds).
3.   S   C
    People / <u>have</u> (many) → problems ← (in their everyday lives).

Exercise 6.12

1.   S
    Mary Ellen / (quietly) <u>collapsed</u>.
2.   S
    Jerome / (always) <u>tries</u> (hard).
3.   S
    Someone / (usually) <u>will respond</u> (after the deadline).

Exercise 6.13

1. Mr. Sokoloff / <u>walks</u> (slowly).
                      C
    Mr. Sokoloff / <u>walked</u> his dog.
2. Clarissa / <u>writes</u> (with a fountain pen).
                  C
    Clarissa / <u>writes</u> many letters.
3. The speeding driver / <u>stopped</u> (suddenly).
                                C
    The speeding driver / (suddenly) <u>stopped</u> his car.

Exercise 6.14 [Make sure that you identified the subjects, complements, and verbs correctly, and drew the slash correctly.]

1.   S   C   C
    Stu / <u>will send</u> (a) map (of the route) and (a) letter (with detailed driving instructions).
2.   S   S
    (A) kettle (of water) and (a) pot (of spaghetti sauce) / <u>were simmering</u> (on the stove).
3.   S
    (One) member (of the audience) / (finally) <u>went</u> (to the stage).

Exercise 6.15

1. Most middle-class families / <u>had</u> money. They / <u>weren't spending</u> it on luxuries.
2. Taxes / <u>were rising</u>. Voters / <u>were demanding</u> new economy in government.

Exercise 6.16 [Square brackets show where you should have drawn a box.]

1. The rain / <u>fell</u> in the wrong places.
    The reservoirs / <u>remained</u> empty.
    The rain / <u>fell</u> in the wrong places **[, and]** the reservoirs / <u>remained</u> empty.
2. Forecasters / <u>predicted</u> a shortage.
    Agriculture and business / <u>continued</u> to waste water.
    Forecasters / <u>predicted</u> a shortage **[, but]** agriculture and business / <u>continued</u> to waste water.

Exercise 6.17

1. The umpire / <u>blew</u> his whistle and <u>stopped</u> the play.
    The umpire / <u>made</u> a bad call **[, and]** the manager / <u>became</u> angry.
2. The latecomers / <u>took</u> their seats **[, and]** the professor / <u>began</u> her lecture.
    The professor / <u>closed</u> the door and <u>began</u> her lecture.

3.   We / <u>started</u> for the airport on time **[, but]** the heavy traffic / <u>delayed</u> us.
        We / <u>started</u> for the airport on time but <u>missed</u> our flight.

RULES SUMMARY, Part 1

1.   Every sentence has two parts, a **subject** part and a **verb** part.
2.   A subject answers the question **WHO?** or **WHAT? in front of** the verb.
3.   A complement answers the question **WHO?** or **WHAT? after** the verb.
4.   In this book, words that tell more about other words in a sentence are called **expansion**.
5.   Analyze the structure of a sentence like this:
        a.   First, find the **verb** and **underline** it. Always look for the **verb** first.
        b   Second, find the **subject** and mark it with an **S**.
        c   Third, find the **complement** (if there is one) and mark it with a **C**.
        d   Finally, draw a **slash** between the subject part and the **verb** part.
6.   A compound sentence consists of two sentences connected by a joining word like **and** or **but**.
7.   In a compound sentence, always use a **comma** in front of the joining word.
8.   When we analyze a compound sentence, we draw **two** slashes.

Exercise 6.18

1.   S   C   C   C   C   C
        The Olympic decathlon / <u>includes</u> javelin-throwing, running, pole-vaulting, long-jumping, and six other events.
2.   S   C
        People by the hundreds / <u>report</u> sightings of UFOs every year.
3.   S   C
        The Democratic committee / <u>produced</u> an expensive television campaign **[, but]**
                        S   C
        their candidates for the city council / <u>lost</u> the election.
4.   S   C   C
        The lab technicians / <u>will order</u> several boxes of computer disks and new ribbons for the printers.
5.   S   C   C
        Women in the Old West / <u>cooked</u>, <u>sewed</u>, <u>scrubbed</u>, <u>plowed</u> the land, and <u>fired</u> rifles from the barricades beside their men.
6.   S   C
        Many new immigrants from Spanish-speaking countries / now <u>are entering</u> the United States **[, and]**
                                            S
        bilingual education programs / <u>are expanding</u>.

Exercise 6.19

        Henry / often <u>recalls</u> his first day of driving lessons. His instructor / <u>smiled</u> encouragingly and <u>pointed</u> to the ignition key and the accelerator. Henry / hesitantly <u>turned</u> the key **[, and]** then he / <u>stepped</u> on the gas. The motor / actually <u>started</u> to run. He / <u>looked</u> at his instructor with amazement. Next, the instructor / <u>taught</u> him how to shift gears. Henry / <u>shifted</u> into "Drive" and <u>held</u> on tight to the wheel. His father's Chevrolet / <u>gave</u> a familiar shudder and then slowly <u>edged</u> forward. Henry / anxiously <u>looked</u> ahead. A truck and a car with a "Wide Load" sign / <u>were</u> <u>creeping</u> toward him at 20 miles an hour. Quickly he / <u>slammed</u> on the brakes **[, and]** his instructor / almost <u>went</u> through the windshield. Telling Henry to stop, the instructor / <u>began</u> to open the car door. Henry / <u>tried</u> to obey **[, but]** he / <u>stepped</u> on the accelerator instead of the brake. Henry / <u>had</u> a new instructor for his next lesson.

Exercise 6.20

        People / <u>worked</u> on the night shift, <u>drank</u> in all-night bars, or <u>slept</u> soundly in their beds. Faint tremors, louder thumps, and ominous rumbles / <u>startled</u> them. Seconds later, the ground / <u>shook</u>, <u>heaved</u>, and <u>split</u> open. Within minutes, factories, stores, and homes / <u>were</u> mountains of loose bricks and blazing timbers. For days, a lurid tower of flame and smoke / <u>reddened</u>, <u>darkened</u>, and <u>blotted</u> out [OR, <u>blotted</u> <u>out</u>] the sky. The San Francisco earthquake / <u>was</u> a greater disaster than the sinking of the Titanic, the collapse of the Johnstown Dam, or the Great Chicago Fire.

Exercise 6.21

1. ✘ Information from both books and magazines.   FRAG
      S
Information from both books and magazines / is helpful.   SENT
2.   S
People in the middle-income bracket / pay higher taxes.   SENT
✘ People in the middle-income bracket.   FRAG
3. ✘ A used car with a good engine and low mileage.   FRAG
       S
A used car with a good engine and low mileage / is worth a lot.   SENT

Exercise 6.22

1.   S
My cousin / lives in Oakland.   SENT
✘ And commutes to work in San Francisco.   FRAG
2. ✘ For example, worry about the future of their children.   FRAG
         S
For example, parents / worry about the future of their children.   SENT
3.   S
Some students / never study in the library.   SENT
✘ And never study at home, either.   FRAG

Exercise 6.23

¹Lawrence / used to eat at a local diner.   ¹SENT
²✘ Really enjoyed the great tasting food.   ²FRAG
³✘ Not to mention the low prices. ⁴Then he /   ³FRAG
read a Health Department report on   ⁴SENT
the kitchen. ⁵✘ Roaches, greasy pots, filthy   ⁵FRAG
refrigerator. ⁶It / was hard to believe.   ⁶SENT
⁷✘ But better not to take chances. ⁸He /   ⁷FRAG
found another place to have lunch.   ⁸SENT

Exercise 6.24 [Mark everything that is not exactly as it appears here, except commas.]

1. People facing religious persecution emigrated. ✘ To the New World.
People facing religious persecution / emigrated to the New World.
2. They farmed the land. ✘ And established new communities.
They / farmed the land and established new communities.
3. The native inhabitants taught them to grow new crops. ✘ Such as corn and squash.
The native inhabitants / taught them to grow new crops such as corn and squash.

Exercise 6.25

1.   ✘
The station canceled its regular programs, it was holding a
fund-raising drive.   RUN-ON
2.   ✘
The volunteers were answering phone calls, they were taking
pledges for donations.   RUN-ON
3. With telephones ringing in the background, the announcer / looked
into the camera and pleaded for funds.   SENT

Exercise 6.26 [Remember: Parentheses and italics mark the words that you should have circled.]

1.
                                                    ✗
   Mrs. White rented a cottage for the summer *(she)* loves it.
   Mrs. White / <u>rented</u> a cottage for the summer. She / <u>loves</u> it.

2.
                                                    ✗
   Owning a house is a lot of trouble, *(it)* is better to rent.
   Owning a house / <u>is</u> a lot of trouble. It / <u>is</u> better to rent.

3.
                                                    ✗
   In the 1980s, the price of housing rose sharply, *(that)* hurt middle-income families.
   In the 1980s, the price of housing / <u>rose</u> sharply. That / <u>hurt</u> middle-income families.

Exercise 6.27

1.
                                        ✗
   She cried for a while, *(then)* she got mad.
   She / <u>cried</u> for a while. Then she / <u>got</u> mad.

2.
                                                        ✗
   Mr. Gordon reviewed his insurance policy *(next)* he called the police.
   Mr. Gordon / <u>reviewed</u> his insurance policy. Next he / <u>called</u> the police.

3.
                                                        ✗
   At the end of the first set, Jennifer seemed tired, *(then)* she recovered and won the tennis match.
   At the end of the first set, Jennifer / <u>seemed</u> tired. Then she / <u>recovered</u> and <u>won</u> the tennis match.

Exercise 6.28

1.
                                        ✗
   We waited until 4 PM *(then)* we called again.
   We / <u>waited</u> until 4 PM **[, and]** then we / <u>called</u> again.

2.
                                                ✗
   Express mail is faster than first class, *(it)* costs nearly $10.
   Express mail / <u>is</u> faster than first class **[, but]** it / <u>costs</u> nearly $10.

3.
                                        ✗
   Wallis finished the letters, *(then)* he hurried to the Post Office.
   Wallis / <u>finished</u> the letters **[, and]** then he / *hurried* to the Post Office.

RULES SUMMARY, Part 2

1.   If a group of words doesn't have both a subject and a verb, it is not a sentence but a **<u>fragment</u>**.
2.   Correct most fragments by connecting them to a **<u>sentence</u>**.
3.   If two (or more) sentences are written as if they are one, the result is a **<u>run-on</u>**.
4.   Many run-ons occur when a new sentence begins with a **<u>pronoun</u>**, or with a word like *then* or **<u>next</u>**.
5.   One way to correct a run-on is to rewrite it as **<u>two</u>** sentences.
6.   Another way to correct a run-on is to insert a comma + a joining word like **<u>and</u>** or **<u>but</u>** to make a **<u>compound</u>** sentence.

Exercise 6.29

1. Car insurance is going up every year it now often costs $1000.	RUN-ON
2. Our business manager / <u>wasn't</u> friendly, but she / <u>was</u> never rude, either.	SENT
3. By checking the ads every day, dialing hundreds of numbers, and never giving up.	FRAG
4. Jacqueline is confident about getting this job, her interview went very well.	RUN-ON
5. The meeting began at seven o'clock and ran smoothly, it ended at ten.	RUN-ON
6. To fly halfway across the country, spend a thousand dollars on hotel rooms, meals, and plane tickets, and return without a contract.	FRAG
7. It / <u>'s</u> hard to change old habits.	SENT

8.   For example, to watch less TV.   FRAG
9.   Vitamin C with breakfast, vitamin E at bedtime.   FRAG
10. Getting up early, eating healthy food, and drinking lots of water.   FRAG
11. The space shuttle / gently <u>touched</u> the ground, and the waiting crowd / <u>cheered</u>. SENT
12. The crew members were smiling, they waved at the crowd.   RUN-ON
13. Everyone / <u>applauded</u>.   SENT
14. They made it, they're American heroes.   RUN-ON

Exercise 6.30 [Mark everything that is not exactly as it appears here, except commas.]

Many famous persons / <u>encountered</u> incredible obstacles but <u>continued</u> to pursue
their goals. The composer Beethoven / <u>lost</u> his hearing and then <u>wrote</u> some of his
greatest musical masterpieces, including his most powerful symphonies. The artist and
writer James Thurber / <u>became</u> almost completely blind, but <u>continued</u> his career by
drawing his famous cartoons on huge canvases under bright lights. The great actress
Sarah Bernhardt / <u>became</u> lame in 1905, <u>lost</u> her leg to gangrene in 1914, and / <u>went</u> on [OR, <u>went on</u>]
to play the most famous roles of her career before her death in 1923.

Exercise 6.31 [Remember: Square brackets show where you should have drawn a box.]

1.   Fei-chen / <u>won</u> the boxing match **[, but]** he / <u>was</u> disqualified.
2.   Beverly Sills / <u>was</u> a great singer **[, and]** her fans / <u>adored</u> her.
3.   Luis / <u>loved</u> children **[, and]** he / <u>planned</u> to have a large family.
4.   Ross / seldom <u>receives</u> mail **[, but]** today he / <u>got</u> three letters from old friends.
5.   The snow / <u>is</u> already 15 inches deep **[, and]** it / still <u>is falling</u>.
6.   Savings bonds / <u>are</u> a popular investment **[, but]** they / <u>don't pay</u> good interest.
7.   Kiyoko / <u>won</u> a prize in mathematics **[, but]** she / <u>prefers</u> to major in history.
8.   Angelo / <u>received</u> the pre-medical science prize **[, and]** he / <u>is going</u> to medical school next year.

Exercise 6.32

Computerized telephones / <u>are becoming</u> more and more popular in homes and offices.
They / <u>save</u> people time and trouble. Busy people / <u>are</u> often away from home. While away,
they / <u>'re</u> anxious not to miss important calls from friends and relatives. In the office,
these people / <u>have</u> the opposite problem. At the worst possible moment, a phone
call / <u>will interrupt</u> their work. With computerized attachments, modern phones / <u>solve</u>
these problems easily. After a few rings, a recording / <u>comes</u> on and <u>invites</u> the caller
to leave a message. Sometimes this recording / <u>will answer</u> the caller's main question.
Then there<u>'s</u> / no need to call back. Many smart phones / <u>allow</u> users to dial a single
digit to transfer a call. In fact, some phones / even <u>transfer</u> calls automatically
to another number. In these and in many other ways, computerized phones / <u>help</u> people
to do their jobs with less stress.

Exercise 6.33 [Remember: Square brackets show where you should have drawn a box.]

1.   S   S   C
     The transmission and windshield wipers / <u>made</u> strange noises.
2.   S   C   C
     Her car / <u>got</u> low gas mileage and <u>burned</u> oil.
3.   S
     The engine / <u>sputtered</u>, <u>choked</u>, and <u>started</u> slowly on cold mornings.
4.   S
     The roof / <u>leaked</u>.
5.   S   C   S   C
     Annie / <u>owned</u> a car **[, but]** it / <u>was</u> a wreck.
6.   S   C   S   C
     However, that old Ford / <u>was</u> her first car **[, and]** she / <u>loved</u> it.

Module 7: *Verb Agreement*

Exercise 7.1

                                    S
          Every day some very fast planes / <u>leave</u>
                                    S
Heathrow Airport in London. They / <u>arrive</u> in New
                                            S
York only three hours later. The seats / <u>cost</u> a lot.
                            S
But some business people / <u>need</u> to meet deadlines.
              S   S
So they / <u>take</u> these planes to save time. They /

<u>complete</u> their business in New York quickly.
                  S
Often they / <u>return</u> home the same day.

                                    S
          Every day a very fast plane <u>leave[s]</u>
                                    S
Heathrow Airport in London. It / <u>arrive[s]</u> in New
                                          S
York only three hours later. A seat / <u>cost[s]</u> a lot.
                          S   S
But Colin Walker / <u>need[s]</u> to meet deadlines. So he /
                                        S
<u>take[s]</u> this plane to save time. He / <u>complete[s]</u> his
                                                        S
business in New York quickly. Often he / <u>return[s]</u>

home the same day.

Exercise 7.2

1.   Americans / **eat** too much red meat.
2.   I / **count** fat grams, not calories.
3.   You / **lose** weight by eating fruit.
4.   Salt and animal fat / **kill** millions.
5.   We / **study** food labels carefully.

Exercise 7.3

1.   Marietta / **likes** studying statistics.
      She / **likes** studying statistics.
2.   The President / **appoints** ambassadors.
      He / **appoints** ambassadors.
3.   A college diploma / **helps** you to get a job.
      It / **helps** you to get a job.

Exercise 7.4

1.   You / **need** a sense of humor in hard times.
2.   My grandmother / **sees** almost perfectly since her cataract operation.
3.   A dictatorship / **discourages** creative thinking.
4.   In their fifties and sixties, couples / **begin** to look forward to retirement.
5.   I / **buy** special paper for my computer printer.
6.   A medical career / **requires** a lot of training.
7.   Most professions / **demand** at least one graduate-school degree.

Exercise 7.5

1.   The mayor of any big city / **marches** in many parades.
2.   This answer / **misses** the point of the question.
3.   That chef / sometimes **mashes** 50 pounds of potatoes at once.
4.   The museum / never **waxes** its antique wooden furniture.
5.   A good teacher / never **preaches** at his students.

Exercise 7.6

1. A bad driver / **risks** other people's lives, as well as his own.
2. Going to college / **tests** your time-management skills.
3. A person with heat stroke / <u>turns</u> red and **gasps** for breath.

Exercise 7.7

1. When a parent lies, a child / **catches** on quickly.
2. My English teacher / **asks** us to do a long writing assignment every week.
3. This judge / **dismisses** charges against most first-time defendants.
4. A smart parent / **trusts** her children most of the time.
5. A basketball team / **consists** of a center, two forwards, and two guards.
6. The shop manager / usually **rushes** to leave on Friday.

Exercise 7.8

1. **Everyone** / <u>tries</u> to pass the buck.
   Most people / <u>try</u> to pass the buck.
2. **All of us** / <u>like</u> to win.
   Everybody / <u>likes</u> to win.
3. **Few people** / <u>want</u> taxes to rise.
   No one / <u>wants</u> taxes to rise.
4. **Anybody** / <u>appreciates</u> a sincere compliment.
   We all / <u>appreciate</u> a sincere compliment.
5. **Not many of us** / <u>enjoy</u> working all the time.
   Nobody / <u>enjoys</u> working all the time.

Exercise 7.9

1. Someone / always **cries** at weddings.
2. That intersection / **worries** every parent in the neighborhood.
3. The entrance examination / **terrifies** most students.

Exercise 7.10

1. That chicken / **lays** brown eggs.
2. A widower / almost always **remarries** within two years.
3. My sister / often **annoys** me with her nosy remarks.
4. Nobody / **tries** to be unsuccessful.
5. Everyone / **says** that love is blind.

Exercise 7.11

1. The **children** / <u>seem</u> quiet.
2. **She** / always <u>reads</u> as much as possible.
3. The **shadows** / <u>fall</u> at dusk.
4. **She** / <u>looks</u> uncomfortable.
5. **Jo** / seldom <u>arrives</u> on time.
6. **Few people** / <u>know</u> how to pronounce the word *mischievous*.
7. **Everybody** / <u>says</u> that inflation may become a problem again.

Exercise 7.12

1. A safe driver / never **passes** without signaling first.
2. A new style / usually **seems** strange at first.
3. I / never **drive** in the passing lane.
4. An older athlete / **relies** on experience instead of speed.
5. You / always **husk** the corn too soon, before the water starts to boil.
6. Southern customs / **emphasize** good manners and hospitality.
7. An incumbent official / usually **coasts** to easy victory.

8. Today young people / usually **marry** in their twenties.
9. Everybody / **trusts** a respectable-looking older woman.

Exercise 7.13 [Remember: Parentheses and italics mark the words that you should have circled.]

1. The committee / wanted *(to require)* more liberal arts courses.
    The committee / **wants *(to require)*** more liberal arts courses.
2. The university / planned *(to lobby)* for funds.
    The university / **plans *(to lobby)*** for funds.
3. The study group / helped students *(to improve)* their grades.
    The study group / **helps** students *(**to improve**)* their grades.
4. Three professors / intended *(to retire)*.
    Three professors / **intend *(to retire)***.
5. Nobody / wanted *(to go)* to the library.
    Nobody / **wants *(to go)*** to the library. [Be sure that you did not circle *to the library*. It is not an infinitive.]

Exercise 7.14

1. Yes, he / **skates** well and **skis** even better.
2. Yes, she / **worries** too much and **works** too hard.
3. Yes, they / **exercise** in the morning and **study** in the afternoon.

Exercise 7.15

1.   S
    (The) discovery (of those scientists) / **interests** me.
                S
    (The) discoveries (of that scientist) / **interest** me.
2.   S
    Women (with confidence) / **intimidate** some men.
                S
    (A) woman (with confidence) / **intimidates** some men.
3.   S
    (The) programs (on that TV channel) / often **win** awards.
                S
    (One) program (on that TV channel) / **wins** an award every year.

Exercise 7.16

1.   S
    (Several) occupants (of that building) / **plan** to move soon.
2.   S
    One (of those keys) / **unlocks** this door.
3.   S
    (Two) members (of the department) / **share** the corner office.
4.   S
    Some (of those bottles) / **need** to be washed.
5.   S
    One (of the interpreters) / **understands** Swahili.

RULES SUMMARY, Part 1

1. In the **present** tense, a verb must agree with its subject.
2. To make a present-tense verb agree with a **plural** subject or *I* or *you*, add no ending.
3. To make a present-tense verb agree with a singular subject (but not *I* or *you*), add *S* or **ES**.
4. When the verb needs an extra syllable, add **ES** to show agreement with a singular subject.
5. When the verb ends in *SK* or **SP** or **ST**, add **S** to show agreement with a singular subject.
6. These subjects are always singular: everyone   anyone   no one
                                             everybody   anybody   nobody

Exercise 7.17

1. The delivery men / **use** the service entrance.
   The janitor / **uses** the service entrance.
2. Jesse / **designs** toys.
   His partner / **designs** toys.
3. The Congressman / **denies** the charges.
   His supporters / **deny** the charges.
4. Two planes / **leave** for Minneapolis daily.
   One train / **leaves** for Minneapolis daily.
5. Harvey / **asks** many questions in class.
   I / **ask** many questions in class.

Exercise 7.18

My friend Milagros **loves** sewing. She **buys** beautiful fabric in a shop near where she **lives**. She and her mother carefully **lay** out the pattern for her dress. Then Milagros **cuts** it out, **bastes** it, and **sews** it together. She **uses** her iron as she **finishes** each seam. Her brother and her mother **help** her with some of the work. For example, they **adjust** the hem and **fit** the waist. Milagros **says** that she **enjoys** sewing. She not only **saves** money by making her own clothes, but she always **looks** better than the other women in her office.

Exercise 7.19

1.   S
   One (of the faucets) / **leaks** slightly.
2.   S
   (Four) members (of this orchestra) / sometimes **play** together in a string quartet.
3.   S
   (An) increase (in income taxes) / **seems** inevitable.
4.   S
   One (of the exercises) / **tests** your sense of balance.
5.   S
   (The) instructions (on this test) / **confuse** many students.
6.   S
   (The) manager (of these stores) / **needs** some part-time Christmas employees.
7.   S
   All (of those textbooks) / **look** difficult.
8.   S
   (Only) one (out of all these employees) / ever **arrives** early.
9.   S
   (The) leader (of those workshops) / **says** that no prior experience with computers is necessary.
10.   S
    Everybody (in most families) / **acts** irrational at one time or another.

Exercise 7.20 [Remember: Parentheses and italics mark the words that you should have circled.]

(To pay) his bills, Ngo Nhu **has** *(to drive)* his taxi up to 16 hours a day. Even so, he hardly **makes** enough *(to put)* nourishing food on the table for his wife and three small children. *(To get)* through his long day behind the wheel, he **dreams** the American dream. As he creeps through the downtown traffic, he **imagines** relaxing with his family after supper in the backyard of their suburban home—the home he plans *(to buy)* some day. These thoughts keep him going until the restaurants and theaters close and the streets **grow** dark and empty. But when he **gets** home after midnight, he finds his wife in bed and his children fast asleep.

So as each week **drags** on, Ngo Nhu **becomes** impatient with distant hopes and dreams. He **tries** *(to make)* an extra buck by racing ahead of other taxis *(to pick)* up fares. As he **drives** faster and faster, his passengers cringe. When he **switches** lanes without signaling, nervous passengers often

ask *(to get)* out. The cops <u>chase</u> him when he **rushes** through stop signs, and just one traffic ticket <u>costs</u> him a full day's pay.

When Ngo Nhu finally **takes** a day off, however, life once more **seems** good and the future bright. He <u>plays</u> with his children, **talks** to his wife about the week's adventures, and **studies** his manual of English verbs. Then the next morning, he <u>drives</u> away at dawn, and the cycle of dreams and frustrations **starts** all over again for Ngo Nhu.

Exercise 7.21

When Lila **goes** to Europe, she **admires** the wonderful subways there. The cleanliness of the Paris Metro and the Vienna U-Bahn **amazes** her. Maintenance people **polish** the brass railings and **wash** down the walls. Gratefully, she **sinks** into the soft seats and **enjoys** the smooth ride. Excellent maps and clear signs on every wall **guide** her efficiently from one unfamiliar station to another. She **remembers** the sweltering cars, dirty stations, and confusing signs in the subways back home. Certainly, Lila never **gets** homesick when she **rides** in European subway trains.

Exercise 7.22

1.   Lolita / **has** a new pair of sunglasses.
2.   These banks / now **have** evening hours.
3.   Coolidge / always **has** the best answer.
4.   The Harrises / **have** nineteen grandchildren.
5.   Abby / never **has** enough money.
6.   You / **have** a large apartment, don't you?

Exercise 7.23

1.   Shaheed / **does** his math problems carefully.
2.   I / **do** the best I can.
3.   Some people / **do** their best work under pressure.

Exercise 7.24

1.   Aurelia / usually **does** very nice work.
      Of course, Kristie / sometimes **does earn** higher job ratings.
2.   First I / **did** the dishes.
      I / always **do try** to finish all my chores before watching TV.
3.   Those two skaters / **do perform** beautifully together.
      They / **do** the spins in perfect unison.

Exercise 7.25

1.   Rena / really **does** <u>like</u> Hiroshi.
      Both Rena and her sister / really **do** <u>like</u> Hiroshi.
2.   These chairs / **do** not <u>need</u> repairs.
      That chair / **does** not <u>need</u> repairs.
3.   **Does** that store still <u>offer</u> discounts?
      Do those stores still <u>offer</u> discounts?

Exercise 7.26

1.   Sally / often **eats** fish and chicken.
      Sally / **does** not **eat** red meat.
2.   Angus / **does** not **want** a pet.
      Angus's wife / **wants** a little dog.
3.   That night watchman / **does** not **sleep** on the job.
      This night watchman / **sleeps** on the job.

Exercise 7.27

1.   Those new shirts / <u>look</u> good on you.
     Those new shirts / **<u>do</u>** not **<u>look</u>** good on you.
2.   This typewriter / <u>works</u> well.
     This typewriter / **<u>does</u>** not **<u>work</u>** well.
3.   That teacher / <u>tries</u> to help.
     That teacher / **<u>does</u>** not **<u>try</u>** to help.

Exercise 7.28

1.   Those new shirts / <u>look</u> good on you.
     Those new shirts / **<u>don</u>**'t **<u>look</u>** good on you.
2.   This typewriter / <u>works</u> well.
     This typewriter / **<u>does</u>**n't **<u>work</u>** well.
3.   That teacher / <u>tries</u> to help.
     That teacher / **<u>does</u>**n't **<u>try</u>** to help.

Exercise 7.29

1.   She **<u>wants</u>** me to call her back.
     <u>Does</u> she **<u>want</u>** me to call her back?
2.   You **<u>need</u>** a receipt.
     <u>Do</u> you really **<u>need</u>** a receipt?
3.   **<u>Do</u>** their parents ever **<u>return</u>** their calls?
     Their parents never **<u>return</u>** their calls.

Exercise 7.30

1.   Those new shirts / <u>look</u> good on you.
     <u>Do</u> those new shirts **<u>look</u>** good on you?
2.   This typewriter / <u>works</u> well.
     <u>Does</u> this typewriter **<u>work</u>** well?
3.   That teacher / <u>tries</u> to help.
     <u>Does</u> that teacher **<u>try</u>** to help?

RULES SUMMARY, Part 2

1.   The verbs *HAVE* and **<u>DO</u>** are irregular.
     a.   The present-tense form of *HAVE* that agrees with a singular subject is **<u>has</u>**.
     b.   The present-tense form of *DO* that agrees with a singular subject is **<u>does</u>**.
2.   *DO* can be a one-word verb or a **<u>helping</u>** verb in a verb phrase.
3.   The helping verb *DO* must **<u>agree</u>** with its subject.

Exercise 7.31

1.   <u>Does</u> Wolfgang <u>want</u> a new piano? <u>Does</u> he <u>have</u> one picked out? <u>Does</u> he <u>expect</u> to get a discount?
     Yes, he / **<u>wants</u>** a new piano, **<u>has</u>** one picked out, and **<u>expects</u>** to get a discount.
2.   <u>Does</u> Wanda <u>watch</u> her weight? <u>Does</u> she <u>do</u> exercises every day? <u>Does</u> she <u>go</u> to the gym twice a week?
     Yes, she / **<u>watches</u>** her weight, **<u>does</u>** exercises every day, and **<u>goes</u>** to the gym twice a week.
3.   <u>Do</u> the twins <u>ask</u> a lot of questions? <u>Do</u> they <u>get</u> into mischief? <u>Do</u> they <u>keep</u> their parents busy?
     Yes, they / **<u>ask</u>** a lot of questions, **<u>get</u>** into mischief, and **<u>keep</u>** their parents busy.
4.   <u>Does</u> the lab <u>contain</u> twenty computers? <u>Does</u> it <u>have</u> lots of work space? <u>Does</u> it <u>stay</u> open on weekends?
     Yes, it / **<u>contains</u>** twenty computers, **<u>has</u>** lots of work space, and **<u>stays</u>** open on weekends.

Exercise 7.32

   After leaving Chicago, **<u>Oscar</u>** now **<u>lives</u>** on a farm. **<u>He says he wants</u>** a
quiet life in the fresh air. **<u>He gets</u>** up every morning at dawn. Before **<u>he has</u>**
breakfast, **<u>he picks his</u>** way through the cow dung, **<u>opens</u>** the smelly chicken coop, and

holds **his** **nose** as **he** **snatches** the eggs. While **he** **makes** a fire in **his** woodburning stove, **he** **chokes** on the smoke. Then **Oscar** **drives** a deafening tractor out to the field. As **he** **breathes** in the blowing dust, **he** **sneezes** furiously. Until late in the evening, **he** **does** chores in the barn. Exhausted, **he** **goes** to sleep and **dreams** of a soundproof office and an air-conditioned apartment.

Exercise 7.33 [Remember: Parentheses and italics mark the words that you should have circled.]

Somebody **makes** plans *(to break)* most world records as soon as someone else **sets** them. When an athlete **runs** the mile in under four minutes, his rival immediately **starts** training *(to beat)* his time. When a woman **swims** around Manhattan in the summer, another **has** *(to do)* it in the winter. It **seems** heroic *(to try) (to break)* records like these, but some other attempts **do** not **make** sense. We **grieve** if someone **dies** trying *(to fly)* fast, but it **does look** silly for a person *(to eat)* or *(to dance)* himself to death. In contests like these, foolish people often **refuse** *(to stop)*. If a person **has** *(to kill)* himself *(to win)*, he **kills** himself. At that moment he just **wants** *(to do)* one thing—*(to dance)* longer, or *(to eat)* more, or *(to scream)* louder than anyone else in the world.

Exercise 7.34

Marjorie **does**n't **impress** me with her skill at tennis. She certainly **does**n't **understand** how to keep her opponents off balance. Her drop shots, for example, often **do**n't **catch** [OR, **do**n't often **catch**] them off guard. And after a drop shot, she **does**n't **hit** long. Her serves usually **do**n't **land** deep in the court, and her opponents **do**n't **find** it hard to return them. Her friends **do**n't **want** her as a partner, and **do**n't **fear** her as an opponent. All in all, Marjorie's skill on the tennis court really **does**n't **overwhelm** [OR, **does**n't really **overwhelm**] me.

Exercise 7.35

Recent medical research <u>shows</u> that our emotional reaction to life's ups and downs **has** a profound effect on our health. The fifteen billion nerve cells in our brains constantly <u>change</u> our hopes and fears into chemical substances, and those substances in turn either **heal** or <u>harm</u> our bodies. Many people **accept** these facts but <u>insist</u> that this information **does**n't <u>help</u> them. Depression **runs** in their family, they <u>say</u>. But researchers again <u>have</u> an answer: If a person **acts** cheerful, then he <u>begins</u> to feel cheerful. When something unexpected **wrecks** his plans, a smart person <u>looks</u> for a hidden advantage instead of moaning over it. When he <u>gets</u> a chance to say something positive, he **does**n't <u>hesitate</u> to say it. When a sensible person **sees** something beautiful, she <u>takes</u> time out to enjoy it. When a small misfortune **happens**, she <u>turns</u> it around in her head until she **finds** the funny side. (Everything **does** <u>have</u> a funny side.) This positive behavior **produces** positive feelings. Most of the time we **have** the power to do what <u>makes</u> life more enjoyable—to see the bright side, or if that **does**n't <u>exist</u>, to remember that sooner or later things <u>will change</u>. This <u>makes</u> sense, and often **means** the difference between sickness and health.

Exercise 7.36: Review Exercise C

All cat **owners** know that domestic cats belong to the same family of mammals as lions. When a pet cat **pounces** on an insect or licks its paws and **washes** its face, it **looks** just like a lion in the zoo. But in one important way, cats and **lions** are completely different. Outdoors, in pursuit of birds or **mice**, a domestic cat **acts** very independent. Aloof and solitary, it **doesn't** seek help from other cats, but **stalks** its victims alone. But lions, especially the females, tend to live and to hunt in groups. The lions travel together and **bring** down their victims in a coordinated attack.

They treat every member of the group, even a cub, as an equal. If a weak or injured lion **doesn't** keep up with the group, the others prod and push him. If one lion by accident **hurts** another as they scramble over a carcass, the others lick her wounds and **comfort** her. In this cooperative behavior, lions **don't** resemble domestic cats at all—and in fact, they differ from all other members of the cat family.

Module 8: *The Verb BE*

Exercise 8.1

My wife and I **are** trying to raise our children in a non-sexist way, but we **are** unable to control the way other people talk to our four-year olds. The children **are** twins, but Emma **is** much more aggressive than her brother Dominick. The neighbors **are** quick to praise Emma as "a little lady," but then they lift an eyebrow when she **is** too boisterous. At the same time, they **are** apt to look at Dominick and ask, "Why **are** you so quiet today? Did the cat get your tongue?" I **am** not happy to see that sexual stereotyping **is** still alive and well, at least on our block.

Exercise 8.2

1. We / **are** brothers.
2. They / **are** good athletes.
3. I / **am** crazy about her.
4. That boy / **is** too lazy to tie his shoes.

Exercise 8.3

1. Herby / **is** my hairdresser.
2. Those teachers / **are** smart.
3. I / **am** hungry already.

Exercise 8.4

1. You / **'re** rather short-tempered these days.
2. I / **'m** eager to hear from you.
3. Nobody / **'s** perfect.
4. They / **'re** members of the Latin Club.

Exercise 8.5

1. There **is** / only one answer.
   There **are** / several possible answers.
2. Here **are** / three examples.
   Here **is** / the best example I can think of.
3. There **is** / a big oak table in the dining room.
   There **are** / five pieces of furniture in the living room.

Exercise 8.6

"Where **were** you when Kennedy was shot?" This **was** a familiar question when I **was** a child, and the answers **were** always interesting. We **were** at my parents' house last November 22nd, and a replay of the shocking events in Dallas **was**

on TV again. My small daughter suddenly looked up and asked, "Who **was**
Jack Kennedy?"

Exercise 8.7

1. We / **weren't** sure of the answer.
2. My mother / **wasn't** able to finish college.
3. You / **weren't** there when we called.

Exercise 8.8

1. There **were** / two terrible bus accidents in South America last year.
   There **was** / a major train accident last year, also.
2. There **was** / a large celebration for the United States Bicentennial in 1976.
   There **were** / many Bicentennial festivals across the country.
3. There **was** / a scratch on that table before I refinished it.
   There **were** / many scratches on that table before I refinished it.

Exercise 8.9

We **were** new at our jobs as bank tellers, so a counterfeit bill **was** hard for us to detect. But there **were** older tellers in
this bank whose index fingers **were** as sensitive as lie detectors. To their sharp eyes, a presidential face on a large bill **was** as
familiar as their own. Presidents with crooked noses or bent ears **were** as obvious to them as the false smiles on the faces of
thieves.

Exercise 8.10 [Remember: Parentheses and italics mark the words that you should have circled.]

1. Life / **was** hard *(in the twelfth century)*.   PAST
2. Life / **is** more complex *(today)*.   PRESENT
3. *(Last year)*, Mr. Coleman / **was** the chairman.   PAST
4. Caterina / **is** away from her desk *(right now)*.   PRESENT
5. *(In the past)*, it / **was** a disgrace for a man to have a working wife. PAST

Exercise 8.11

1. Reatha / **is** at her sister's right now.
   Reatha / **was** at her mother's last week.
2. You / never **were** wrong before.
   But you / **are** wrong now, believe me!
3. My brother and I / **were** good friends when we were in high school.
   We / **are** still good friends now that we attend college together.

Exercise 8.12

1. Julian still <u>wonders</u> why he **was** so shy when he <u>was</u> a child.
2. My grandparents seldom <u>talk</u> about the days when they **were** young.
3. <u>Do</u> you <u>remember</u> the time when we **were** almost late for the plane?

Exercise 8.13

1.   S
   (The) author (of those new books) / **is** from Argentina.
2.   S
   (The) pressures (of the modern world) / **are** a threat to health.
3.   S
   (The) center (of most people's lives) / **is** still their family.
4.   S
   (A) channel (through reefs and sandbars) / **is** often hard for a ship's pilot to find.
5.   S
   (The) number (of violent crimes in our area) / **is** relatively low.

6.
          S
(The) point (of many jokes) / **is** basically cruel.

7.
          S
(The) targets (of much masculine humor) / **are** wives and mothers-in-law.

Exercise 8.14

1.
              S
(The best) skiers (in yesterday's race) / **were** from Switzerland.

2.
            S
(Each) delegate (to any of the two most recent conventions) / **was** at least 18 years old.

3.
           S
(Several) books (from that set) / **were** on the table last night.

4.
         S
Nobody (from either of the classes) / **was** able to attend the lecture.

5.
           S
(The) monasteries (of Ireland) / **were** centers of Christian learning in the early Middle Ages.

6.
                S
(The first Christian) missionary (to the Germans) / **was** an English monk.

7.
                   S
Before the Revolution, (the principal) religion (of the Chinese people) / **was** Confucianism.

RULES SUMMARY, Part 1

1. The verb *BE* has three **present** -tense forms: *I* **am**; *he / she / it* **is**; *we / you / they* **are**.
2. Forms of the verb *BE* are often **contracted** with their subjects or with the word **not**. Use an **apostrophe** to show where letters are omitted. The contracted form of *I am* is **I'm**.
3. A verb must agree with its **subject** even if the subject follows the verb. Sentences like this often begin with the words *here* or **there**.
4. The verb *BE* has two **past** -tense forms: *I / he / she / it* **was**; *we / you / they* **were**.

Exercise 8.15

1. The city / **is** smoggy.
    Its suburbs / **are** smoggy.
2. My father / **is** a policeman.
    I / **am** a policeman.
3. My friends / **were** active children.
    I / **was** an active child.
4. A T-square / **was** ready on the architect's table.
    A set of pens / **was** ready on the architect's table.
5. There **are** / some Indian carpets in that museum.
    There **is** / a beautiful Persian rug in that museum.

Exercise 8.16 [Remember: Parentheses and italics mark the words that you should have circled.]

Parents often **like** *(to imagine)* that their children **are** very talented. Sometimes a father **wants** his son *(to be)* a movie star, and so he **teaches** the boy how *(to sing)* and *(to dance)* almost before he **knows** how *(to walk)* or *(to talk)*. A mother **thinks** her daughter **is** sure *(to be)* another Pavlova, so she **sends** the child to school *(to learn)* ballet before she **is** able *(to read)*. It **is** true that every now and then a Shirley Temple **turns** up and **makes** a million dollars before she **is** four years old; and once every four or five centuries a Mozart **writes** a symphony when he **is** only nine. But much more often, these children **are** remarkable only to their parents. And when a so-called child prodigy **grows** up, he never **wants** *(to see)* a piano or *(to dance)* a step. He **becomes** a plumber or a policeman, which **is** just what he **wanted** *(to be)* from the start.

Exercise 8.17

1. Charlotte / **is** an excellent pianist.
    Charlotte / **is playing** the piano in the studio.
2. I / **am** ready to leave.
    I / **am going** to the store.
3. It / **was snowing** last night.
    The temperature / **was** less than 32 degrees.

Exercise 8.18

1. We / **sang** well last night.
    We / **were singing** Handel's *Messiah* for the first time.
2. I / always **work** hard.
    I / **am working** harder than ever these days.
3. That show / first **ran** on Broadway forty years ago.
    Now it / **is running** again.

Exercise 8.19

1. The defendant / **was robbing** the store when the police walked in.
2. Bertram / **is planning** to go to Trinidad for a vacation this winter.
3. Those clerks / **are filing** our computer output.
4. Jordana / **was writing** a poem.
5. Since the rookie / **is batting** .300, he plays in almost every game.

[If you made any mistakes in Exercise 8.19, it would be a good idea to review the Spelling Rules in Appendix A. Throughout the rest of the Answers, be sure to check the spelling of every *ING* main verb.]

Exercise 8.20

1. I / **am working** for a computer software company now.
2. Those departments / **are cutting** down on their staff.
3. Irina / **is trying** to start her own business.

Exercise 8.21

1. Until recently, unemployment / **was declining**.
2. I / **was hurrying** to catch the bus when I twisted my ankle.
3. **Were** you **hoping** for a raise?

Exercise 8.22

1. We / **are trying** right now to get this job finished.
2. They / **were paying** too much for car insurance last year.
3. My two sisters / **were planning** to go skating yesterday.

Exercise 8.23

1. Often school-aged brothers and sisters / **will** quarrel and compete with each other.
2. My friend Jewel / **is** studying Spanish and hoping to make a career as a bilingual secretary.
3. The oncoming drivers / **were** slowing their cars and staring at the accident.
4. The student government / **is** preparing petitions, collecting signatures, and organizing a campaign to establish a daycare center on campus.
5. A volunteer / **will** answer the phone and accept your donation.

RULES SUMMARY, Part 2

1. The verb *BE* can be either a one-word verb or a **helping** verb in a verb phrase.

2. Use the helping verb *BE* + the <u>**ING**</u> form of a main verb to tell what <u>**is happening**</u> right now or <u>**was happening**</u> in the past.
3. The helping verb *BE* must <u>**agree**</u> with its subject and show the appropriate <u>**tense**</u>.
4. Often a helping verb is not repeated before a second <u>**main**</u> verb.

Exercise 8.24

Hello, Josie, I<u>**'m calling**</u> from the union hall. They<u>**'re going**</u> to take a strike vote soon. They<u>**'re telling**</u> us to accept the contract, but we<u>**'re going**</u> to turn it down. It <u>**'s**</u> just no good. It<u>**'s cutting**</u> back our benefits, and there<u>**'s**</u> no more money in it anywhere, except for the managers.... Yes, that<u>**'s**</u> right. I<u>**'m**</u> afraid that it<u>**'s going**</u> to be a long strike. We<u>**'re**</u> probably not <u>**going**</u> to get that new refrigerator, after all.... I<u>**'m**</u> sorry, Josie, but I<u>**'m**</u> glad that you<u>**'re**</u> so understanding. You<u>**'re**</u> the best wife in the world.

Exercise 8.25 [Remember: Parentheses and italics mark the words that you should have circled.]

Aunt Mattie, like many people over sixty, <u>**thinks**</u> all her young relatives <u>need</u> *(to know)* how great the good old days <u>**were**</u> – before TV, when she and her sisters <u>**were**</u> <u>growing</u> up. Every Sunday, my brother Jake <u>**watches**</u> her coming up the block, <u>frowns</u>, and <u>mutters</u> that trouble <u>**is**</u> on the way. She always <u>**rushes**</u> into our kitchen with a big hello, but then she <u>**acts**</u> like a lady preacher. There <u>**are**</u> a thousand things she <u>**likes**</u> *(to criticize)*. While we <u>are eating</u> dinner, Auntie M. <u>tries</u> *(to get)* our attention, and if she <u>**doesn't**</u>, she <u>thumps</u> the table, <u>demands</u> silence, and <u>**begins**</u> *(to preach)* a sermon against modern times. She <u>says</u> it <u>**is**</u> a scandal that girls these days <u>**are**</u> <u>wearing</u> sexy jeans and that boys <u>are kissing</u> girls they <u>don't</u> even <u>know</u>. And there <u>**are**</u> those loud radios all over the place! When she <u>was</u> a girl, she <u>**declares**</u>, things <u>**were**</u> a lot different. She <u>**says**</u> life was better when times <u>**were**</u> harder. And then she <u>asks</u> what <u>**I'm**</u> [OR, **I am**] <u>doing</u> with all the money that I <u>**earn**</u>. We <u>**try**</u> *(to be)* polite, but she really <u>**tests**</u> our patience. Jake usually <u>jumps</u> up and <u>**leaves**</u> the room at some point long before Aunt Mattie's final amen. The next time she <u>wants</u> *(to visit)*, we <u>are</u> ready *(to tell)* her that we <u>**have**</u> *(to go)* out!

Exercise 8.26

Who <u>**am**</u> I? Well, sonny, my name <u>**is**</u> Bill Williams, and I <u>**am**</u> 95 years old. In World War I, I <u>**was**</u> a fighter pilot. The Red Baron and I <u>**were**</u> <u>stalking</u> each other up there in the clouds. Fragments of shrapnel <u>**were**</u> <u>flying</u> all around me, but I <u>**was**</u> not one bit scared. Here <u>**is**</u> an old photograph of me in my uniform. I <u>**was**</u> twenty years old at the time. Those campaign ribbons on my chest <u>**were**</u> my pride and joy then, and they still <u>**are**</u> now. And here on this table <u>**are**</u> some more souvenirs – a couple of old brass artillery shells that now <u>**are**</u> lamps. It <u>**is**</u> hard to believe, but these shells <u>**were**</u> once in a German cannon. And now they <u>**are**</u> <u>decorating</u> my living room. I <u>**was**</u> one high flyer in the Great War, child, and I still <u>**am**</u>.

Exercise 8.27: Review Exercise D

These days, baby toys <u>**are**</u> <u>selling</u> briskly, and toy manufacturing <u>is</u> big business. In the past, toys for infants <u>**were**</u> mostly simple plastic rattles and terry-cloth balls. Now toy makers <u>**are**</u> constantly <u>trying</u> to come up with new gimmicks that <u>will appeal</u> to parents and expectant parents. In fact, they<u>'re turning</u> for inspiration to research on babies, even on unborn babies. Investigators recently <u>discovered</u> that soft music <u>was</u> able to soothe not only a pregnant woman but also her unborn child. So an ingenious manufacturer <u>is</u> now <u>selling</u> "Babyphones," lightweight stereo speakers that a mother-to-be <u>wears</u> around her waist. A cassette player <u>**hooks**</u> onto her pocket or purse. If the fetus <u>starts</u> kicking, the expectant mother <u>**switches**</u> on "womb tunes" (as the maker <u>**calls**</u> these tapes). What else <u>**does**</u> the fetus <u>hear</u> besides violins or guitars? One favorite <u>**is**</u> a home-made tape of Mom and Dad singing lullabies. Then to help the newborn to make the transition from the familiar womb to the scary outside world, toy makers <u>**have**</u> yet another helpful invention. For nine months the baby <u>was listening</u> to the sounds of its mother's body and the beat of her heart. After birth, the parents <u>**are**</u> able to buy a tape player to put in the baby's bed, where it <u>**plays**</u> the same comforting rhythms. Toy manufacturers <u>**are**</u> also <u>publicizing</u> the discovery that babies <u>**enjoy**</u> the high contrast of black and white. Now zebras, pandas, and other black and-white animals **are** making big bucks for them. They **'re** also promoting black-and-white mobiles to hang on the crib. In this age of the consumer, the manufacturers **exploit** the idea that nobody **is** too young for an expensive toy.

Module 9: *Past-Tense Verbs*

Exercise 9.1

	past tense	past participle	*ING* form
1.	said	said	saying
2.	went	gone	going
3.	saw	seen	seeing
4.	left	left	leaving
5.	brought	brought	bringing
6.	bought	bought	buying
7.	paid	paid	paying
8.	had	had	having
9.	was/were	been	being
10.	put	put	putting [*PUT* is one of a small group of irregular verbs that are

the same in the present tense, the past tense, and the past participle. Most verbs like this end in *T.*]

Exercise 9.2

1. On September 30, 1829, George Worsham, a Virginia farmer, **got** his tax bill in the mail.
2. He **paid** forty cents per slave, ten cents per horse, and one cent per two-wheel carriage.
3. On May 1, 1862, he **bought** his grandson Henry a new horse for $120.
4. Henry's mother **brought** a box of cornbread to the verandah and **put** it in his knapsack.
5. Henry **said** goodbye and **rode** away to join the First Virginia Cavalry in the Shenandoah Valley.
6. On February 27, 1865, the Confederate States of America **sent** Mr. Worsham $2965 in worthless currency for his dead horse, and nothing for his dead grandson.
7. One by one, the freed blacks **left** the farm, and Worsham **sold** his livestock.
8. On June 1, 1870, Worsham and his sons **spoke** to their lawyer and **told** him to file for bankruptcy.

Exercise 9.3

1. In 1861, the Civil War **began** with Confederate victories at Fort Sumter and Bull Run.
2. For many months after that, the timid Northern generals **ran** away or **did** nothing.
3. Early in 1862, Ulysses S. Grant **came** to Lincoln's attention as the first Northern general to win a battle.
4. The subsequent battles at Shiloh and Antietam **were** bloody but indecisive.
5. The following year, Grant **saw** a chance to win control of the Mississippi Valley.
6. On July 4, 1863, Grant **drank** a victory toast at Vicksburg, and his troops **sang** *Yankee Doodle* on the banks of the Mississippi.
7. After this triumph, the tide of the war **swung** in favor of the North.

Exercise 9.4

1. According to Joseph Smith, in 1829 a heavenly messenger **presented** him with a Bible-like book which he **called** the Book of Mormon.
2. Because he and his followers **practiced** polygamy, an angry mob **lynched** him in 1844.
3. The leadership of the Mormon Church **passed** to Brigham Young.
4. Thousands of Mormon converts **followed** Young to Salt Lake City where they **established** a new community.

Exercise 9.5

1. Grace / **planted** a garden and **grew** tomatoes.
2. The shortstop / **stole** third base and then **scored**.

3. Mr. Ericson / **taught** my high school Spanish class and **passed** all his students with a B.
4. The child / **caught** chicken pox and **developed** a high fever. [The *P* is not doubled because *develop* is not accented on the last syllable. See Spelling Rule A3 in Appendix A.]
5. Everybody / **sat** in his seat and **pretended** to be working.

Exercise 9.6

1. During the 1940s, American factories **relied** on millions of women workers while their men **carried** arms in World War II.
2. Most of these women **enjoyed** their earning power and independence, but **buried** these feelings when their husbands and sweethearts returned.
3. Then throughout the 1950s, most wives **stayed** home and once again **played** a traditional role.
4. The post-war "baby boom" and sentimentalization of family life **delayed** modern feminism for an entire generation.

Exercise 9.7

After the bank **collapsed**, the investigators **laid** the entire blame on the bank officials. They **said** that the officers **relied** on inside information about stock investments and **delayed** paying interest on loans. As usual, the officers **denied** the charges, but the depositors **paid** dearly for these illegal practices.

Exercise 9.8

1. I / **hoped** to get a B in my philosophy course last semester, but I didn't really expect to.
   Edmund / **hopped** four miles last year to win a bet.
2. Somebody / **robbed** the liquor store on the corner last week.
   The graduates / **robed** in the hall before the ceremony.
3. Who / **rapped** on my door a minute ago?
   The Romans / **raped** the Sabines.
4. That group / **planned** the conference two years in advance.
   The carpenter / **planed** the door so it would fit better.
5. We / **stared** at each other in disbelief.
   The film / **starred** William Hurt and Glenn Close.

Exercise 9.9

1. Every morning when the alarm clock rings, they / **jump** out of bed.
   Every morning when the alarm clock rings, she / **jumps** out of bed.
   When the alarm rang yesterday, they / **jumped** out of bed.
   When the alarm rang yesterday, she / **jumped** out of bed.
2. Cassie and her husband / always **have** a miserable time when they go camping.
   Cassie / always **has** fun when she goes to the beach.
   Last year in California, Cassie and her husband / **had** a wonderful vacation.
   Cassie / **was** sorry when she **had** to come back home.

Exercise 9.10

As the storm battered the coast, the men on board the small fishing boat **grasped** the ropes and furled their sails. Desperately, they **flashed** distress signals to the shore. But the waves **surged** savagely, overturned their boat, and **threatened** to drown them. All night, they **clutched** the hull of their craft with aching fingers. At dawn, while the storm still raged, helicopter pilots **risked** their lives when they hovered over the fishermen, dropped ladders, and **plucked** them out of the sea.

Exercise 9.11

1. Millions / **used to die** of smallpox.
2. Some middle-income folks / **used to have** cooks and chauffeurs.
3. Some retired Americans / **used to save** money by living abroad.

RULES SUMMARY

1. All verbs are either **regular** or irregular.
2. To form the past tense of most irregular verbs, **change** the whole word.
3. The past-tense forms of the irregular verbs *LAY*, *PAY*, and *SAY* are **laid**, **paid**, and **said**.
4. To form the past tense of regular verbs, add **D** or **ED**.
5. Some regular verbs need **spelling** changes before adding a past-tense ending.
   a. If a verb ends in a **consonant** + *Y*, change the *Y* to **I** before adding *ED*.
   b. If a verb ends in a **vowel** + *Y*, don't change the *Y* to *I*.
   c. If a verb ends in a single vowel + a single consonant, **double** the final consonant before adding *ED*.
6. In most sentences with more than one verb, every verb must be in the **same** tense.
7. Be careful not to leave off the **D** ending in the expression *used to*.

Exercise 9.12

They **bought**
They **brought**
They **caught**
They **taught**

Spell all these verbs with **A U G H T** or with
<u>O</u> **U G H T** in the past tense.

They **threw**
They **knew**
They **grew**

Spell all these verbs with **E W** in the past tense.

They **stole**
They **rose**
They **froze**
They **chose**

Spell all these verbs with an **O** in the past tense.

They **said**
They **laid**
They **paid**

Spell all these verbs with **A I D** in the past tense.

They **rang**
They **swam**
They **began**
They **drank**
They **sang**

Spell all these verbs with an **A** in the past tense.

They **sent**
They **lost**
They **spent**
They **kept**
They **felt**
They **slept**
They **left**

Spell all these verbs with a **T** in the past tense.

They **quit**
They **cut**
They **hit**
They **hurt**
They **put**

These verbs all have **no** change in the past tense.

Exercise 9.13 [Be sure to check the spelling of every past-tense form.]

1. Yes, he / **washed** the dishes, **dried** them, and **put** them away.
2. Yes, it / **rang**, **stopped**, and **began** ringing again.
3. Yes, she / **worried** about money, **shopped** very carefully, and **paid** all her bills.
4. Yes, she / **attended** school, **kept** house for her family, and **studied** every weekend.
5. Yes, I / **woke** up [OR, **woke up**] at 9 AM, **had** breakfast, **listened** to the morning news, and **went** back to bed.
6. Yes, he / **prayed**, **read** from the Bible, **led** a hymn, and **said** the benediction.

Exercise 9.14

1. Whenever she finishes early, Muriel / **goes** straight home.
   When she finished early last night, Muriel / **went** straight home.
2. Before my brother moved to Chicago last year, he / **bought** a new car.
   Every time my brother makes a big change in his life, he / **buys** a new car.

3. Whenever their parents disapprove of something, Maggie and Joan / **are** eager to do it.
    Although their parents disapproved, Maggie and Joan / **were** eager to become models.
4. If a person is ambitious, he or she / **does** the best job possible.
    Because Latrelle was ambitious, she / always **did** her best work.
5. Every night, when Edith's husband comes home, she / **asks** him how he **feels**.
    Last night, when Edith's husband came home, she / **asked** him how he **felt**.
6. Whenever she had time, Mrs. Franklin / **stopped** and **bought** a newspaper to read on her way to work.
    Whenever she has time, Mrs. Franklin / **stops** and **buys** a newspaper to read on her way to work.

Exercise 9.15

1. Last year, a number of people **dropped** their senile parents at the door of an emergency room and **drove** away.
2. If Congress **passes** that controversial bill, the President will veto it when it **reaches** his desk.
3. When I'm writing at my computer, time **flies** , and I **lose** myself in whatever I am doing.
4. A working mother often **shops** for groceries on the way home and **rushes** to start dinner before her husband arrives.
5. While he **washes** the dishes, she lies down on the sofa and **watches** TV.
6. Recently, a deranged man **hid** a hammer under his coat, and then attacked the famous statue of David and **chipped** its toe.
7. When the doorbell **rang**, Brenda looked to see who was there before she **unlocked** the door.
8. A young child is hard to live with because she **asks** questions constantly and **gets** into a lot of mischief.
9. There **are** several drugs which prolong the lives of AIDS victims, but until doctors **find** a cure, the disease will continue to spread.
10. Before the game started, Roseanne **sang** *The Star-Spangled Banner* off key and almost **caused** a riot.

Exercise 9.16 [Remember: Parentheses and italics mark the words that you should have circled.]

1. Some people / <u>drink</u> *(to forget)* their problems.
    Some people / **drank** *(to forget)* their problems.
2. Stocks / <u>begin</u> *(to rise)* when interest rates <u>fall</u>.
    Stocks / **began** *(to rise)* when interest rates **fell**.
3. AIDS victims / <u>try</u> *(to obtain)* this experimental drug.
    AIDS victims / **tried** *(to obtain)* this experimental drug.
4. It / <u>costs</u> too much *(to travel)* abroad.
    It / **cost** too much *(to travel)* abroad.
5. A close call / <u>teaches</u> us *(to drive)* more carefully.
    A close call / **taught** us *(to drive)* more carefully.
6. These immigrants / <u>are</u> always happy *(to help)* their friends.
    These immigrants / **were** always happy *(to help)* their friends.
7. We / <u>have</u> *(to run)* fast *(to stay)* in the same place.
    We / **had** *(to run)* fast *(to stay)* in the same place.
8. It / <u>is</u> dangerous *(to accept)* his favors.
    It / **was** dangerous *(to accept)* his favors.
9. He / <u>plans</u> *(to demand)* repayment.
    He / **planned** *(to demand)* repayment.

Exercise 9.17

The 14 leading cars **carried** tents and equipment, and the next seven <u>transported</u> the animals. In the fading light of June 22, 1918, the crew **hitched** the four sleeping cars to the end of the train. The flagman <u>signaled</u> to the engineer, and the Hagenbeck-Wallace Circus **clattered** out of Michigan City. In the wooden sleepers, 300 circus people <u>chatted</u> and **played** cards, or <u>climbed</u> into their bunks and **dreamed** of the next day's opening performance in Hammond, Indiana.

Near the town of Ivanhoe, the circus train <u>pulled</u> into a side track while the crew **tried** to fix an overheated brake box. The Pullman cars <u>extended</u> out onto the main track, so Ernest Trimm, the flagman, <u>propped</u> up emergency flares and **checked** to make sure that the signal lights <u>were</u> <u>flashing</u> warnings. Suddenly, an unscheduled troop train **thundered** down the track, hurtling toward the circus cars. Asleep at the throttle, Engineer Alonso Sargent never **slowed** down. As the oncoming train **passed** through the yellow caution lights, Trimm <u>waved</u> his lantern frantically and then **hurled** it through the engineer's window. But the speeding locomotive **ripped** past the red stop lights and <u>plowed</u> into the fragile wooden sleeping cars, crushing and killing most of the performers. Gas lights <u>started</u> fires in the wreckage, and the animals <u>bellowed</u> in terror as the flames **licked** toward them. Trapped in their cages, some **burned** to death. Their roars **terrified** the townspeople, and hysterical reports <u>traveled</u> from house to house. According to so-called eye witnesses, lions and tigers <u>jumped</u> from the train and **roamed** the streets.

On the evening after the wreck, the circus **opened** on schedule. Performers and acts from all over the country **rushed** to Indiana and <u>substituted</u> for the victims of the crash. For years afterwards, the people of Ivanhoe **used** to sit around on summer evenings, talking about that terrible night when one exhausted man **destroyed** almost an entire circus.

Exercise 9.18

In the Middle Ages, marriage customs **used** *(to be)* strange and cruel, especially for women. While brides **were** still in their cradles, their parents **used** *(to arrange)* their weddings. Sometimes a girl never **saw** her husband until they **met** at the altar rail, and all too often this meeting **turned** out *(to be)* quite a shock. But no matter how she **felt** about him, the marriage contract **made** it clear that he **had** *(to have)* an heir. If the wife **failed** *(to deliver)* a child within a year or two, her husband often **used** *(to get)* an annulment, and then he **married** someone else. The man **was** free *(to take)* a mistress, but if his wife even **looked** at another man, he **beat** her. Some women **thought** that it **was** better not *(to marry)* at all, and **chose** *(to enter)* the convent instead.

Exercise 9.19

Last week when I **got** out of the elevator in my apartment building, my neighbor Sam **warned** me *(to be)* careful. He **reminded** me about the rise in street crime during this past year. I just <u>laughed</u> as I <u>pushed</u> open the front door. After I <u>stepped</u> onto the sidewalk, I **stopped**, <u>buttoned</u> up my coat, <u>pulled</u> on my gloves, and **picked** up all my packages again. It never **occurred** to me *(to see)* if I <u>had</u> everything. I <u>entered</u> the bank on the corner and **asked** *(to apply)* for a credit card. The guard **opened** the gate into the office area. I **went** inside and **got** an application *(to fill)* out. But when I <u>reached</u> for my purse *(to get)* a pen, my purse <u>wasn't</u> there. I <u>started</u> *(to **scream**)*. I <u>shook</u> the gate and **yelled**, "Somebody <u>stole</u> my purse! Somebody **robbed** me!" The guard <u>told</u> me *(to **stop**)* for a minute and *(to try)* *(to think)*. I <u>admitted</u> to him, "Yes, maybe I <u>left</u> it on the street when I <u>stopped</u> and <u>put</u> my gloves on." In a panic, I <u>ran</u> all the way home. There I **saw** Sam, just inside the door, with my purse in his hand. He **said**, with a look of astonishment, "Some stranger <u>found</u> your purse by the door and **gave** it to me." This week Sam **switched** the topic of his conversation from crime to the weather.

Exercise 9.20

I **was** not a suspicious person, but I **knew** something **was** wrong. Whenever I <u>left</u> the house, someone **followed** me. I never **saw** him, but I **knew** that he **was** there. I **heard** the sound of feet behind me when I **walked**. As I **stopped** to glance into shop windows, I **caught** a glimpse of someone who **stood** off to one side, but when I **turned** around, he **was** not there. I **felt** his presence in crowds. As I **chose** a magazine, he **looked** over my shoulder. As I **bought** toothpaste or **paid** for my groceries, he **passed** near and **counted** my change. As I **hurried** home, I **felt** his eyes on my back. I **went** out less and less. He **watched** me through my windows. When the phone **rang**, I never **answered**. I **slept** very little. My friends **thought** that I **was** paranoid, but I **wondered** if they **were** in league with him.

Exercise 9.21: Review Exercise E

My grandmother <u>grew</u> up in the Great Depression of the 1930s, when it **cost** just eight cents *(to buy)* a loaf of bread. Even with such low prices, her parents **were** too poor *(to put)* a good meal on the table every day. She and her family **saw** some really hard times. Since almost everybody **was** in the same boat, though, they **laughed** off their troubles and <u>waited</u> for the economy *(to **recover**)*. They and their neighbors **were** right *(to believe)* what President Roosevelt always <u>said</u> on his weekly radio broadcasts, that prosperity <u>was</u> just around the corner.

Compared to the Great Depression, recent years <u>seem</u> prosperous to most people. Parts of the economy **are** <u>thriving</u>, and one of my own neighbors **has** two BMWs and a vacation home. But the lives of many working people today <u>aren't</u> much different from my grandmother's. For example, my nephew, a recent high school graduate, <u>is having</u> a hard time finding a decent job, and not one of his friends **owns** a car. There **are** people in the middle, like me and my husband. We <u>pay</u> our bills and <u>drive</u> an old station wagon, but our dream of owning our own home **gets** dimmer and dimmer. Our future **seems** just as likely *(to get)* worse as it <u>is</u> to get better, as America **moves** toward the year 2000.

Module 10: *Understanding Sentences II*

Exercise 10.1 [Dark print shows the expansion words which you should have circled.]

1. Ms. Montoya / <u>will teach</u> a Saturday morning section (**if** enough students register for it).
2. People / sometimes <u>tell</u> lies (**when** they're under pressure).
3. Children / sometimes <u>become</u> angry (**because** their parents neglect them).

Exercise 10.2

1. Wendell / <u>bought</u> a bicycle (**when** he moved to Palo Alto).
    The expansion tells **when** Wendell bought a bicycle.
2. Most people / <u>will lose</u> weight (**if** they exercise).
    The expansion tells under what **condition** most people will lose weight.
3. Many elderly people / <u>have</u> difficulties (**because** they live on fixed incomes.)
    The expansion tells **why** many elderly people have difficulties.

Exercise 10.3

1. You / <u>will</u> not <u>get</u> that job (**unless** you're willing to travel).
2. Minneapolis / <u>held</u> a tickertape parade (**after** the Twins won the World Series).
3. Coast-to-coast trips / <u>were</u> a rare event (**before** plane travel became common).
4. Mr. Liang / <u>will repair</u> your shoes (**while** you wait).
5. Jo Beth / <u>stopped</u> watching TV (**so that** she would have more time to read).
6. Children / <u>become</u> confused (**unless** parents agree about discipline).

Exercise 10.4

1.   S   V
    Mr. Reyes / <u>was traveling</u> in Mexico (**when** he met his future wife).
2.   S   V
    You / <u>will see</u> a small explosion (**if** the experiment succeeds).
3.   S   V
    Many older students / <u>attend</u> college (because they want a career, not just a job).

Exercise 10.5

1.   S   V
    ✗ (**When** times are good).   FRAG
                              S   V
    People / <u>spend</u> money (**when** times are good).   SENT
2.   S   V
    Robin / <u>is</u> cooperative (**if** people treat her politely).   SENT
              S   V
    ✗ (**If** people treat Robin politely).   FRAG
3.   S   V   S   V
    ✗ (**Because** the weather was bad and only four people attended).   FRAG

S   V
The meeting / <u>ended</u> early (**because** only four people attended).   SENT

Exercise 10.6 [Be sure that you used a comma after expansion at the beginning of a sentence.]

1.   Putting money in the bank / <u>doesn't</u> <u>make</u> sense (**if** the inflation rate is high).
      (**If** the inflation rate is high) , putting money in the bank / <u>doesn't</u> <u>make</u> sense.
2.   The leaves / <u>turn</u> red (**when** there is an early frost).
      (**When** there is an early frost) , the leaves / <u>turn</u> red.
3.   Most Japanese children / <u>are</u> taller than their parents (**because** their diet contains more portein than in the past.
      (**Because** their diet contains more protein than in the past) , most Japanese children / <u>are</u> taller than their parents.

Exercise 10.7

1.   Few people / <u>like</u> to speak (**before** somebody else breaks the ice), (**unless** they have something important on their minds).
2.   (**When** someone teaches us something (**before** we are ready to learn it)), we / <u>will</u> not <u>understand</u> it.
      [OR, (**When** someone teaches us something)(**before** we are ready to learn it), we / <u>will</u> not <u>understand</u> it.]
3.   (**After** Marco dealt out the cards), he / <u>repeated</u> the rules (**so that** everyone would understand).

RULES SUMMARY, Part 1

1.   A special kind of verb expansion begins with **expansion words** like **when**, **because**, and **if**.
2.   A sentence that is expanded in this way has two parts: a **base sentence** part and an **expansion** part.
3.   Verb expansion words can **combine** sentences by changing one sentence into **expansion** of the other.
4.   This special kind of expansion contains a **subject** and a **verb**.
5.   Verb expansion by itself is a **fragment**, even when it contains a subject and a verb.
6.   This kind of verb expansion can come either at the **end** of a base sentence or at the **beginning**.
7.   When this kind of verb expansion comes at the beginning of a sentence, a **comma** is needed to separate it from the base sentence.

Exercise 10.8

People and information / <u>continue</u> to hurtle through space at higher and higher speeds. (When John Adams traveled from Boston to Williamsburg in the 1770s), he / <u>was</u> on the road for more than a week. Today the trip / <u>takes</u> 90 minutes by plane. (After Andrew Jackson was elected President in 1828), a month / <u>went</u> by (before some voters heard the news). Today most people / <u>know</u> the new President's name (before the polls close). However, one notable exception to this law of progress / <u>is</u> the daily mail. The pony express / <u>was</u> faster in the 19th century than some modern mail trucks. Back in the 1930s, the postman / <u>came</u> to my grandmother's house twice a day (unless the snow was more than three feet deep). (When she mailed a letter in the late afternoon), it / usually <u>arrived</u> the next morning at a friend's house fifty miles away. (If her friend wrote back that morning), Grandmother / sometimes <u>got</u> her reply the same day. This kind of service / <u>used</u> to cost just two cents. Today I / <u>pay</u> over $9 for Express Mail (so that an important letter will get to its destination overnight). In fact, (although it runs up my phone bill), I / often <u>phone</u> long distance instead of writing, (because the mails are so undependable). Today's postal service / <u>seems</u> to be an example of progress in reverse.

Exercise 10.9

[1]In 1492, (while Spain was still a great European power), Christopher   [1]SENT
Columbus / <u>set</u> sail with three ships from a port near Seville. [2] ✗ (After the   [2]FRAG
Spanish monarchs Ferdinand and Isabella had financed his voyage). [3]Columbus   [3]SENT
/ <u>sailed</u> west to find new lands. [4] ✗ (Although he told a different story later).   [4]FRAG
[5] ✗ According to this later story, (because he was seeking another route to   [5]FRAG
Cathay or "the Indies.") [6](If that story was true), Columbus / <u>organized</u>   [6]SENT
a strange expedition. [7]There <u>were</u> / no diplomats or soldiers on his ships.   [7]SENT

⁸✗ (Although Europeans well knew the wealth and power of those eastern lands).   ⁸FRAG
⁹✗ (After Columbus and his crew had sailed for 64 days). ¹⁰✗ (Until they landed   ⁹FRAG
on an island in the Caribbean). ¹¹(When they returned to Spain), their   ¹⁰FRAG
ships / carried some gold and a number of captive "Indians," but no news   ¹¹SENT
of eastern civilizations. ¹²✗ However, (because the strange tale of sailing   ¹²FRAG
west to India persisted). ¹³We / still call those islands the West Indies and   ¹³SENT
refer to the native inhabitants of the American continent as Indians.

Exercise 10.10

1.   Everyone will be able to hear. ✗ (**If** the audio system operates properly).
     Everyone / will be able to hear (**if** the audio system operates properly).
2.   Customers were growing irritated. ✗ (**Because** the lines were very long).
     Customers / were growing irritated (**because** the lines were very long).
3.   ✗ (**When** their children become teenagers and begin to do things on their own). Parents worry.
     (**When** their children become teenagers and begin to do things on their own), parents / worry.

Exercise 10.11

1.   ✗
     Sarah is nervous, she has a job interview tomorrow.
     Sarah / is nervous (**because** she has a job interview tomorrow).
2.   ✗
     Many people look forward to retirement, they will be able to travel.
     Many people / look forward to retirement (**so that** they will be able to travel).
3.   ✗
     The tenants ended their strike, they received a rent reduction.
     The tenants / ended their strike (**after** they received a rent reduction).

Exercise 10.12

1.   ✗
     Ursula lost her voice, she won the speech contest.
     Ursula / lost her voice (**after** she won the speech contest).
2.   ✗
     I practiced the piano sonata, I played it perfectly.
     I / practiced the piano sonata (**until** I played it perfectly).
3.   ✗
     The bus arrives soon, we will be late.
     (**Unless** the bus arrives soon), we / will be late.
4.   ✗
     People eat out more frequently, they have more money.
     People / eat out more frequently (**because** they have more money).
5.   ✗
     Josephine goes shopping, she always looks in the newspaper for sales.
     (**Before** Josephine goes shopping), she / always looks in the newspaper for sales.

Exercise 10.13   [Remember: Square brackets show where you should have drawn a box.]

1.   ✗
     Martinique was 21 years old, she filed papers to become a citizen.
     a.   Martinique / was 21 years old. She / filed papers to become a citizen.
     b.   Martinique / was 21 years old **[, and]** she / filed papers to become a citizen.
     c.   (**When** Martinique was 21 years old), she / filed papers to become a citizen.
          OR, Martinique / was 21 years old (**when** she filed papers to become a citizen).
2.   ✗
     Social services like education are suffering, the public resists raising taxes.
     a.   Social services like education / are suffering. The public / resists raising taxes.
     b.   Social services like education / are suffering **[, but]** the public / resists raising taxes.

c.   (**Although** social services like education are suffering), the public / resists raising taxes.

RULES SUMMARY, Part 2

1.   Most fragments which begin with verb expansion words can be corrected by **connecting** them to a base sentence.
2.   There are at least three ways to correct a run-on:
   a.   Rewrite it as **two** sentences.
   b.   Rewrite it as a **compound** sentence, using a comma + a joining word like **and** or **but**.
   c.   Rewrite it by changing one of the sentences into **expansion** of the other.

Exercise 10.14

1.   (While Claire prepared for her examinations), her husband did the shopping. ✗ (So that she was free to study).
     (While Claire prepared for her examinations), her husband / did the shopping (so that she was free to study).
2.   ✗ (Before the cost of living became so expensive). Most women stayed at home (while their husbands worked).
     (Before the cost of living became so expensive), most women / stayed at home (while their husbands worked).
3.   ✗ (Before Bertha arrived). They hid the presents. ✗ (Because they wanted to surprise her).
     (Before Bertha arrived), they / hid the presents (because they wanted to surprise her).
4.   (Although everyone feels angry at times), anger is a dangerous emotion. ✗ (If we don't control it).
     (Although everyone feels angry at times), anger / is a dangerous emotion (if we don't control it).

Exercise 10.15 [Be sure to check for commas. Commas in brackets are acceptable but not essential.]

(When the brutal emperor Caligula ruled Rome), he / had complete power to do anything, no matter how inhuman. On the hottest days, he / often removed the canopies at the outdoor theater. Then he / refused to let anyone leave[,] (so that the spectators collapsed from sunstroke). (When Caligula was sick once), a friend / promised to commit suicide[,] (if the gods spared the emperor's life). Later (after Caligula got well), he / compelled his friend to keep that promise. He / forced important administrators to trot beside his chariot[,] (because he enjoyed making them look ridiculous). (When two officials failed to announce his birthday), he / removed them from office and sent them into exile. (If he liked the looks of a woman), he / took her home with him[,] (even if she was unwilling). (Until he died at the hands of an assassin), Caligula / continued to brutalize others[,] (because other people's suffering was, for him, the best entertainment).

Exercise 10.16

1.   ✗
     I am taking typing lessons now, (when I go to graduate school), I will type all of my papers.
     I / am taking typing lessons now. (When I go to graduate school), I / will type all of my papers.
2.   ✗
     (If you want the best coffee), you will grind the beans yourself, whole beans stay fresh longer.
     (If you want the best coffee), you / will grind the beans yourself. Whole beans / stay fresh longer.
3.   ✗
     The babysitter lived twelve blocks away, (before I went to work), I had to take my son to her house.
     The babysitter / lived twelve blocks away. (Before I went to work), I / had to take my son to her house.
4.   ✗
     (Although Marie is dedicated to her job), she also makes time for her family, she is always there (when they need her).
     (Although Marie is dedicated to her job), she / also makes time for her family. She / is always there (when they need her).
5.   ✗
     (When I left the store), I waited on the corner for the light to change, (while I waited), I thought about all my chores.
     (When I left the store), I / waited on the corner for the light to change. (While I waited), I / thought about all my chores.

Exercise 10.17 [Be sure to check for commas. Commas in brackets are acceptable but not essential.]

Although Albert Einstein was perhaps the greatest scientist of all time, he was a very simple human being. When he joined the faculty of the Institute for Advanced Study at Princeton, he had to name his own salary. The director had to plead with him to accept more money[,] because he asked for such an impossibly small amount. As a child, he was slow in learning new things[,] so that his teachers saw no special talent in him. After he became a renowned physicist, his colleagues at Princeton smiled in disbelief when he asked them to pause and repeat their statements again[,] because his mind understood new things so slowly. If famous scientists and world leaders visited him, he greeted them wearing his usual outfit, an old sweater, baggy pants, and a pair of sandals. When some children came knocking on his door one Christmas Eve, he followed them through the streets of Princeton[,] while he accompanied their carols on his violin.

Exercise 10.18: Review Exercise F [Be sure to check for commas. Commas in brackets are acceptable but not essential.]

In 1935, a scientist named Charles Richter developed a scale[,] using numbers to measure the intensity of earthquakes. Few people feel an earthquake rated 1 unless they're very sensitive to faint tremors. Most people do notice a number 2[,] although nothing seems to move. Almost everyone sees and feels the effects of a number 3 earthquake because it makes hanging objects swing. Beginning with number 4, an earthquake makes sounds. Dishes rattle. Glasses clink. Sometimes they even tumble from the shelf. A number 5 earthquake is frightening[,] because it's strong enough to break windows and to crack walls. A number 6 injures people and even kills them when loose bricks and weak chimneys come crashing down. A number 7 destroys whole buildings and often buries thousands in the rubble. A number 8 shakes the earth strongly[,] so that even hills move. Although more violent earthquakes are theoretically possible, none stronger than an 8 is presently on record.

Module 11: *More about Verb Phrases*

Exercise 11.1

1. Someone / **has** my notebook.
   Someone / **has taken** my notebook.
2. No one / **had** the answer.
   No one / **had answered** the last question.
3. Many cities / **have** financial problems.
   Many cities / **have grown** smaller in population in the last ten years.

Exercise 11.2

1. Poland / **has** begun to trade with the West.
   Poland and Czechoslovakia / **have** begun to trade with the West.
2. **Have** you beaten the computer at chess?
   The computer / **has** beaten me at chess.
3. My brother / **has** had to borrow money.
   I / **have** had to borrow money.

Exercise 11.3

	past tense	past participle	*ING* form
1.	saw	seen	seeing
2.	went	gone	going
3.	bought	bought	buying
4.	paid	paid	paying
5.	had	had	having

Exercise 11.4

1. By the end of the 1970s, sales of American cars / had **gone** down.

2. Before we knew it, Japan / <u>had</u> **taken** the lead.
3. For years, American companies / <u>had</u> **chosen** to ignore the problem.
4. Congress / still hasn't **done** much about it.
5. Prices / <u>have</u> **risen**, and profits / <u>have</u> **shrunk**.
6. This shift in the balance of trade / <u>has</u> **taught** us some harsh lessons.
7. We / <u>have</u> **had** to change our ways.

Exercise 11.5

1. In the early 1990s, we / **saw** big changes in Eastern Europe.
    We / <u>have</u> **seen** more big changes recently.
2. In 1990, the two Germanys / once more **became** one nation.
    Before that, several countries with Communist governments / <u>had</u> **become** democracies.
3. Soon the Baltic States / **broke** away from the Soviet Union.
    By the end of 1991, the Soviet Union / <u>had</u> **broken** up.

Exercise 11.6

past tense	past participle	ING form
1. talked	talked	talking
2. smiled	smiled	smiling
3. expected	expected	expecting

Exercise 11.7

1. Doctors / <u>have</u> **learned** how to save premature babies.
2. Modern medicine / <u>has</u> **prevented** many childhood diseases.
3. Infant mortality / <u>has</u> dramatically **decreased**.

Exercise 11.8

Over the centuries, triskaidekaphobia—the fear of the number 13—<u>has</u> **terrorized** many people and <u>caused</u> them to act in strange ways. In all ages and in all countries, people <u>have</u> **refused** to hold celebrations on the 13th of the month, and in some societies, they <u>have</u> even **drowned** children born on this evil day. Recently, architects <u>have</u> **learned** to deal with triskaidekaphobia by giving the number 14 to the floor after 12. In this way, also, hospitals <u>have</u> **tricked** patients into accepting beds on the 13th floor. Yet despite this superstition, for almost two centuries Americans <u>have saluted</u> a flag with 13 stripes, and immigrants <u>have</u> **flocked** to pledge allegiance to it from all over the world.

Exercise 11.9

1. Some serious accidents / <u>have</u> **occurred** in my apartment building this winter.
2. Several elderly tenants / <u>have</u> **slipped** on icy sidewalks.
3. They / <u>have</u> **applied** to the landlord for compensation.
4. He / <u>has</u> **denied** any responsibility.
5. The tenants organization / <u>has</u> **planned** a protest meeting for next week.

Exercise 11.10

1. Pilar / **has** <u>liked</u> Rafael for six months, and she still does.
    Pilar / **had** <u>liked</u> Tomas, until she saw him with Emilia.
2. Ruby and Dee / **have** <u>been</u> friends for years; they live next door to one another.
    Ruby and Vikki / **had** <u>been</u> best friends until Vikki married Ruby's brother.
3. Stavros / **has** <u>taken</u> the bus to work every day this week.
    Stavros / **had** <u>taken</u> his bicycle to work, until the weather became colder.

Exercise 11.11

My sister **was** in the kitchen. She **had been** there for less than an hour. She **had baked**
two pies already. She **planned** to make two more.

Exercise 11.12

Russ **is** in the garage. He **has been** there all afternoon. He **has changed** only one snow
tire. He **is** too tired to finish the job.

RULES SUMMARY, Part 1

1. *HAVE* can be either a **one word** verb or a **helping** verb in a verb phrase.
2. The present-tense form of *HAVE* that agrees with a singular subject is **has**.
3. With the helping verb *HAVE*, use the **past participle** of the main verb.
4. To form the past participle of most **irregular** verbs, change the whole word.
5. To form the past participle of regular verbs, add **D** or **ED**.
6. In verb phrases, the **helping** verb, not the main verb, shows **tense**.
7. Use verb phrases with the **present** tense of *HAVE* to mean that something began in the past and is still happening or is
    still true in the present.
8. Use verb phrases with the **past** tense of *HAVE* to mean that something happened or was true in the past, before
    something else happened.

Exercise 11.13

1. Last week, Minnie / **drove** to work.
    For the past month, Minnie / **has driven** to work.
    Until she wrecked her car, Minnie / **had driven** to work.
2. Last year, Pedro / **was** the store manager.
    For the last five years, Pedro / **has been** the store manager.
    Before the store was closed, Pedro **had been** the store manager.
3. Last month, Noreen / **read** romance magazines and **wrote** in her diary.
    For the last six months, Noreen / **has read** romance magazines and **written** in her diary.
    Until she eloped, Noreen / **had read** romance magazines and **written** in her diary. [Remember that the helping verb
    may be "understood" in a second verb phrase, so **has written** and **had written** would also be correct.]

Exercise 11.14

1.   Last week, Charlene / **made** her rounds as a traffic patrol officer. She / **checked** parking
    meters, and she / **wrote** tickets for violators. Drivers / often **were** angry with her. But
    Charlene / never **relented**, for she / **was** proud of her reputation as a heartless meter maid.
2.   For the last six months, Charlene / **has made** her rounds as a traffic patrol
    officer. She / **has checked** parking meters, and she **has written** tickets for violators.
    Drivers / often **have been** angry with her. But Charlene / never **has relented**
    [OR, **has** never **relented**], for she / **has been** proud of her reputation as a heartless meter maid.
3.   Until a driver attacked her, Charlene / **had made** her rounds as a traffic
    patrol officer. She / **had checked** parking meters, and she / **had written** tickets for
    violators. Drivers / often **had been** angry with her. But Charlene / never **had relented**
    [OR, **had** never **relented**], for she **had been** proud of her reputation as a heartless meter
    maid.

Exercise 11.15

For the last seven years, every morning at 11 AM, Heinrich Count von Schlegel **has visited**
the west bank of the blue Danube. His neighbors **have noticed** that, at almost the same hour, Frau
Hilde Hindenberg, the banker's widow, **has gone** to the same spot. Behind their shuttered
windows these nosy neighbors **have whispered** about the count and the widow. But all
this gossip **has been** nonsense. Each time these two **have gone** to the embankment,
they **have sat** about three meters apart. The widow **has closed** her eyes for a snooze.

The count **has waited** for her first snore before he **has rolled** up his pants to the knee
for a sunbath. Then he **has buried** his head in a book, while she **has snored** gently on.
If he **has felt** the slightest interest in her plump form, he certainly never **has given**
[OR, **has** never **given**] any sign of it.

Exercise 11.16

1. **Did** they **try** to find summer jobs last year?
2. After Delma pays her bills, she / usually **does** not **have** enough money left to buy lunch.
3. **Do**n't most people **feel** nervous when they see a black cat?

Exercise 11.17

1. My uncle / had **lived** in this neighborhood for years.
    He / doesn't **live** here any more.
2. I / have **tried** to be reasonable.
    But you / don't even **try**.
3. Daisy / still doesn't **use** a typewriter.
    Her sister / has **used** a word processor for two years now.
4. Nothing / had ever **bothered** Marsha except her husband's smoking.
    It / didn't even **bother** her that he left his wet towels on the bathroom floor.
5. I / have always carefully **stopped** for a yellow light.
    One time I / didn't **stop**, and of course I / got a ticket.

Exercise 11.18

1. You / **will see** us tomorrow.
2. Alvin / **may** not **accept** your nomination.
3. I / **might** not **paint** my house until spring.
4. You / simply **must meet** Mr. Fowler.
5. We / **shall** always **remember** this occasion.
6. Deitra / **could**n't ever **find** that committee list.
7. Felix / **can** never **forget** the past.
8. You / **should** not **leave** the scissors on that table.

Exercise 11.19

1. Your brother / **can** borrow my motorcycle.
    Your brothers / **can** borrow my motorcycle.
2. They / **would** appreciate a card or a letter.
    She / **would** appreciate a card or a letter.
3. Alice / **might** need more time.
    Alice and Ray / **might** need more time.

Exercise 11.20

1. You / **can complete** this form at your convenience.
2. No one / **will answer** my question.
3. Aaron / **should stay** until two o'clock.
4. We / **shall overcome** all obstacles in our path.
5. Raul / **might arrive** early.

Exercise 11.21

1. I think that I **can** do it.
    I thought that I **could** do it.
2. By this afternoon we **will** be ready to go.
    We promised an hour ago that we **would** be ready to go by 3 PM.
3. Last year, students **could** not major in business at that school.
    This year, they **can** major in business or computers.

Exercise 11.22

1. She / **would** **prefer** not to talk about that.
   She / **'d** **prefer** not to talk about that.
2. He / **will** **be** there before midnight.
   He / **'ll** **be** there before midnight.
3. They / **would** rather **fight** than switch.
   They / **'d** rather **fight** than switch.
4. I / **will** be home soon.
   I / **'ll** be home soon.
5. We / **would** rather take our time.
   We / **'d** rather take our time.

RULES SUMMARY, Part 2

1. With the helping verb *DO*, use the **base form** of the main verb.
2. Never use a **past participle** in a verb phrase with *DO*.
3. The nine special helping verbs called modals are:
   | **will** | **can** | **shall** | **may** | **must** |
   | **would** | **could** | **should** | **might** | |
4. Modals don't have different forms to **agree** with their subjects.
5. With modal helping verbs, use the **base form** of the main verb.
6. Modal helping verbs don't have **past**-tense forms. But *could* is often used as the past tense of **can**, and *would* is often used as the past tense of **will**.

Exercise 11.23

1. On last October 1, Kim balanced her checkbook. She **paid** all her bills, and she **planned** her budget. Then she **wrote** a letter to her father and **asked** him for money.
2. On the first of the month every since she left home, Kim has balanced her checkbook. She **has paid** all her bills, and she **has planned** her budget. Then she **has written** a letter to her father and **asked** [OR, **has asked**] him for money.
3. Every month until she lost her job, Kim had balanced her checkbook. She **had paid** all her bills, and she **had planned** her budget. Then she **had written** a letter to her father and **asked** [OR, **had asked**] him for money.
4. Tomorrow, Kim should balance her checkbook. She **should pay** all her bills, and she **should plan** her budget. Then she **should write** a letter to her father and **ask** [OR, **should ask**] him for money.

Exercise 11.24

Mickey **has**n't **been** a very satisfactory child. As an infant, he **would**n't **eat** his cereal. At two, he **could**n't **feed** himself. At four, he **could**n't **tie** his shoelaces. Now at six, Mickey **is**n't the star pupil in the first grade. He **does**n't **read** well and **is**n't very good at arithmetic. His teacher **does**n't **paste** gold stars on his papers. Furthermore, he **can**'t **draw**, he **can**'t **sing**, and he **does**n't **know** when to keep quiet. Mickey **is**n't a winner, and he **does**n't even **seem** to know it. His parents **are**n't proud of him. **Do**n't **mention** his name. They **wo**n't **beam** with delight. [Remember that *won't* is an irregular contraction.]

Exercise 11.25

Geraldine **wants** to lose weight. She **plans** exactly what food she **will buy**, and how much of it. She **has** even **memorized** the layout of the supermarket, because she **knows** that if she **can stay** away from the ice cream and candy, she **will lose** five pounds in one week. She **says** that she **is going** to stick to her diet until she **can get** into every outfit which **is hanging** in her closet, especially those velvet slacks which she **has**n't **been** able to wear for years. But, of course, Geraldine **has made** these plans before. Her friends **do**n't **think** that she **will** actually **lose** a pound.

Exercise 11.26

1. We <u>knew</u> that last year Einar <u>had</u> **hoped** to get a larger apartment, but now he <u>has</u> **given** up on it.
2. We <u>have</u> **done** this so often that it <u>**has**</u> almost <u>become</u> a habit.
3. Old Mrs. Benson <u>had</u> **gone** to the play, but she <u>did</u> not **stay** for the second act.
4. Homer **does**n't ever <u>drink</u> alcoholic beverages; he **would** rather <u>have</u> soda pop.
5. Several students in this course <u>have</u> **taken** journalism before, or <u>have</u> **worked** for the student newspaper.
6. After deregulation, the price of plane tickets <u>didn't</u> **drop** as much as the airlines <u>had</u> **promised**.
7. Our deadline for filing applications <u>**has**</u> now been <u>extended</u>.
8. The Governor **has** <u>asked</u> the State Assembly to cut the budget because he <u>had</u> solemnly **promised** in his campaign never to raise taxes.
9. We <u>must</u> **remember** to turn out the lights before we <u>leave</u>; Irma <u>didn't</u> **remember**, and she <u>has</u> recently **received** an enormous electric bill.
10. My father <u>has</u> **studied** Chinese history in a local college ever since he <u>returned</u> from his trip to China.
11. He **would** rather <u>study</u> the Chinese language, but the college <u>doesn't</u> **offer** it.

Exercise 11.27

In 1981, President Reagan <u>chose</u> Dr. C. Everett Koop as Surgeon General of the United States because he <u>had</u> openly **opposed** abortion. But once the Senate <u>had</u> **confirmed** his appointment, this conservative doctor **astonished** everyone. The President <u>had</u> **asked** him to write a report showing that abortion was harmful to women's health. Koop **believed** that abortion <u>was</u> morally wrong, but, when he **studied** the evidence, he **saw** that it <u>failed</u> to prove that abortion necessarily <u>caused</u> physical or psychological damage to women. So he **explained** to the President that he, as an honest scientist, <u>could</u> not <u>write</u> this report. Then he **turned** his attention to smoking and AIDS. The Administration <u>had</u> not **expressed** much interest in these problems, but, according to Koop, they **were** health hazards which the Surgeon General's office <u>could</u> and <u>should</u> <u>do</u> something about. Within a few years, his warnings on cigarette packages <u>had</u> **caught** the attention of every smoker, and many <u>had</u> **kicked** the habit. Next, his report on AIDS **showed** that for the first time someone in the government <u>had</u> <u>taken</u> the deadly virus seriously. He strongly **encouraged** early sex education and the use of condoms. The Administration <u>was</u> angry, and the liberals **were** happy. Both <u>said</u> that he <u>had</u> **changed**. Koop <u>answered</u> mildly that he <u>had</u> not **budged** from his original position on any issue. By the time he **left** office in 1989, many of his early opponents <u>had</u> <u>turned</u> into supporters, and some of his former supporters **claimed** that he <u>had</u> **betrayed** them. In TV interviews after his retirement, Dr. Koop <u>insisted</u> that his views <u>had</u> never <u>altered</u>. The problem, he said, <u>was</u> that no one <u>had</u> **bothered** to learn what his convictions really **were** in the first place.

Exercise 11.28

1. ACTIVE
   PASSIVE
2. ACTIVE
   PASSIVE
3. ACTIVE
   PASSIVE
4. ACTIVE
   PASSIVE
5. PASSIVE
   ACTIVE

Exercise 11.29

1. Lots of money / <u>is</u> **lost** on Wall Street every day.
2. Sardines / <u>are</u> **caught** in nets.
3. His windshield / <u>was</u> **broken** by a rock.

Exercise 11.30

1. Every day the same routine tasks / <u>are</u> **performed** by dozens of workers.

2.   His old trunk / **is** now **used** as a coffee table.
3.   Emily / **was annoyed** by that remark.

Exercise 11.31

1.   Nowadays the supplies / **are** usually **carried** by trucks.
     Ten years ago the supplies / **were carried** by trains.
2.   When I was a child, I / **was fascinated** by complicated puzzles.
     I / **am** still **fascinated** by puzzles that are hard to solve.
3.   These days teenagers / **are** often **influenced** by peer pressure.
     In the past, teenagers / **were influenced** by their families as much as by their friends.

Exercise 11.32

1.   We / **were driving** our cars to the airport.
     My mother / **was driven** to the airport by my cousin.
2.   Iris / **is eating** the last crumb of pie.
     That entire pie / **was eaten** by just two people.
3.   We / **are taking** our places now.
     This seat / **is** already **taken** by my wife.
4.   All these vegetables / **were grown** by my husband.
     This summer my husband / **is growing** corn and peas.
5.   The trees / **were shaking** in the wind.
     The trees / **were shaken** by the wind.

Exercise 11.33

1.   Somebody / **gets injured** seriously every season playing football.
2.   Benita / **got promoted** last month, so her friends gave her a party.
3.   Last night, Ali / **got robbed** in front of his own house.
4.   Miss Ecklestein / **gets paid** much less than she deserves.
5.   The arsonists / **got sentenced** to a long prison term after a very short trial.
6.   Basil and Vera / **got divorced** just two months after they **got married**.

Exercise 11.34

1.   Now that they have lived in the tropics for ten years, they / **are used** to the heat.
2.   Next year, food prices / **are supposed** to go up again.
3.   Cordelia / **is used** to her father's bad temper, so she hardly notices it any more.
4.   The painter / **was supposed** to finish this job yesterday.
5.   We / **were used** to getting our own way when we were young.

RULES SUMMARY, Part 3

1.   A sentence is **active** when the subject is doing the action of the verb. A
     sentence is **passive** when the action of the verb is happening to the subject.
2.   For an **active** sentence with the helping verb *BE*, use the **ING** form of the main verb.
3.   For all **passive** sentences, use the helping verb *BE* with the **past participle** of the main verb.
4.   The helping verb *BE* must **agree** with its subject in both the present tense and the **past** tense.
5.   Sometimes the helping verb **GET** is used instead of *BE* in passive sentences.
6.   Be careful not to leave the **D** ending off the past participles *used* and **supposed**.

Exercise 11.35

1.   Rosita / **is beating** eggs for the meringue.
2.   The eggs / **aren't** yet **beaten** stiffly enough to add the sugar.
3.   Something / **was frightening** the animals.
4.   The animals / **were frightened** by something outside the house.
5.   Those children / **are being** suspiciously quiet.
6.   The leader / **is selecting** a date for the workshop.
7.   The grass / **was growing** so quickly that we had to mow the lawn twice a week.

8. The cold temperature / was **freezing** the road surfaces throughout a three-state area.
9. All those candidates / were **chosen** for interviews by the committee.
10. That couple / was **married** by a ship's captain.
11. The students / were **writing** essays about the book they had just discussed.
12. This novel / was **written** by James Baldwin.

Exercise 11.36

1. Last week, when Monique was **driving** her car through town at 50 miles an hour, she was **overtaken** by a patrol car and given a ticket.
2. Silver is **tarnished** by exposure to air, so Heloise has **stored** all her silverware in plastic bags.
3. I'm not yet **used** to digital clocks and watches, even though they have been common for more than a decade.
4. My sister was **supposed** to go back to work on Monday, but instead she is **taking** another week off.
5. During the winter the pipes had **frozen**, and the floor was **ruined** by the water.
6. Professor Parnell was talking to each of his students while they were writing their papers.
7. Kip is being difficult these days, and his parents are **annoyed** by his attitude.
8. When Cecil and Jerilyn got **married** last May, they were given a large check by his parents.
9. Chadwick has **been** sick for several weeks, so he has not **done** as much work as he was **supposed** to.
10. Too many couples get **divorced** before they have really tried to solve their problems.

Exercise 11.37 [Remember: Parentheses and italics mark the words that you should have circled.]

Every culture **forbids** people *(to perform)* certain acts which **are called** taboos. Some modern taboos **were** not always **considered** evil in the past. In ancient Egypt, royal siblings often **got married** to each other. American Indian warriors **used** *(to eat)* the hearts of enemies that they **had killed**, *(to show)* respect for their courage. Now both incest and cannibalism **have become** almost universal taboos. We **are horrified** by incest. And if anyone **eats** human flesh today, that person **is condemned** as a monster. In 1972, a famous plane crash in the Andes **illustrated** how strongly this taboo **is felt** in modern times. Although some survivors **kept** themselves alive by eating the bodies of the passengers who **had perished** in the crash, the taboo against cannibalism **was** too strong for most of them. Instead they **chose** *(to die)* of starvation.

Exercise 11.38

Since my wife and I **began** to do crossword puzzles together, we have bought a lot of reference books, including a new edition of *The Guinness Book of World Records*. This book has certainly **helped** us with our puzzles, but it **has** also been a source of fascinating information. It **does**n't just tell about recent sports records. Each edition **tries** to include every amazing and amusing feat of the human race. Here are some we will always remember: (1) Although Strombo the Maniac has **established** the longest official record of 65 hours for lying on a bed of nails, that record was totally **demolished** by Silki the Fakir, who **did** the same thing for 111 days—but only his followers saw him do it. (2) Lightning has **struck** one living man seven times—Roy Sullivan, a Shenandoah park ranger. His body was hit in five different places, and twice his head was **burned** bald. (3) Steve Weldon of Texas has **eaten** the longest meal in the shortest time: 100 yards of spaghetti in 28 seconds. (4) By the time he died in 597 AD, St. Simon Stylites had **chalked** up the all-time pole-sitting record: 45 years on top of a stone pillar. (5) And what book has **sold** the most copies in the past 25 years? *The Guinness Book of World Records*, of course!

Exercise 11.39: Review Exercise G

My mother has often tried to tell me that crime **does** not pay. But then, my mother **has** never run for office. I have never told her about what **happened** when I was a sophomore in high school. I had **campaigned** hard to be class president, and election day had finally **arrived**. Just before the vote was **taken**, the teacher **reminded** us, "Don't vote for yourself. Each student must **write** down somebody else's name on the ballot." But I was **scared** that I might lose the election by one vote. I knew that I should not have **done** it, but when the slips were passed around, I voted for myself. I **have** never

<u>forgotten</u> the moment when the votes **were** all <u>counted</u> and the teacher <u>said</u>, "There <u>are</u> 31 votes for Mary Williams and one vote for Ted Collins." As soon as the teacher **announced** the results, Ted <u>jumped</u> up to say that I <u>had</u> not <u>cast</u> my vote for him. But then he <u>sat</u> down even more quickly. It **took** me a day to figure out that Ted <u>had voted</u> for himself, too. He <u>could</u> not <u>accuse</u> me without accusing himself. So even if I <u>did</u> **commit** a crime, on that occasion I <u>wasn't</u> **punished**. In fact, the teacher even **praised** me because I <u>had</u> **given** my vote to my opponent.

Module 12: *Understanding Sentences III*

Exercise 12.1

1.   S   C
   (Most)→families←(in the United States) / <u>own</u> (several)(television)→sets.
2.   S   C
   Inhabitants←(of large cities) / <u>receive</u> (many)→channels←(carried by cable networks).
3.   S   C
   People←(living in rural areas) / <u>need</u> (special)→equipment←(for TV reception.)

Exercise 12.2 [Remember: Dark print shows the expansion words which you should have circled.]

1. S   C
   I / <u>met</u> a woman←(**who** knew you in high school).
2.   S   C
   Coleen / <u>needs</u> an apartment←(**which** has at least two bedrooms).
3.   S   C
   Racism / <u>is</u> a problem←(**that** concerns us all).

Exercise 12.3

1.   S
   New courses←(**that** explore cultural diversity) / <u>are being offered</u>.
2.   S   C
   A subject←(**which** too many women students avoid) / <u>is</u> mathematics.
3.   S   C
   People←(**who** learn to think optimistically) / <u>may</u> actually <u>add</u> years to their lives.

Exercise 12.4

1.   S
   A person←(**who** expects good results) / <u>makes</u> better decisions.
   A person / <u>makes</u> better decisions.
2.   S
   The newspaper / <u>interviewed</u> the community leaders←(**who** organized the boycott).
   The newspaper / <u>interviewed</u> the community leaders.
3.   S
   The children / <u>told</u> a story←(**that** their parents could hardly believe.
   The children / <u>told</u> a story.
4.   S
   Senior citizens←(**who** need long-term health care) / often <u>become</u> penniless.
   Senior citizens / often <u>become</u> penniless.
5.   S
   A car←(**which** has special safety features) / <u>gets</u> a reduction on insurance.
   A car / <u>gets</u> a reduction on insurance.

Exercise 12.5

1.
                                           S   V
My younger brother / <u>bought</u> a computer ←(**which** he uses nearly every day).

2.
                         S   V
Gladys / <u>has</u> a nephew ←(**whom** the whole family calls *Bubba*).

3.
                                   S   V
The owl species ←(**that** the scientists discovered) / <u>was</u> nearly extinct.

Exercise 12.6

1.
                      S   V
The people ←(**who** arrived late) / <u>didn't seem</u> at all embarrassed.

2.
                                           S   V
Dorcas's biology teacher / <u>assigned</u> two textbooks ←(**which** cost at least $45 each).

3.
                              S   V
The only books ←(**that** interest many teen-aged boys) / <u>are</u> science fiction fantasies.

Exercise 12.7

1.
                                             S   V
✗ An old Harley-Davidson motorcycle ←(**which** Jake inherited
from his uncle).   FRAG

                                             S   V
Jake / <u>drives</u> an old Harley-Davidson motorcycle ←(**which** he inherited
from his uncle).   SENT

2.
                                     S   V
Neighbors / <u>avoid</u> the young men ←(**who** loiter in the hallways).   SENT

                                 S   V
✗ The young men ←(**who** loiter in the hallways smoking and drinking beer).   FRAG

3.
                             S   V
✗ Some children ←(**who** cause trouble and demand attention).   FRAG

                             S   V
Some children ←(**who** always cause trouble) / only <u>want</u> attention.   SENT

Exercise 12.8

[1]Pattie / <u>is planning</u> a surprise party for her   [1]SENT
husband. [2] ✗ (**Who** is having a birthday next week).   [2]FRAG
[3]All their friends / <u>will meet</u> on Friday night at a   [3]SENT
local restaurant. [4]She / 's also <u>inviting</u> some   [4]SENT
of the people (**who** work with him). [5]There <u>are</u> /   [5]SENT
several restaurants in the neighborhood. [6] ✗ (**Which** [6]FRAG
serve large parties). [7]Which one <u>has</u> she <u>chosen</u>?   [7]SENT

Exercise 12.9

1.   This is a fact. ✗ (**Which** almost everyone recognizes).
       This / <u>is</u> a fact ←(**which** almost everyone recognizes).

2.   We all trust a person. ✗ (**Who** tells the truth).
       We all / <u>trust</u> a person ←(**who** tells the truth).

3.   The two teenagers discovered a cave. ✗ (**That** contained broken pottery and arrowheads.)
       The two teenagers / <u>discovered</u> a cave ←(**that** contained broken pottery and arrowheads.)

Exercise 12.10

1.   Donald / <u>did</u> something ←(**which** bothered me).
2.   Kalliope / <u>married</u> a man ←(**who** was old enough to be her father).
3.   The director / <u>made</u> a film ←(**which** shocked the public).

Exercise 12.11

1.   The canoe capsized in the rapids (**that** Dudley repaired).
      The canoe ← (**that** Dudley repaired) / <u>capsized</u> in the rapids .

2.   The cat brought home a dead bird (**which** Luci adopted).
      The cat ← (**which** Luci adopted) / <u>brought</u> home a dead bird.

3.   The doctor saved many patients (**who** developed the new surgical procedure).
      The doctor ← (**who** developed the new surgical procedure) / <u>saved</u> many patients.

Exercise 12.12

1.   The police officer ← (**who** was shot in the robbery) / <u>wore</u> a bullet-proof vest ← (**which** saved his life).
2.   Someone ← (**who** loves movies) / <u>hates</u> people ← (**who** talk during the show).
3.   The readings ← (**which** our teacher assigned) / always <u>treated</u> controversial subjects ← (**which** were in the news).

RULES SUMMARY, Part 1

1.   A special kind of noun expansion begins with the expansion words **who**, **which**, and *that*.
2.   Noun expansion beginning with *who*, *which*, and *that* always contains a **subject** and a **verb**.
3.   The nouns *who*, *which*, and *that* are often **subjects** in the expansion they create.
4.   Even when noun expansion contains a subject and a verb, expansion by itself is a **fragment**.
5.   Most fragments caused by noun expansion words can be corrected by **connecting** them to a base sentence.
6.   Noun expansion words **combine** sentences by changing one sentence into **expansion** of the other.
7.   Noun expansion must directly **follow** the noun it expands.

Exercise 12.13

Modern medicine / now <u>approves</u> some of the folk remedies ← (which our ancestors swore by). In the past, doctors / <u>warned</u> against old women ← (who treated fever with willow bark). They / merely <u>laughed</u> at country druggists ← (who recommended chicken soup for colds). But today many doctors / <u>prescribe</u> these remedies, ← (which recent research shows to be effective). For centuries, people ← (who had heart trouble) / <u>chewed</u> foxglove. Digitalis, a modern drug ← (which is widely used for heart disease), / <u>comes</u> from this herb. However, not all folk remedies / <u>are</u> helpful. Movie cowboys ← (who gulp down a bottle of whiskey for snakebite) / <u>get</u> up and <u>ride</u> away. But in real life, anyone ← (who drinks whiskey for snakebite) / <u>helps</u> to spread the poison by dilating the blood vessels. Putting cobwebs on open wounds / only <u>multiplies</u> the germs. Some so-called cures ← (which are still popular) / <u>are</u> actually killers. A heatstroke victim ← (who climbs into an ice-cold bath) / <u>is</u> likely to have a heart attack. A folk remedy ← (that sometimes causes tetanus) / <u>is</u> manure on a bee sting. So folk medicine / still <u>deserves</u> skepticism. Your doctor's advice / <u>is</u> best.

Exercise 12.14

1.	✗ The new accountant ← (who was hired last week).	FRAG
	A new accountant / <u>was hired</u> last week.	SENT
	The new accountant ← (who was hired last week) / <u>seems</u> very competent.	SENT
2.	The accident ← (which Mrs. Antoine witnessed) / <u>involved</u> three cars.	SENT
	✗ The accident ← (which was witnessed by Mrs. Antoine).	FRAG
	The accident / <u>involved</u> three cars.	SENT
3.	Students ← (who attend college at night) / often <u>have</u> trouble budgeting their time.	SENT
	✗ Students ← (who work all day and attend college at night).	FRAG
	Some students / <u>work</u> all day and <u>attend</u> college at night.	SENT
4.	✗ A fact ← (which almost everyone recognized).	FRAG
	That / <u>was</u> a fact ← (which almost everyone recognized).	SENT
	Almost everyone / <u>recognized</u> that fact.	SENT

5.   Anyone ←(who considers the risks) / <u>will</u> not <u>try</u> hang gliding.   SENT
      ✗ Anyone ←(who considers the risks).   FRAG
      Only a foolhardy person / <u>will try</u> a dangerous sport like hang gliding.   SENT

Exercise 12.15

[1]Animals / <u>have</u> elaborate systems of movements and sounds ←(which resemble human communication). [2]✗ Systems ←(which some people describe as language). [3]Certainly most animals, / in one way or another, <u>communicate</u> fear, pleasure, or sexual desire. [4]✗ For example, the songs ←(that birds sing). [5]✗ (Which have some of the qualities of human speech). [6]Each melody ←(which we hear) / <u>signals</u> food, danger, or a sense of territory. [7]There <u>are</u> / studies of the sounds ←(which dolphins make). [8]✗ Curious underwater vibrations ←(which are like the pulses of Navy sonar equipment). [9]One scientist / <u>considers</u> these sounds to be the equivalent of human speech. [10]✗ And the complicated dances ←(which bees perform). [11]These intricate movements / <u>tell</u> other bees about sources of nectar. [12]Scientists / <u>are</u> now <u>studying</u> animals ←(which seem to be able to learn human language). [13]✗ A woman ←(who invented a signal system) ←(which resembles the finger talk of the deaf). [14]She / <u>taught</u> it to a chimpanzee ←(which now has a vocabulary of over 100 words). [15]But not even this smart monkey / <u>uses</u> sounds or signals ←(which are exactly like human language). [16]✗ Sounds ←(that express general and original ideas).

[1]SENT
[2]FRAG
[3]SENT
[4]FRAG
[5]FRAG
[6]SENT
[7]SENT
[8]FRAG
[9]SENT
[10]FRAG
[11]SENT
[12]SENT
[13]FRAG
[14]SENT
[15]SENT
[16]FRAG

Exercise 12.16

1.   Americans / <u>value</u> democracy, education, and economic opportunity.
2.   For centuries, the Vikings / <u>attacked</u> England, <u>stole</u> its treasures, and <u>returned</u> to their homeland to enjoy their loot.
3.   Food, shelter, and love / <u>are</u> basic needs for every child.

Exercise 12.17 [Remember: Square brackets show where you should have drawn a box.]

1.   There <u>is</u> / no proof of visitors from outer space[, but] many people / <u>believe</u> in them.
2.   Tania / <u>will work</u> in June[, and] then she / <u>will go</u> to summer school.
3.   Elderly people / <u>may become</u> difficult to please[, or] they / <u>may mellow</u> with age.

Exercise 12.18

1.   (Because latex paint is soluble in water), it / <u>is</u> easy to use.
2.   (Until the barbarians invaded from the east), Rome / <u>ruled</u> the world.
3.   (After the Civil War ended), many Confederate soldiers / <u>returned</u> to ruined homes and farms.

Exercise 12.19

1.   Parents / <u>worry</u> about their children's safety. However, they / <u>must permit</u> their children to experiment and explore.
2.   The candidate / <u>was</u> highly qualified. Also, he / <u>had</u> the backing of the local newspaper.
3.   The wedding / <u>was</u> held right after Grandfather died. Nevertheless, it / <u>was</u> a joyous occasion.

Exercise 12.20

1.   ✗
      Most young people are in college to prepare for a career, however, they often shortchange themselves.
      Most young people / <u>are</u> in college to prepare for a career. However, they / often <u>shortchange</u> themselves.
2.   ✗
      Many students do not study history, also, they seldom take a foreign language beyond the basics.
      Many students / <u>do</u> not <u>study</u> history. Also, they / seldom <u>take</u> a foreign language beyond the basics.

3.   **X**

The global economy is becoming interdependent, therefore, the ability to speak a foreign language will often translate into higher pay.

The global economy / <u>is becoming</u> interdependent. Therefore, the ability to speak a foreign language / <u>will</u> often <u>translate</u> into higher pay.

Exercise 12.21

1. These are **joining** words, which are used to create compound sentences.
2. These are **expansion** words, which turn one sentence into expansion of another.
3. These are **transitional** words, which show logical relationships, but never join sentences.

Exercise 12.22

1. a. Women / <u>need</u> more iron than men**[, and]** many women / <u>take</u> mineral supplements.
    b. (Because women need more iron than men), many women / <u>take</u> mineral supplements.
    c. Women / <u>need</u> more iron than men. Therefore, many women / <u>take</u> mineral supplements.
2. a. Americans / <u>are</u> very health-conscious**[, but]** most of us / <u>eat</u> diets rich in sugar and fat.
    b. (Although Americans are very health-conscious), most of us / <u>eat</u> diets rich in sugar and fat.
    c. Americans / <u>are</u> very health-conscious. Nevertheless, most of us / <u>eat</u> diets rich in sugar and fat.

Exercise 12.23

1. Cholesterol can damage your heart. **Also**, most foods rich in cholesterol are fattening.
2. Exercising regularly takes discipline. **However**, it pays off in many ways.
3. Being well organized saves time. **However**, it also takes time.
4. The idea was truly brilliant, **and** she thought of it all by herself.
5. During the Great Depression of the 1930s bread cost only eight cents, **but** some people didn't have eight cents.
6. Los Angeles is in a valley surrounded by mountains. **Therefore**, the air is often heavily polluted.
7. People are marrying later, **and** they are having smaller families.
8. **Although** Eubie was well prepared, he seemed nervous.

RULES SUMMARY, Part 2

1. Use commas to separate the items in a **series**.
2. In a compound sentence, use a **comma** in front of a joining word like **and** or **but** or *or*.
3. When verb expansion comes at the beginning of a sentence, use a comma to separate it from the **base sentence**.
4. Use commas to separate **transitional** words from the rest of a sentence.
5. Transitional words like *however*, *therefore*, and *furthermore* cannot **join sentences**.

Exercise 12.24 [Be sure to check for commas.]

1. (When the list of contributors reaches one thousand), the woman ←(who organized this drive) / <u>will</u> <u>make</u> a large donation.
2. (Because Beauregard wants to be fashionable), he / <u>wears</u> fancy boots ←(which hurt his feet).
3. The antique table ←(which was standing in the hall) / <u>collapsed</u> (when Amos put the package on it).
4. (Unless you send it by Express Mail), a letter ←(which is mailed this afternoon) / <u>will</u> not <u>arrive</u> by Thursday.

Exercise 12.25 [Commas in brackets are acceptable but not essential.]

Michelangelo was a 16th century sculptor who also painted. His huge paintings on the ceiling of the Sistine Chapel in Rome are in every art history book, but his marble statues are perhaps even more famous. Because marble was plentiful in the hills near Florence, he always used this beautiful stone. While he was planning his statues, he seemed to hear voices speaking from inside the uncarved marble. One day he was painting a prince's portrait which he wanted to finish before sunset[,] when his helpers carried in a large chunk of marble. After they left, Michelangelo sensed the presence of an invisible person in the room, but he continued to paint. He turned and saw the marble, and then he understood. When he touched the rough surface, Michelangelo felt a figure which moved

in the marble. It was Moses, the prophet, who was waiting for Michelangelo to set him free.
The prince who had ordered the painting would have to wait[,] because at this moment a more
important person was giving Michelangelo orders. With a shout of joy, he lifted his hammer
and struck the first of the ten thousand blows which would free the prophet from his marble
prison.

Exercise 12.26: Review Exercise H [Mark anything that is not as it appears below, except commas.]

Our ancestors died of many **diseases which** the modern world knows little **about,**
like bubonic plague and smallpox. In the Middle Ages, bubonic plague killed **thousands.**
In fact, the populations of entire cities died of this **scourge, which** recurred every
few generations. Doctors could only lock the city **gates. They** had no cures. People
shuddered when anyone mentioned its **name. They** called it the Black Death. Up to the
18th century, smallpox was another killer. Even if the victims recovered, the pockmarks
which it left on their faces disfigured them for **life. This** was particularly dreadful
for women. However, because of the miracles of modern **medicine, smallpox**, like bubonic plague,
has become merely a memory. Past success in eliminating these diseases
encourages **researchers who** are now seeking cures for AIDS and cancer.

Appendix A: Spelling

Exercise A.1

1.	fi**el**d	1
2.	c**ei**ling	2
3.	**ei**ght	3
4.	rec**ei**pt	2
5.	fri**e**nd	1
6.	vi**e**w	1
7.	v**ei**ns	3

Exercise A.2

Do you **believe** in magic? When people play the lottery or enter a sweepstakes, they always
believe in their hearts that they're going to win. It's hard to conceive that the odds against
winning a sweepstakes are millions to one. Did you ever have a **friend** who won a big state
lottery? Probably not. But most of us have friends and neighbors who consistently play their
lucky number and lose. These people might not spend a dime without a receipt, and they would
be outraged if a **thief** took **their** hard-earned dollars. However, again and again they **deceive**
themselves and squander money that never can be **retrieved**, all on a brief fantasy of magical
gains. (Do you believe that you have a lucky number?)

Exercise A.3

1. s t r **(a)** p   h **(a)** v **(e)**   t **(o) (u)** c h **(e)** d   **(e) (e)** r **(i) (e)**
2. **[s] [t] [r]** a **[p]**   **[h]** a **[v]** e   **[t]** o u **[c] [h]** e **[d]**   e e **[r]** i e

Exercise A.4

1.	plays	played
2.	marries	married
3.	enjoys	enjoyed
4.	replies	replied
5.	terrifies	terrified
6.	X-rays	X-rayed

Exercise A.5

1. grinning
2. rained
3. starring
4. mattered
5. repellent
6. repealing
7. shopped
8. swimmer
9. preferred
10. covered

Exercise A.6

1. The choir members were **robing** in the vestry.
   The gang has been **robbing** small shops in the neighborhood.
2. **Planning** next year's schedule is the chairman's responsibility.
   The carpenter is **planing** the boards.
3. In American society, **staring** at strangers is considered to be impolite.
   Many actors who have **starring** roles on television never work in motion pictures.

Exercise A.7

1. carries	carried	carrying
2. worries	worried	worrying
3. tries	tried	trying
4. replies	replied	replying
5. studies	studied	studying

Exercise A.8

1. Incidents involving guns are **occurring** with alarming frequency.
2. People these days are **marrying** at a later age.
3. There is an old **saying**: "Handsome is as handsome does."
4. The senators believed that the witness was **lying**.
5. To children, **writing** is a lot like drawing pictures.
6. The missile did not succeed in **hitting** its target.
7. People in photographs are usually **smiling**.
8. Few students who get low grades really enjoy **studying**.
9. Many Native Americans are striving to keep the old ways of their people from **dying** out.
10. **Worrying** about problems seldom helps us to solve them.

Exercise A.9

   Reading, **'riting**, and 'rithmetic have been called the three R's of education, the basics that
every child should have **studied** and **mastered** by the end of elementary school. Now some educators
are **saying** that the new basics will be **reading**, **writing**, and **computing**. But the computer
should not be **identified** only with **studying** arithmetic and numbers. For example, word **processing**
is much more than just **typing**. Young children have **tried using** a word processor before they have
even **studied** the alphabet, and their teachers are **saying** that **writing** on the computer has **helped**
them to read sooner and with more **understanding**. A special computer language called LOGO
applies reasoning skills by **having** children draw pictures on the screen. Some people are
worried that children will become too dependent on machines, but the ones who are **worrying**
the most are usually not the ones who have **tried** to teach in this new way.

Exercise A.10 [Dictionaries may divide words into syllables in somewhat different ways. Count your answer
correct if it is exactly what appears in your own dictionary.]

1. commercial   3   com-mer-cial

2.	environment	4	en-vi-ron-ment
3.	studying	3	stud-y-ing
4.	athletic	3	ath-let-ic
5.	representative	5	rep-re-sen-ta-tive
6.	vehicle	3	ve-hi-cle

Appendix B: Possessives

Exercise B.1 [Remember: Parentheses and italics mark the words that you should have circled.]

1.

We sent a thank-you note to grandfather's *(friends)*.

2.

The government's new *(policy)* was announced at a press conference.

3.

An old union motto is, "A day's *(work)* for a day's *(pay)*."

Exercise B.2

1. **Jennifer's** scarf
2. **one month's** pay
3. **Robert Frost's** poems

Exercise B.3

1. **James's** new pen
2. **one class's** assignments
3. **Garcia Marquez's** novels

Exercise B.4

1. **some cooks'** equipment
2. **three days'** time
3. the **doctors'** offices

Exercise B.5 [Parentheses and italics mark the endings that you should have circled.]

1. society*('s)* problems
   society
2. the mothers*(')* group
   the mothers
3. his parents*(')* income
   his parents
4. my teachers*(')* advice
   my teachers
5. one city*('s)* budget
   one city

Exercise B.6

1. **my brother's** tools
   my brothers' tools
2. **one woman's** career
   many women's careers
3. **one person's** opinion
   many people's opinions
4. **my boss's** schedule
   our bosses' schedule

5.   **a man's** responsibilities
      men's responsibilities

Exercise B.7

1.   To make most nouns possessive, add **apostrophe + S**.
2.   Most plural nouns end in S. To make most plural nouns possessive, add **apostrophe only**.
3.   Irregular plural nouns (for example, *men*, *women*, and *children*) do not end in *S*. To make irregular plural nouns possessive, add **apostrophe + S**.

Exercise B.8

1.   **Jean-Luc's** parents
2.   **our professor's** lectures
3.   **our professors'** tests
4.   **that woman's** enormous hat
5.   **ten years'** hard work
6.   **the students'** oral reports
7.   **the government's** new policy
8.   **my little sister's** skinned knees and stubbed toes

Exercise B.9

   Our grandparents' house was crowded. In the recreation room, **Tasha's** stereo was blaring rap music while the cousins checked out **one another's** new dance steps. In the kitchen, the wonderful aroma of roast turkey wafted from **Grandma's** oven while **Uncle Joe's** yam casserole and **Aunt Betty's** mince pies were displayed for **the assembled guests'** approval. In the living room, **our grandparents'** photo albums were being passed around, to **everyone's** amusement. "Look at **our aunts'** miniskirts! Get a load of **Joe's** haircut!" From the den, where **Grandad's** television was tuned to a football game, came the occasional roar of **men's** voices. **The family's** yearly Thanksgiving Day reunion was in full swing.

Exercise B.10

1.   Penelope was surprised by **her husband's** plan.
2.   The young woman stole the money from **her employers'** account.
3.   Many parents know little about **their children's** friends.

Exercise B.11

1.   Valerie says that her sister's cooking is better than **hers** and even better than mine.
2.   The jury asked **its** foreman to request a copy of the judge's instructions.
3.   Sid's brother and sister-in-law were both married for the second time, and the couple always joked that their children were "his, **hers** and **ours**."

Exercise B.12

1.   **Who's** the person who wanted to borrow **Melvin's** notebook?
2.   We **haven't** seen any apartment as attractive as ours, except perhaps yours.
3.   **It's** been predicted that the finance committee will deliver its report only after the **Senate's** last meeting of year.

Exercise B.13

1.   Both **women** waited for the **letters** to arrive.
2.   **Teachers' salaries** were raised last year.
3.   Many **customers** objected to the **salesmen's** high-pressure **tactics**.

Exercise B.14

It's becoming almost a habit: The University raises its tuition nearly every year, and when it does, **it's** certain that a small group of students will protest against the **administrators'** decision. They lock themselves into the **President's** office and hang banners out the windows. After a **week's** delay and negotiation, the administrators call the police. They always say that the decision **hasn't** been easy, but that the students **who've** gone on strike are interfering with other **students'** right to an education.

Exercise B.15

My two **sisters' babies** were born just two **weeks** apart, so the **children** grew up together. **Rosa's** little girl and **Chita's** little boy were both healthy **infants**, but their **mothers** often wondered why the **children's personalities** were so very different. Little **Robert's** temperament was sunny, but his cousin **Estella's tantrums** became famous in the family. Still, the two **children** got along together very well. Perhaps **opposites** attract. At any rate, they never fought over **each other's toys**, and they happily shared their **cookies** and **treats**. In fact, their **relatives** always called them "the **twins**."

Index